THE ATTORNEY'S COMPLETE GUIDE TO PRACTICE DEVELOPMENT

How to Build Your Practice and Career

ROGER F. SMITH JAMES H. MITCHELL

PRENTICE HALL, Englewood Cliffs, New Jersey 07632

Library of Congress Cataloging-in-Publication Data

Smith, Roger F.

The attorney's complete guide to practice development : how to build your practice and career / by Roger F. Smith and James H. Mitchell.

p. cm.

Includes bibliographical references and index.

ISBN 0-13-558982-7

1. Practice of law—United States. I. Mitchell, James H. II. Title.

KF300.S63 1991 91-11787

340'.023'73—dc20 CIP

Editorial/production supervision
and interior design: **Barbara Marttine**
Cover designer: **Bruce Kenselaar**
Prepress buyer: **Kelly Behr**
Manufacturing buyer: **Susan Brunke**
Acquisition editor: **John Willig**

Published by Prentice-Hall, Inc.
A Simon & Schuster Company
Englewood Cliffs, New Jersey 07632

The publisher offers discounts on this book when ordered in bulk quantities. For more information, write:

Special Sales/College Marketing
College Technical and Reference Division
Prentice Hall
Englewood Cliffs, New Jersey 07632

ISBN 0-13-558982-7

90000>

9 780135 589823

Printed in the United States of America

10 9 8 7 6 5 4 3 2 1

ISBN 0-13-558982-7

Prentice-Hall International (UK) Limited, *London*
Prentice-Hall of Australia Pty. Limited, *Sydney*
Prentice-Hall Canada Inc., *Toronto*
Prentice-Hall Hispanoamericana, S.A., *Mexico*
Prentice-Hall of India Private Limited, *New Delhi*
Prentice-Hall of Japan, Inc., *Tokyo*
Simon & Schuster Asia Pte. Ltd., *Singapore*
Editora Prentice-Hall of Brasil, Ltda., *Rio de Janeiro*

To Amelie and Cathy

Contents

PART 2

THE ASSESSMENT PROCESS: LEARNING WHERE YOU ARE NOW, WHERE YOU WANT TO BE LATER

PART 4
IMPLEMENTATION

Foreword

A law firm that does not take marketing seriously is going to have a tough time surviving. Clients are growing up to expect the best from their lawyers. The only way to deliver the best is to respond to clients' needs. The real test of legal services is the extent to which our services meet the needs of our clients. Clients are the recipients—the benefactors, if you will, of our skill and training. The market place for legal services has changed, overnight, it seems to many lawyers. Many lawyers now wonder how they should respond. How can they meet their clients' needs?

Some lawyers have discovered that they must learn and apply the art and practice of marketing. This is a new discipline for the legal profession. As we reach out for new ways to respond to clients' needs, we tend to accept the easy solutions first. The easy solution is to adopt the tools of marketing such as newsletters, brochures, and advertising. These tools of marketing are now common in many law firms and have been for the past ten years. Are these tools enough? Many lawyers have discovered they are not. A brochure is of little help unless it is in response to a particular client need.

Client needs are at the heart of marketing and this book is the first, for lawyers, that begins with a discussion of a client-focus theory. The authors develop this book from the principle that the fulfilment of your own goals depends on how well you focus on your clients' needs. Practice follows principle and what this book gives in good measure is the practice of marketing. Today's clients increasingly turn their backs on arrogant and surly lawyers—those who assume they know what is best for their clients. Clients want a new breed of lawyer—one who offers courtesy, promptness, and value. This is more complicated than you might imagine. You cannot copy what other firms do and pretend you are meeting your clients' needs.

This book teaches many lessons but the one it teaches well is the necessity to survey, analyze and research what clients want. This information is necessary to understand clients' needs. This book gives many practical tools for ways you can discover your clients' needs. This book lays to rest any idea you may have had that you can market without understanding your clients' needs.

You cannot meet your clients' needs without clear goals and objectives for your firm. Clear goals and objectives are hallmarks of a firm with a plan. A firm without a plan is difficult to market. A good plan helps to develop and promote the value of clients. The authors add to my excitement about this book, when they prove that planning, management, and good marketing practices go hand in hand. They show, for example, the effect of docketing and compensation systems on marketing plans. A successful law firm must move toward an organization able to learn to adapt to the growing demands of clients. To accomplish this a law firm must select, train, and empower its people to meet clients' needs, and reward them for so doing.

These authors deliver a strong message: We must improve not only what we do for clients but how we do it. Fortunately, this book is full of advice of what it is we must do and how to do it. As importantly, this book explains why it must be done. The authors don't assume all clients are the same. They go so far as to explain four personality types: The thinker, the director, the relator and the socializer. They show us the importance of understanding these client personalities.

If you only have time to read one book on marketing, read this one. If we can thank the authors for anything, it's for developing a comprehensive theory of client needs and practices. Underlying this theory is the idea that the client is king and we must serve. Clients make a law firm, not lawyers. Clients are the foundation of a law firm. This book demonstrates the breadth and complexity of marketing. Lawyers will have to spend a lot more of their time learning how to meet their clients' needs. The authors show us how this can be done. The easiest thing about marketing is spending money. The hardest thing is to spend it wisely. This book shows us how to spend wisely. If you spend your time reading and applying the lessons from this book you will know you have spent wisely.

MILTON W. ZWICKER

Preface

For most attorneys, the 80/20 rule of marketing is valid: eighty percent of revenue comes from 20 percent of the clients.

A recent study further points out that the 75/5 rule of marketing is also valid: of the 20 percent of clients representing 80 percent of revenues, 75 percent were not clients five years ago, and additionally, 75 percent will not be clients five years from now.

No matter how it is analyzed, client loyalties are changing. Legal services are becoming increasingly competitive. Pressures will continue to build due to graduation and admission rates far exceeding the market needs. The trend toward lower average compensation for all attorneys will continue. Only those who address the changing marketplace will obtain the work to meet their personal and financial needs.

Today's society demands goods and services for *individuals*. Mass marketing today is more a process of segmenting the market and identifying profitable niches to serve. As a result, the very nature of the practice of law is changing to reflect the personalized demands of the market.

This book is a reflection of these changes. But more, it is a guide to the new face of practice of law, a "how to" for the delivery of legal services required in the contemporary market place.

The *Bates and O'Steen* v. *Arizona* decision permitted advertising of legal services. But advertising is a very small part of marketing. This book provides complete information on the total marketing picture as relevant to attorneys.

Authors' Commentary and Acknowledgments

An attorney once said to us "At our firm, we only pick the low-hanging fruit." We asked what this means and he said "We go after the work that is easiest to get."

This simple idea became the genesis of this book—to show attorneys clearly how to find the low-hanging fruit and how to get it.

No author could ever complete a book of this nature without considerable help from multiple sources. The attorney who described the easy-to-get idea is one of them. Also of tremendous value were our attorney clients, their colleagues, and their peers who gave us in-depth background on a wide range of subjects. Their suggestions and contributions were priceless.

Though one of us had written two other books for Prentice Hall and one of us is a public relations and media writer by profession, nothing in our collective experiences prepared us for this undertaking.

Both of us have a history in sales and marketing for service-oriented firms. We became involved in business development for attorneys when the interest in marketing among our attorney friends began to grow significantly. In our analysis with them, we found it logical to apply proven marketing theories to their practices. It seemed to us that marketing techniques appropriate for an accountant or architect or other service providers also would apply to attorneys.

ATTORNEYS DON'T GO TO LAW SCHOOL TO LEARN MARKETING

Our experience has proven us both right and wrong. Attorneys are a unique breed, highly trained and intelligent about the law but frequently naive and uninformed about marketing. Law school training has and continues to focus on the practice of law, with very little emphasis on practice management issues. Marketing is becoming an integral part of every attorney's practice. Yet attorneys lack a solid foundation in its theory. Most have very little knowledge of how to do it. Further, the motivations that drew the attorney into law were most likely not related to anything remotely connected with sales or promotion.

On the other hand, professional service providers such as accountants and—to a greater degree—architects have understood and embraced marketing concepts and practices wholeheartedly. The nature of their professions evolved so that aggressive marketing, brochures, sales presentations, and so on are now an essential part of the business.

So for the attorney who now realizes that marketing will play a larger and larger role in their future practice, we prepared this book. It is written for all levels of interest and understanding. For the sole practitioner with limited resources and time, each concept is evaluated so that the attorney can decide which activities are most worthwhile. For the more advanced marketer, there are many details presented here to fine-tune existing programs. The book also offers the theory and academic framework for marketing—material sorely missing in most attorney-marketing books and articles.

Many details are presented. Too many? We as authors debated how to handle this. We finally decided that checklists of how-to items are helpful so that attorneys can review specifics as they plan for and carry out activities. When we say an obvious thing like "Bring an extension cord for the slide projector," we are not insulting the attorney who is thinking "Oh my god, I know that . . ." but reminding them of last-minute details that can make or break an otherwise sterling presentation.

DYNAMIC DUO? YOU BE THE JUDGE

Having dual authors created synergism. When one of us would have a concept, the other would fill in the details. We critiqued each other's work and shared our own separate experiences to include real-world case histories. Some concepts and theories are mentioned more than once in this book, done purposefully for emphasis. This also aids the attorney who turns to a single chapter looking for specific guidance. Each chapter provides a proper understanding of the activity and its context within a larger marketing program.

While dual authorship enhances creativity, it sacrifices efficiency. Playing no small role in this book was Deborah Stark Harrington who drew together our separate theories, styles, and approach to the many subjects discussed herein. She was our controller on style and organization. In the end, she was extremely helpful in many ways. She improved our prose and organization, and served as traffic cop and referee to keep the whole project on track. Because of her efforts, we were able to assemble a unified whole rather than a grouping of unrelated dissertations. Without her, we may never have finished, much less on time.

Also of great assistance at the end were Tiffany Heston and Heather Mills. They kept our many revisions of chapters all up to date and in order, and even suggested minor copy changes that improved the complete manuscript.

Our editors at Prentice Hall, Paul Becker and John Willig, both gave invaluable guidance and encouragement. We also deeply appreciate the direct input into our original manuscript from several attorneys and bar association personnel, located in various parts of the country and practicing in different areas of the law. Their comments and notes were carefully evaluated and used to improve the second and final draft. Of special assistance were Kevin McMurdo, J.D., Practice Development Manager, Stoel, Rives, Boley, Jones & Grey, and Dean Emeritus Orlando J. Hollis of the University of Oregon, School of Law. Both gave immense personal assistance in their review of the manuscript. Their criticisms and suggestions for revision and reorganization were especially helpful. We deeply appreciate their commitment of time and energy.

The facilities at the University of Oregon Law Library allowed us easy access to extensive volumes for research and knowledge to develop as accurate and complete a book as possible.

Finally, we acknowledge the tolerance of our spouses Amelie and Cathy for the irregular hours and shutting ourselves into isolation with our word processors, while ignoring family and social obligations. This allowed us to juggle full client work loads while doing our research and writing. Their help researching subjects and reading the manuscript goes beyond anything in the marriage vows.

John Viscount Morley wrote in his *Life of Gladstone,* "Success depends on three things: who says it, what he says, how he says it; and of these three things, what he says is least important." An anonymous quotation summarizes our feelings: "Success is getting what you want; happiness is wanting what you get."

We trust this book will help give success and happiness.

ROGER F. SMITH
JAMES H. MITCHELL

How to Use This Book

This book is written for the individual attorney. It focuses on the requirements for the individual attorney to develop his or her own practice. Information is applicable to attorneys with varied backgrounds in legal services marketing.

An estimated 19.4 percent of the approximately 850,000 attorneys in America practice as individuals, i.e. sole practitioners in single-attorney offices, according to a survey by the consulting firm of Hildebrandt, Inc., of Somerville, N.J., and this group is growing! Some jurisdictions report over 40% practicing solo. The most often mentioned reason for this is the sole practitioners' control of their practice.

This book therefore addresses the various situations in which attorneys practice—the shared office, the two- or three-partner practice, or law firms of various sizes. The following suggestions will assist in the understanding of this book's organization, enhancing the attorney's use on a regular basis.

Glance through the Table of Contents. Note the four sections, each of which is a sequential step in the practice development. Also in the Table of Contents, read the chapter titles. Turn to chapters of interest and read the summary at the beginning of each chapter.

In this way, the reader understands how specific activities fit into the larger marketing effort. The reader can then focus his or her attention on individual activities as necessary, depending on individual needs and interests at the moment.

PART 1: STRUCTURE

This section lays the foundation and establishes the significance of the *client-focus* approach to marketing. This section also discusses the successful approach to marketing planning.

PART 2: ASSESSMENT

This section stresses the role of research and feedback to develop a marketing plan. It describes the importance of assessment of both the *internal* and *external* markets, including colleagues, staff, clients, potentials, and others.

PART 3: PREPARATION

This section prepares the attorney to maximize business development plans through proper allocation of resources.

PART 4: IMPLEMENTATION

The section identifies the many specific tactics that can be undertaken to communicate effectively with your target audiences.

Introduction and Overview of Legal Services Marketing

By describing in brief narrative the contents and rationale for this book, perhaps the reader will be able to gain more insight into the business development and planning processes.

We feel, and there is certainly substantial empirical evidence to support our feeling, that marketing planning and implementation are the critical keys for success, no matter what your personal and practice objectives. By following sound marketing principles, *you can get what you want from your practice of law.*

We have looked at the available literature and find little that is written and organized with the individual attorney in mind, regardless of their practice structure or environment. This book is valuable to all individual attorneys, whether a sole practitioner, in a small or medium-size firm, in a megafirm serving as business development chair, or working in a corporate counsel office.

We have organized this book to follow the planning process. From the basis laid down in Part 1 (theory) and Part 2 (assessment), the implementation of business development programs has a solid foundation for the next step, explained in Part 3 (preparing for marketing). In Part 4 (implementation), by far the largest section, no fewer than 50 specific activities are described. Each one of these activities has its own variation for individual attorneys, depending on their intended audience, geographic location, working environment, and so on.

WRITING LONG, BUT READING SHORT

We have learned that lawyers may write long for legal purposes, but read short, due to time pressures. We have kept this constantly in mind as we put this book together. Each chapter is short to facilitate *use,* not just reading and filing. Typical plans and budgets have been included for a variety of attorneys, serving as models for building new programs.

Case histories are relevant and meaningful only if one understands the theories behind their strategies and tactics; in other words, it is far easier to accept and adopt specific tactics if one understands *why* they work the way they do. Therefore, this book only tells the *what* and *how,* but also the *why.* Setting goals and objectives is the keystone upon which everything else is built. *What do you want from your practice?* This book helps individual attorneys recognize the value of

- Understanding what efforts may be required for various alternatives to measure your performance against your expectations.
- Learning that the most important concept, the client-focus, starts with considering niche strategies, something given a lot of lip service but little understanding.
- Asking what clients are thinking to provide feedback for positive action. We'll give you some tools to ask questions that will result in meaningful answers.
- Analyzing existing clients on several different planes to continue the client-focus process. Attorneys and staff think they know their clients until they analyze them systematically. New areas of law may not be self-apparent. The bigger issue is understanding external forces working on the marketplace.
- Preparing for marketing to get "all your ducks in a row," including human resources and facilities *before* beginning implementation. Extensive damage often occurs when implementing marketing programs without being prepared to handle the results.
- Planning for marketing to begin implementation of a program. Some management issues related to client relations are a part of marketing, including time management, docket and calendar control, value billing, compensation, and client evaluations.
- Getting started with the internal market—the attorney's colleagues, administrative, and support staffs. Very specific ideas to initiate a

market program internally are presented since these are subjects not taught in law school.

- Communicating to the internal market to initiate the implementation phases.
- Setting budgets and schedules for practice development by objective as well as some more traditional techniques.

For attorneys interested in practice development, the first step is usually to approach the external market. This normally gets the most attention because many people, lawyer and nonlawyer alike, believe "doing something" such as developing publicity or creating a brochure is all there is to marketing. Our approach to the subject, however, is to offer a comprehensive look at the total process, suggesting alternatives and reporting on results by other attorneys, whenever possible. Included also are some unusual ideas with which others have had success. Those chapters read like a litany of tactics but represent the most visible and effective marketing elements.

The Table of Contents should serve as a valuable guide to find the desired information.

The Future of the Practice of Law

When considering the future of the practice of law and, specifically, the nature of marketing legal services in the future, the best guide is empirical data of two kinds: (1) law-specific data combined with (2) information from the mature unregulated service professions.

Both data indicate the same trends: There will be an ever-increasing trend to multinational megafirms. *But* there will also be an ever-increasing trend to boutiques and even highly successful sole practitioners. Simultaneously, a decrease in individual attorney loyalty to law firms' institutionally will continue.

Those firms clearly doomed to extinction are the "general-practice" or "full-service" midsized firms. Whether your firm, like the dinosaurs, is headed for the tar pits or not is a function of the size of your target market segments, defined in terms of geography, demography, or industrial classification.

Therein lies the clue to future success: The survivors will know their target client group inside out and upside down. The depth of information will greatly exceed that of an occasional social encounter or friendly neighbor relationship.

If there is a new trend, it will be toward a greater segmentation and establishment of relationships along psychographic lines, that is, life-styles and values.

Considerable attention will continue to be given to the legal profession by both the business and popular press. Subjects such as lawyer incomes, firm structures, mergers, and legal trends, all command significant space in the press and attention by the electronic media.

LIMITED CONSOLIDATION

One trend that will not come to fruition is a Big Eight or Big Five as has happened in the accounting profession. Why? There are two contributing factors:

1. Law is more complex with more separately identified practice areas. For example, P.I.C.'s National Law List, edited by Altman and Weil, Inc., identifies more than 100 main practice areas plus many subspecialties (see Appendix 16 for the complete list).
2. By its nature, the practice of law requires stronger egos which probably translates into more individuals wanting to be the big frogs.

Not incidentally, law requires a closer relationship between attorney and client, whether the practice be "transactional" or "advice and counsel" (relationship) in nature (if the reader does not understand these differences, see Chapter 1 of this book).

A frequent recurring issue will be alternatives to conventional legal service. While alternate dispute resolution (ADR) is touted as a promising trend to lower litigation incidence and costs, ADR is by no means the only issue. Legal technicians, legal clinics, storefront law offices, do-it-yourself legal software, and fill-in-the-blank legal documents are all getting wider attention. To a certain degree, they will be successful in capturing legal fees.

Why? It is not just a matter of the cost of legal services but perceived value as well. It's no secret that the level of distrust by the lay public of both civil and criminal courts has risen, reflecting a lack of faith in the legal system altogether. Therefore, as a profession, law needs to reassess what it can do to reverse this alarming trend and implement proactive strategies.

CLIENT SERVICE

Ideally, all attorneys—public and private alike—must assure that their clients are being well served, specifically making sure they are getting the results they want, to the extent allowable.

For lawyers in private practice, this is just another reason for niche marketing, which calls for specialized expertise to be focused for a unique clientele. It is neither practical nor possible to "be all things to all people." The best approach is to pick a niche and then to serve the clientele or constituency to the greatest extent possible.

A final trend is that in order to better serve the business and corporate clients, megafirms will own other professional firms, such as engineering, public relations, land use consultants, and on and on.

In sum, the obvious conclusion is that the profession will become more crowded. There will continue an even more rapid attrition of practicing attorneys. Opportunities will exist in abundance for those who are smart marketers—those who deliver what the market needs, focusing on niches, and those who do a good job of building recognition and credibility without losing sight of their single best source of new business and referrals, their existing client base.

Whether in multinational megafirms, boutiques, or solo, lawyers need to be sensitive to the nature of a maturing profession. In the simplest of all terms, client-focus is the answer to the future.

PART 1

The Client-Focus Theory

Most attorneys attend law school for two reasons: to reach personal and financial objectives. Attorneys who are happy in their practice of law today are attaining both goals, at least to some satisfactory degree.

If these goals are not being met, for whatever reason, the attorney logically takes corrective action. It is clear that attorneys cannot practice the law they want without the clients who need the expertise the attorney can provide. It is also clear that attorneys cannot earn the dollars they want without clients who can and are willing to pay. So the clients must be found and maintained. This search for clients is called *business development,* or marketing.

The client-focus theory holds that fulfillment of the attorney's personal and financial goals comes through a focus on client needs. When the right clients are found and served well, it is a win-win situation, allowing attorneys to practice what they want and with whom they want.

For the attorney, finding the right clients means the clients will receive superior legal service. The clients will obtain desired results. In the process, the attorney will be satisfied with his or her practice and, presumably, be compensated for this service.

Some essays on legal marketing divide all attorneys into two groups. One group of attorneys is *production* or *practice centered.* These attorneys are oriented toward the practice of specific areas of the law. They know which area of the law they like to practice, and they are usually very good at it. The other group is *client centered,* focusing on client needs. The client-focus theory says that being client centered is ultimately the only valid orientation for successful attorneys. Being client-focused means having an active plan to deliver superior legal products and services to clients at the time they want to buy.

UNDERSTANDING CLIENTS

Understanding clients goes beyond knowing a little about their business or a few things about their personal lives. Real understanding means knowing what causes a client to make a particular decision. It means developing a personal relationship with each client, upon which a foundation of trust can be established. Individual attorneys must foster these relationships. The client, therefore, becomes the center on which the attorney's world turns.

The client-focus theory is the key to ultimate attorney success. It removes the clutter from the marketing matrix by narrowing the attorney's efforts to serve the client.

Attorneys will always need to remain legal practitioners of the highest quality. But through the adoption of a client-focused attitude, and the embracing of practical methods to enhance client service, the attorney will also see the practice grow and prosper, ultimately fulfilling his or her personal and financial goals.

CHAPTER 1
Transaction versus Relationship Marketing for Lawyers

SUMMARY

Depending on the individual attorney, law is practiced based primarily on *relationships* or on *transactions.* Understanding the basis of marketing legal services for relationship versus transactional practices puts the discussion of planning and implementation into perspective. This leads to more effective business development, which in turn, will lead to a more satisfying and rewarding practice.

This chapter discusses

- the importance of interactive relationships between attorney and client.
- the necessity of maintaining stability in attorney-client relationships.
- the transactional approach to attorney practice development.
- the relationship approach to attorney practice development.
- applying the six Ps of marketing to attorneys.

A basic marketing tenet is the concept of delivering what the market needs—not what the provider wants to sell. This places the emphasis on the consumer or client, which is the driving force behind a client-focused marketing agenda.

How does this client-focus impact attorneys who want to increase the professional and financial success of their practices? Research shows that clients perceive law as a service business. Yet a common criticism from clients is that law seems to provide "work products" more than it provides a service. This means clients want to buy solutions to their problems, not papers. Many attorneys simply are not providing what the market wants: law as a service rather than as a product.

The most important difference between legal practices can be classified as being either transaction oriented or relationship oriented. The difference is between providing clients with discrete transactions or with ongoing advice and counsel.

Swedish School of Economics and Business Administration Professor Christian Gronroos calls this approach to business "relationship marketing." He states that a significant portion of what the client expects to receive in return for payment is the establishment, maintenance, and enhancement of a mutually interactive relationship. This is accomplished by a mutual exchange and fulfillment of promises.

Conversely, Gronroos calls another approach to business as "transaction marketing," which is less flexible and more tangible.

Taking these definitions one step farther, Gronroos provided a marketing continuum (for purposes here, adapted to the law profession) which demonstrates the differences between relationship marketing and transaction marketing or between the marketing of a service and a product.

In the case of a transactional approach to marketing legal services, probably the most visible and significant strategy will be the aggressive, overt marketing efforts. A fairly obvious illustration would be the retail or consumer market for legal services. The marketing strategy and implementation is geared specifically to provide a stream of discrete transactions for many customers. Communication tends to be more reactive, except while actually engaged in client matters. However, this strategy can be equally appropriate for attorneys serving business and corporate clients, such as litigation, real estate transaction work, and Initial Public Offering (I.P.O.) and Leveraged Buy Out (L.B.O.) securities work, to name the more obvious types.

On the other hand, a relationship approach to marketing legal services would imply a more or less continual, ongoing relationship between attorney and client providing advice and counsel. Often this type of practice will involve not only a variety of law practice areas but, on occasion, frequent referral out for more specialized assistance. Illustrative cases could include individual consumer clients as well as business and corporate clients.

The marketing strategy for this type of practice will, as the name

Marketing Strategy Continuum	Transaction Marketing		Relationship Marketing
Dominating marketing function	Traditional advertising and public relations Marketing mix dominated		Interactive marketing dominated. Personal communication surveys, etc.
Quality dimension most important for a competitive advantage	Output related Technical quality dominated "Document oriented"		Process related Functional quality dominated Advice counseling
Price sensitivity	Clients very price sensitive		Clients willing to pay premium fees
Interface between marketing and other functions, e.g., organizational behavior/ personnel	Limited or nonexistent; interface of no significant strategic importance		Substantial; interface of strategic importance; department differentiation
Typical marketing situations continuum	Packaged goods marketing	Tangible services	Services marketing
Legal services continuum		Transactional Retail consumers plaintiff Personal Injury Bankruptcy Divorce Immigration Business Real Estate Bankruptcy Securities	Relationship (advice and counsel) Business/corporate clients Business planning Corporate law Labor law Regulated industries

Figure 1-1 The Marketing Strategy Continuum. The critical differences between transactional and relationship orientations are demonstrated within this graph. Note the differences between relationship and transactional marketing illustrated in this model. While a service (represented by relationship marketing) is chiefly influenced by interaction with clients, a product (represented by transactional marketing) is affected by more traditional marketing methods such as advertising and public relations. Adapted with permission from Christian Gronroos, "A Relationship Approach to Marketing: The Need for a New Paradigm," Swedish School of Economics, Helsinki, Finland, February 1989.

implies, be focused on developing and maintaining a close attorney-client relationship. Far less effort is aimed at overt marketing activities, but rather concentrated on identifying all the legal needs of clients, regardless of practice area involved. (See Figure 1-1.)

For example, the attorney's marketing efforts focus on client need and satisfaction surveys, client newsletters, "client alerts," legal audits, relatively frequent semisocial occasions, emphasis on developing relations between legal staff and clients' staff (when appropriate), and other devices specifically for the purpose of enhancing the relationship. In other words, more concentration on interactive communications.

In recently completed research, Dr. Lawrence Crosby of the Arizona State University marketing department points out that business clients want not only reliability and quality but, more important, a stable relationship with their service providers. Clearly this means that for lawyers serving business and corporate clients, a strategy aimed at ongoing interactive communications is critical to establishing and solidifying relationships.

THE SIX PS OF MARKETING

Another concept important to understand before a successful marketing program can be developed is the six "Ps" of marketing. These elements form the heart of any marketing effort, which in turn affects the formation of business development strategies. Let us, however, begin at the beginning with Jerome McCarthy, of Michigan State University who originated the four "Ps" model with these ingredients: price, product, place, and promotion.

McCarthy's four "Ps" are applicable to law business development. *Price* clearly refers to the hourly rate or value billing standard; *product* refers to needs satisfied; *place* refers to the method of distribution (clinics, do-it-yourself operations, public attorneys, private attorneys, and so forth); and *promotion* refers to public relations, advertising, personal marketing, and similar activities. Any combination of the four "Ps" becomes the "marketing mix."

Following McCarthy's development of the four "Ps," two additional "Ps" were identified by Philip Kotler of Northwestern University: *politics* (legislative, regulatory, and judicial) and *public* (beyond the targeted clients and direct recipients of services). These are also considered important ingredients of the marketing mix. All six "Ps" can be used to help identify why an individual attorney is serving a particular niche or segment and how that attorney can shift to an additional or perhaps altogether different niche.

For example, an attorney might analyze his current clients and assess that most (although not all) of his efforts are devoted to corporate real estate acquisitions. How do the six "Ps" affect this?

- *Price:* a billing rate to be geared toward the typical value of real estate acquisition legal services.

- *Product:* contract and financing review service.
- *Place:* for client convenience or only at law office? Where? The location may speak to corporate versus small business or alternately individual clients.
- *Promotion:* includes image, reputation, various activities to gain visibility, and so on.
- *Politics:* legislative, executive, administrative, land use zoning, tax treatment, environmental, and so on. The way current events affect the practice may show that the need in this area is great and has regulatory impact.
- *Public:* public opinion toward proposed projects. The perception people have of the practice can combine with the other "Ps" to reinforce the current practice area and determine the type and caliber of any new clients.

Clearly price, product, place, promotion, politics, and public can be influenced by the attorney to guide his or her practice development. Viewing these elements as ingredients to the marketing mix and consequently adjusting for their individual impacts will determine the course of all practice development efforts. The fact that law as a profession has not consistently paid attention to all six "Ps" contributes to current perceptions.

BIBLIOGRAPHY

GRONROOS, CHRISTIAN. "A Relationship Approach To Marketing: The Need for a New Paradigm," Swedish School of Economics, Helsinki, Finland, February 1989.

KOTLER, PHILIP. "Mega-Marketing," *Harvard Business Review,* May/April 1986.

CHAPTER 2
Understanding Service Quality

SUMMARY

Services provided by attorneys are seen by clients in two ways. The first is the technical or "what" element of the service (a will, a contract, a bond sale, etc.). The second is the functional or "how" element of the service, or the clients' perception of the manner in which the technical service was delivered. These two elements, when combined with the attorney's "image" in the mind of the client, will determine the quality of service that the client thinks they receive.

This chapter discusses

- the technical element or "what" quality of service.
- the functional element or "how" quality of service.
- the effect of image or impression on perception of service quality.
- the expected versus received service.
- the perception of received service.

Here is a case history that illustrates a common dilemma for attorneys and solutions on how to overcome difficulties through client research.

> Attorney Jones did not understand why his practice was not developing more quickly. He had been in practice for seven years and had been an associate with a respected firm for three years prior to branching out on his own. His academic record was excellent; he graduated in the top third of his class at a well-known law school. Jones' professional record was also good. He, more often than not, provided the results his clients wanted.
>
> Some of Jones' clients had developed relationships with other attorneys and had discontinued their work with him. Jones felt that to some degree this would continue to happen and that this was not always within his ability to control. The number of potential clients referred to him had decreased over the past year. He was not sure what had caused this.
>
> Jones had always felt that by providing competent legal services, his record and reputation would attract clients. But Jones was watching his income decline and was concerned about the future. He decided to talk with two former clients with whom he felt most comfortable and ask why they no longer used his services. He knew that the work products were complete and delivered on schedule. He wanted to hear firsthand from the clients why that had not been enough. Although this might not be "scientific," at least he could get some idea of what was wrong.
>
> He was surprised by what the first client told him. The client said that Jones' work was more than satisfactory and his billing rate was very fair, but he did not like the way Jones' staff treated him. Although he felt that they may perform their tasks well, he did not feel that the receptionist or support staff appreciated him. As a result, the client believed that Jones did not appreciate him.
>
> After talking with the second former client, Jones began to realize what the problem might be. The second client had told him that he did not think he was being billed fairly. He did not understand why the professional rates on Jones'

bills fluctuated. The client believed that Jones was charging what he needed to receive in order to match an income expectation for his practice.

Jones realized that he had based his analysis of his practice on his own perceptions. Without asking his clients' opinions, he planned and adjusted his practice according to what he thought would be areas of need for improvement. He altered his schedule for the next two weeks and took time to call his existing clients and many former clients asking their general opinions, in addition to calling several referral sources. He asked for their specific recommendations: What would they do, if they were Jones, to improve his practice?

None of the clients or referral sources seemed to mind the interruption in their schedules, and several actually seemed to enjoy sharing their opinions. In fact, a few former clients mentioned the possibility of future work with Jones. In this case, the facts were what the clients believed them to be.

THE SERVICE/QUALITY CONCEPT

Everyone seems to "know" when they receive good service, whether in auto repair or restaurant or legal services. Yet defining service quality seems to elude easy explanation. To deliver good service consistently, it is imperative to understand what constitutes good service.

Defining the abstract concept may not be as difficult as imagined. Christian Gronroos presented these simple concepts to the American Marketing Association. Service delivery can be simply diagrammed, he said. Total quality is a composite of *technical* or the "what" of the service and *functional* quality or "how" the service is delivered.

Technical. This element is often the only one the service provider considers when determining performance. In simple terms, the technical quality deals with whether the results are good—specifically, if the will or contract review gives the client peace of mind and satisfaction.

Functional. This element is easy to control in theory, but in practice may take more conscious continual effort, since the facilities' ambience and staff impact *how* service is delivered. In fact, they may have more than one-third weight toward service/quality perception in the clients' minds.

Image. This element is an umbrella which includes reputation, advertising, public relations, physical facilities, pricing strategies, personal selling and external factors of ideology, word of mouth, and traditions.

All those elements together describe the service experience. In straightforward terms, the interaction of these service elements determine the *perception* of the service quality delivered.

Total service *quality* is the difference between *expected* service and *perceived* service received. (See Figure 2-1.) Often a client will retain an attorney with clear expectations about the results (technical quality) or the manner of delivery (functional quality) of legal services. However the attorney delivers somewhat different results and in a different manner from what the client had in mind. As a result, the client is very disappointed and upset, even though the attorney did all that was possible under the legal circumstances.

People have similar feelings toward an airline when a connection is missed due to traffic or even weather. Most tend to blame the airline because they did not receive the result (destination) in the manner (schedule) as expected. Learning client expectations becomes crucial to building a perception of quality legal services (later chapters further discuss client engagement techniques).

Once these simple marketing concepts of service delivery and service quality are understood, it is much easier to see why the application of the ideas in this book will work.

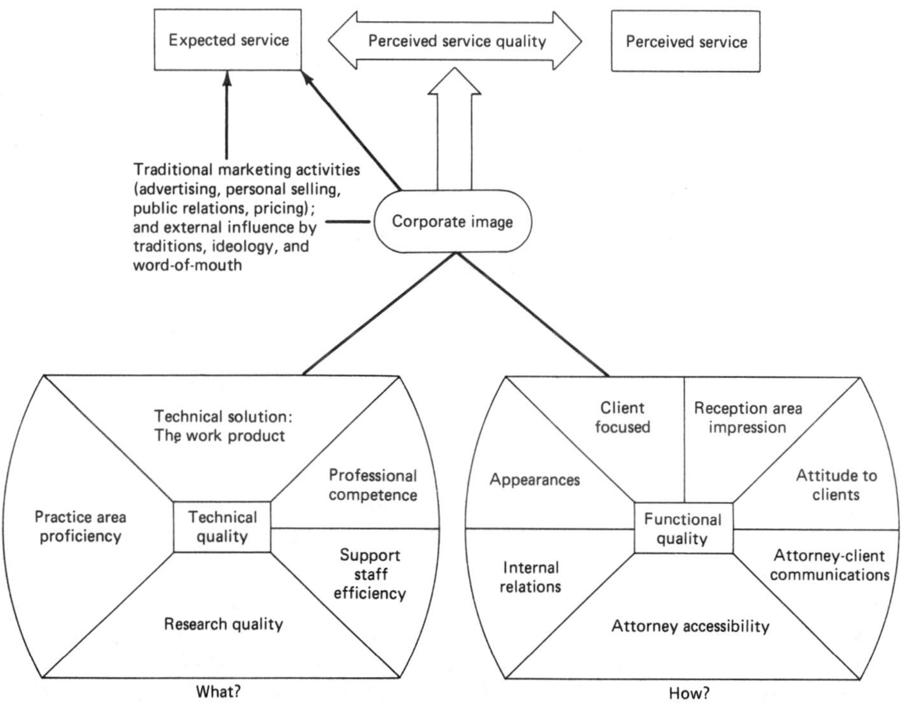

Figure 2-1 Service/Quality Concept. Adapted with permission from Gronroos, Christian. "A Service Quality Model and Its Marketing Implications," European Journal of Marketing, Vol. 18, no. 4, 1984.

BIBLIOGRAPHY

GRONROOS, CHRISTIAN. "A Service Quality Model and Its Marketing Implications," *European Journal of Marketing*, Vol. 18, no. 4, 1984.

CHAPTER 3
Strategy Options for Business Development

SUMMARY

The key point in developing a marketing strategy is a focus on clients. They are the easiest source of new work. In seeking new clients, attorneys can avoid coming head to head with strong competition by making good strategic decisions in their business development efforts. Marketing strategies can be defined in military terms—taking the offense, taking the defense, attacking where the "enemy" (i.e., competition) is vulnerable, and using guerilla tactics.

This chapter discusses

- the nature of the real competition for clients.
- why positioning is all important.
- when to go on "offense" and when to go on "defense."
- practical implications for any practice development plan.

As an attorney considers a business development program, there are many strategy options available. Selection of a strategy is critical since it will determine most of the specific marketing activities related to it. Just as a military general selects the strategy (say, to attack the enemy's left flank), many specific actions or tactics result from that strategy (such as creating new supply lines and relocating artillery).

The importance of this strategic approach is as important for attorneys as it is for anyone involved with the delivery of goods or services to the marketplace. Some attorneys argue that law firms cannot effectively practice the type of marketing strategies that other businesses use to plot out the direction of their marketing campaigns. Further, they would say that this type of language and thinking would be even less applicable to an individual attorney, whether affiliated with a firm or a sole practitioner.

This chapter is not written to provide the point that attorneys need to develop marketing strategies identical to those of manufacturers of products. Rather, it explores some of these concepts as they apply to individuals. From them, attorneys may begin to think in terms of developing their own strategy for marketing.

COMPETITION FOR THE MARKET

Al Ries and Jack Trout, astute analysts of marketing strategies, have written the two hallmark books: *Positioning: The Battle for Your Mind* and, more recently, *Marketing Warfare*. They see marketing as serving the client but also a war with the competition over turf, or clients. Both books deal primarily with mass marketing consumer products, yet both books teach a great deal about business development strategies.

The works of Philip Kotler and Paul Bloom, who authored *Marketing Professional Services* and other books and articles, also illustrate some of the options available to individual attorneys. Through these materials, highways to marketing success can be opened for the attorney to drive with ease rather than taking bumpy back roads.

The most likely success rate in terms of business development is incurred by the attorney who attempts only to maintain the status quo by providing the same service to the same clients. Since this is a close to effort-free strategy, why not adopt it?

A four-component square (Figure 3-1) illustrates this basic concept. The greatest amount of effort possible is assumed by the attorney who provides a new service (new to that attorney, at least) to an untried type of client. Clearly that attorney's efforts involve his or her own capabilities in providing service as well as understanding what this new client type needs.

Client: Same Services: Same 1 Minimal Effort	Client: Same Services: Different 2 Modest Effort
Client: Different Services: Same 3 Modest Effort	Client: Different Services: Different 4 Significant Effort

Figure 3-1 Client/Services Difficulty Scale. This simple grid assumes some basic concepts of the marketing effort. Philip Kotler and Paul N. Bloom, *Marketing Professional Services*, © 1984. Adapted by permission of Prentice-Hall, Inc., Englewood Cliffs, New Jersey.

An easy-to-understand assessment of how all effort pans out in terms of legal services and clients is demonstrated on an expanded version of the four-point grid, showing in the effort matrix, a 16-square grid. (See Figure 3-2.) Eight elements combine in pairs to create unique situations. Four client-related elements combine individually with four practice-related elements to provide a client/practice combination. The four client-related elements are

- Current client type (lowest effort)
- Same client type (lower effort)
- New, but similar, client type (higher effort)
- Never-served, different client type (highest effort)

The four practice-related elements are

- Same service (lowest effort)
- Related service, same practice area (lower effort)
- Similar service, related practice area (higher effort)
- New practice area (highest effort)

Combinations of these elements provide 16 variations of effort potential. Imagine that the number for each listing represents a degree on an effort thermometer. Relatively effort free would be defined by number 1. High effort would be defined by number 16. Numbers 2 through 15 represent gradations between lowest-effort and highest-effort client-related, practice-related elements. Type of activity and effort required to accomplish is as follows:

1. Current client type/same service (lowest effort)
2. Same client type/same service (lower effort)
3. New, but similar, client type/same service (low effort)
4. Never-served, different client type/same service (moderate to low effort)
5. Current client type/related service, same practice area (moderate effort)
6. Same client type/related service, same practice area (moderate to medium effort)
7. New, but similar, client type/related service, same practice area (medium to moderate effort)
8. Never served, different client type/related service, same practice area (medium effort)
9. Current client type/similar service, related practice area (medium effort)
10. Same client type/similar service, related practice area (medium to probable effort)

More effort required* →

	Current Client Type	Same Client Type	New Similar Client Type	Never-Served, Different Type
Same Service	1	2	3	4
Related Service, Same Practice Area	5	6	7	8
Similar Service, Related Practice Area	9	10	11	12
New Practice Area	13	14	15	16

↓ More effort required*

*Effort required varies by individuals according to their practice strengths in client relations and work products.

Figure 3-2 Effort Grid. This grid develops the effort analysis concept further, demonstrating the relative role of the client versus technical proficiency in determining relative marketing effort required.

This grid is based on the assumption that serving the existing client is not only preferable but in fact easier than developing new clients. The effort required varies by individuals according to their practice strengths in client relations and work products.

Most businesses would agree that serving the existing client base is easier, less risky, and therefore more profitable than is developing a new one. Quite obviously less effort and expense are required to communicate interest and expertise to a smaller group that already knows your qualifications than to get established with a new client or client group.

Within the structure of this grid are gradations of risks and opportunities so that no alternative becomes a precise black-and-white situation.

Many opportunities fall in between the more extreme or corner points of the grid. When determining the points on the grid for any given combination of client/practice area, one must make judgments about the relative strengths of each axis for each individual.

This grid also operates on the assumption that the "client" axis is more important than the practice area axis. The reasoning behind that assumption is that in the final analysis, client orientation is the most important. Without the client component in the grid, the whole issue becomes moot.

When assessing any specific opportunity, be it practice area or client group, the closer we move toward the lower right-hand corner, the greater the effort required for success, the higher the expense, and the greater the difficulty of achieving success.

11. New, but similar, client type/similar service, related practice area (probable to medium effort)
12. Never served, different client type/similar service, related practice area (probable effort)
13. Current client type/new practice area (probable to high effort)
14. Same client type/new practice area (high effort)
15. New, but similar, client type/new practice area (higher effort)
16. Never-served, different client type/new practice area (highest effort)

Should every attorney seek out the activities requiring the lowest effort and greatest likelihood of success? Not automatically. The decision to accept and even welcome hard work and a chance of failure depends on the individual involved. For some attorneys, one combination might require too much effort for their individual inclinations and therefore be unsuitable. For other attorneys, the same combination might not allow enough room for growth and development.

Each attorney must outline his or her capabilities in a personal profile (discussed in Chapter 13), assess his or her existing practice and client base (discussed in Chapters 13 and 14), and then make an effort judgment.

The final judgment is based on the placement of the attorney's existing practice and desired practice within the 16-square effort grid. How much effort is involved with the attorney's current practice and clientele? How much effort will be involved in the desired practice and clientele? How many gradations are there between those two levels of effort? If the existing practice is a number 1, which is to say the lowest possible effort, and the attorney wants a practice and clientele in number 16, the highest possible effort, he or she should make gradual steps toward that goal. If the difference between the status quo and the desired status is only 1, 2 or even 5 gradations, the attorney can make a much more rapid change.

POSITIONING IN THE MARKETPLACE

One of the key points of "positioning" is that the first person to hold a position will have the very important advantage of being first and therefore being dominant. For example, the first attorney in a town to establish himself or herself as an environmental litigator will naturally be perceived as the best and most expert if he or she maintains position and does a good job.

In the process of becoming so established, an attorney would presumably be quoted in news articles as the expert, would conduct continuing legal education (CLE) sessions, or would otherwise be recognized as a leader in the field. All of these are communications which will further reinforce the image of expertise. Also by traditional means, that attorney would develop relationships with other attorneys which would result in referrals. So by all these methods and perhaps others as well, the attorney would be recognized as the leading environmental litigator in the area.

That person may not necessarily be the most qualified or the most competent lawyer, but he or she would "own" the position in that market by virtue of first arrival.

With the growth of that area of law, such a position would be enviable. If that person were reasonably successful in court or negotiations, their practice would be fairly rewarding, up to a point.

From a strategic standpoint, the established environmental litigator has both the best and most difficult position—*best* by virtue of being first and therefore "owning" the position and *most difficult* because the dominant leader cannot attack the competition in an offensive stance but must be on the defense.

In this context, as with sports or warfare, defense means that one must be on guard to react to the moves and strategies of the competitor's offense. The defense's objective is to hold the position.

At some point the work available would exceed the capacity of the leader to care for it. The attorney could allow some of the work to go to other attorneys and perhaps lose the leadership position or could pursue a marketing option called a "defensive offense."

THE LEADER'S DEFENSIVE OFFENSE

One of the few options open to leaders in a marketplace is to compete with themselves, or as Ries and Trout say, "attack yourself." This method is virtually the only way they can go on the offense. For example, the established attorney might set up a complete *department* focusing on environmental litigation. In this manner, the leading attorney would in effect be attacking himself by using other attorneys in his or her own firm. Each attorney would naturally have slightly different techniques both technically and functionally; that is, each attorney in the department would not only use different methodologies for the legal aspects of a matter, but each likely would establish relationships with clients by a different manner.

Through all of this, however, the first lawyer would still be perceived as the leader and in fact would probably *strengthen* his position by virtue of being the leader of a department.

What about other attorneys who want to take over the leader's position or "attack"? The key question for the others is: Where would the leader be vulnerable? The only likelihood for a successful offensive attack would be if the leader had an inherent weakness and other attorneys had enough strength to mount and sustain an attack against that weakness. Clearly it is a judgment call whether the leader has a secure hold on his clients, or turf, and whether the attackers could be successful in their challenge.

FLANKING MOVE

Another method to attack the market leader is to carry out a flanking move. For instance, a large firm, presumably with substantial resources, that wanted to take on the market leader could hire an environmental litigator. If they discovered a portion of the market unserved, such as residential property developers, then the firm's offense has a chance to succeed by quickly attacking a weakness of the market leader versus going head to head. To assure successful achievement of their objective, the second firm should attack quietly and quickly because the surprise element will be important for them.

Coincidentally, since the second firm found that the residential developers were not well served in other practice areas, they could establish a department *by client area* and in fact own that turf outright! This "flanking move" in essence means that the second firm has broken off an unserved segment which the leader may not even miss! Of course, the second firm would now be the leader in that segment and potentially subject to other competitive moves against them.

GUERILLA MOVES

A third approach is for a firm to take "guerilla action" against the market leader. This scenario is for small firms and even sole practitioners who have been watching the growth in a certain practice area. Using the example of environmental litigation again, many attorneys are in a position where they understand that virtually every sale of land represents a potential client matter. At the same time, that attorney does not think they have the resources to compete with either of the existing firms in the market. What's left for them to do?

Most attorneys can then adopt a guerilla strategy rather than trying to take on the leaders in a frontal attack or even a flanking move. They should target and hit small segments that are left unprotected. Perhaps no single target represents a significant segment, yet several together could well support a small practice.

For example, the suburban developers may not be well served. The environmental issues of the suburban developer's real estate transactions are being handled by a downtown law firm that may be expensive and hard to access. The action then for sole practitioners and small firms already located nearby is to establish expertise and credibility in environmental litigation. By doing this, they can hope more easily to capture enough turf, or clients, to generate sufficient fees to be profitable in that area of law.

Their strategy is to emphasize ability to provide more cost-effective service on terms and conditions better suited for the local market.

DELIVERING WHAT THE MARKET NEEDS

Many times, the marketing strategies of individual attorneys and firms are not based on client needs or what portion of the market is underserved. Rather, they are based on a practice area which an attorney wishes to pursue, regardless of entrenched competition. Instead, what passes for strategy is really a collection of marketing tactics, coupled with a vague idea of how to apply those tactics aggressively, be they newsletters, advertising, entertainment, joining clubs, and so forth. Usually this is done with no clear objective in mind such as whether to develop a relationship or transaction practice (see Chapter 1). All too frequently a legal practice is structured for the attorney rather than the client. Very few firms—large, medium, or small—are departmentalized along client or industry lines. The fashion is to organize according to legal practice area. Implicit in that concept is that law is practiced for the attorney rather than the client. Further evidence is the production-oriented practice that flies in the face of sound marketing, which is based on delivering what the client needs.

Concentrating on serving the client is the most effective method of all.

BIBLIOGRAPHY

Kotler, Philip, and Paul N. Bloom. *Marketing Professional Services.* Englewood Cliffs, NJ: Prentice Hall, 1984.

Ries, Al, and Jack Trout. *Positioning: The Battle for Your Mind.* New York: McGraw-Hill, 1981.

Ries, Al, and Jack Trout. *Marketing Warfare.* New York:McGraw-Hill, 1986.

Chapter 4
The Powerful Value of Clear Goals

SUMMARY

Firms and individual attorneys need to articulate set goals and objectives. Although this may be difficult due to training and orientation of the law profession, this process is key for attainment of success and happiness in personal and professional life.

This chapter discusses

- the difficulty of goal setting due to orientation.
- the impact of lack of commitment.
- the rewards of focused efforts.
- the satisfaction of attainment.

Setting objectives and goals is a simple concept, but hard to do. It is a commitment to achieve specific results.

Far easier is the option of "I'll do the best I can" or "We'll keep our options open" or "We'll do whatever is possible in our market." Unfortunately that strategy usually results in little attainment, a great deal of frustration, and much wasted energy and resources.

Salespeople, whom most people normally think of as goal oriented, often have no clear objective. Many sales managers and salespeople have considerable difficulty articulating and committing to specific targets. No wonder that attorneys, whose training and experience normally have less to do with overt goal orientation, have so much difficulty focusing their energies.

Many people use the terms "objectives" and "goals" interchangeably, but they should not. *Goals* are statements of intended direction. *Objectives* are time-specific quantifiable targets to hit. Setting both goals and objectives is crucial to establishing the planning process.

Law firms and individual attorneys must engage in soul searching occasionally to articulate objectives and goals. A good part of the difficulty is that attorneys, due to their training, find it difficult to visualize the future without substantive evidence. Setting objectives and goals is important because the establishment of these is really a statement of what is desired to achieve. That statement should be the guiding force for all efforts to succeed.

Many lawyers work very hard, are very capable, but lack any central direction. As a result, they waste time and energy pursuing activities and clients that were inconsistent with their personal and financial objectives.

Today, those objectives have less to do with money and more to do with personal and professional satisfaction. Financial rewards, although important, are usually secondary.

Coincidentally, those that have attained the highest levels of professional development, either by focusing on a narrow well-defined practice area or concentrating on the special needs of a client group, have been rewarded materially. It is certainly not an original revelation to suggest that if seeking professional excellence is primary, the money will come in due time.

It is prelude to success, no matter how defined, that clear objectives and goals be set, so that energies and resources will be focused rather than used, bit by bit, with no direction. No matter whether considering a newsletter, value billing, cross-selling, or any other subject, approaching the issue with a clear objective in mind will ensure a greater chance of success.

CHAPTER 5
Proactive Marketing To Get the Desired Quality of Work

SUMMARY

Proactive practice development is nothing more than marketing focused on a specific client profile. The antithesis is reactive, that is, taking whatever work and clients show up regardless of desirability. Establishing a priority system to rank the client profile types is an important step in gaining control.

This chapter discusses

- setting specific client profiles.
- focused activity planning.
- establishing a priority system.
- determining which clients and matters to refer out and which to develop.

Consider this passage from *Alice in Wonderland:*

> "Cheshire-puss," she began, rather timidly, "would you tell me which way I ought to go from here?"
>
> "That depends a good deal on where you want to get to," said the cat.
>
> "I don't much care where . . ." said Alice.
>
> "Then it doesn't matter which way you go," said the cat.
>
> —Lewis Carroll

Successful legal services marketing, as achieved through the client focus, is not a broad-based program but an individualized effort. It is one attorney's decision to recognize the power of client relationships. The client focus is based on two important facts:

1. Clients buy solutions to problems rather than legal products.
2. Clients develop trust and dependence based on their relationships with individual attorneys rather than law firms.

Many attorneys have no sense of direction to their practice. An extension of this is that they also do not have a sense of the value of their clients.

Successful attorneys are those who follow a clear practice development plan, focusing on the client, to achieve what they want, be it wealth or satisfaction with their professional expertise.

Highly successful attorneys are those who focus on the client and/or practice area they enjoy and, not incidentally, their income is at a level they desire. As a lawyer friend remarked, "It is unlikely anyone would go into the private practice of law with life-style in mind. Income opportunity is probably the most significant reason."

Once the attorney commits to providing solutions to clients' problems and emphasizing personal relationships, the marketing process can begin.

There is a sound intellectual basis for this approach to marketing. The following chapters in this introductory part discuss fundamental concepts basic to business development efforts that are especially relevant to attorneys.

Many professionals, particularly attorneys, do not like to think of themselves as businesspeople. The matters of marketing and business development, for them, equate with "sales" and detract from the joy of unadulterated professional work. But the glut of lawyers in the marketplace has tremendously increased the competition for clients. According to trend analysts, the situation is becoming more serious. This means Darwin's survival of the fittest theory is à propos in the law arena. Only those attorneys with marketing and business development savvy will survive the tests of competition for client recruitment and retention.

Attorneys who have come to this realization are broadening their scopes. Not only are they sharpening their professional skills, but they are also working toward becoming better businesspeople. They are developing "macrovision." For these attorneys, macrovision means understanding the world in which a legal practice operates. It includes knowledge of the risks involved in any practice development effort as well as the mechanisms and processes involved in delivering services to clients.

To establish and build a successful legal practice, the actual operation of that practice must be fully understood by the individual attorney. The practice is affected not only by the attorney's legal knowledge and expertise, but by many other outside mitigating factors.

Joel's professional time was out of control; at least he felt he had little control. Clients and prospective clients he was not interested in were frequently calling him. It seemed to Joel that they were always asking for free legal advice or to prepare a comment with an immediate deadline.

The more he thought about it, the more Joel realized that his time was not his own to work for the clients he preferred. He was spending virtually all of his time reacting to someone else's pressures. Joel decided to do something to correct his situation.

He decided that his problems primarily stemmed from the fact that he did not have a clear idea who his clients should be. He only vaguely knew who he did not want them to be, which was not granting him much control. Joel knew from a research report he had read that many small business people were extremely reluctant to use an attorney for preventative matters. To them, lawyers equated with trouble rather than precaution.

First, Joel developed a profile of his ideal client and made precise statements regarding whom he was seeking. He knew he wanted clients to be close to his age and have many interests in common with his, so that he could form close relationships. He preferred his clients to be relatively sophisticated in legal matters. Even though they might understand some aspects of law and might not need an attorney as much as other potential clients, the favorable trade-off would be that Joel would not have to spend so much time and frustration educating them about legal processes. He had never found the client education process to be very rewarding, and it was something he would just as soon avoid.

Second, Joel began to plan his activities around his interests and those of his ideal client. He had noticed several potential clients at his athletic club. From conversations and casual comments, it was apparent that they were reasonably sophisticated users of legal services. He noticed that they did not exhibit an attitude of mistrust and anxiety about attorneys.

Third, Joel made a few discreet inquiries about some of the people he had seen at the club and was able to engage some of them in casual conversation about the nature of their business. He was careful not to imply that he was interested in providing them legal services, since his jurisdiction's bar had ruled against personal solicitation.

ASSIGNING PRIORITIES

The next step was slow, but Joel found it rewarding to know that at last, he was developing a strategy to get control of his time. With the information he had developed about his fellow club members, he sat down and assigned priorities, in the form of letters, "A," "B," "C," and "D." "A" represented what Joel felt would be an excellent potential for quality and volume of work, "B" represented a somewhat lesser quality and volume, "C" an average or moderate potential, and "D" represented little to no potential.

After Joel completed his cursory evaluation of the potential clients, he felt he had a target at which to aim. The only problem was that the process did not eliminate the telephone calls from people whose needs were not in an area of law in which he wanted to spend any appreciable time.

Taking the final step was the most difficult, but he reasoned that most successful lawyers at some time must also take it: learning to refer to another attorney prospective clients that Joel had the skills but not the desire to serve. At first, Joel was almost afraid to see work go out the door, but he exercised enough self-discipline to begin gradually to refer potential clients, even though he was not fully booked.

Joel began to experience a great deal of satisfaction for a relatively simple reason: he was now devoting more of his time to doing the work he enjoyed. In the process, he began to realize what he had heard was true. He was working fewer billable hours but doing a better job and enjoying the work more. He knew this would eventually lead to better revenues, either through higher hourly billing rates or value billing.

PROACTIVE PRACTICE DEVELOPMENT

Many attorneys feel they don't have complete control of their time. Clients and prospective clients require contacts which do not always result in business. Many ask for free legal advice or want a proposal within a short deadline. Much of time spent within a law office can be lost reacting to someone else's pressures. Achieving practice objectives by becoming proactive rather than reactive in regard to marketing requires some decision making on the attorney's part.

The first conclusion must be a clearer understanding of the ideal client, which means identifying whom the attorney really wants to serve. The second decision is how the attorney's time will be geared toward increased contact with potential ideal clients. The final choice, often the most difficult, involves when an attorney should turn away business because the potential client does not meet the established "ideal" criteria.

Identifying desired clients begins with the development of a profile. A number of elements can factor into this model, for instance: age, professional and social interests, and level of sophistication with respect to legal matters. (Profiling ideal clients is further discussed in Chapter 10.)

This profile should be followed by an investigation of how to find these clients in the marketplace. For example, this could be the result of a club membership or professional association. This investigation includes a ranking of actual potential in terms of business development—which activities and potential clients appear to be most promising for quality and volume of work.

Turning away potential business is always tough, particularly for the marketing-conscious individual or the attorney who needs to increase billable hours. Yet many times it is the only way to eliminate calls and visits from people whose needs do not match the attorney's practice objectives. Ultimately, referring work to other attorneys results in greater professional satisfaction as well as development in a market niche.

Proactive marketing for attorneys might just as well be called proactive practice development. It is an attitude as much as a method. The desire and commitment to take control is as important as the actual means to achieve that end.

CHAPTER 6
Market Segmentation and Niche Strategy Applied

SUMMARY

It is no longer enough to offer "full service" to the entire market. People want services designed to fill their specific needs. Breaking the market into logical homogeneous segments is the first step in the process. The objective is to focus on a segment which has a unique and viable legal need. This segment or "niche" becomes the particular position to occupy providing a specific service for a specific segment.

This chapter discusses

- thinking in terms of market segments.
- reasons behind success of niches.
- personalized attention as a key to success within a niche.
- how to develop and serve a profitable niche.

To make strategic choices without regard to competition, a few relatively simple concepts are often overlooked.

Many attorneys are responsible for developing their own clientele. This is obvious for sole practitioners, but is also true in firms of all sizes. Certainly, individual attorneys are responsible for legal service that will satisfy the client and retain them as future sources of business. Attorney salary and progress are determined, to a great extent, by his or her success in satisfying clients.

An approach to obtaining and retaining an attorney's clientele is to develop a "niche strategy." Attorneys are hearing many colleagues say, "I think I have found my niche." In short, finding a niche means focusing on a narrow market and delivering only what it needs.

The essence of marketing based on an understanding of niches is to interpret sociological trends so that goods and services can be tailored to meet specific needs and desires of the marketplace. Taking this one step farther, "niche" marketing starts with segmenting or breaking the marketplace into identifiable groups or segments with consistent characteristics.

Successful manufacturing companies use niche strategies extensively. This has come about because significant sociological developments occurring in the last few years changed the way people do business, both as buyer and seller. People no longer are apt to accept generalists to provide products and services. They want specialists, which allowed them choices. Providers of goods and services could no longer just say "here it is" and expect customers to be satisfied. Customers have come to expect more. It is reasonable to assume that law clients expected the same. Providers of legal services are guilty of not thinking in terms of market segments.

MARKET SEGMENTS

Market segmentation is the process of dividing the market (existing and potential clientele) into logical homogeneous groups. A market segment is a uniquely individual component of a more general market. A niche is a specialty within a small segment. For example, real estate for commerical developers includes finance, land use, and environmental niches within the smaller segment.

Some attorneys avoid niche marketing in favor of "full-service" practices. The usual end result for small- to medium-sized practices that try to be full service is an overextension of too few resources and poor results in filling a broad range of needs. With over 100 practice areas and many subspecialties (niches) identified by P.I.C.'s National Law List, edited by Altman & Weil, Inc., (see Appendix 16 for a complete list) how can one firm or even one attorney possibly expect to cover all the bases?

CLIENTS WANT PERSONALIZED SERVICES

Everyone who provides a product or service must think in terms of segments, according to Theodore Levitt, author of *Marketing Imagination*. The point is to focus on a group to serve, not the whole market. Avoiding niche marketing is to ignore indicators pointing the way to increased practice success. (The selection of segments and niches is discussed further in Chapters 13 through 16.)

Niche marketing allows attorneys to offer their clients personalization of service. By knowing and understanding the segment of society to which a client belongs, the attorney can tailor services, that is, practice area, to meet exact needs and expectations.

Clients want services which particularly suit them. This follows the trend for the general buying public. Four doors and four wheels is not enough any more—car buyers want a product that expresses their personality and are willing to pay for that personalization. Today, everyone wants personalized attention, whether they are retail consumers, decision makers for large corporations, or law clients.

BIBLIOGRAPHY

LEVITT, THEODORE. *Marketing Imagination.* The Free Press, New York, 1986.

PART 2

The Assessment Process: Learning Where You Are Now, Where You Want to Be Later

The cornerstone of successful legal services marketing programs is a clear understanding of the client. Knowing who you work for is critical for a realistic assessment of the practice. Too many professionals mistakenly believe they have this understanding—based, of course, on their own perceptions. They forget the importance of client perceptions!

A realistic assessment of clients and potential practice areas, both existing and desired, acts as a guide along the marketing course. The assessment lets the attorney know if he or she is headed in the right direction. All of the elements of assessment provide the map which helps the attorney win the marketing race.

The first step is an assessment of three areas: the attorney's practice, client development strategies and techniques, and client retention tracking.

Assessment is important for attorneys whether in a sole practice "boutique" or a multinational megafirm. It allows the attorney to look at a practice area, trends within it, expectations for business development, and actual business growth. Client development assessment provides an opportunity to analyze how prospects become clients and whether this rate of development meets attorney needs and expectations. Assessment of client retention lets attorneys know if their clients perceive their legal counsel and legal products as competent.

CLIENT SURVEYS

Someone once said, "If your clients are not complaining, you have no communications with them." The burden is on the attorney to inspire and maintain an open line of communications, even when the practice seems to be successful and all the clients seem to be happy. Client feedback is always a positive influence because it eliminates the doubt created by assumptions.

Any systematic polling of clients can be called a client survey process since the intent is to learn the clients' perceptions. To be valuable, the process must always be ongoing because perceptions may change quickly, even overnight.

An attorney with an established business, real estate, and land use practice claimed that all his clients loved him and his work. He had himself so convinced that he was beginning to convince his partners and associates, although they privately shared their doubts. His staff also confided that there were some problems with client relationships.

For the purpose of fine-tuning his marketing efforts, the attorney decided to conduct a client survey. He felt he could show his partners and associates how law should be practiced in a way that both pleased clients and was profitable. As a result of his survey efforts, he had a few surprises! His clients' feelings were not always what he expected. But the attorney was able to examine the criticisms and begin to think from a client perspective. Now he bases his practice development decisions on client feedback rather than on his own assumptions.

QUALITATIVE VERSUS QUANTITATIVE SURVEYS

The two principal classifications of surveys are qualitative (the "what") and quantitative (the "how much"). Qualitative surveys emphasize depth of information, whereas quantitative surveys emphasize the amount of information. A choice of one method over the other can be appropriate in various situations. For instance, to gather perceptions regarding practice "image," a small sampling of the client base may be asked a few general open-ended questions so that the information received is very comprehensive (qualitative research). On the other hand, if potential new practice areas are being studied, a large portion of the client base may be asked detailed questions regarding needs (quantitative research).

CHAPTER 7
Qualitative Individual Surveys: Learning What Clients Feel

SUMMARY

All attorneys can and should interview clients regularly to learn the clients' perceptions of attorney professional activities. Performance in areas of timeliness, accessibility, communications, billing, and competence all need to be examined from the clients' perspective. Postinterview follow-up is nearly as important as the interview itself.

This chapter discusses

- the advantages and disadvantages of using interviews to learn about client attitudes.
- how to create the appropriate setting for effective interviews.
- issues important to clients that interviews can raise.

The most personal technique to learn client perceptions is conducting one-on-one qualitative interviews. The process can be time consuming, but it generates a wealth of valuable information and demonstrates concern for client sensitivities. All attorneys should do a client qualitative survey no less than once every 12 months, and more frequently is highly recommended. The relatively few clients that account for 60 to 80 percent of the revenue of the attorney should all be interviewed as a minimum.

Some attorneys feel uncomfortable receiving criticism, and some clients feel uncomfortable giving constructive criticism face to face with the attorney. However, the discipline required on the parts of the attorney and the client in dealing with these problems often develops a better channel for two-way communication. If the qualitative interviews are an ongoing process, as they should be, eventually a greater comfort level can be established, and the quality and sincerity of the feedback improves.

As an alternative, if the attorney cannot overcome the comfort obstacle with one-on-one interviews, an outside consultant can be hired to conduct interviews and interpret results.

SELF-ADMINISTERED PERSONAL INTERVIEWS

Setting. It is vitally important to the objectivity of the process that the interview be conducted in an arbitrary, nonsocial setting. The client should not be a guest of the attorney in the attorney's office or conference room. The interview should never be conducted during a meal paid for by the attorney or in any situation where the client may feel some social obligation to be "kind" to the attorney. The purpose of the whole process is objective, even if negative, feedback.

On more than one occasion, attorneys have invited clients to their offices or taken clients to lunch or dinner to discuss their feelings. The attorneys have returned from the interviews feeling good about a client's perceptions and their practice services only to be surprised later when the client changed attorneys! The attorneys had let themselves hear what they wanted to hear while at lunch. The clients, of course, did not feel comfortable being completely candid in a social setting and felt an obligation to be pleasant. The true purpose of the meeting, to uncover possibly yet undisclosed client perceptions, ended up being one of the casualties of a very comfortable meal.

The best place to conduct a personal interview is the client's office (or home, if the person is a retail client). Besides showing an interest in them and their environment, the interview time spent remains clearly distinct from any billable time in the attorney's office. Client research that benefits the attorney's practice should never be billed to the client, and the client should understand this.

Preparation. A list of questions should be carefully prepared prior to the interviews and strictly followed during the interview so that all interview results can eventually be compiled. This also helps to ensure that all subjects important to the attorney's practice will be covered, meaning the discussion will stay on track.

Individual questions should be based on issues important to the attorney, firm partners, associates, and most of all, clients. All of the responses by the clients may or may not be based on fact. That is immaterial. What do clients think they are getting? This is the real concern.

Active listening on the part of the attorney is vital. One way to do this is to paraphrase client statements verbally immediately after they are said to confirm understanding. Key words and phrases should be noted with as much additional detail as needed to reconstruct the conversation later.

Notes may be reviewed with the client at the close of the interview to confirm a mutual sense of emphasis and priority.

QUALITATIVE ISSUES

There are four general areas where client surveys can provide significant information on attorney performance. They are communication, work response, competence, and billings.

Communications and Accessibility. Communications and accessibility can be a source of contention between attorneys and clients. An attorney must know client perceptions regarding this matter.

Do telephone calls and written requests receive a *prompt* reply? Some law firms have a goal of returning telephone calls within 24 hours. Is this satisfactory? Should calls be handled more promptly, even if by someone else? Some clients have said that even if their attorney is not available, they still want to hear from someone in the office, whether a secretary, paralegal, or associate familiar with the client. It is often better for someone else to respond with apologies for a specific attorney than it is to let the call go unanswered.

Does the attorney keep the client informed regarding the work in progress? Does the client have to ask how things are going? A frequent complaint of clients is that they don't feel informed. Even during protracted matters, clients have said they like to know what they are waiting for, why, and when it is likely to occur.

Work Response. Another issue is the work response. Is the client satisfied with the work response time? More than one client has asked an attorney to review a contract before execution, but, by the time an attorney response was received, the issue had become moot because a negotiation deadline had passed. The burden is on the attorney to determine needs and expectations in each situation. What the attorney can reasonably do is not always satisfactory. Responsiveness goes beyond merely returning phone calls, but speaks to ability and willingness to complete work in a timely fashion, according to the needs of the client.

Competence. Competence is another area of client perceptions. Is the client confident in the quality of work and expertise? Most clients will not feel competent to judge an attorney on legal knowledge and application. Clients have more pragmatic criteria. Did the attorney always make deadlines for courts, agencies, and negotiations when known in advance, particularly when by statute? Did the attorney understand the client's business? Most important, did the client get the results she expected or needed?

Research is often perceived by clients to disguise a lack of competence. From the attorney's point of view, it is better to research an issue carefully than to advise improperly. But often the client's perception is that researching simple issues should not be necessary. The attorney must share with the client the nature of the research and the results as soon as they are learned.

Clients often judge their attorney's competence by matters of appearance. Do documents and correspondence always appear correct and efficient? Clients have been heard to complain that too often a document is incorrect or needs to be redone. Detail has a huge impact on the client.

Billing. This issue of billing is emotion laden by its very nature. Were the bills reasonable for the task accomplished? Were they fair in relation to the value of the work? Were the amounts in keeping with expectations? Are they understandable? Had a clear understanding, with written confirmation, been reached before the matter was undertaken? Billing may be one of the most critical communications of all. The billing process affects the client's perceptions of value, fairness, and competence.

FOLLOW-UP AFTER THE INTERVIEW

Not only should the attorney verbally thank the client for his or her help, but follow with a letter specifically citing the areas discussed. If remedial action was indicated, the client should be advised as to when (or not) the action will be implemented. The attorney's skills in active listening will be critical at this point.

There may be areas mentioned by the client which are clearly out of the attorney's hands. The attorney should tell the client when that is the case but also indicate that an effort will still be made to effect change.

In a situation where clients complained of staff ignorance on certain matters, one attorney considered follow-up action to be complete when offending staff people were disciplined or terminated. Naturally, the client may have felt responsible for a termination that perhaps was not necessary. The attorney, on the other hand, was able to "hide" from the main point that the client was trying to make—which was that staff members were not informed by the attorney. Further, the client became less willing to give feedback after that incident.

CHAPTER 8
Qualitative Group Surveys: Multiplying the Value of Individual Interviews

SUMMARY

Focus groups often uncover issues which are important to clients, yet are not mentioned in individual interviews. Bringing small groups of people with some commonality develops creative assessments available no other way. Success can be defined in terms of feelings expressed both in breadth and depth. The key is to use an experienced and disinterested moderator.

This chapter discusses

- the appropriate person to moderate a focus group.
- location considerations.
- specific equipment and setup requirements.
- establishing agendas and time frames.
- postsession evaluation.

If individual interviews cannot or will not be used by an attorney to gather client information, a group interview or "focus group" is an effective option. In the case of firms and even practice groups, the technique uses panels of clients to focus on broad concerns.

Focus groups are loosely structured meetings with a third-party moderator. The selection of a qualified and experienced moderator is vitally important for ultimate success. The moderator's experience does not necessarily need to be specifically as a focus group facilitator, but should include extensive experience with group dynamics. The moderator's qualifications should include an understanding of the challenges of the legal profession. Using an attorney from the firm or someone affiliated with the firm is not normally recommended.

The moderator's challenge is to keep the discussion moving, yet focused on client-related concerns. He or she needs to draw out the shy as well as control the aggressive participants so that participation is relatively well balanced.

The moderator and the participants should have copies of the discussion agenda. This agenda could consist of nothing more than broad derivatives of the basic issues described in Chapter 7. Other issues might include

- Are you generally satisfied with your legal service?
- Are there ways in which the attorney could improve?
- How did you choose your attorney?
- Do you feel your attorney fully understands your needs?
- Would you recommend your attorney to someone else?

Often the inexperienced moderator will have a list that is too long to be practical. Normally, a group can only attack a very short list of items adequately. The inexperienced moderator can also tend to get unduly nervous and talk too much using his or her overly long list, inadvertently squelching discussion.

A recording device (either audio or video, depending on the comfort level of the participants with the method selected) is helpful for review and analysis, as well as editing for later use. The recording must be of good quality since transcriptions will be valuable for later study. Pretesting the recorder is highly recommended, including the placement of microphones, so that all participants will be recorded clearly. Multiple microphones may be necessary to record all remarks.

The moderator should explain the purpose of the resulting recording (transcription, study, etc.).

The value of transcribing recorded remarks is that all information will be extracted, including comments which might otherwise be lost in nuances or non sequitur remarks.

THE FOCUS GROUP SETTING

The value of focus groups is in the creative synergy developed by bringing together people with presumably similar interests. Everything possible should be done to enhance that atmosphere. Physical arrangements should be well lit and comfortable. A roundtable seating arrangement has proven to be most conducive to discussion. Paper and pens should be provided for participants to make notes for themselves.

Refreshments such as coffee, tea, and soft drinks should be available, but no meal should be furnished at that time since a meal tends to make the meeting too social. A neutral setting such as a club or hotel room is preferable.

There should be no distractions. Possible distractions could be a room with an outstanding view or noteworthy pictures on the wall. All outside interruptions, such as ringing telephones or room service, should be avoided during the course of the discussion.

MEETING LENGTH AND PARTICIPANT SELECTION

To be most effective, the focus group should meet for 60 to 90 minutes. Less than 60 minutes prevents the full development of ideas while longer than 90 minutes results in loss of attention. Offering a meal following the discussion is an appropriate token of appreciation and also a chance for members of the group to socialize.

Six to 10 people should constitute the group. Each should represent the attorney's ideal client criteria. If the attorney wants to market services to a particular audience, the attorney should have the understanding of that audience provided by this type of research. A logical first focus group could include the attorney's leading clients, if they match the ideal criteria.

If the attorney wants more information than is provided by the first focus group, additional meetings should be planned. Participants in these additional meetings could include particular practice area segments or nonclients drawn from a client group the attorney may want to attract.

MEASURING FOCUS GROUP SUCCESS

Success should be judged in terms of the breadth and depth of client feelings expressed. From the attorney's first efforts in this area, subjects will likely be uncovered that will warrant further exploration in future focus groups. Because the focus group method is considered qualitative research, little statistically reliable data are provided since only a small number of people is involved. In terms of statistics, focus groups are often used to define issues which warrant quantitative research.

One in-house marketing director used focus groups to find out how clients felt the practice could improve. By playing audiotapes for the attorneys, they could learn client perceptions in very candid terms. The attorneys learned a great deal about issues of communication and access, response, and billing as well as client feelings in relation to parking, the reception area, and a host of items which seemed small. The attorneys realized that if these "small" issues were not of importance to the clients, they would not have been mentioned.

CHAPTER 9
Quantitative Research: Measuring the Extent of Perceptions

SUMMARY

Gathering a large amount of information is to proceed with a solid marketing program. To learn this information, quantitative research is employed. Careful adherence to many common sense considerations in the research will assure more accurate client survey results. Understanding and limiting both the objective and questions for which you want answers will improve quantity and quality of responses. Analysis of the quantitative results will often pinpoint unknown or underutilized opportunities.

This chapter discusses

- when and how to use quantitative surveys.
- questionnaire construction.
- setting objectives for research.
- determining potential subjects.
- pretesting to improve results.
- research project planning and schedule.

A group of partners and associates at a law firm in a medium-sized city felt they needed to get a complete understanding of where the firm stood in the eyes of its target market (ideal clients), particularly in relation to other firms serving the same market. Because they wanted to gather the opinions of a number of people in a relatively short amount of time, the personal interviews that go with qualitative research were ruled out. The firm decided to undertake a quantitative research project.

A list of important existing and former clients was made. Clients the firm hoped to recruit were added to the list. Possible referral sources were also included. The firm then began to elicit responses from every person on its list, asking the same questions of each respondent.

Firm partners learned that their assumptions regarding their reputation and visibility did not match the research results. They also discovered that several cross-selling opportunities, that is, opportunities to provide additional services to clients, were not being utilized to their full potential.

A firm strategy meeting was called, and the attorneys agreed to take remedial steps to change the firm's course. Their goals as a result of the research focused on the firm's image and a greater level of awareness of all practice areas among all their existing and potential clients as well as within the firm.

WHY QUANTITATIVE RESEARCH FOR LEGAL SERVICES?

Quantitative research essentially is a methodical discovery of a large amount of relatively simple data, usually involving a number of responses to multiple questions. Mail surveys generally are the method used for professions and businesses. Telephone surveys are utilized for retail consumers. For example, mail surveys require more turnaround time due to logistics inherent in the process. Conversely, some specificity of the recipient is assumed. Telephone surveys to businesses and professionals will not be as successful in eliciting detailed responses, because it is difficult to build trust and to get the respondent's attention for any length of time. Experience has also shown that the respondent may or may not be the person actually involved in the organizational decision process.

With those caveats, telephone surveys will produce quick answers to simple questions. For instance, some researchers have used telephone surveys to validate mail surveys. However, this choice can depend on several considerations such as response time requirements, the number of issues to be explored, and the proximity of locations of audience to be assessed.

When the issues deemed important by qualitative research must be asked of more clients than are practical to interview personally, quantitative research becomes an ideal choice. Other reasons for using quantitative research can be that the practice serves a relatively large number of clients, a need exists to determine as yet unvoiced responses (such as relative performance compared to other law firms), or the desire to plan more realistically according to anticipated needs.

The obvious advantage to quantitative research is that it allows a large number of people to be asked a relatively large number of questions. This method is believed to be statistically reliable, if performed appropriately. The disadvantage is that responses must be quantifiable which may not allow for sufficient deviations. Some client respondents feel they are not able to express adequately their opinions and perceptions with this method. When evaluating relationships and service, respondents often wish to describe their experiences, especially to third parties. That by definition is not quantifiable. A quantitative survey with sufficient items and response variants would be difficult to administer.

RESEARCH PITFALLS

Research can be a dangerous thing when attempted by someone not versed in the construction of questions and format. As litigators understand, the very way in which a question is asked can determine its answer. A flawed question, by virtue of its prejudice or its inability to communicate a purpose clearly, can lead a novice researcher to incorrect conclusions resulting in ill-advised actions. The format of a questionnaire definitely has impact—if it is a hobbled mix of multiple-choice questions, ratings, and open-ended questions, it can be difficult to construct and answer and a nightmare to assess.

A few caveats exist which can reduce the possibility of a faulty questionnaire and consequently flawed data.

DRAFTING A QUESTIONNAIRE

Scope. Many projects start out with too many objectives despite evidence that the less a respondent is asked, the more likely he or she is to respond. A questionnaire should be narrow in scope, dealing specifically with what needs to be learned from a predetermined target audience. A consensus on the questionnnaire's objective and target audience by all those who expect to benefit from the research is mandatory for success.

Target. A great deal of energy should be placed to determine who will be asked to provide opinions. Should all clients or just a group, such as a practice area clientele, be asked to share their feelings. Attorneys engaging in the research must have a clear vision of who will be reading and answering the questions, so that the appropriate questions can be included. In many cases, a third-party researcher will be a *must* to get much unbiased responses, particularly when the target audience reaches beyond the existing client list.

A cover letter should be included with any mailed questionnaire, telling why the research results will be important to the respondents as opposed to the attorney or firm. Each respondent should feel a sense of ease, flexibility, convenience, and confidentiality. Included in the cover letter can be an appropriate inducement, such as a donation to the respondent's favorite charity made in the respondent's name. Clearly the type of inducements used by consumer marketing researchers, such as $1 bills or prizes are not appropriate for a law office. A stamped, self-addressed envelope should be enclosed, and the single most important element of the cover letter must be included: a thank you from the attorney!

The questionnaire should be attractive and easy to read, which is simply produced by many word processing software programs. If a desktop publishing system is available, it should be used to make the form more graphically appealing. Ultimately, a professional typesetting service can make a very dramatic professional statement.

Simple, interesting, and nonthreatening questions should begin the questionnaire with the crucial and/or controversial items placed well into the body. Multiple-choice questions tend to receive greater responses since they are easier for the respondent (as well as easier to score and evaluate). Open-ended questions normally generate more information, although they are much more time consuming and difficult to assess accurately. If an ordered mixing of multiple-choice and open-ended questions is used, it can be appropriate, such as: "How would you rate our service?

Poor ____ Fair ____ Below Average ____
Above Average ____ Good ____ Excellent ____
Why?

This type of structure gives the respondent the option of providing a more involved response.

The last few questions in the questionnaire should be easy marks. For example: "Is there anything else you think is important for our survey?" or "How long have you been a client?"

It may seem obvious but can be a deceptively simple mistake to make: do not even subtly suggest answers. The introduction of bias will affect the validity of the entire research project, particularly if items are interrelated.

PRETESTING THE QUESTIONNAIRE

An attorney or firm planning to use a questionnaire to gather quantitative data should first ask someone not involved in the project to complete the intended survey. That person should be interviewed immediately afterward for their opinion. Depending on the size of the actual respondent target audience, it can be beneficial to ask a small group (five to ten) of the target group to repeat the process.

With those caveats you may feel that due to budget constraints, and the fact that you have the time or inclination, you will leap out into the gray clouds and manage the project yourself. At least start with a few basic questions which have worked well for other law firms.

A sample questionnaire is shown that can easily be adapted and used by attorneys. (See Figure 9-1.)

A. Is our location convenient?

Poor ___ Fair ___ Below Average ___
Above Average ___ Good ___ Excellent ___

B. Is your attorney accessible?

Never ___ Sometimes ___ Adequately ___
Frequently ___ Almost Always ___ Always ___

C. Is work done on time (such as document preparation, document review, filings)?

Never ___ Sometimes ___ Adequately ___
Frequently ___ Almost Always ___ Always ___

D. Were fees, costs, and their basis explained before the work was done?

Never ___ Sometimes ___ Adequately ___
Frequently ___ Almost Always ___ Always ___

E. Were fees and costs in line with expectations?

Never ___ Sometimes ___ Adequately ___
Frequently ___ Almost Always ___ Always ___

F. Did your attorney understand your needs?

Never ___ Sometimes ___ Adequately ___
Frequently ___ Almost Always ___ Always ___

G. Was our staff helpful and friendly?

Never ___ Sometimes ___ Adequately ___
Frequently ___ Almost Always ___ Always ___

H. How did your select your attorney?

Reputation ___ Community/Proximity ___
Industry involvement ___ Outside Referral ___
Other (please identify)

I. If by referral, would you please share by whom?

Friend ___ Banker ___ Accountant ___
Another Lawyer ___ Other ___

J. Would you recommend your attorney to others?

Yes ___ No ___
Why or Why Not?

Figure 9-1 Sample Questionnaire

CONDUCTING THE RESEARCH

A realistic time frame must be established in which the work can be completed. It is pointless to spend so much time drafting the perfect questionnaire and using perfect methodology that issues change and the results become outdated before they can be utilized. Whether the research is being conducted by one attorney or an international partnership, at least one person should be placed in charge of managing the project. Accountability can help to move the project along a predetermined timeline.

Depending on the size of the practice and the number of clients/respondents involved, most law practices should hire a third party to conduct research. By hiring a professional marketing research organization, greater reliance on the results becomes possible, a greater impartiality is achieved, and often a greater number of responses can be garnered.

Professional research firms can be located by asking for referrals from well-known advertising agencies in town, checking with a local chapter of the American Marketing Association, or asking the marketing department of a university or college.

As with hiring any professional, the final selection should be based on an understanding of the attorney or firm's need as well as a history and reputation for excellence with similar projects.

CHAPTER 10
Getting To Know Those You Work For

SUMMARY

An understanding of client characteristics enables the attorney to speak the client's language, understand client needs, and reach clients where they normally seek information. The more information known about clients, the more valuable that information becomes, owing to potentially interrelated facts. In simple terms, the cumulative effect of information helps paint an accurate picture, whereas single items contribute little.

This chapter discusses

- establishing factual client profiles.
- gathering data for profiles.
- using profile data for business development.

Personal information about clients eases the relationship-building process that is part of a successful law practice. Knowing the client well and making sure the client is aware of that knowledge adds to attorney-client trust.

Client profile information can be used by attorneys to set up data bases from which they can effectively track client developments, referrals, interrelationships, and such.

Imagine these statements when spoken by an attorney to a client: "Hello . . . how is your son enjoying college life?" or "I understand House Bill 234 can have a serious impact on your business" or "I see your local zoning board meeting next week will be pivotal for your development plans." These sort of statements demonstrate an interest in the client beyond billable hours.

Tracking clients to anticipate their needs can also lead to other opportunities for the attorney. Information about clients that is organized and accessible is more important than statute or case law knowledge when enhancing a practice is concerned. Software programs now available can help the attorney and staff organize this information in a cohesive, usable manner.

ESTABLISHING A DATA BASE

To gather and organize information pertaining to clients, the attorney should begin by making a list of existing, former, and potential clients. Oddly enough, this basic and relatively simple task is often overlooked in office procedure—more than one lawyer has tried to send holiday greeting cards only to learn that a list of names and addresses of clients was not readily available.

Next, a list of areas of interest should be made and input into a format. This means that the type and amount of information gathered will be consistent from client to client. For example, some areas of interest and relevance might be

Date updated:

Name:

Business address:
Residence address:
Business phone:
Residence phone:

Occupational title:
Age and/or date of birth:
Gender:
Marital status:
Children:
Religion:
Relatives and/or associates:
Graduate/professional school year of graduation:

School alumnus:
College year of graduation:
School alumnus:
High school year of graduation:
School alumnus:
Business and/or professional associations:
Outside interests and hobbies:

Dominant personality type: (Amiable) (Analytic) (Expressive) (Driver)

Probable career track:

The only substantive difference between an individual profile and a profile drawn up for a business or corporate client is that the information gathered begins with the organization. This means the format will be somewhat different:

Name of organization:

Address/location:
Billing address:

Nature of business (SIC* code(s)):
Economic trends and anticipated events:
Legislative, regulatory, and legal environment:
Estimated annual revenues:
Number of full-time employees:
Number of part-time employees:

Primary decision maker:
(insert personal profile here)

Secondary or alternate decision maker:
(insert additional personal profiles here)

Corporate officers or directors:

How does the attorney find all of this information regarding clients? Hopefully most of it will already be known as a result of being client focused. But even points about the client or client organization which are known should be verified for accuracy. This often can be accomplished by an administrative or support staff person who contacts the client's administrative or support staff. One conversation between attorney and client secretaries can provide a wealth of information.

It is very important that the information gathered for a client profile (Figure 10-1) is frequently updated. It can be embarrassing in the least to

*Standard Industrial Classification.

Name of company: Williamson Development Corporation Atty: DLH

Billing address: Post Office Box 2276, Kansas City, MO 64658
Office Location: 515 North Main, Kansas City, MO 64658

Primary Decision Maker: Paul Williamson Phone: 555-2009
Alternate Decision Maker: Spencer Boone Phone: 555-2276

Nature of Business (SIC code): 1620 (Bridge/Heavy Construction)
Estimated Annual Revenue: $12–15 million

Key Personnel: (Name, Title, Function, Personality Type, Notes)

Otis Williamson	Chairman of the Board (retired) Chief Executive Officer Expressive Founded company as young man, leaves most decisions to grandson Paul
Alan Craig	President Chief Financial Officer Driver Been with company for 35 years, oversees all finances
Taylor McKenna	Vice President Administrative Driver Administrates directives of Board, CEO, and CFO

Last Marketing Contact Date/Person/Subject/Result/Recommendation: 00/00/00 Taylor McKenna Labor contract review Received go-ahead for review and recommendations. Hourly billing with amount to be discussed if more than $7,500. Promised progress report in two weeks (secretary responsible).

00/00/00 Taylor McKenna Labor contract review Contacted regarding progress report (on schedule).

Agreed to go ahead with finalization and present final contract in two weeks.

00/00/00 Taylor McKenna Labor contract review

Established 00/00/00 at 00:00 A.M. as date and time for contract presentation and discussion with Board.

00/00/00 Board of Directors/Taylor McKenna Labor contract review Presented and agreed upon labor contract with Board.

Future work to be decided upon a need basis.

Figure 10-1 Client Profile

operate with outdated information and could do more damage than good. This task can also be assigned to a staff person.

CHAPTER 11
Understanding Basic Personality Types

SUMMARY

Understanding basic personality types is valuable for development of a strong client focus and good relationships. Recognizing the two basic client characteristics of assertiveness and responsiveness is the beginning of the process. Varying degrees of each feature and the relative interaction constitutes the root of the system. With this knowledge one can decide how much of what kind of information will be important to a given client.

This chapter discusses

- the thinker: slow moving, information oriented, detailed.
- the director: fast moving, goal oriented, factual.
- the relator: slow moving, relationship oriented.
- the socializer: fast moving, outgoing, opinionated.

Many attorneys do not really understand what clients need. They may feel they understand their client's legal needs and are active in client trade and community groups. But personal relationship with each client may not progress as the attorney once had envisioned it might.

For instance, attorneys can make a concerted effort to provide very detailed information with all their work so clients would understand the comprehensive nature of the services offered. For some clients this did not seem enough, while for others the detail was overwhelming. One client may actually become upset with a lengthy report, impatiently interrupting the attorney's explanation by demanding, "What's the bottom line?" Attorneys can have doubts that they will ever find a middle ground that satisfies all their clients. One solution is to learn the client's personality types and speak their individual "languages."

CLASSIFYING CLIENT PERSONALITIES

Despite the similarity of most practice area work, client personalities can make similar tasks seem dramatically different. One client asks to be inundated with information. Another client wants concise counsel and depends on the attorney to keep supporting information on target.

A simple personality classification system can help sort through personal idiosyncrasies and ease diversity of the client base. Of course a doctorate degree in psychology might reasonably argue that this system goes beyond simple to simplistic. Yet many businesspeople and professionals have made this system work for them.

Personality classification is based on a comprehensive system originated in the book, *Non-Manipulative Selling* by Tony Alessandra, Phil Wexler, and Rick Barrera. It is a method of intensely studying client behavior and then responding accordingly—attorney behavioral adaptation! The benefit to the client is that the attorney works and communicates in a way to which he or she can relate and feel comfortable. The benefit to the attorney is a better relationship with clients.

PERSONALITY CLASSIFICATION

The basis of this personality classification is that human (in this case client) behavior can be broken down into a two distinct personality characteristics: assertiveness and responsiveness. Assertiveness is proactive while responsiveness is reactive. Personalities exist in combinations of these two general characteristics. Everyone is, to some degree, somewhat proactive and somewhat reactive. It is the degree of each as well as their combination that makes each person unique.

Combinations of the two characteristics result in four personality combinations according to this methodology:

- self-contained/indirect
- self-contained/direct
- open/indirect
- open/direct

Each combination results in a personality type which can be identified and named: thinker, director, relator, and socializer.

Thinker (self-contained/indirect). As the name implies, this personality type tends to be motivated by detailed facts and task-oriented problems. Thinkers are generally slow moving, relatively low in self-esteem, and in need of detailed information to make a decision.

Director (direct/self-contained). This type is very assertive although not very responsive. Directors' concerns are with tasks to the extent that tasks and facts will contribute to goal attainment.

Relator (open/indirect). This type usually is more interested in relationships and much less in tasks. They tend to be susceptible to the suggestions of anyone on which they feel they can rely. It is difficult for them to make decisions on their own.

Socializer (open/direct). This type is opinionated and a risk taker. They are highly relationship oriented and fast paced. They can make quick decisions enthusiastically. Since they are gregarious, they are great referral sources if they are pleased.

Attorneys can ascertain their clients' personality types by observing their behavior and reaching conclusions regarding past behavior. A few generalizations about a particular client's business style will show a tendency toward one personality classification. After that, the attorney can watch for indications that the client's style is changing or has changed and can assign a new classification when appropriate.

Of course people do not always conform to one personality classification but generally have strong tendencies and "backup" styles which they will adopt when they perceive certain stimuli. What causes one to either raise or lower their assertiveness or responsiveness varies according to the individual. To make the classification system work, the attorney must be able to recognize changes and even their causes in order to produce appropriate responses.

The attorney must develop a specific style of his or her own to deal with each personality situation. Specific recommendations:

Thinkers. These clients will need lots of detail, almost to absurdity, and sometimes only remotely relevant. The attorney's strategy should be to inundate them with information and then guide them to a decision. This information must be well organized and offer tangible evidence of its worth. Analytics are more comfortable with written information and correspondence than personal or telephone conversations so the attorney should always follow each meeting with this client type with a summarization and written recommendation.

Directors. These clients are goal and results oriented. They require efficiency and organization without much emphasis on personal relationships. The attorney should allow this client type to discover things rather than be told. The attorney-client relationship should be businesslike without an attempt to move into a more casual, personal relationship (unless the client actively seeks it). Disagreements should be argued on the basis on facts, not personal feelings.

Relaters. These clients will value relationships, people, and relative values. They have difficulty making a strong stand on any given issue. The attorney should support their individual feelings and emotional inclinations to establish personal bonds. They should be treated like close friends. The attorney must be careful to seek out and understand what this client type really wants rather than what the client may think the attorney wants to hear. Debates with amiables should be based on feelings rather than on facts, and all communication should be slow, informal, and open.

Socializers. These clients will be risk takers with strong opinions. They have a great potential as referral sources for the attorney. While they value relationships, they like ideas to be their own and they like to argue points. The attorney should help these clients to talk about their opinions, ideas, and dreams and offer support for those things. These clients do not like to lose arguments, so the attorney should make sure all alternatives are explored with mutual enthusiasm. Expressives can be influenced by references and referrals from entrepreneurs and companies they admire, so the attorney should make these available when seeking new clients and serving established clients.

PUTTING THE INFORMATION TO WORK

So how did our attorney friend do after reading this information? After a few months, he began to react to client needs according to his increased understanding of their personality styles. He began to enjoy client relationships more and feel less agitated by personal reactions which he felt were beyond his control. His clients seemed to appreciate his professional services more as well.

He began using the classifications in business as well as social settings. He developed strategies for dealing with people as outlined in *Non-Manipulative Selling.* Particularly with clients, he found treating them the way they wanted and speaking their language was not only fun but gratifying as well. The more he used the system, the more he understood why he had difficulty dealing with certain people in the past.

BIBLIOGRAPHY

ALESSANDRA, TONY, PHIL WEXLER, AND RICK BARRERA. *Non-Manipulative Selling.* Prentice-Hall Press, New York, 1987.

CHAPTER 12
Where Does The Revenue Come From? What About Profit?

SUMMARY

Determining revenue sources is both a simple and valuable process. Although sophisticated profit measurements are available for larger firms, most law practices need a simple numerical analysis. By measuring effort versus results, the essence of profit can be accurately derived. Actual cash receipts aren't totally conclusive, but often reveal information many practices have not carefully analyzed. The results can have a significant impact a practice's future course.

This chapter discusses

- reasons for misperceptions of client values.
- simple but useful profitability measures.
- graphs to see relative contributions and trends.
- staff and associate commitment.

An attorney, a member of the executive committee of a midsized law firm, wondered about the profitability of his firm. Firm clients represented a broad range of interests. Each client received the same amount of attention with regard to public relations, that is, a holiday card mailed each December and occasional gifts as tokens of appreciation. The attorney thought that more attention should be paid to clients generating the most income, but no one seemed to know who they were with any confidence.

The attorney decided to conduct a revenue analysis, categorizing clients by the amount of work generated in contradistinction to the amount of income received. The attorney discovered that relatively few clients (and related matters) accounted for most of the firm's revenue. The rest of the clients were either hit and miss with their needs and lacked consistency in revenue for the firm or required a lot of partner work with little leveraging opportunity and negotiated bill write-downs so that profitability was not good.

The attorney concluded that the firm needed to pay more attention to the few real consistent revenue producers. The loss of some of these clients could have a severe impact on the organization's fiscal health.

ANALYZING CLIENTS BY REVENUE

Many attorneys react too much to the "squeaky wheel" and not enough to those clients that are truly important to the practice. Key clients require special attention because of their immediate economic impact, their value as referral sources for similar potential clients, and the damage to reputation and revenue that would result from the loss of such a client. The process starts with the identification of which clients are key.

If attorneys asked each person in their office, from the receptionist to the paralegal to the partners, who the key clients were, they would probably find that each person would provide a different answer. Each person views clients in a very personal way. The receptionist might think that the client who calls the office frequently is the most important client. The paralegal might assume that the client generating the most labor-intensive work is the greatest revenue generator for the firm. The partners, most likely, would be able to name the top revenue generators, but they might not be able to name the most profitable clients.

Few practices, whether solo or a firm, have an accurate listing of revenue and/or profit by client. Attorneys can establish a clear picture of which clients should be considered crucial to the success of their practice by analyzing

- client work required.
- billable hours generated.
- billable hours actually billed (no time write-downs).
- income received.
- any other mitigating factors.
- leveraging opportunities.

The attorney's bookkeeper, accountant, or even the attorney (if interested in conducting such an analysis) should be able to assemble a breakdown of all these factors and piece together "the big picture" in terms of revenue and profitability for the firm. For most practices it will be a matter of devoting the labor to compiling the data, since it is the most simple data required.

USING GRAPHICS TO TELL THE STORY

The single most effective device in the analysis of quantifiable data, in this case client revenue, is the use of graphics. Not only is graphic display valuable for attorneys, it has other value. When shared with staff, they can become more involved and committed. Graphic display does not require the exposure of detailed financial data which should be kept confidential; it only requires an honest evaluation of a practice's financial status.

The receptionist who thought the client calling the office frequently was the most valuable client may learn that person generated very little revenue for the practice. By providing a clear indication of the attorney's key clients, the receptionist is able to treat them in the manner they probably expect and most definitely deserve, without making the other clients feel they are missing anything.

One way to illustrate client revenue graphically is the use of a bar graph. (See Figure 12-1 and 12-2.)

Another way to illustrate client revenue graphically is the use of a pie graph. (See Figure 12-3.)

Both methods clearly demonstrate key revenue-generating clients. By looking at revenue and profitability of clients, an attorney can do a more efficient and rewarding job of assigning energy and resources to take care of clients. Further, by identifying strengths and opportunities, an attorney can make well-informed decisions about business development resource allocations.

Attorneys should make such a graph available to partners, associates, and staff on a regular basis, as often as is necessary to ensure that it is current and relevant.

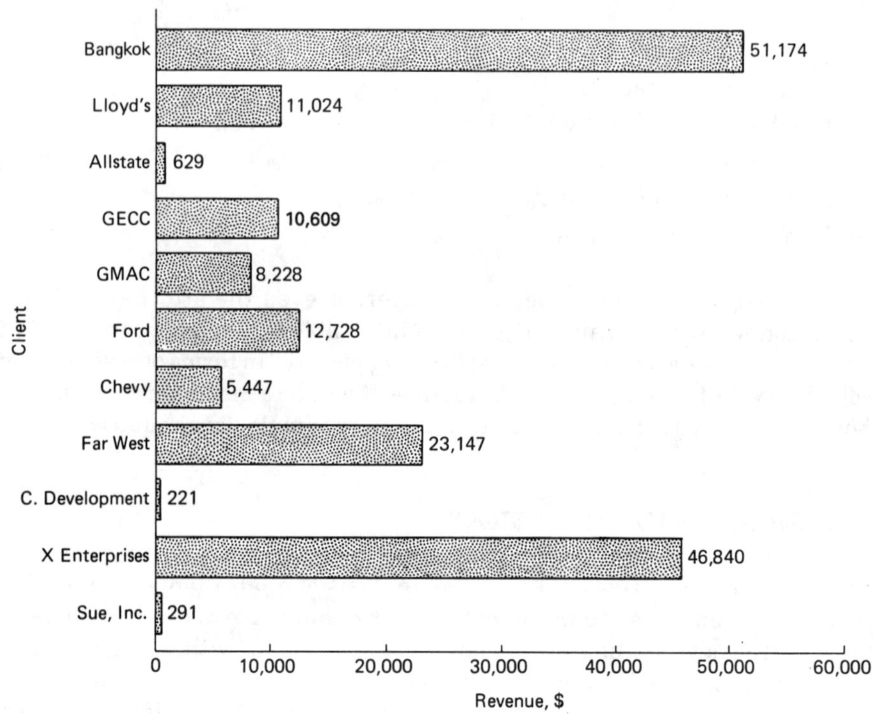

Figure 12-1 Clients by Revenue Bar Graphs

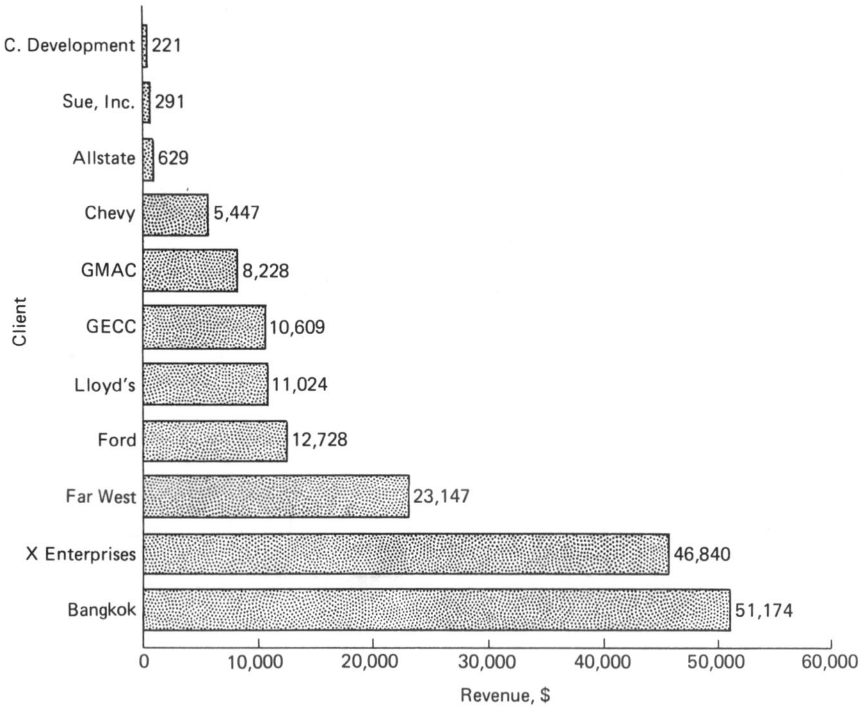

Figure 12-2 Clients by Revenue Bar Graphs

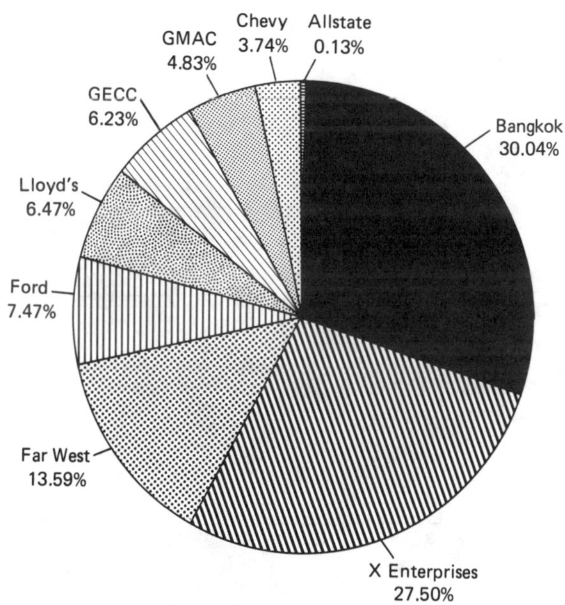

Figure 12-3 Clients by Revenue Pie Graph

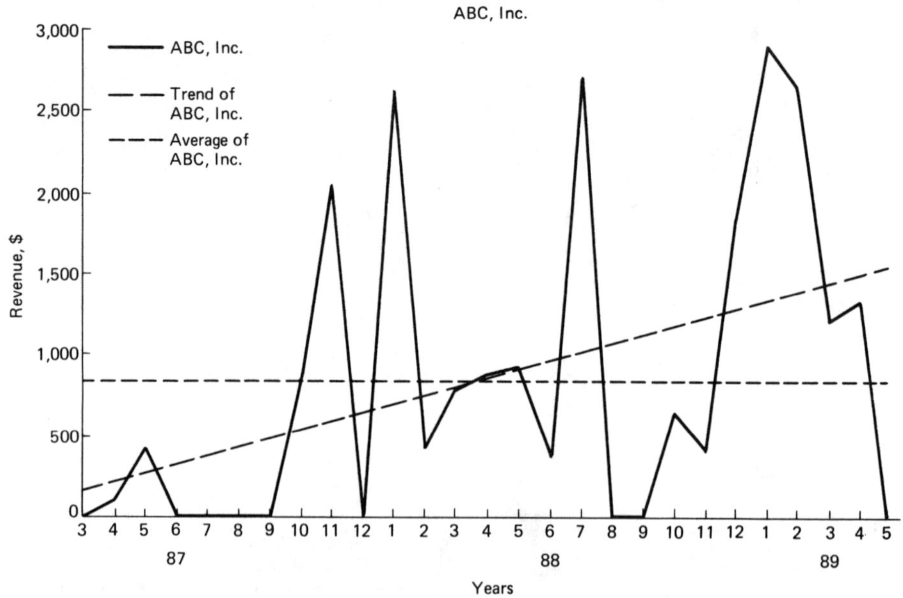

Figure 12-4 Line Graphs of Revenue

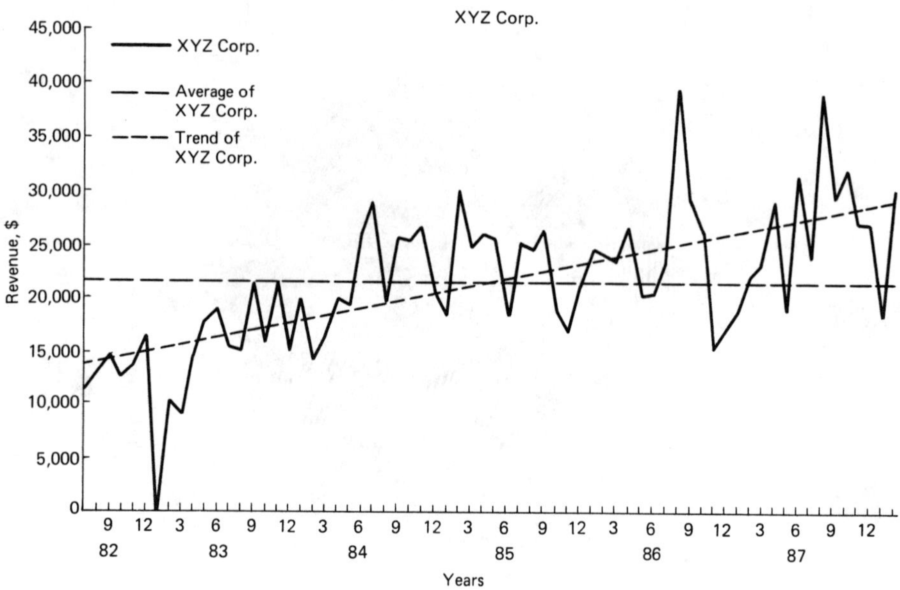

Figure 12-5 Line Graphs of Revenue

PLOTTING CLIENT REVENUE TRENDS

A simple line graph depicting client revenue trends can help the attorney ascertain which clients may be slipping in loyalty and perhaps receiving legal services elsewhere. (See Figures 12-4 and 12-5.)

An attorney who discovers that the work and revenues from one or more clients is steadily decreasing should take immediate remedial actions to increase communications with those clients. The attorney should also investigate and seek replacement work. Seeing a negative trend as it just begins to take shape helps the attorney to alter its course before impact, which is more hopeful than making reactionary plans in its wake.

The point of this analysis is twofold: *first,* by understanding your clients' changing needs, you can better adapt and change for their and your benefit, and *second,* and perhaps even more basic, by better understanding your revenue sources by clients, it will be easier to identify other potential clients with the same needs and profiles.

CHAPTER 13
Finding Your Practice Niche: Internal Practice Analysis

SUMMARY

Finding a niche is relatively easy once the decision is reached to focus a legal practice. Economically and professionally, a focused practice may be more rewarding on different levels. An analysis of an attorney's practice will reveal clients who prefer—and will pay for—one expert in a field more than a generalist.

This chapter discusses

- understanding the niche concept.
- simple techniques to start the analytic process.
- revenue analyses of practice areas.
- relative criteria according to individual interests.

Many attorneys feel there is an increasing importance to focus on selected practice areas. Part of this is a reflection of a growing need to establish niches (see Chapter 6). Very simply, emphasizing practice areas, or for that matter even client groups, allows lawyers to become increasingly expert in the needs of the clients. By the same token, most clients appreciate the value of that expertise and are willing to pay accordingly.

How does an attorney find a practice niche? Should that niche be based on what the attorney likes to do? Should it be based on what appears to be the most profitable or shows the most dramatic propensity for growth? The answer is: "It depends." It depends, first, on what the attorney is willing to accept and sometimes even to sacrifice. It also depends on the attorney's competitive market.

There are several methods of analysis which can help an attorney find a niche that will be both satisfying and rewarding. Whether attorneys choose just one or all of these methods will be affected by their belief in the priorities of relative benefits of finding the right practice area.

> The managing partner for a midsized firm in a city of about 100,000 felt that his firm could be considered a full-service firm. After all, they provided a wide range of practice area services, including some retail client needs; first-party and insurance defense litigation; and business, real estate, tax, franchise, and corporate work. The practice group that was the most active varied each year, depending on the local market conditions.
>
> But practice area emphasis was the center of some debate in the firm as a result of declining revenues, particularly from key clients. Two partners thought by trying to be full service, the firm was covering too many practice areas with limited resources. The business development partners were asked to investigate options and make a recommendation at the next partners' meeting.
>
> They began by inviting a legal services marketing consultant to the office to discuss the issue. They explained the problem and asked how he might proceed, if retained by the firm. The consultant told them he would start by conducting an internal analysis to find possible growth areas as well as drains on the firm's resources.
>
> The firm retained the consultant who immediately began his analysis. The consultant and the firm's administrator examined the firm's gross client revenue (in contradistinction to billable hours). Then they plotted the revenue for each practice area by year for the last five years. They used graphs to compare client revenue and practice area revenue. From this comparison, they were able to draw a few preliminary conclusions which they presented in a report to the firm's partners.
>
> The partners agreed that some of their perceptions of client revenue and practice area revenue had been wrong. One partner said that because of her own interest and experience, she thought that one practice area was very profitable for the firm. She was surprised to find that it had provided a great deal of work but had not been a substantial source of profit for the firm. Other partners described their misconceptions similarly.

They discussed those areas which were the most successful for the firm which they enjoyed and in which they felt most competent. The most difficult even wrenching decision was actually to eliminate some practice areas. Other firms had internal battles over this very issue. The practice areas they decided to discontinue were ones which provided the least revenue and the least professional satisfaction for the partners.

By narrowing the firm's practice scope, based on the recommendation of the consultant, a potential niche was identified for the firm based on its size, remaining practice areas, clientele, and anticipated revenue. The anticipated revenue, although negatively affected in the short term, was expected to increase over the long term. This revenue increase would result from two factors: the enhanced reputation of the firm due to its focus and increased client satisfaction due to attorney expertise in the selected areas.

DISCOVERING WHAT WORKS

Attorneys who want to specialize certainly are not alone. Many professionals and businesses are discovering that specialization is a key to survival in a very competitive marketplace. Clients are often no longer satisfied with an attorney who knows a little about a lot of things when an attorney who knows a lot about a particular need is available.

For some attorneys, finding a practice niche is easy. They may be particularly proficient at land use or real estate law or may be "natural" defense litigators. For most attorneys the choice is not quite so simple. With a broad range of practice areas from which to choose, narrowing a practice down to a few areas may be difficult.

Here are some simple methods and rules which should be used to find the proper niche or verify the appropriateness of a selected niche. The information to utilize these is in the attorney's office—the only work required is the discipline to access and analyze that information.

First, the attorney should examine client revenue for at least the past five years (see Chapter 12). Billable hours can be examined as an altogether different exercise to determine attorney efficiency, but client revenue is a more important factor in predicting profitable growth areas.

Next, the attorney should list all practice areas in which he or she has at least some experience. With this list, the attorney then can track practice area revenue.

Finally, a compilation, comparison, and trend analysis is used with the information already gathered. The most effective way to accomplish this task is with a business analysis software program. Using bar graphs, pie graphs, line graphs, or any other graphic form, the attorney can readily visualize what type of practice area work occupies most of his or her time while at the same time producing the most revenue. (See Figures 13-1 through 13-4.) With this information, a choice (albeit sometimes a difficult one) can be made. The attorney can select the practice area that appears to be the most positive.

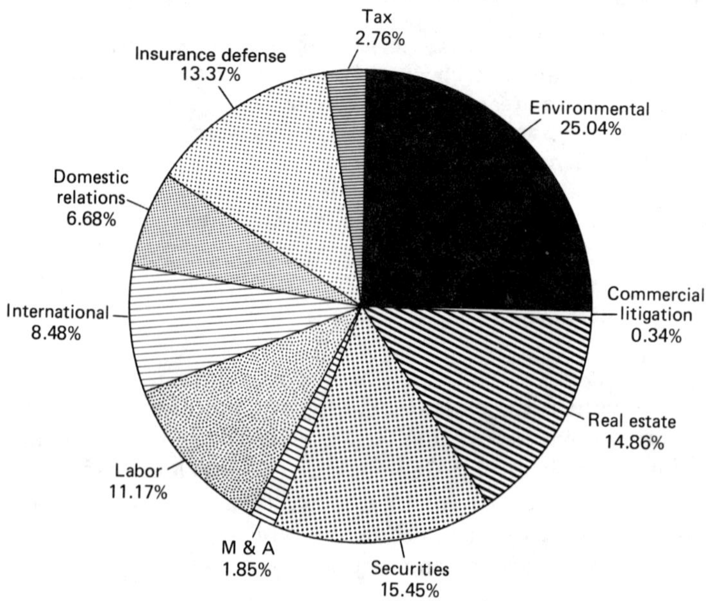

Figure 13-1 Pie Graph

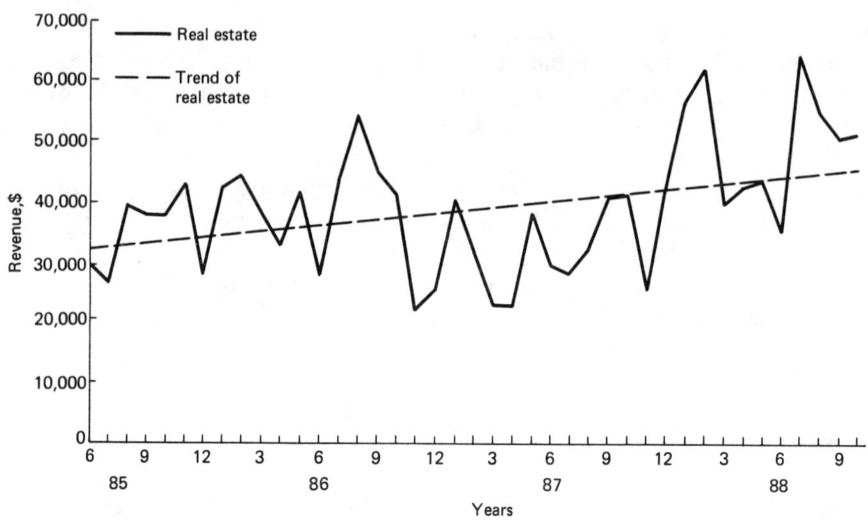

Figure 13-2 Real Estate Trend Lines

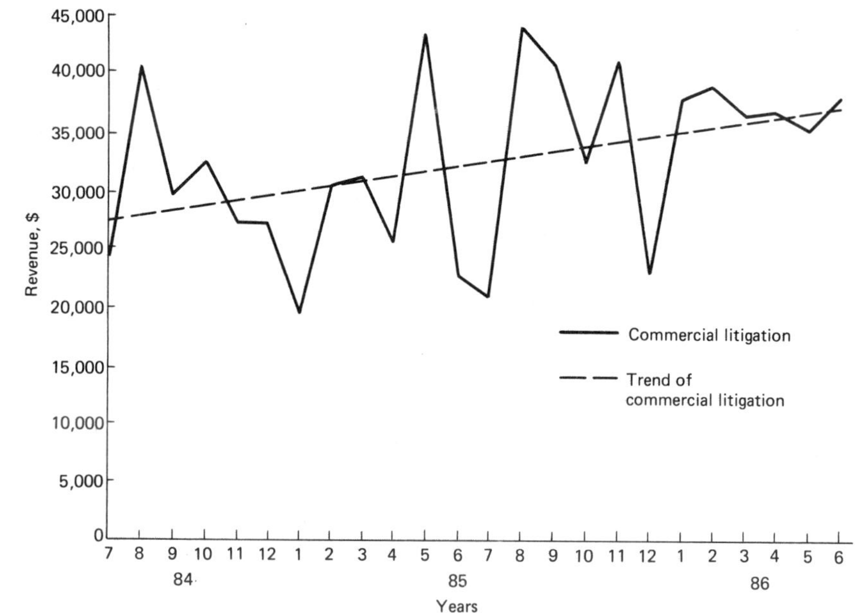

Figure 13-3 Commercial Litigation Trend Lines

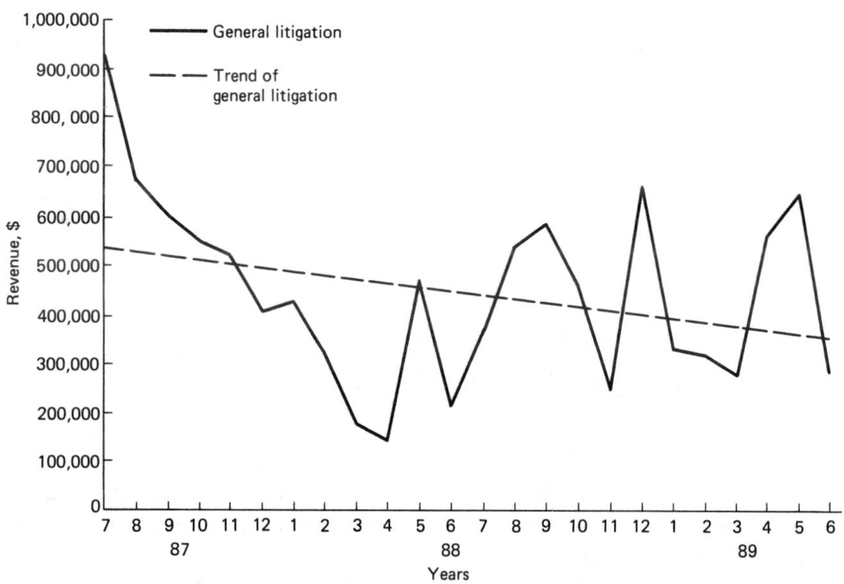

Figure 13-4 General Litigation Trend Lines

NARROWING THE SCOPE

Once the attorney chooses the practice areas on which to focus, the most important next step is to commit all energy into those new areas. Conversely and more difficult yet, disregard CLE's, potential clients, and other developments in a discarded practice area. In the words of Mark Twain, "Put all your eggs in one basket and watch that basket!"

The attorney should watch for continuing legal education sessions on the emphasized practice areas and, to the extent that the attorney's existing practice and resources permit, should attend them all. The attorney should also attend community conferences and join associations, where practical, that will further knowledge in that area and introduce the attorney to others in the field.

After becoming increasingly versed in the selected practice areas, the attorney can begin to seek speaking engagements and article-writing opportunities. This will generate a more recognized presence in situations where information is needed about the selected practice areas. The attorney should not speak as an attorney at these opportunities, attempting to impress the audience with "legalese." Instead, the vernacular of that particular industry or group should be used to demonstrate expertise in that area and using the law credentials only as a "hook" (see Chapters 64 and 70 on specific methods for attracting client attention to an attorney's expertise in a practice area).

The most important point is that the practice area niche should be one in which the attorney has established quantifiable potential resulting from internal analysis and one to which he or she is completely committed. The ideas presented here are as useful to an individual attorney as they are to a large firm.

CHAPTER 14
Analyzing External Data for Niche Cues

SUMMARY

Deciding what has been profitable and what was rewarding is only part of the niche answer. One should look at market opportunities relative to future trends before deciding on a practice niche. Market segment size will indicate opportunities. Library resources and computer data bases are all quick and easy sources of valuable information.

This chapter discusses

- using business periodical indices creatively.
- building practice niche on personal history and interests.
- analyzing potential impact of trends.
- luck as contribution to practice niche.

Let's follow an attorney through an analysis of information about potential practice areas and the results of the analysis on the attorney's current practice.

> June had conducted an internal practice area analysis but wanted more information before deciding on which areas to focus. She was more concerned with personal satisfaction than with financial gain, although she did not think she needed to choose one over the other. She wanted to gain a better understanding of trends while at the same time considering her personal interests.
>
> Her first stop was the local municipal library. Since her home and practice were in a large metropolitan area, the library resources available were quite substantial. June compiled a list of her own top five practice areas from the past five years, based on the internal analysis of client revenue and frequency of work. She consulted a periodicals index to look for stories about the industries those practice areas touched. She started with the annual business periodicals index dated ten years and tallied the articles regarding the industry and practice area issues. She continued the process through each annual index up through the current year and made monthly totals for that.
>
> Using her periodicals tally she narrowed her list to the top five practice areas showing the most growth potential. She kept the other five areas on a separate sheet, not completely rejecting them without further study.
>
> Next she talked with clients, professional colleagues, and trusted friends to ask their opinions regarding the potential for future work. She informally noted and tallied their responses.
>
> Later, she conducted further comprehensive statistical research. She also consulted business and law trend analysis articles and books. Finally, she contacted her undergraduate university career placement center, asking for their information on areas of career placement growth.
>
> Her conclusions led her to retain the top three related practice areas she had initially selected after consulting the library periodicals index. She staked her current practice on her decision by referring existing clients who were not in those areas to other attorneys and focusing her attention on clients who were. Her focus became more client centered than practice centered.
>
> At first, her practice revenue declined because of her reduced client work load. But over time, her increasingly substantial reputation for expertise in her chosen niche led to more client referrals, and eventually she regained and even surpassed her former client work load and income.

GOING AFTER TRENDS

How can attorneys determine, with some degree of assurance, what hot new areas or trends are worth pursuing as practice niches? One method is content analysis, which is watching, reading, and analyzing the news and business media for frequency of issues. A watered-down although less time-consuming variation on this method is counting articles on a target subject.

Three issues that must be identified with regard to each potential trend are

- What peripheral issues will this trend introduce?
- Who will the key players be?
- What will their objectives be?

Answers to these questions provide more definitive parameters for the trend and demonstrate more clearly the trend's potential for continued importance and recognition.

Politics also plays a significant role in this process. By following local, state, regional, and national legislation and litigation through news journals and even bar journals, an attorney can develop a keener sense of political trends.

Whatever the emphasis, be it an issue, an industry, or a political position, it is important to be objective in conducting content analysis. Specifically, the attorney should rely on a number of seemingly objective sources of information to avoid prejudice.

DEVELOPING PERSONAL INTEREST AREAS

Just because a practice area shows potential for being a hot new trend does not necessarily mean it will work for a particular attorney. The practice area should also coalesce with the attorney's personal interests.

For example, one attorney had an undergraduate degree in chemical engineering. Further, she had worked for a petrochemical firm before attending law school. Her decision to serve that clientele was natural. She understood and could speak their language. Additionally, she was particularly well suited to become involved in many environmental issues dealing with wastes and chemical accidents. Her practice area development decision, however, was a direct result of studying media coverage. She knew her skills alone would not provide success. She had to establish that her market needs would provide work and income.

Another example is an attorney who was introduced to literature and theater as an undergraduate liberal arts major. His interest grew into an important avocation as he continued to serve on boards and became involved in theater production. His practice area emphasis came to serve professionals in contract negotiation, tax, and general commercial work.

These lawyers are finding satisfaction personally and professionally. The chemical engineer/attorney developed her practice by combining her legal training with a studied interest and by assessing her practice potential through trend analysis. The theater enthusiast/attorney found satisfaction by combining his legal training with an outside interest.

Luck has been a significant contributor in the selection of more than one practice niche. For example, a retired law school professor has told of three cases where freshly minted attorneys were barely on the job with a law firm when they were given files to study and pursue. In all three cases the new attorney recognized that the matters represented great opportunities because they were areas of law which had no extant expertise. By becoming the experts they developed highly successful practice niches based on luck. Luck in what their employer asked them to do! Perhaps as Shakespeare would have said it, "Greatness was thrust upon them."

External practice area analysis can increase the odds for success in developing a practice niche.

CHAPTER 15
Focusing on Industry Groups for Practice Niches

SUMMARY

A relatively easy but seldom employed tactic for successful marketing of attorneys is for the attorney to associate professionally and socially with a target setment. Many clients appreciate lawyers that not only understand their legal needs but understand their day-to-day operations as well. Specific involvement in trade associations by reading trade literature, presenting a physical appearance and speaking the language of the market segment requires an intense client-focus orientation.

This chapter discusses

- how to become identified with an industry.
- methods of focusing on clients.

- the value of personal involvement.
- the value of appearances and image.

Several members of Carl's family worked in various parts of the heavy construction business. As a result of his familiarity, it was a logical choice for him, as an attorney, to focus on the legal needs of that industry.

For years, he had heard some of their unusual problems discussed at family gatherings. One thing Carl had noticed even before he selected a practice area was that his family commented on the lack of lawyers in their area who were even vaguely familiar with the day-to-day workings of construction. Since Carl had worked every summer and most vacations since high school for the family, he felt he had a fairly keen sense of the industry problems even if he did not know much about construction law yet.

Carl set his practice objective to serve the smaller home builder segment of the industry. His rationale was that he did not as yet feel comfortable with the more sophisticated labor law requirements of large-scale general contractors. Also, the larger projects often involved environmental liability issues as well as multiparty financing which usually required additional expertise.

Having set his practice objective, Carl began the process of assessing the environment in which he would be working. He paid a visit to his local chamber of commerce and to the local branch of the Home Builders Association. He checked the organizations' information on local growth trends in the home construction industry over the last three years. Those figures were confirmed by the county building department.

All indicators pointed to solid growth for at least ten years. Surveys published in the general business press, government reports, and Home Builders Association reports projected substantial construction to keep pace with local economic growth as a result of more young families needing homes and population influx. This growth was underwritten by long-term world events which benefited the basic industries in the area. The projections seemed fairly safe and conservative.

Carl's competition appeared to be two or three larger law firms in the area and sole practitioners who spent most of their time primarily on land use tax and environmental issues. His industry sources told him that one of the larger firms put out a "canned" newsletter, but nobody really seemed to address the local home-building market.

The state bar's Construction Law Section chairperson told Carl that most of their activities were oriented toward heavy construction and commercial building contractors. Carl enrolled in that section anyway and the Business Law Section.

He joined and began attending Home Builders Association meetings. Through his regular attendance, he began to learn the principal problems facing the industry. He also began regularly reading three of the national trade journals and subscribed to and read the local *Construction News*.

By becoming familiar with supplier/builder/purchaser conflicts and the relations with subcontractors and labor (mostly non-union), Carl learned that like most closely held businesses, frequent topics of conversation were succession, sales planning, and difficulties with local regulatory agencies.

Finally, Carl set some very specific billing goals to be attained from the builders within a certain time frame. He felt that if he could not meet those goals on schedule, he would seriously consider some other market segment on which to focus his energy and resources.

He met his goals easily because he was genuinely concerned about the needs and challenges of his industry. Construction business owners came to know Carl personally through his association memberships. His determined presence within the industry secured his success.

TARGETING AND WINNING OVER A SEGMENT

Attorneys can identify potential industry markets using the same techniques required for internal and external practice analysis. Assessment of potential, revenues, existing activities, trends, and personal interest and luck often point to a general area and sometimes even to a distinct segment.

But it is not enough just to target a market. The attorney must embrace the issues which face that segment and become personally involved.

An example of the importance of this personal involvement is an attorney who was not as qualified or experienced as several others in town to serve a particular industry segment. For advice and counsel, this attorney relied on an older, more experienced colleague from a larger firm which chose not to have a stake in the industry. As a sole practitioner, this attorney had the time to spend with the targeted client group. The attorney addressed their association meetings, wrote for their monthly bulletin, and worked on their association constitution and bylaws.

Ironically, two other attorneys, both more experienced and qualified in the practice area, were also active and visible at trade association meetings. However, they spent most of their time at these meetings talking with each other. They also wore suits and white shirts, even though their potential clients were much more casually dressed.

Needless to say the younger, less experienced attorney wore the same style clothes and avoided "legalese," opting instead for industry jargon. The perception of the target audience was that the younger attorney was the only attorney who really cared! It should be no surprise that she captured virtually all the client work, which was substantial.

CHAPTER 16
Where Will You Practice? Identifying Geographic Markets for Business Development

SUMMARY

A practice niche can be identified not only in terms of client groups or practice areas but also in terms of geography. Segmenting the market potential by area often seems obvious but can be overlooked. Implementing a geographic marketing image utilizes the same principles as that of the client industry focus.

This chapter discusses

- using the 80/20 rule to spot potential.
- simple methods to analyze and quantify business development opportunities.
- importance of a commitment to an area.
- developing an affinity for an area.

Camille was a recent law school graduate and new associate with a large metropolitan firm. After her undergraduate work and prior to law school, she had worked for a property development firm as a land use consultant. Therefore after law school, it was logical for Camille to put her efforts into land use law. She felt that her knowledge of commercial real estate from a developer's point of view would help in her dealings with developer clients.

Camille gathered information from her own firm regarding commerical developer client matters, including past revenue. She outlined the top revenue-producing clients and marked on a map the area in which these clients had offices. She then gathered information regarding all commercial property developers within this area and through members of her firm and colleague contacts, attempted to pinpoint upon whom these developers depended for legal services.

Camille's objective was to build her practice by aiding the efforts of her firm in serving its current clients but also to add to the firm's client roster by winning new profitable clients. Her rationale for client potential was based on her geographic analysis. In a word, the area was underserved to say the least. Her modus operandi was a very active role in the targeted community. Because she lived far away enough from the area to require a 45-minute drive on the expressway, Camille moved into the area. Her living expenses increased as a result, but she anticipated future income would be her just reward.

THE 80/20 RULE

The 80/20 rule says that 20 percent of all clients constitute about 80 percent of all revenue. As a generalization this rule may be unscientific and unspecific, but it has many applications in business operations, including law firms. This rule can be used to guide market research and definition and more specifically, geographic markets.

Attorneys who decide to serve a specific geographical area need to know their real boundaries. Although they may believe that their clients live and work within a certain metropolitan or regional area, they are better served by a closer analysis. To target a geographic area successfully, they need to know the location of the 20 percent of clients producing 80 percent of their revenue. Clearly this provides the geographic area which holds the most potential for business development.

An attorney can begin this process by analyzing U.S. Postal Service zip codes. Which area zip codes represent 80 percent of the law practice's clients? Which zip codes represent 80 percent of the practice's revenue? What relationship exists between these two geographic areas and to what extent does the 80/20 rule apply?

It should follow that the attorney's best opportunities for additional business are found in the geographic area defined by this quick 80/20 analysis. Even if the attorney wants to change his or her practice focus to another "uncharted" or "unknown" geographic area, he or she should be able to go through this exercise on a hypothetical level, using intuition to gauge where the 80/20 rule might apply. Obviously intuition must be grounded on logic and facts.

APPLICATION

Having determined where most clients and revenue come from, how can this information be utilized? To start, once a preliminary geographical area has been outlined for client development, the attorney can focus energies and resources toward a smaller target.

Consider the attorney practicing in Cook County, Illinois. That attorney is more likely to build a successful practice by attempting to focus on one part of the Chicago area. The same is also true of an attorney practicing in a less densely populated, albeit even rural, area. A more successful practice will result from a rifle rather than shotgun approach to a target market.

Many lawyers do not define their geographic market. Their practice theory is that by building a better mousetrap, success will surely follow. Geographic convenience is an often-overlooked criterion of attorney selection.

COMMITMENT TO THE AREA

To serve clients and fill their needs effectively, it is important to understand all their concerns, not just their legal problems. In the geographic segment context, this is relatively easy. By becoming active in community and civic affairs, an immediate difference will become apparent!

These activities should not be approached with the idea of gaining recognition and exposure for the attorney's practice, as is usually espoused, but rather with the opportunities to learn and truly understand the objectives of the market area targeted. Activities in which the attorney is particularly interested must be selected or involvement will inevitably be short-lived. All manner of community and civic organizations are in desperate need of talented volunteers. To the extent that the attorney can resolve conflict and/or liability exposure, as interpreted in their jurisdiction, a lending of professional expertise can be appropriate and helpful.

Organizations need parliamentarians; writers; and interpreters of constitutions and bylaws, contract reviews, and similar matters. Beyond that, they need good advisors on their boards and of course fund-raisers.

One attorney took his geographic market to heart and became involved with a local amateur theater festival. In the process of serving on the board of the local theater festival company, he learned a great deal regarding his community's concerns for performing costs in time and money. At the same time, he became acquainted with some of the influential people in the community whose views shaped the community's agenda. Incidentally, his tax practice flourished, not because he deliberately tried to leverage his contacts but because a good deal of mutual respect evolved between him and his new clientele. The theater festival was a big event socially, artistically, and economically. By becoming heavily involved, he in essence demonstrated community affinity.

CHAPTER 17
Applying Demographic Data to Practice Development

SUMMARY

The demographic makeup of society is changing and always will. These changes can be examined in national, regional, and local contexts. Accessing and creatively studying these data may point the way for practice development opportunities.

This chapter discusses

- sources of demographic trends.
- highlights of some national trends.
- practice development implications.
- demographic focus opportunities.

Demographics is a methodical breakdown of any population grouping into similar characteristics which are defined by the person doing the demographic research. These characteristics can be age, gender, education, occupation, income, marital status, or a host of other qualities. Demographics can be used to classify existing client characteristics (as outlined in Chapter 10) as well as to define possible new clients.

DEMOGRAPHICS FOR THE ATTORNEY

To the attorney studying areas of possible practice emphasis, demographics can highlight and even pinpoint areas with the greatest propensity for success. An attorney whose area demographics show a majority of the population as aging should consider offering services to accommodate the needs of the aging. Similarly, an attorney whose geographical area demographic statistics show a high level of education and sophistication could consider investment-related matters or other issues related to this market's needs.

Demographics fine-tunes the market research process, allowing the attorney a greater level of sophistication in decision making regarding practice services than would otherwise be possible. It provides a way for the attorney to get to know existing and potential clientele personally.

What follows in this chapter is a detailed description of how demographic research was conducted by one attorney and the results that occurred. Through this description, an understanding of the concept can be easily grasped.

> An attorney had read a good deal about the possible general impact of demographic trends on her law practice. However, she had not done much research on specific implications and ways to make these implications beneficial to her. Her work had been primarily routine business-related matters like drafting contracts, advising small businesses, representing clients' collection interests, drafting simple wills for small-business owners, handling real estate, and handling other asset sale closings and similar matters.

She had reached a point where she did not like having little significant or unique expertise. She felt that she was not giving clients the quality they deserved or which would be rewarding to her professionally and personally.

In a discussion with an office colleague, she learned that this attorney regularly used a computer modem to access a wealth of statistical data. She wondered if specific demographic data might be available through this means, and he agreed to help her find out. They searched for demographic trends in the business information section of the associate's data base. They learned that 204 listings were available, which meant 204 articles or journal paper abstracts on demographic trends might be accessed.

Her colleague printed out a list of titles so she could select which abstracts might be worth her time to read. She also highlighted a few articles which she wanted to read in greater detail. Using the computer modem, he printed out abstracts and articles.

After reading the information, the attorney discovered that several important demographic trends were evident. The total population of her geographical base was growing slowly with some areas growing more quickly than others. In terms of age, most members of that area were in the 30- to 50-years-of-age range, with small age groups, younger and older, on each side. Several ethnic groups were becoming significant in parts of her area, enough to suggest special marketing efforts by retailers geared to their needs. Hispanic growth was continuing rapidly in several parts of her area, and Asian immigrants, particularly from Southeast Asia, were settling in large numbers in one section.

Several of the business articles discussed how business marketing efforts were being prepared to take advantage of demographic trends. Other articles reviewed demographic trends and their impact on various industries, which could become good investment opportunities.

The attorney decided that rather than concentrate on a narrow selection of law practice areas, focusing on a *client group* made more sense. She wanted to target the dominant age group, the 30- to 50-year-olds, in a unique way. She felt that as this population aged, its dependence on health care would logically increase. The health care industry's needs were multifaceted and very challenging. Nursing homes and extended care facilities were clearly industries with growth potential. At the same time, retirement and recreational facilities of all types seemed to have growing markets to serve.

By becoming involved in her target market's aging needs now, the attorney felt she would have the time to develop her expertise and build a more secure client base. She drafted a marketing plan which began with work in her target market's current need areas, such as wills and estate planning, and the remainder in aging health care issues. Her ten-year plan eventually led to health care issues as her sole area of expertise.

She decided that by outlining her professional future according to her demographic analysis, she would have a greater chance at achieving her professional goals. She was relieved that she had actually done the research and seriously considered its implications, as it afforded her the time to plan accordingly.

CHAPTER 18
What Does Corporate Counsel Want?

SUMMARY

Understanding corporate general counsel is of growing importance to many attorneys and law firms. Corporate counsel is looking for the same traits as other clients: cost containment, results, and attention. Like any client, relationships between corporate general counsel and lead attorneys in outside firms must be one of trust and confidence both in legal areas and project management. Corporate counsel expertise is improving, which requires higher performance of outside counsel.

This chapter discusses

- what corporate general counsel looks for in outside counsel.
- when corporations need outside counsel.
- how corporate counsel evaluates outside counsel.

Many law firms seek corporate clients as much for prestige as for potential revenue and profits. In the process, they overlook the fact that often, a corporate client is interested in cost containment as well as effectiveness. Consequently, the negotiated fees end up to be on the low side of current market trends. For certain tasks, some will consider and negotiate value billing. In speeches, panel discussions, and journal articles by corporate counsel, it is abundantly clear what they want.

In attracting corporate clients, brochures can be practically valueless, particularly if they are just sent out in a random search effort. This is because the attorney or firm must respond to specific client needs. A brochure is normally too general to do this and can only be a supplement to a client-based approach.

It is up to the attorney to discover specific needs, such as merger and acquisition, securities, environmental litigation, product liability, or some other area. Outside attorneys whose firms provide complete legal services are of no importance to a particular corporate client. Clients need only one thing at any given time and at any particular locale.

WHAT CORPORATE CLIENTS LOOK FOR

Corporate law departments have been slowly evolving so that they no longer depend solely on outside counsel for resolution of matters. Now, many matters are handled internally due to larger staffs and increased specialization of corporate attorneys. The work which is passed on to outside counsel is more focused and requires a great deal of specialization. As a result, greater partner involvement has become necessary as firms are no longer able to pass much of the work onto lesser skilled associates.

Whereas several years ago an attorney or firm providing legal advice and expertise to a corporate client might have been given a good deal of free rein, now corporate clients require greater control over the management of matters. This means less variation between original proposals and final results (as well as bills).

Perhaps a great deal of this tightening of the corporate legal belt is due to an increased concern for efficiency. Corporate legal department budgets certainly seem to be under greater scrutiny these days. Corporate law matters are considered to be business rather than law oriented. Detailed billings are often required to demonstrate work accomplished and results achieved as compared to expenses incurred.

The key to attracting corporate clients is multifaceted. According to current trends, the attorney must be

- specialized to handle a particular need.
- able to demonstrate good project management skills.
- efficient in operations.
- on target with regard to ability to follow through on proposal objectives and budgets.
- uniquely knowledgeable (the more so the better) regarding the corporate client's business.

The crucial factor, though, remains the personal relationship. The attorney must establish and maintain a significant amount of trust and confidence. As corporations have stated, they seek attorney referrals from trusted referral sources. Law firm advertising, public relations, and general reputation may help influence the hiring decisions of corporate counsel, but they will never supersede the power of solid referrals.

In the final analysis, it boils down to the relationship between the corporate client and the lead outside attorney rather than between the corporation and the law firm. For the attorney just starting out on the trail of corporate clients, the listing in *Martindale-Hubbell Directory* is only a starting place to establishing name recognition.

In a broad sense, corporate general counsel's decision processes are no different from that of the local closely held business that needs either to change attorneys or is seeking expertise in a particular area. Much of the decision will be based on the personal relationship.

PART 3

Preparations for Marketing

The one theme that permeates all discussions in this book is the necessity of careful planning before action can take place. The choices for attorneys of specific practice development activities are numerous—too many in fact for any individual or firm to conduct them all. Therefore, a plan must be established. Then the actions that are taken are most effective.

This part provides the fundamentals of preparing to market. The preparations involve some additional assessment. But what's more important, they stress the importance of properly identifying the target market, ensuring that all the internal building blocks are in place (i.e., good staff, good facilities, management practices) and that internal agreement is present. Finally, this section discusses the preparation of the plan, incorporating the all-important financial considerations.

CHAPTER 19
The Role of Your Human Resources in Practice Development

SUMMARY

Even though an attorney is committed to building a practice, partners, associates, and staff may not share the commitment. Therefore, a commitment must be instilled. Everyone in the firm must feel a sense of ownership in vision, objectives, and goals. Marketing success depends to a great extent on the synergetic force created by united office effort. Firms with nonattorney administrators seem to understand this and develop human resource programs more efficiently.

This chapter discusses

- human resources as a large expense that receives little attention.
- the importance of getting to know staff.
- the need for objective self-evaluation of the attorney.
- staff assessment and the importance of staff opinions.
- keeping staff assessment current.

Too often, attorneys think that because they are committed to building a practice, their partners, associates, and staff will share their commitment. They eventually discover that this type of enthusiasm does not exist simply for its own sake. They learn that a marketing program, in order for others to embrace it fully, must have its purpose clearly communicated, its strategy logically outlined, and its expectations fully understood.

Just as a new practice area can change the way a firm operates, a decision to become proactive with regard to marketing impacts everyone in the firm, from the senior partner to the receptionist. Marketing success depends, therefore, to a great extent on the synergetic force created by a united office effort.

> Jayne was a proficient and well-known attorney in her state. She had 3 well-respected partners in addition to 6 associates and 12 staff members. Her reputation as a litigator was unassailable. Despite her expertise as a lawyer, Jayne did not feel her office atmosphere was always pleasant for herself, clients, or staff. She noticed animosity between staff members despite her efforts to assign staff according to their obvious abilities. She felt that the salaries her firm offered were very competitive with other firms' scales and that other amenities such as benefits and vacation time were generous.
>
> In an effort to take control of the situation, Jayne persuaded her partners to hire a human resources consultant. The consultant spent two weeks in Jayne's office. He interviewed each staff person individually and in groups of two and three. He analyzed work requirements, employee hours, and productivity. His final analysis was delivered to Jayne and her partners in presentation form as well as a written report. Jayne found herself taken aback by many of his conclusions.
>
> As far as Jayne was concerned, the consultant more or less accused her and the other partners of not really knowing or understanding their employees. He said that most of the staff believed they were receiving good salaries but that they were bored with their jobs. Furthermore, the consultant said staff did not

believe they played an important role in the operation of the firm since they were not attorneys.

Jayne felt betrayed. She felt their importance was an unspoken absolute and they understood this as well as she. Her partners mentioned the salaries and benefits as evidence of employee importance. The consultant said these did not replace an employee's confidence in a sense of genuine caring from an employer. Jayne and her partners discussed other issues with the consultant and agreed they had a larger problem than they initially recognized. She asked the consultant to help them begin immediate remedial steps to correct the now apparent problems.

One of the first things Jayne did was call an office meeting of partners, associates, and staff. With her partners' permission and encouragement, Jayne asked everyone to submit a list of their professional goals. She told associates and staff that the firm partners wanted to know the employees' capabilities and aspirations. Jayne told employees that in the future they would be assigned work with more attention to their interest as well as ability.

Jayne also asked all associates, staff, and even her partners to write down suggestions for making the office more efficient and a more pleasant place to work. She said all suggestions submitted could be anonymous. She promised to circulate a compilation of all the submissions. After everyone had a chance to read the suggestions, Jayne told the staff that they would have a chance to discuss and even vote on possible changes.

Jayne noticed her staff's watchful acknowledgment of her effort to be a more effective supervisor. She also noticed an impact on the staff's own efforts to be effective on other employees. Based on this, she made a personal commitment to place more emphasis on her own human resource management skills.

MANAGING HUMAN RESOURCES

Firms with nonattorney administrators seem to understand and develop programs for human resource needs more effectively than firms headed by attorneys. The most likely cause is that attorneys are trained to be production oriented. Further, there is little taught in law school or available in today's CLE system that would help an attorney develop human resource management skills. Those attorneys which are good people managers are either self-taught or are intuitively equipped to be good managers.

For the attorneys who are not necessarily "naturals" at the art of human resource management, the time and expense taken to learn such skills can lead to two end results:

- more satisfaction on the part of the attorney and staff
- more time and cost-efficient practice operation

An attorney's human resources are a larger direct expense than any other resource. Yet, ironically, this area often receives less attention than libraries, office decor, and computer systems, both in terms of initial acquisition and maintenance.

As a result of human resource mismanagement, attorneys often experience high staff turnover. This results not only in the costs of lost productivity during replacement and training, but also disrupts the relationship between staff and client. A client who speaks with a different receptionist, secretary, or paralegal each time he or she telephones or visits the office will undoubtedly note the lack of consistency in personnel and wonder as to the reason.

GETTING TO KNOW STAFF

What can the lawyer do who is not directly involved in management? For that matter, what can the solo practitioner do? The primary concern should be to establish regular two-way communication with others in the office. This sounds relatively simple and easy, but what does it really mean? Using a marketing approach, it means that the attorney must first discover staff needs. This is the antithesis of the typical adversarial or caste relationship that exists between many lawyers and staff, both administrative and, most especially, support staff.

Attorneys need to know as much about their staff and they want to know about their clients. What are their personal and career objectives? What are their avocational interests? Why do they want to work for the attorney and what do they expect to receive in return, in addition to a salary? Attorneys are often surprised to learn that money is rarely a sole motivating factor for employees (for more information on employee job satisfaction see Chapter 43). A competitive salary in a position which is not satisfying will eventually lead to that person's poor performance or transition into a more satisfying position, often at another firm. Staff employment must include a recognition of employees' nonmonetary needs such as recognition for good work, opportunities for learning and advancement, and a satisfying work atmosphere.

Attorneys must demonstrate real interest and concern in their employees. This means finding out what can be done to help staff members in their personal pursuits and a conscious effort to stay informed with regard to staff activities. In practical terms, this could mean tasks as simple as bringing a newspaper or magazine article clipping of interest to them or making sure events they care about (and not just vacations) are placed on the office calendar.

USING ATTORNEY RESOURCES

The most difficult resource for a person to manage in all likelihood is "self." That is, an objective self-evaluation of the attorney is the first step to the successful development of any practical plan. But attorneys who want to effect a more efficient and motivated staff begin with a very thorough and objective self-analysis.

> An attorney, assigned responsibility of personnel management in a 25-attorney firm, saw the motivation of his office staff as a problem. The attorney identified his personal strengths and weaknesses, both in personality traits and skills. He listed major areas of expertise and wrote positive and negative comments he felt were reasonable. He asked a colleague whom he trusted to evaluate his list objectively and note any additional comments.
>
> With his completed self-analysis, the attorney was able to decide what sorts of human resources management skills he might most effectively learn and use. Initially he had planned to hold a twice-monthly informal breakfast with staff to discuss current office events and clear up possible misconceptions. His self-analysis demonstrated that he was uncomfortable in casual conversations with staff so he tended to be domineering and impatient with chitchat. The attorney crossed the staff breakfast plans off his list and decided, instead, upon a regular, formal, and anonymous staff feedback system. Employees were urged to submit questions and concerns which were answered personally by the attorney. He also made a concerted effort to track staff birthdays, anniversaries, and special events (with help from his personal secretary) and sent cards to employee homes congratulating them on such events.
>
> The staff recognized the attorney's effort at making them happy and responded accordingly. They felt, for perhaps the first time, that this particular attorney, and by extension the whole firm, really cared. The consequences of breakfast meetings would not have been as positive. The staff would not have felt equally satisfied with the results as they knew the attorney did not enjoy his visits with them.

STAFF ASSESSMENT

As with clients, in order to understand staff, the attorney must not rely on assumptions but rather on staff opinions. This means staff must be asked how they feel in regard to issues and procedures.

One firm opted to assess staff performance and personality traits and marked the file "confidential." The list, despite efforts to keep it secret, fell into the wrong hands. The damage was irreparable. Very personal comments were made known to peers, supervisors, and subordinates. Some staff members left the firm as a result while others became defensive and consequently less productive. Employees felt an unnecessary sense of competition based on their own inability to control very private information about themselves.

A staff analysis must be confined to the enumeration of skills and experience. From this, the staff person being evaluated can develop plans to either improve strengths or overcome deficiencies. All staff, from receptionist to paralegal, should be assessed in this manner to understand their needs. It is as important to keep this analysis process current as it is to initiate it. Imagine the employee receiving an anniversary congratulations card in the mail after a recent divorce! Or acknowledgment of an employee's promotion several months after it occurred. Staff needs and personal information will change frequently, and so analysis should be conducted regularly.

Chapter 20
Motivating and Training Staff with Interactive Reviews

SUMMARY

Low morale, internal friction, and lack of ambition among attorney staff can be caused by two things: lack of motivation to succeed and low expectations from the attorneys. A method to improve morale and motivation is a good staff review process. It will not only measure for potential growth within the attorney's organization, but also give staff the feedback they need and want.

This chapter discusses

- staff review as a two-way process.
- opportunity for supervisors to praise staff.
- feedback and discussion as invaluable in staff training.
- how to rate staff on their skills and experience.

A firm of 10 attorneys in a large city relied on 12 staff members to keep office operations running smoothly. All of the attorneys agreed that the employees were meeting the firm's basic expectations. No one felt that more could be expected from the staff because of the limits of staff education, training, ability, and even desire. One former staff member had resigned to enroll in law school the previous year, but the attorneys agreed that this particular case was an exception to the norm and that the rest of the staff had limited career aspirations.

The surprise for these attorneys came when consultants were called in to create a new firm brochure. The consultants insisted on interviewing all of the attorneys and several key staff to piece together a complete firm identity. As a result of the interviews, the attorneys received not only a new brochure, but some unexpected news from the consultants: the staff was far from motivated to meet their full potential.

The attorneys invited the consultants to a meeting to explain this information more fully. The consultants said that in speaking with firm employees, they had discovered low morale, internal friction, and lack of ambition to make sure all tasks were well done. The reason, according to the consultants, was very low expectations from the attorneys.

The attorneys subsequently called a firm meeting, inviting all staff members. One attorney with a comfortable rapport with the employees acted as the meeting's moderator. He told the staff about the conclusions drawn by the consultants and the concern this raised for the attorneys. He then asked staff to submit suggestions, anonymous if necessary, on how firm morale could be improved. He told the participants that all suggestions would be read and discussed by the attorneys and then discussed again with the staff. From this basis, a more concerted effort would be made to improve morale and motivate everyone to reach their full potential.

The attorneys were surprised at the responses they received! The most frequent suggestion was for a review process by which employees could be measured for professional growth within the firm. The attorneys had ceased to hold review meetings almost two years before because the meetings only seemed to increase employee anxiety regarding employer-employee relations. Since then, staff supervision had consisted primarily of scheduling vacations and sick leave and monitoring whether employees arrived at the office on time and stayed within meal and break time limits. The employees, in their own words, suggested that they wanted a better method by which they could be evaluated and, they hoped, rewarded.

The firm held another meeting with all the attorneys and staff and decided by democratic process on a review system which could be fair to the attorneys as well as staff. Everyone agreed to evaluate the system in six months and accept, reject, or alter the program. Six months later, the staff made a few adjustments but expressed their general satisfaction. The attorneys noted their delight at staff's interest in the firm's well-being and their increased expectations regarding staff potential.

EMPLOYEE REVIEWS AS A MOTIVATIONAL TOOL

The employee review process is often regarded with fear and trepidation by employers and employees and for good reason. In most cases, it tends to be a one-sided process, where the staff member is called into an attorney's office and seated across from the attorney. With a large desk in between and usually stacked with paperwork, the employee is asked a few general questions before a judgment is rendered. The staff member is usually too inhibited to voice concerns and generally agrees to whatever the attorney suggests.

A far more effective system would be a two-way review process. This would allow the staff person to review his or her own performance based on the same criteria the attorney uses. A review meeting is then held in which the employee and attorney discuss each point, the comments on that point made by each, and possible improvements or rewards. By providing the employee an equal opportunity to vocalize regarding his or her performance, that employee feels a greater sense of ownership in the process and accountability for conclusions reached.

Managers who use this system report that employees frequently rate themselves lower than supervisors do. This provides a uniquely beneficial opportunity for the supervisor to praise the employee's good points, reassuring the employee and instilling a less adversarial atmosphere.

The opportunity for feedback and discussion is invaluable in training staff. At the same time, this process can be and should be used to map out career and training paths with employees.

The program generally receives considerable positive feedback from staff and attorneys who have used it. The only negative response is that the process takes more time than the traditional "one-sided" review meeting. Still, the increased attention paid to each individual employee does not require the time often devoted to far less important items such as libraries, decor, and computers.

EMPLOYEE REVIEW POINTS

A number of criteria can be used to evaluate law practice staff. The points should always be used in a positive, not negative, sense. A scale by which to rate the employee should also be used so that conclusions are not "yes" or "no." Some examples of criteria might be attendance, organization, impression, general attitudes, and skill areas. These allow different employees with different strengths to be recognized for their individual qualities. Figure 20-1 presents a form for this use. It is not recommended that attorneys use any written form to evaluate or discuss staff personality traits. The reason is that such forms are sometimes not kept completely confidential and can be very damaging to staff morale.

1 = Needs attention 2 = Poor 3 = Below average
4 = Above average 5 = Good 6 = Excellent

ATTENDANCE	1	2	3	4	5	6

1. Arrives on time, or early, to begin work.
2. Returns promptly from lunch and breaks.
3. Makes appointments in timely fashion.
4. Gives adequate notice if unable to work.

ORGANIZATION	1	2	3	4	5	6

1. Uses time effectively.
2. Displays resourcefulness and ingenuity.
3. Completes tasks in timely manner.
4. Keeps work area well ordered and clean.
5. Completes work accurately and neatly.

SKILL AREAS	1	2	3	4	5	6

1. Exhibits proficiency in skill areas.
2. Seeks improvement in abilities and skills.
3. Has acquired new skills.
4. Seeks additional responsibility.

Figure 20-1 Employee Rating Scale. Adapted from Roger F. Smith, *Sales Management: A Practitioner's Guide*. Englewood Cliffs, NJ: Prentice Hall, 1987 © Roger F. Smith.

CHAPTER 21
The Impact of Staff Involvement on Practice Development

SUMMARY

Actively involving staff with practice objectives will influence their attitudes regarding work quality, clients, and their relationships with the attorney. One result will be more care and attention to clients, a critical factor in successful practice development.

This chapter discusses

- the importance of setting examples of behavior expected from staff.
- the impact of negative communication or performance.
- the impact of internal communications on client relations.

As a partner in a small boutique firm, Jeff diligently worked to communicate the firm's practice objectives to staff. He and his partners had decided to work toward an efficiently run law office that would permit them a reasonable amount of personal time. He wanted staff to understand the importance of their role in making this possible. He also wanted them to know that he respected their expectations for the same life-style.

First, Jeff discussed the firm's practice objectives in "working hour" rather than "billable hour" terms. Jeff explained that he and his partners had made the choice to place an importance on their family lives. This meant that they expected to accomplish professional tasks within normal working hours and would work beyond that when necessary but would not regularly seek out work which would demand extra time.

Second, Jeff shared with his staff that he and his partners felt their community and client industry activities were important to the success of the firm. He said he hoped these activities would demonstrate his interest in improving the conditions in the community and industry he served while at the same time leading to new work.

Third, he candidly shared with them that, by building up the practice, they would all be able to emphasize the type of work which would be more profitable. His generosity and frequent expressions of appreciation made it clear to staff that they would share in the success of the practice.

Fourth, Jeff met with staff for one hour every other Monday morning to critique relations with each client and to discuss ways in which those relations could improve. Staff input was valuable since employees usually implemented actual communication with clients and often were involved in substantive matters under Jeff's direction. Staff brainstorming sessions were particularly productive in developing ways to improve service quality.

Jeff did not stop with these techniques. He went on to make the firm's staff tasks as easy as possible. He and his partners made sure that staff had constant access to all firm information so that their work on projects would not stumble upon gaps in information. Each partner carefully explained the flow of information which they preferred, so that staff could process the information most efficiently. At the biweekly staff meetings, Jeff outlined the partners' calendars for the coming week so staff would know when to expect the partners to be in the office as well as what issues might be critical at what times. Jeff and his partners also designated the final half hour in the working day as a catch-up period, to be interrupted only by emergencies. Within this 30-minute period, staff was allowed to organize their own information and leave the office on time.

Jeff's time spent on staff influenced staff attitudes regarding work, clients, and their relationships with Jeff and his partners. By devoting time and attention to very specific points, he conveyed to staff the importance of each matter and eliminated the potential for misunderstandings. The end result was that the firm's partners and the office staff worked together to develop a very profitable and personally satisfying practice.

STAFF ATTITUDES

Attorneys often have problems relating to staff. As a result, staff turnover in law offices is often higher than desirable, and the relationships occurring between attorneys and staff are frequently adversarial. It is within the power of the attorney to change this to a greater extent than it is possible for staff to effect any changes.

Attorneys must start by recognizing the value of their staff. Staff capabilities are almost consistently underestimated and underutilized by professionals. By recognizing the potential of each individual staff member, a realistic set of expectations may be drawn on the parts of the attorney and the staff.

There are several specific things attorneys can do to make staff relations less adversarial and more productive. The attorney can begin by introducing staff (whether receptionist, paralegal, or associate) to clients. This places a value on staff input and lets the staff member know the attorney is proud to have that person in the office.

Attorneys can also set an example of the type of behavior they expect from staff. Staff tends to emulate the "boss," and so the attorney must live by the rules set for staff. This may mean more time spent on organization, prompt return of telephone calls, or an increased priority placed on client relationships.

IMPACT OF NEGATIVE COMMUNICATION

Attorneys communicate volumes by how they refer to clients in the presence of staff. Whatever they communicate will be implicitly communicated by the staff to the clients. Unless a client truly is not important to the practice (and what client is not?), negativity should never be expressed in regard to that person or business.

For example, consider the client who is less than pleasant. This person is unusually demanding, slow to pay bills, and disrespectful of others' time.

In the absence of the client but the presence of staff, the attorney may refer to the client in less than complimentary terms. Hearing this, the staff begins to think of this client as less than important to the practice. Eventually the client's work does not receive proper attention from the staff in terms of timeliness and quality, and what's more important, the staff begins to treat the client coolly. The results were predictable to an outsider but less obvious to the attorney, staff, and even the client. This client will eventually find another attorney more willing to cater to his demanding nature. No great loss? Wrong. The biggest loss was not just the client's fees but staff awareness that the attorney did not hold client interests in high esteem.

The most effective way to prevent staff misunderstanding is a rule most people learn from their parents as children: do not say about a person what you would not tell that person directly. In the law office, this philosophy should be rigidly adhered to. Client interests should always be placed as top priority, no matter who the client is. Staff also deserves this kind of attention. An attorney should never complain about a staff person, associate, or even partner to anyone else in the firm, unless the comment is called for and appropriate.

For details on processes and techniques to communicate with staff, see Chapter 43.

CHAPTER 22
Enhancing the Role of Staff in External Marketing

SUMMARY

Specific training programs for attorney and staff will improve overall service quality. Training for business development involves workshops, seminars, and courses aimed at sharpening client/service skill. Such training can be provided by using in-house resources or the more common use of outside consultants. Some staff will be eager to seek out training opportunities while others will not. Attorneys need to respond to both. Training is important to the ultimate success of marketing programs.

This chapter discusses

- training impact on overall service quality.
- types of training available.

- in-house training resources.
- how to deal with differing interests in training.
- training as component of marketing.

Other chapters discussed the importance of the attorney's human resources in the total marketing effort. Specific activities are discussed to analyze these resources and use them to full advantage. Chapters 30 and 32 suggest methods of building internal consensus so that a unified marketing effort is put forth. This chapter examines specific training programs for attorney and staff to improve overall quality of service, thereby supporting the client-focused marketing effort.

TRAINING PROGRAMS

Training for business development involves workshops, seminars, and courses aimed at sharpening client/service skills. It involves programs for attorneys, professional staff, and support employees. In larger firms, training can be provided using in-house resources. Examples are

- communication from successful rainmakers to other partners who have the personal interest and style necessary for rainmaking. Information shared is specific techniques that the rainmaker has found to work within the firm's client groups and geographical market.
- an in-house marketing coordinator meeting with attorneys to report on a marketing analysis of new files. Important in this kind of meeting is information on type of work, type of client, and reasons each new file was opened (sometimes analysis of why a file was opened reveals a successful marketing process!).
- the office manager meeting with secretaries and receptionists to review office procedures, standard correspondence formatting, computer technologies, and so on.

Far more common for attorneys is the hiring of outside consultants for in-house training or sending attorneys, staff and others to outside seminars. Consultants can be found to instruct in every topic from sales management to desktop publishing. Outside courses are taught through educational institutions, law-related organizations that offer CLEs, and private companies whose sole purpose is personnel training and development.

TRAINING PROGRAM GUIDELINES

Because training for client service and marketing involves attorney and staff time as well as out-of-pocket costs, there can be considerable expense involved. Therefore, training is legitimately an element in the marketing budget. Its cost should be realized and addressed.

Marketing training and improvement of client/service skills should be part of the job for every attorney, staff, and other firm employee. Over the course of a year, the degree of training and involvement will vary greatly among individuals, depending on their seniority, interests, and job responsibilities. Persons with jobs of marketing or administration may spend 15 percent of their time either attending or giving marketing-oriented training sessions. Clerical staff may spend less than 5 percent. Some partners may spend none.

By identifying training in the marketing budget, employees realize its importance to the firm. Some employees will eagerly seek out training opportunities, while others will not. Attorneys need to respond to both situations.

For employees who seek out classes, their enthusiasm needs to be encouraged but addressed by limiting the time and out-of-pocket commitment that the firm can make to the individual. Some firms have allocated a fixed out-of-pocket amount to the employee for training, depending on the individual and position. Additional training is at the employee's expense. For instance, a clerical employee may be allocated $300 per year for training in computers, office procedures, time management, and so on or whatever he or she wishes to study.

For the reticent types who do not show their own initiative for outside training, the firm should tell the employee that, during the next 12 months, the firm wants the employee to attend at least one one-day training session on a topic of the employee's choosing that, in the opinion of the employee, would be helpful to his or her job. Attorneys are frequently and pleasantly surprised to see what the employees come up with!

EDUCATIONAL ASSISTANCE

Training can take place during the individual's personal time, so there is no "loss-of-revenue" cost to the attorney or firm. This applies particularly to administrative and clerical employees who enroll in educational programs through local community colleges or universities and obtain credit for their study. Courses taken are usually technical in nature, such as computer lessons or bookkeeping, although they can be oriented toward advanced degrees.

Generally, this kind of training by employees should be encouraged.

One method to do this is through educational assistance programs (EAPs), programs where the employer pays the employee for costs related to their study, typically around 80 percent (although they can range from 20 percent to 100 percent). They are common in corporations and can work well within law firms, no matter how small. EAPs specify what type of course work is eligible for reimbursement and the rate at which costs will be paid. Effective EAPs stipulate that the coursework must be related to the employee's current job responsibilities.

Attorneys usually stipulate in the EAP a reimbursement rate to the employee. This usually depends on several factors, such as total costs, grade received, and value to the firm. For instance, one law firm has an EAP that says employees taking an approved college-level course will be reimbursed at 50 percent of the employee's cost of both books and tuition if they receive a "C" in the course, 75 percent if they receive a "B," and 100 percent if they receive an "A."

From graduate programs in economics to half-day sessions on good telephone techniques, training is important to the ultimate success of individuals and firms. Because marketing for the client-focused attorney is not "selling" but rather "service," training to improve employee job and service skills plays a critical role in attorney success.

CHAPTER 23
Personal Planning: The First Step to Getting What You Want

SUMMARY

Successful marketing of legal services requires a personal commitment by each attorney. The personal commitment is demonstrated by development of individual marketing plans. For attorneys other than sole practitioners, these plans need to be coordinated with other attorney plans in the organization. Plans must be tailored to fit the individual, understanding that marketing skills and interest are not equal.

This chapter discusses

- the erroneous belief that *firms* rather than *individuals* should be marketed.

- the importance of individual marketing plans.
- the development of clear and concise individual objectives.
- how to conduct successful planning that includes the clients' best interests, meets practice objectives, and provides measurable results.

Whether partners in a multinational megafirm or sole practitioners in a rural area, attorneys are responsible for their own success. An attorney cannot expect the success of the firm or colleagues to determine to any great degree his or her own individual practice success. It is personal commitment to building the practice, utilizing time-proven marketing skills, which reaps the bounty of success.

As the proverb says, the longest journey begins with the first step. So it is with business development and, more specifically, law practice development. A successful legal marketing program must begin with an initial, however small, effort and a determined commitment to continue.

The successful attorney must be his or her own time manager, personal planner, and evaluator of practice efficiency and effectiveness. Although professionals may be retained, the final outcome is dependent on the attorney's execution.

Because personal planning and time management are not emphasized in law school, the attorney must use his or her own initiative to learn as much as possible to become proficient in these areas. The end result will be greater professional and personal satisfaction as well as a commensurate reward in terms of financial success.

Two large firms, each determined to improve and expand their business practices, decided to implement marketing plans. Their purpose was to achieve the same basic objectives: to increase firm efficiency as well as profitability and to attract more clients in business practice areas. Here are descriptions of two situations that law firms may encounter:

> A 15-attorney, general practice firm spent a greal deal of partner and attorney time discussing goals and objectives, client profiles, past experience, and expectations. Firm members noticed a distinct improvement in accounts receivable after the marketing plan was completed and implementation had begun. The reason was that one of the plan's goals was to reduce nonpaying work on matters or clients that did not fit their "ideal" client profile. By limiting work to clients of higher value, they eliminated some of the unrecoverable time and financial expenses spent on matters and clients not in line with the firm's vision.
>
> Despite the success in this area, another one of this firm's goals still had not reached fruition. Progress toward recruiting and retaining new clients was not matching expectations. Firm members had expected that by focusing internally on the type of work they wanted, they would logically begin to receive

> more of its type. They did not realize that more action on their part was necessary to achieve results.
>
> A second, similar firm also decided to draft and implement a marketing plan, but employed a different methodology. They hired a high-profile public relations firm to develop an external marketing communications program. The public relations firm provided news releases, improved media relations, and produced a firm brochure, firm resumes, and similar products all of very high quality.
>
> The partners and associates in this second firm experienced a great deal of pride regarding their organization as a result of their improved external image. They distributed brochures to friends, hosted monthly open houses for key accounting firms and financial institutions, made substantial contributions to local philanthropic organizations, and provided pro bono work for important community projects.
>
> Despite all this, the second firm suffered the same lack of expected results as the first firm: there was no significant number of new clients. Handling clients of dubious potential was still an ongoing problem.

The specific workings of both firms' plans and the nuances of their implementations were different, but the results were the same: they did not provide all of the results expected or desired. The firms had missed a commonly overlooked but nonetheless crucial point: successful legal services marketing requires a personal commitment on the part of each attorney involved.

INDIVIDUAL COMMITMENT

Unique to successful legal services marketing is the personalization of the marketing plan and implementation program. Client engagement and referral source development efforts simply cannot be delegated to the firm as a whole or to an intervening third party, such as a public relations firm. Much of the professional service is based on personal trust and confidence between the client and attorney.

Yet few firms pay attention to this basic principle when dipping their toes into the marketing pool. They make great effort and incur huge expense to study market potential, analyze the competition, and identify areas of law and types of clients without significant individual involvement. Too often associates and even partners feel that marketing is something *the firm* should do, not *the individual*. This demonstrates that they do not clearly understand marketing's potential benefits or do not know how to engage in professional services marketing.

PERSONAL PLANNING

Whether part of a larger, firmwide marketing plan or as a guide for marketing a solo practice, a personal marketing plan must be written for each attorney, partner, or associate. These plans can differ in terms of detail but must include an accurate and complete assessment of the attorney's own practice situation and past and current marketing efforts.

Marketing efforts might be quite general. For instance, an attorney may state as an objective, "To become active in the local downtown business association." They also can be as specific as, "Schedule a lunch meeting with Hazel Williamson, CPA, to discuss referrals." Other marketing efforts might include speaking opportunities or written contributions to trade journals.

PERSONAL PLANNING OBJECTIVES

There are four basic objectives which must be satisfied by the individual attorney's personal marketing plan. The plan must

- be in the best interest of clients.
- meet firm or practice objectives.
- be appropriate for the attorney's abilities.
- provide measurable results.

Why would an individual attorney's marketing plan be in the best interest of that attorney's clients? Because ultimately the clients will determine that plan's very success. This goes beyond mere marketing exposure to include efforts at self-education regarding client needs and concerns. It begins with an active role in client groups and interests. While the attorney is expected to have an extensive knowledge base regarding law, the unique quality of his or her marketing plan will be his or her extensive knowledge regarding client business.

Although the attorney's personal objectives may be different from firm or practice objectives, they must be in line with the general vision. This requires a real understanding by the attorney of the broader objectives.

In terms of an appropriate personal plan, the attorney must be capable of achieving the plan's objectives. For instance, an attorney who knows very little about theater and has little interest in this area should not set as an objective an involvement on the local theater board of directors. Likewise, an attorney who dislikes public speaking should not establish an objective which includes many speeches. Both cases would be contradictory to successful objectives. The attorney, without regard to all the best intentions, should not set objectives which cannot be successfully realized.

Finally, some measurability must accompany the marketing plan. Results are difficult to identify and assess because they are often intangible. Ways to make the intangible more real, for purposes of measurement, might include an assessment of impact on the attorney's practice. Is the attorney gaining new clients as a result of the plan? Is the attorney able to devote more time to matters and clients of value? Are billable hours with respect to such matters and clients on the increase? The answers to these questions will provide some measurement (see Chapter 33 for a discussion on program evaluations).

CHAPTER 24
Managing the Most Critical Resource: Your Time

SUMMARY

Time management is a simple yet frustrating problem for attorneys. A personal practice plan allocates more time to be spent effectively pursuing goals and objectives. The plan can be marketing oriented or developed for some other purpose. But creating a personal agenda will provide focus for activities, leading to attainment of objectives.

This chapter discusses

- setting individual objectives, both personal and professional.
- ensuring that tasks are commensurate with objectives.
- "batch" work to streamline the effectiveness of work efforts.
- tackling small portions of larger tasks.

Attorneys agree that one of the most frustrating problems impacting professional and personal lives is time management. Juggling time for CLEs, business development, billing time, personal time, and social affairs, not to mention family life, puts a great deal of pressure on every attorney.

One solution is a personal practice plan. With a personal plan, more time can be spent effectively pursuing goals and objectives. The plan can be primarily for marketing or other purposes to help the attorney reach practice objectives. It creates a personal agenda which the attorney can follow to cut out unnecessary, time-absorbing tasks.

THE IMPACT OF PLANNING ON TIME MANAGEMENT

The first, most important, and usually most difficult element to conceptualize is an individual objective. The attorney must identify in very specific terms what he or she wants to accomplish and receive from professional practice and personal life. What motivates the attorney—income, recognition, social responsibility—or is there another stimulus? The attorney must clearly understand his or her primary objective and then write it down. It will be the beacon which guides all additional planning tasks.

Once a personal objective has been identified, putting the tools of time management to work can be relatively easy. Alan Lakein, in his classic work on time management *How to Get Control of Your Time and Your Life,* developed a simple, easy-to-use concept of prioritizing tasks. To condense, he advocates that the time manager make three lists of tasks, an "A," "B," and "C" list. All items placed on the "A" list are of the highest impact and are very time sensitive. Issues and matters on the "B" list have a lower priority, and items on the "C" list are the lowest priority of all tasks to be accomplished to the point that they are of little consequence.

Lakein suggests that all items belong on either the "A" list or "C" list. Lakein additionally recommends that only small portions of large tasks be tackled at once, to avoid procrastination.

Another time management technique is "batch" work. This is simply lumping together similar activities to streamline work efforts. The efficiency of the batch process comes from the time saved by not duplicating similar efforts. For the attorney, this may mean combining all trips outside the office into one long errand, or spending one section of time with the secretary in the morning to outline work for the day rather than sporadically throwing "to do" papers on his or her desk.

Striking a balance between client work and a role in office administration, business development, education, and all other time conflicts becomes less frustrating if time is used efficiently. The question an attorney must continually ask is: "Is this the most important thing I can be doing with my time right now?" Self-discipline helps to assign priorities among professional tasks and personal items.

EFFECTIVENESS

Peter Drucker, in his book *The Effective Executive,* lists five elements as being important to effectiveness:

1. Effective executives know where their time goes. They work systematically at managing their time.

2. Effective executives focus on outward contributions. They gear their efforts toward results rather than work.
3. They build on strengths, not weaknesses.
4. They concentrate on a few major areas where superior performance will produce outstanding results.
5. Effective executives make effective decisions. They know that judgments are always based on dissenting opinions rather than on a consensus of facts and that to make any decision fast means to make the wrong decisions.

Although many business managers and executives read Drucker's works to learn more about management theory, many of his management effectiveness theories are time management directives as well.

BIBLIOGRAPHY

DRUCKER, PETER F. *The Effective Executive.* New York: Harper & Row, 1966.

LAKEIN, ALAN. *How to Get Control of Your Time and Your Life.* New York: P. H. Wyden, 1973.

CHAPTER 25
Docket and Calendar Control: Keys to Malpractice Avoidance

SUMMARY

Missed deadlines and statutes result in many malpractice actions. An attorney's inability to schedule work adequately is interpreted as incompetence or at worst negligence. This has a negative impact on overall practice development. A centralized docket and calendar is critical.

This chapter discusses

- docket and calendar as separate but equally important entities.
- accountability and control by using a manually produced monthly calendar.

- methods for attorneys to track work schedule.
- staff benefits derived from control.
- sophisticated use of time management computer software.

According to Duke Nodlinger Stern, who serves as risk manager for several state bar associations, missed deadlines and statutes result in up to 70 percent of all malpractice actions taken against lawyers. Who can blame the clients? The self-discipline required to meet deadlines is unspoken, yet implicit in the attorney-client relationship. An attorney's inability to schedule his or her own work adequately is interpreted at the very least as incompetence and at worst, as negligence.

Here is how mishandling of docket and calendar control can affect an attorney's livelihood.

> One small firm in a large metropolitan area lost two major clients within six months, substantially hurting the firm's accounts receivable as well as attorney and staff morale. A special partner meeting was called, and all agreed that the firm could not tolerate another such loss, particularly since both instances could easily have been prevented.
>
> Both clients had left after the firm had missed two or three important filing deadlines on small matters, apparently ignoring those for larger more lucrative matters. The clients accused the firm of wanting only their most profitable work and not really caring about their overall well-being. The attorneys and staff involved in those cases had been called in to private meetings and had been reprimanded, but the firm's partners were concerned that the same thing might happen again without more dramatic remedial steps.
>
> The partners agreed to begin putting a great deal of emphasis on one centralized firm docket and calendar. They realized that *dockets* deal with legally prescribed and binding dates, whereas *calendars* refer to dates dealing with strictly firm related dates. They also understood that the two clearly impact each other, so keeping them interrelated on one document makes sense in most situations.
>
> They decided that the general office manager would be responsible for its overall ongoing maintenance while individual partners and attorneys would be required to input all significant dates as soon as they became aware of them. The office manager would release a three-sheet program on the first day of every business week, listing important dates for that week on one sheet with considerable detail regarding the nature of the deadline, matter, or event. Dates for the current and next month would be listed on another sheet with some detail about the nature of their importance and, finally, on a third sheet, dates for the current month and following 11 months would be listed with names of the partners, attorneys, and staff involved in the matter.
>
> The partners decided that failure on the part of attorneys or staff to input data in a timely manner or update them when necessary would result in a verbal

warning from the partners for a first offense, a written warning for the second offense, and a penalty to be decided at that time based on the nature of the lack of compliance for the third offense. Firm partners agreed that to make sure attorneys and staff understood how seriously they viewed the situation and the calendar, a fourth offense would result in dismissal of staff or associates and a distribution reduction for partners.

An immediate difference was noticed. Attorneys were reminded of all deadlines by the receipt of their weekly calendar from the general office manager. Firm partners and even colleagues made mention of the more important deadlines, since they too were now aware of them. Many of the attorneys, associates, and even staff began to take their time management efforts more seriously.

After the system had been in place three months (with no additional clients lost because of missed deadlines), the partners announced that firm meetings would be held each Monday morning. The purpose of the meetings would be to discuss the calendars and allow each attorney, associate, and staff member to note important but perhaps unmentioned facets of particular matters. The partners found that soon a lesser sense of friction and a greater sense of cohesion existed within the office since everyone understood when a particular attorney or staff member was under pressure for a deadline.

One year after implementing the system, the entire firm evaluated its effectiveness. Not one client had been lost because of inadequate time management or missed deadlines by firm members. Additionally, because of greater firm efficiency, more time was spared to bring in new clients, which the firm expected would soon occur.

SEEKING ACCOUNTABILITY

The problem just described required a simple solution, easily implemented and with very little additional maintenance: accountability. This is the only key to successful docket and calendar control. It can be delegated to a staff person or may be retained by the attorney, but all attorneys and staff associated with client work should be aware of important matters and related deadlines as well as who is accountable for making sure they are handled appropriately.

CONTROL METHODS

It is not necessary for a docket and calendar control method to be sophisticated, although such methods are available. Control may be asserted simply by using a manually produced monthly calendar, with updated versions distributed weekly throughout the attorney's office, listing matters, deadlines, and persons responsible. Dates for filing, discoveries, adversarial deadlines, and statute of limitations can be entered when the files for those matters are initially opened.

This serves a number of purposes. For one, it allows the attorney to keep track of his or her own work schedule. It gives an indication of matter priority and provides a sense of how much attorney time is still available for new client work. Such a calendar also allows partners, other attorneys, and associates to realize what will be holding that attorney's attention in the very near future. Partners will be less likely to make promises to clients which their attorneys and staff cannot reasonably keep. Attorneys and associates will have a greater awareness of the individual attorney's availability for other matters as well as social accessibility.

Staff benefits because the calendar demonstrates the areas of work for which they will be held responsible and that they are accountable for meeting deadlines.

This system can become more sophisticated through the use of a time management computer software program. Firms may find such a method beneficial.

Chapter 26
Alternative Billing Practices: Beyond the Billable Hour

SUMMARY

There are two basic reasons for using a billable method not based solely on time actually spent on matters. Both justify implementing "value billing." The standard hourly based program carries income limitations related to an implied billable hour ceiling. Further, value billing allows a client to be sure of anticipated expenses, plus paying the worth of a matter rather than its costs.

This chapter discusses

- alternative billing methods as widespread as ethical limits permit.
- billing by job or project.
- contingency variations outside litigation cases.
- benefit-conferred billing.

- blended fees of those involved.
- the "hunch" method of determining value.
- standardizing billing procedures for simplicity.

Many attorneys charge based on the billable hour. But there are two basic reasons for using a billing practice that does not rely solely on time actually spent on matters. One is internal while the other is external. Both provide excellent justification for considering and implementing an alternative billing practice. Such an alternative is widely known as value billing, or value-based billing, since the dollar amount billed is based on a value derived from methods other than the traditional hourly cost basis.

The internal reason for using an alternative billing method is that the standard hourly based program carries income limitations related to an implied billable hour ceiling. An alternative billing program allows the attorney a greater opportunity for profit. The old formula that hours worked equal profit must be more closely examined. Often, it is more accurate to say that hours worked equal revenue, which does not necessarily mean profit. That specific issue is not within the scope of this book.

The external reason for alternative billing practices is marketing oriented because it fills a client need by allowing the client to be sure of anticipated expenses as well as pay for what a matter is worth rather than what it costs. This enhances the attorney-client relationship. It also makes a value statement with regard to the attorney's practice, since the client ultimately assigns the value which, with the attorney's guidance, provides an equitable agreement for all involved.

ALTERNATIVE BILLING POSSIBILITIES

To the extent permissible by ethics considerations, the number of alternative billing possibilities is limited only by the attorney's creative imagination. Billing practices can be so attorney and situation specific that they are virtually unduplicated anywhere else in the world. For the attorney who wants to find a billing practice right for his or her practice—and just as important, his or her clients—there are several options from which to draw.

Among the most often used alternative billing methods available to attorneys are

- billing by job or project.
- contingency variations.
- benefit-conferred billing.

- blended fees.
- the "hunch" method.

Billing by job or project often is most liked by clients. It is easy to understand and eliminates client fears regarding what matters will actually cost versus what attorneys say they will probably cost.

The *contingency variation billing method* is related to the amount of the transaction. If the client has a $500,000 matter, the attorney's fee can be negotiated on the basis of that amount. Of course it is not always easy to pin an exact dollar value on a client matter, particularly with regard to litigation. But this is an alternative which can be more satisfactory than hourly billing in many situations and has been used successfully in divorce and estate matters.

Benefit-conferred billing is a third option available to attorneys. This is appropriate when the attorney shares some of the risk involved. It is in the form of a contingency fee related to successfully negotiated or pursued matters. Real estate and land use matters may lend themselves to this alternative.

The *blended-fee option* places a value on the whole legal service without regard to which partner, attorney, associate, or staff member provided the service. This means a bill will show only hours provided, with the same hourly rate applying to whoever the individual service provider might be.

The *"hunch" method of billing* is the most risky for both attorney and client. The amount of the bill is determined according to what the attorney believes the matter is worth to the client, what the client feels the matter is worth, and what the client is willing or able to pay.

STANDARDIZING CERTAIN PROCEDURES

Ultimately, the attorney is seeking a time value which will equal profitability. A sure way to do this is through the use of standardized forms and procedures. Because so many legal tasks are repetitive, especially with regard to how the attorney or office handles matters internally, a great deal of time and therefore expense can be spared by standardizing frequent procedures to the extent possible. Personal relationships must be unique, but tasks do not have to be.

Alternative or value billing has significant potential for client relationships as well as revenue. It places greater emphasis on value rather than cost, which, of course, is what the client ultimately wants. It results in fewer surprises for the client when the bill arrives because the legal expenses would presumably be in line with the value perceived by the client for services rendered.

CHAPTER 27
Attorney Compensation and Its Effect on Overall Practice Strategy

SUMMARY

Attorney compensation is central to every other law practice decision. It is crucial to marketing in a program's strategy and orientation. Pages of practice management books and law journals have lengthy analysis of the subject. Examining several plans shows how they relate to practice development and can have a significant impact on the ultimate success of marketing programs.

This chapter discusses

- objective of practice as a compensation determinant.
- compensation rewarding "rainmaking" for survival.
- trust as a critical element in subjective systems.
- how compensation plans often contradict firm's stated objectives and priorities.
- case histories of three situations.

What are some of the options and issues regarding attorney compensation? This one issue is central to every other decision in a law firm, especially the firm's strategy and direction.

Certainly this is one of the most often discussed subjects of law practice management, since by definition it affects all attorneys. The pages of practice management books and law journals have more lengthy analysis of more types of plans than one would think possible to exist.

Someone once made the comment that for every 20 law firms there must be at least 25 different compensation schemes—just for partners! This chapter discusses a few plans, as they relate to practice development and marketing, and looks at their results achieved over time.

Articles in the *New York Law Journal* and *Legal Economics* have presented views on both *subjective* and *objective* formula approach to compensation. Arguments for both sides were presented and had merits. However, there are two other and more important aspects in the procedure to determine compensation.

BASIC ISSUES OF COMPENSATION

Perhaps the most important issue of all is the objective of the practice. If the objective is to increase production, then rewarding production through the compensation system is clearly the most appropriate strategy to pursue. It boils down to the simple concept that if behavior is rewarded, it will be repeated.

However, one would suspect that readers of this book are considering methods to modify their practice in any one of several ways, presumably by way of selected marketing tactics. Therefore, a compensation system which rewards "rainmaking" is preferable. That sounds obvious, but many lawyer compensation plans contradict the stated objectives and priorities of the firm.

Second, the most important factor is *trust*. When discussing compensation with attorneys, the subject of trust often comes up, either implicitly or explicitly. Whether pay is determined by the Executive Committee or a separate compensation committee, it requires that those subject to their decisions must trust their motives and the system itself to reward their contribution.

THREE CASE HISTORIES

Here is a firm that encouraged associates as well as partners in the business development process:

> A small firm of four partners and seven associates with a fairly focused practice emphasized land use and real estate law. Their partner pay is predicated on contribution to profitability as determined by a formula that includes billable hours, leveraged hours, and collections. However, their plan departs from the norm in that associates receive 5 percent of annual billings of clients they obtain, in addition to salary. Obviously new business is a high priority, and performance is rewarded.

Here is an example of a firm that encouraged cross-selling but put the primary responsibility for retention on the attorney that brought the client into the firm.

> A law firm, practicing in estate planning and employee benefits, uses a system based on "responsible" and "billing" attorney. When a client is brought to the firm by a partner, that partner receives 5 percent of billings for as long as the partner remains with the firm, no matter who in the firm does the work. The "billing" partner is directly responsible for the work, even that of paralegal and associates, as well as his own. In return, the billing attorney receives 30 percent of all revenues generated by the client.
>
> This system works well for them because "rainmaking" is rewarded, as are billable work production, supervision, and personnel development. Leveraging

> is encouraged in addition to passing matters on, or cross-selling to others for purposes of work load balancing. But the system is based on trust of different levels—trust that someone else will do quality work for "my" client and trust that each partner will get proper credit for business development. It is also based on trust that the system will remain in place long enough to reward business development and contributions to the firm. Additional time, such as for marketing planning, library, computer office management, firm management, and other duties, is done voluntarily with no direct remuneration in the belief that serving the firm will be rewarded indirectly.

This third example describes a firm that is fairly traditional, but does in fact reward nonproductive time, while filling important needs mandated by the firm's management committee.

> A general practice firm uses a system similar to the longevity-based "lockstep" method except small "credit" is given toward billable hours requirement for extra duties, such as associate and staff development, marketing, library and computer management, and so on. The basis is still production oriented so little incentive exists for business development.

Whatever the formula for compensation, it is clear that no other factor says as much about the firm's objectives and strategic planning than the compensation structure. Even the traditional lockstep method which rewards largely on the basis of longevity and acceptance to a structured partnership is based both on trust and firm objectives.

A detailed discussion and analysis of compensation is not within the scope of this book and is more properly addressed in law firm management books as well as practice-oriented journals. Of particular merit in this area is Prentice Hall's newsletter service, *Of Counsel.* Overall, no single other item will influence a firm's direction to the extent of compensation.

CHAPTER 28
What Clients Want: Client Evaluation Criteria and Expectations of Attorneys

SUMMARY

Considerable research has explored the criteria and expectations of both business and retail clients when evaluating attorneys. Most people buy legal services on the basis of the attorney rather than the firm. This can be the core of a legal services marketing program. Understanding the criteria will enable attorneys to meet the expectations of clients better.

This chapter discusses

- the importance of value setting by the client.
- the reasons for business clients changing attorneys.
- ranking of specific client expectations.
- retail client criteria and expectations.

Considerable research has been conducted concerning the criteria used by business and retail clients when evaluating attorneys. Since clients buy legal services from attorneys, not firms, an understanding of clients' evaluation criteria can contribute to shaping a practice development program.

In a paper entitled "Business Executive Evaluations of Various Aspects of Outside Legal Services," presented to a 1983 American Marketing Association Symposium on Services Marketing, Jackson, Brown and Keith developed a comprehensive analysis of business client behavior.

The results of their study indicated that clients evaluate attorneys on several different criteria. It is interesting to note that several different factors which reflect interpersonal relationships with clients were especially important. Personal interest in the client's legal matters, keeping the client informed of progress, verbal skills and personal interest in the client's business were very important.

This is consistent with later studies using other methodology, including a survey done for a law firm's internal use which queried their clients and former clients. Other research using different methodology found that the most important criteria when evaluating service firms was reliability followed by quality of work, overall value and expertise.

VALUE

The client assigns value. As if with blinders to block out hourly rates, value billing and other attorney costs, it is the client who assigns intangible values which have nothing to do with dollar figures. Clients use selective facts to rationalize their conclusions and often may have difficulty articulating the reasoning behind their valuation and subsequent choice of attorneys. No matter how the question is asked, the results are similar. The point is no matter how sophisticated the client, results and communications are vital to the attorney-client relationship.

GETTING ANOTHER ATTORNEY'S FORMER CLIENT

Few businesses, unless new, hire an attorney for the first time. Clients usually hire attorneys because they have rid themselves of their former attorneys. A research report presented at an American Marketing Association Services Marketing Conference indicated that 34 percent of business changed legal counsel in one year. Empirical data would certainly indicate at least the same rate year after year.

Listed in this research were four reasons for a client's termination of a relationship with an attorney:

1. Expected work quality resulted in higher fees.
2. Reaction time did not meet expectations.
3. Needs required specialty work not available.
4. Conflict of interest prevented effective counsel.

Marketing guru Theodore Levitt pointed out that the client does not know what he or she is supposed to get until they do not. When the client does not receive an expected but intangible result, then the client makes real the intangible and realizes its absence.

Early in the attorney-client relationship, the attorney must expend considerable effort to learn the client's expectations in the matter. If nothing else, it provides the attorney with the opportunity to assess how realistic client expectations are. Unrealized expectations are explicitly a significant source of adversity between client and attorney.

The attorney should also become proactive in this process by keeping the client informed regarding pending matters, by sending copies of paperwork, memorandums, correspondence, and progress reports. Since many matters require extended periods of time before final resolution, clients need to know the process is continually ongoing and that attorney effort and concern are continuous as well.

CHAPTER 29
Getting Started: How to Build the Foundation for a Good Program

SUMMARY

The successful marketing of any attorney depends on establishing an internal agreement on the long-range vision of other firm members (if any). Getting started in marketing often involves a specific activity, such as a brochure or new letterhead. These seemingly easy tasks raise more complex questions that must be resolved within the larger group before effective marketing can occur.

This chapter discusses

- the "first steps" of marketing to avoid.
- the issues that must be resolved before getting started in marketing.
- the role of "simple" issues like brochure paper and color in prompting serious and beneficial marketing discussions.

Attorneys in larger firms frequently say "Well, I know what I'm doing, but I have no idea what the folks down the hall do." It's said in jest, but the statement rings true all too often.

What it points out is that all too frequently, attorneys in one part of a firm may not be aware of other activities within their firm. It happens in a two-person office and is almost guaranteed in larger firms. Business development activities are less effective when attorneys and staff within a firm lack overall knowledge of the work of others.

Clients are best served by attorneys who know what they do best, have utmost confidence in their ability to deliver results, and who know the capability of those around them, professionals and support staff alike.

The successful practitioner begins the external business development program with an internal look, and carries out these activities:

- Information gathering within the firm to determine strengths and weaknesses
- Consensus establishment on who the firm is and where it is going
- Communication with everyone in the firm about goals and objectives
- Development of a plan that achieves these objectives
- Attorney and staff training to carry out the business development plan

This process of establishing consensus, ensuring good communication and training personnel for both marketing and for client service, is critical for both the single attorney and a large firm. The level and scope of activities are all that changes.

By addressing these issues, the attorney concentrates resources onto those situations where the greatest results will occur. It lessens the chaos in the office of a general practitioner by emphasizing certain legal areas of service. It provides guidelines and criteria for the acceptance of new work. It provides a common purpose toward which all attorneys can strive.

It is the basis for a good internal marketing program, which helps attorneys bridge the information gap "from the folks down the hall." But it also increases efficiencies and improves client service. It enables attorneys to respond more quickly to situations and information. Internal communication helps to avoid duplication of effort.

In short, it is the basis for a well-planned, effective marketing program.

GETTING STARTED

Why is it so hard to launch a coordinated marketing program in a law firm? Because law firms are conceptual ideas. They are comprised of strong-willed individuals who by personality and training are fierce in their convictions. Since most attorneys have an opinion about marketing, initial agreement between two or more attorneys on how to begin almost never exists.

Marketing involves the blending and molding of individuals into unified groups with a common purpose. Attorneys in the same firm may not agree on their own common purpose, virtually prohibiting the development of a unified group and the subsequent coherent marketing program!

Most attorneys begin marketing by creating some sort of printed piece, usually a brochure or similar device that attempts to describe the attorney or firm capabilities, areas of practice, expertise, and so on. What a difficult task to undertake as the first step.

To represent a law firm in print is difficult, translating living energy into frozen words on paper. It requires not just creative thinking but arduous soul-searching. It is a process of taking vision and transferring it into graphics, of taking soul and describing it in words.

To some degree, every law firm goes through an agonozing start-up phase of marketing. Many issues are raised. Take, for example, the intellectual process of simply preparing a brochure. Brochures raise not only graphic design issues but also more philosophical ones. Another example is a logo and letterhead, which are always needed. If they move away from white bond paper and standard typefaces, it disturbs many attorneys, representing a break from the conventional and smacking of something unprofessional. Clearly, even this is territory to be entered with trepidation.

POWER OF THE PRINTED WORD

The power of graphic design to communicate is immense, but so too is the power required to create it. Attorneys, document oriented by training, intuitively know that every printed piece, whether a contract summary or an individual biography, represents the firm and therefore must be complete and correct. Maybe this explains a frequent attempt to avoid errors and omissions by including everything in a single brochure.

If an attorney accepts an earlier premise—that individual law firms are concepts difficult to summarize—then the attorney understands that a unified vision of the practice of law is the bond of a firm and a prerequisite to effective marketing. Through things like brochures is that vision transferred to print. This process forces the first main hurdle along the way to successful brochure production—consensus of vision.

SIMPLE QUESTIONS, TOUGH ANSWERS

The creation of a marketing program prompts issues that strike to the heart of law firms. Using again the example of a brochure, a simple question about design ("Should we list all our practice areas on one page?") may raise a more complex question ("Are our practice groups clearly defined?"). Simple questions. Frequently tough answers.

Other decisions that are necessary for successful marketing prompt soul-searching responses. For instance the question "What colors do we want to use?" really strikes at firm culture: "Are we conservative, formal, and stuffy? Or are we contemporary, approachable, and responsive?" A firm may be shades of both, and colors of ink and paper can reflect that. Law firms are conservative, so are black and white. An attorney can be sophisticated yet warm, and so are silver and burgundy. A traditional, stable law firm of aggressive litigators is both gray and red. Casual, friendly attorneys are shades of green and peach.

In sum, lawyers will always have difficulty implementing plans without total internal consensus. But on a practical level, the process of the creation of marketing materials raises significant internal issues, the resolution of which is often of greater value to the attorneys than the creation of the material itself! The outcome is a firm with a clearer picture of its current position and a united vision for its future.

CHAPTER 30
Building Consensus: A Prerequisite to Meeting Individual Attorney Needs

SUMMARY

Individual attorney interests and needs must be identified for successful practice development. Successful marketing efforts are grounded in the identification of internal disagreements and subsequent building of internal consensus. Methods to gain information for planning purposes are individual interviews, internal focus groups, firm retreats, and written surveys.

This chapter discusses

- the importance of conducting a firm's internal analysis.
- methods for successful and accurate queries.
- items to be assessed for the firm.
- methods for individual assessment and analysis.
- necessity for building agreement among attorneys on marketing efforts.
- an approach to marketing when agreement cannot be reached.

Successful practice development, whether conducted by the sole practitioner or the 100-attorney firm, requires that individual attorney interests and needs be identified. Ideally, these interests and needs are met within the framework of the firm as currently structured. But the first step to meeting needs is to identify them.

INDIVIDUAL ANALYSIS

To understand fully the needs of the individual, attorneys can follow steps laid out in many of the popular self-help books that offer guidance to job seekers. Examples are *What Color Is Your Parachute?* by Richard Bolles and the classic *Passages* by Gail Sheehy. These books and many others recommend that the reader perform an internal evaluation to determine their own skills, strengths, weaknesses, and a host of other self-analysis characteristics. Following subsequent analysis of what they want to do (be in control, be independent, be powerful, etc.), the reader is then advised to follow certain steps leading to a discovery of exactly the right kind of career choice.

The job-seeking process works for individual attorneys because, essentially, the attorney is looking for new work all the time and therefore needs to develop the skills of self-analysis. Analysis leads to a conclusion which is the basis for future direction.

GROUP ANALYSIS

Because the firm by definition is composed of more than one person, the individuals' needs must be considered in order to develop a responsive firm. Different approaches can be taken by the firm to gather this information and to understand the diverse individual needs. Effective ways to accomplish this analysis in law firms is through the following techniques:

- Attorney interviews
- Internal focus groups
- Firmwide retreats
- Written surveys

All four methods are designed to solicit opinions and feelings from people. There are no "right" or "wrong" answers during the analysis phase. The activity is to gather information to see if general agreement is apparent and to identify areas of conflict.

Here is a list of questions that, when presented to attorneys of a firm, will solicit information of value:

- What sets this firm apart from other law firms?
- What are the firm's three greatest strengths? Are these the same reasons clients seek our services?
- What are the firm's three biggest weaknesses? Are these the same reasons clients do not seek our services?
- In terms of business development and marketing, how do these strengths and weaknesses affect us?
- What are the values that most or all of the attorneys agree are important?
- What do you feel is the greatest area of potential growth for the firm?
- How do you feel we should achieve this growth—internally through associate development or externally through hiring of associates, laterals, or mergers? Please explain.
- One year from now, describe your practice of law. Where? With whom? Areas of emphasis? Types of clients?
- Five years from now, describe your practice of law. Where? With whom? Areas of emphasis? Types of clients?
- What do you think is the most effective way to increase our firm's profits?
- What are the five most effective methods of business development?
- Is the firm's billing methods satisfactory to you and your clients?

Honest answers to these questions very quickly paint a picture of the attorney's attitudes, beliefs, and goals. Here is a review of the four methods used successfully by attorneys to obtain answers to these questions.

INTERNAL INTERVIEWS

This is the preferred method of soliciting answers to the foregoing questions. Within 20 minutes, a good interviewer can solicit answers that paint a fairly clear picture of the individual's opinions. The interviewer (either an in-house administrator or outside consultant but never a group member) can conduct the interview efficiently so attorney time commitment is kept to a minimum. The interviewer will later assemble the responses, using appropriate research-based techniques, and analyze the data to report on areas of agreement and disagreement among the firm's attorneys.

FOCUS GROUPS

In focus groups, information is gathered from up to ten attorneys at one time, usually comprised of attorneys within an identified grouping, such as from the same department or by seniority within the firm. The process takes about 90 minutes. A facilitator leader asks the questions listed and encourages discussion among the group. An assistant takes notes or records the discussion for later transcription. The meetings can take place in the attorney's offices, providing no interruptions are allowed. An off-site meeting location is preferable.

The facilitator may be an internal administrator but is usually an outsider. The facilitator must be a "neutral party" who does not express his or her own opinions or feelings. The facilitator summarizes opinions expressed as the meeting continues and pinpoints key issues and sometimes (but now always) draws conclusions. Creative expression and/or idea friction is healthy as the group tries to deal with issues. The facilitator does not allow strong negatives to interfere with the conversation flow. In larger firms, numerous focus groups are necessary.

Individual interests are then concluded from a review of comments from all the focus groups. As with individual interview techniques, a report to senior partners is developed on areas of agreement and disagreement among the firm's attorneys.

FIRMWIDE RETREATS

Common to law firms, retreats are opportunities to discuss a range of issues in a relaxed environment. The retreat is approached in much the same way as the focus group, except more time is devoted to the process. Retreats allow partners the time not only to raise issues but also to resolve them.

A strong facilitator is required in a retreat environment, primarily for two reasons: the larger number of people involved and the diversity of the group. The practical number of people that can be included in a single discussion in a retreat environment is no more than 25. Who is included in this group depends, of course, on the size of the firm. For many firms, a group of 25 will include partners and associates alike.

Since the purpose of the retreat is to solicit opinions, the facilitator's skills will allow equal voice to all concerned. The discussion succeeds if every attorney feels that his or her opinion was heard and considered. The firm's leadership will ultimately make the key decisions regarding future direction and business development policies.

WRITTEN SURVEY

Distributing questionnaires that require a written response are usually the worst way to solicit valuable information from attorneys. They are to be avoided if possible, particularly in the difficult area of gathering attorney opinions about substantive and personal issues.

If they must be used, the questions should be listed on a single sheet, with attorneys encouraged to use a separate piece of paper for their responses. This allows greater freedom of expression, which should be encouraged to show depth of feelings from the individuals. Questionnaires that ask open-ended questions and leave only two or three lines for an answer create bias by implying that every attorney's feelings on the subject should be expressed in a limited space. This works against the very purpose of the survey!

Questionnaires are time sensitive, and a deadline for their return must be stated. Further, senior management of the firm must totally endorse the survey process and indicate the importance of each attorney response.

RESOLVING CONFLICTS

For larger firms, analysis often leads to conflicts that may or may not have been previously discussed. So the process to resolve internal conflicts is important for attorneys to understand. When too many attorneys of a single firm operate as if they are sole practitioners, their goals and those of the firm in which they work are not met.

Almost every attorney is familiar with the 25-person law firm that is headed in 30 directions. Small firms of 3 and megafirms of hundreds can easily be working hard, practicing law, yet moving in many directions all at the same time. Over the short term, there are activity and cash flow; over the long term there are dissatisfaction and defections. A lack of leadership results in many individual practices under one roof. The net gain for those involved is significantly less than it could be.

Through the information-gathering processes, the divergence among attorney goals, attitudes, and expectations for the future can be identified. Even in the most homogeneous of firms, the analysis reveals surprising information about attitudes that may not be in concert with those of colleagues.

This is not immediate cause for alarm. It is normal and part of the natural growth process for attorneys and firms. But given the situation, the attorney needs immediately to undertake two activities:

1. Development of a marketing program based on the areas of agreement
2. Work to build consensus in areas of disagreement

In the second case, total agreement is not necessarily mandatory. What is important is to understand areas in which the attorney and the firm do not agree. This may be on a specific business practice, a client/service issue, or a proposed marketing technique.

A CASE HISTORY

Here is an example of how the consensus process of resolution can work for a 20-attorney law firm.

> The firm consisted of 8 partners (5 named) and 12 associates. The primary area of emphasis was insurance defense, with particular expertise in medical malpractice litigation. Insurance defense constituted approximately 50 percent of gross annual average fees over the last ten years. Other practice areas of the firm, none of which averaged more than 10 percent of gross fees, were in areas of admiralty law and transportation law, primarily railroads. A smattering of additional business came from various sources, including wills and probate, some personal injury, and simple labor law involving a close friend or relative of one of the attorneys.
>
> During a two-week period, 15 of the attorneys were privately interviewed for their opinions on the firm, strengths, weaknesses, and future growth potential. An analysis of the data revealed
>
> - everyone agreed that insurance defense was the firm's greatest strength.
> - three senior partners and several other partners believed that insurance defense would continue to remain the backbone of the firm for the foresee-

able future. They also felt that the firm should recruit and seek out laterals to maintain its position in this market.

- the remaining attorneys felt that because of changing conditions in the insurance industry, the amount of work available from all insurance companies would decrease. This market was drying up, they said.
- although the firm did very little corporate or general business law, 9 of the attorneys said that this was an area where they felt the firm needed to gain exposure.
- the one partner and two associates who worked in medical malpractice felt this area of law offered great potential and wanted more emphasis there. They wanted to hire laterals and nonattorney medical specialists, and they wanted to train younger attorneys in this area.

How did the members of this firm resolve their differences? The managing partners hired a research consultant to conduct two analyses: one of their current client base and the other of the future of the insurance defense industry (see Chapters 13, 14, and 15 for discussion of the analysis process).

Armed with hard numbers and facts, the firm scheduled a two-day weekend retreat for all attorneys at a destination resort about 75 miles from their offices. Most attorneys were permitted to leave early Friday to travel to the site and prepare for the meeting, which began at 9 A.M. Saturday morning.

A managing partner spent the first hour of the day reporting on the findings of the internal analysis. The research consultant then spent two hours presenting his findings. Time for questions on the facts was allowed. Discussions on the firm's response to the information was held over until the afternoon.

An outside facilitator was brought in after lunch to lead the group. The purpose of the afternoon was for attorneys to express the reasons for their feelings as stated in the individual analysis and to reach agreement in as many areas as possible.

The firm considered the research regarding the future of insurance defense. They agreed that, because of factors beyond its control, the amount of work in this practice area would decrease. They also agreed that the subspecialty of medical litigation was a growing area. They decided to continue discussions on the hiring of laterals and expansion of associate training in this area.

The firm then addressed the ground swell of enthusiasm for corporate work expressed by the associates. The senior partner announced that he would consider a merger or acquisition of some kind that would enable the firm to establish a larger presence in the marketplace. It seemed logical to him that discussions could be explored with another firm who had corporate clients. This was a major breakthrough for the firm and created a great deal of support throughout all levels.

FOUNDATION FOR SUCCESS

In this case history, the firm was successful in obtaining agreement on virtually all the substantive issues. But in circumstances where agreement was not obtained, attorneys understood that no effort was wasted to pursue or promote an activity which does not have the support of the whole firm.

The attorneys also found internal meetings useful to resolve issues and build agreement. These are scheduled and planned like the focus groups described elsewhere in the book. Essentially these meetings became "miniretreats" with the same components—report of research findings, then discussion to arrive at consensus.

The resolution of disagreements and the building of future plans can be a lengthy process. But with the techniques described here, attorneys can use their time efficiently and build a foundation for marketing success.

BIBLIOGRAPHY

Bolles, Richard Nelson. *What Color Is Your Parachute? A Practical Manual for Job-Hunters and Career Changers.* Ten Speed Press, Berkeley, CA, 1990.

Sheehy, Gail. *Passages. Predictable Crises of Adult Life.* E. P. Dutton and Company, New York, 1976.

Chapter 31
How to Develop a Generic Plan

SUMMARY

Many attorneys have difficulty in establishing and maintaining plans. If the attorney does not establish a plan with specific objectives, chances of meeting those objectives are less, and the attorney will not be completely satisfied. Four crucial elements to an effective plan are the objective, assessment, strategy, and implementation.

This chapter discusses

- the difficulty of attorney planning.
- the need for establishing and maintaining plans.
- four crucial elements to effective planning.
- the importance of conducting a complete planning process.

To summarize many of the concepts discussed elsewhere in this book, business development plans typically have the following components:

- *Situation Assessment.* A narrative description of the current status of the attorney or firm. This is the "here is where we are" statement.
- *Goal.* An overall statement on "where we are going."
- *Objectives.* Specific statements, both short range and long range, that lead to the attainment of the goal.
- *Message Theme.* A single concept that is woven throughout all business development activities and helps to focus efforts. It is one easily understood and memorable fact about the attorney or firm.
- *Audiences.* Identification of the specific people and groups important to business development. These will be clients, past clients, potential clients, referral sources, and so on.
- *Strategy.* A general statement that outlines the general approach to business development. This is the "how we will get there" statement.
- *Tactics.* The specific activities that develop from the overall strategy.
- *Budget.* The cost for carrying out each of the tactics.
- *Schedule.* The time frame in which all activities will take place.
- *Evaluation.* Process to control the marketing activities and provide feedback on their success.

KEEPING IT SIMPLE

Business development plans should not be complicated. Too much time can be spent developing the plans and budgets, and too much time can be spent controlling them. At the same time, the process of planning and budgeting can itself be time consuming while at the same time enlightening for an attorney. The process requires not only specific decisions on future action but also an acknowledgment by the attorney and other partners that this activity is important.

Every attorney and many staff members within a firm should be incorporated into the planning process in some way. Every attorney should have assigned to him or her some sort of marketing budget, however modest. This emphasizes that *marketing is everyone's responsibility* and that everyone is encouraged to include at least some marketing activities in their normal job responsibilities.

An attorney was once overheard commenting, "Lawyers are about the worst at planning; they seldom do any!" Perhaps that perception was because the simple basics of planning are not taught in law school, and nowhere else in their experience have attorneys been exposed to planning techniques. Some attorneys are good planners by default, coming by the skill naturally. But many attorneys have some difficulty in establishing and maintaining plans.

Whether planning a major practice emphasis change, office move, or practice restructure, or a special event such as a holiday open house, the planning concepts are the same. The important bit of wisdom to remember in terms of planning is, "If you don't know where you are going, you are never going to get there!" Similarly, if the attorney does not establish a plan with objectives, those objectives will never be met, and he or she will never be completely satisfied.

DRAFTING THE PLAN

There are four crucial elements to an effective plan. These are the objectives, assessment, strategy, and implementation. Anything else is an instrument to tailor the plan to fit a unique sutiation.

First, the *objectives* list what the attorney specifically wants to accomplish. Is the foremost objective an increased number of clients, increased profits, success in a new practice area, or an open house for clients? Whatever the case, additional objectives must be established which will help the attorney reach the primary objective. For instance,

- if the attorney's primary goal is to increase the number of clients, specific objectives might include membership in certain clubs, increased communication (such as correspondence, telephone calls, or visits) with potential clients, and so on.
- if the attorney's primary goal is to increase profits, specific objectives might include a greater emphasis on time management to increase hourly billings, new negotiation terms with clients to increase the

financial value of work completed, or increased response from accounts receivable.

- if the attorney's primary goal is an open house for clients, specific objectives might include comprehensive cleaning and refurbishing of the office area; scheduling of a caterer; and some entertainment, development of an invitation list, and so on.

Next, some form of *assessment* regarding the plan's development and effectiveness should be introduced. Such an assessment vehicle would address issues such as

- What resources are available to the attorney?
- What *internal* factors exist which might influence the plan's outcome?
- What *external* factors exist which might influence the plan's outcome?
- What are the negative factors, or competition, for the attorney's attention?

The assessment provides the attorney with a clear vision of how practical the plan is and what sort of time line might be necessary for its effective implementation.

After an assessment of the environment in which the plan must operate, a *strategy* must be decided and clearly understood by everyone involved in its eventual success. This is when the attorney must decide which objectives are time-specific, quantifiable goals and to whom these goals should be delegated. For example, in the event of an open house, the office receptionist might be asked to schedule food and entertainment, the office manager might be asked to supervise cleaning and office rehabilitation efforts, and the attorney might want to retain supervision of the guest list.

Finally, the last step is the *implementation* process. This is where the attorney is rewarded for the sometimes tedious process of planning. If all the elements of the planning process have been satisfied, then the implementation of the plan is destined to be successful. Unfortunately, many attorneys jump right into the implementation process without setting objectives, conducting an assessment, or outlining a strategy. Because of this, many do not achieve the success otherwise possible.

A vast wealth of literature has been written and is available to attorneys with regard to all types of planning: strategic, marketing, and social event planning, to name a few areas. Successful planning essentially boils down to a rule of thumb: with very few exceptions, the amount of time spent making the perfect plan will multiply to create the perfect plan outcome.

CHAPTER 32
Developing the Internal Program

SUMMARY

External business development efforts depend heavily on the internal marketing program. Where an internal plan does not exist, the results of a marketing effort can at best be ineffective and at worse chaotic and embarrassing. Just as external programs frequently measure the audience to see if their needs are being met, so too does a good internal program. The internal component serves four purposes: to motivate, inform, coordinate, and educate. An internal program is a vital part of the external plan.

This chapter discusses

- the internal plan components and value to attorney and staff.
- specific issues to address in internal plans, such as authorship, scope, implementation, and reviews.

Here is the story of a 75-member firm in a large metropolitan area whose lack of an internal plan caused initial embarrassment and subsequent loss of business.

> The firm was young and very aggressive in its marketing efforts. Besides having several excellent rainmakers as partners, the firm hired a full-time marketer to capitalize on earlier scattered efforts. The marketer was excellent in sales and promotion. He was able to attract much attention to the firm and provide opportunities for the attorneys to obtain additional work.
>
> The problem arose as the attorneys began to believe in their own promotional materials. The marketer had been given permission to write brochures and news releases touting the firm's success in many areas.
>
> But the successes and depth of skill in several of those areas were questionable. This fact came home to haunt the firm in several ways.

Due to the marketer's strong efforts to interest the news media in the firm's success, a major article on worker's compensation appeared in the city's largest newspaper. It gave the impression that the firm had significant depth in this area of the law. Believing this to be true, the marketer had embellished the firm's capabilities with the reporter. While the individual attorney who was quoted extensively knew the law very well, the article created the impression that the firm's worker's compensation department was larger than it actually was and could handle virtually any situation.

The reality was that this department was highly specialized and not capable of handling a variety of cases. Subsequent clients were disappointed in the results. Since internal consensus was missing, there was a profound lack of direction. Internal communication was nonexistent, and the marketing strategy was seriously flawed (or, more correctly, the marketing strategy was not really developed at all). Obviously, the attorney and staff were not trained in marketing techniques to make the whole thing work together. The basic problem is that the firm lacked an agreed-upon plan.

In a more common if less dramatic situation, attorneys frequently promise a new client excellent and continual communication on all matters related to a case. But if the firm or staff does not internally agree or understand this (at least to the level expected by the attorney and the client), then the whole effort becomes suspect.

WRITING THE INTERNAL PLAN

The internal plan is a component of the external marketing plan. Internal plans have the same components of external plans—the "target audience" of the plan is the various segments of the firm—partners, associates, staff, and so on. Just as external programs frequently measure the audience to see that their needs are being met, so too does a good internal program. The internal component will *motivate* colleagues and staff, *inform* them as to overall marketing efforts, *coordinate* their activities, and *educate* them about marketing results and so on.

Guidelines for the specific process to write the plan are discussed in the preceding chapter on generic marketing plans. The important issue here is to recognize that an internal program is an important component of the external plan.

Here are the specific issues that need to be addressed in the internal components of a complete plan.

- *Authorship.* Committees can rarely write anything, but if consensus is established, a commitee *can* and in many cases *should* write a plan.

Individual attorneys or administrators are likely candidates to draw up the first draft.

- *Personalities.* It is important to fit strategy and tactics to the personalities of those involved.
- *Scope.* The plan must involve everyone in the firm—from the senior partners to the newly hired secretaries.
- *Addressing needs.* Strategy and tactics must fit the needs and desires expressed by the attorneys in the internal surveys.
- *Plan components.* An internal program uses many of the same elements as an external one.
- *Implementation.* Who will be responsible and control the plan?
- *Reviews, revisions, and edits.* The internal plan should be read every month, edited every four months, and reviewed/revised every year.

CHAPTER 33
Program Evaluation and Feedback: What You Don't Know Can Hurt You

SUMMARY

The most overlooked element in successful marketing programs is the evaluation of ongoing activities. This forms the basis for taking correct action and making future programs successful. But good evaluations are possible only when clear and quantifiable objectives have been set. There is never one reason why a client hires an attorney, so all the factors affecting the decision must be considered.

This chapter discusses

- the role of evaluation in a successful marketing program.
- the setting of appropriate objectives to enable effective and meaningful evaluation.
- typical marketing activities and the most common methods to evaluate their success.
- the interrelationships of all marketing efforts.

In business development, there are four phases to every successful program: the situation analysis, the planning stages, the implementation steps, and, finally, the evaluation of program results.

These are sequential steps, with each one being as important as the other. Which one usually gets the least attention? Invariably, it is the evaluation phase, the part of the program that answers the questions: "How did we do? What worked and what didn't? If our program needs adjustment, what needs to be fixed?" The answers provide information that is absolutely essentially to successful marketing programs in the future.

Here are two stories of marketing by attorneys where evaluation would have been of great value:

> A sole practitioner had developed a modest business in handling real estate transactions for individuals and small, family-owned businesses. She was interested in expanding her practice to include other kinds of services such as wills and estate planning. She embarked on a six-month program, purchasing advertising and mailing a newsletter to potential clients. After a time-consuming and relatively costly effort that produced minimal results, she abandoned the marketing effort.
>
> A 70-member law firm felt the municipal bond market was underserved in their state. They brought in a lateral and several young associates to meet this need. After making the appropriate announcements, the firm engaged in an aggressive publicity and seminar program to attract attention. One year later, the firm had been unsuccessful in attracting any significant new bond business and had actually seen its existing bond work decline. The other partners were discouraged by the cost of the effort and quietly dismantled the bond department.

In each of these cases, the attorneys involved were asked why their programs failed. Although the situations were entirely different and the attorneys had opinions on what happened, their answers were essentially the same: they didn't know—they had performed no *meaningful evaluation* of the programs.

ROLE OF EVALUATION

Although the evaluation phase comes last in the business development process, it is really the first phase of the next program. As illustrated in Figure 33-1, the business development process is guided by assessment of ongoing activities. In practice, each phase is not so neatly compartmentalized due to the continually overlapping nature of the process.

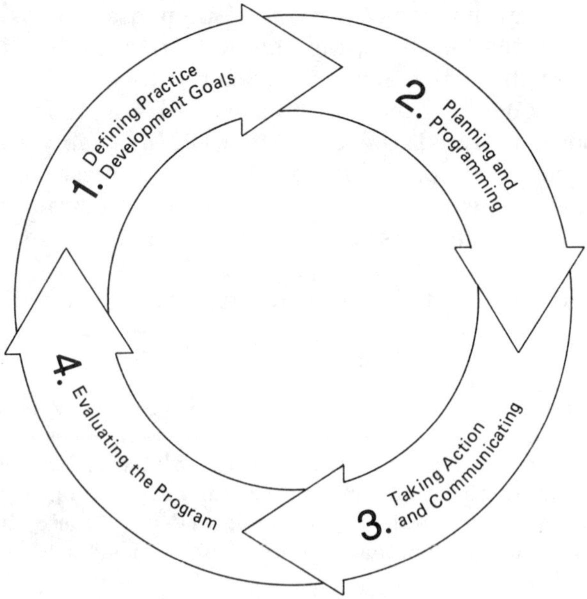

Figure 33-1 Four-Step Marketing Process. From Cutlip, Center, Broom, *Effective Public Relations,* 6th ed., ©1985, p. 200. Adapted by permission of Prentice Hall, Inc., Englewood Cliffs, New Jersey.

In both case histories, knowledge of "what went wrong" is essential to plan future business development activities. In many marketing programs, this question is not answered correctly. Subsequent adjustments in future programs are therefore inappropriate. The attorney may actually fix the component that was not broken!

Here is what a good evaluation of the two case histories revealed.

> The sole practitioner's advertising was wasted because the marketplace was flooded with other attorneys after the same business, many of whom were more aggressive in their advertising and siphoned off any potential new clients. Through the newsletter, her existing clients were aware of her services but had no immediate need to act on it. The attorney was therefore doing the right thing, but failed to recognize the time required before results would accrue. Instead of abandoning the entire program as she did, a good evaluation would have told her to discontinue advertising while continuing her newsletter efforts.
>
> In the 70-member firm after the bond market, their efforts failed because of entrenched competition and because they did not recognize the increasing price sensitivity of the public sector. They relied on the goodwill and reputation of the lateral. However, when tough decisions were made by bond-issuing en-

tities, public pressure forced them to respond to the aggressively marketed services of other attorneys who were offering a lower price. Appeals by the lateral to recognize the importance of his experience and high-quality service were acknowledged but essentially ignored.

WHAT IS EVALUATION?

Evaluation is a process of determining, in terms of both quantity and quality, if the goals and objectives of a program were met. The information it provides is essential to create and carry out future programs. It plays an essential part in the total marketing process, as shown in Figure 33-1.

Evaluation is closely related to goals, both large and small. A large goal of a business development program can be to "build a practice that is satisfying to the attorney's personal and financial goals." The evaluation process can measure success in reaching those goals. An immediate goal could be to "establish personal contact with vice presidents at seven software companies in our area with annual sales of $1 million or more." An evaluation will reveal not only if those contacts were made but their depth and future potential.

Evaluation dissects each marketing activity of the attorney or firm, enabling the "weak link" in the marketing chain to be identified. Here are the typical variables in a marketing effort and questions attorneys can ask themselves:

- Was our analysis of the marketplace correct? Did we have the right information to identify the right audience?
- Was our message appropriate? Were the content and organization correct?
- How was the quality of the message(s), in terms of style, format, and "packaging"?
- Did we send enough messages? Was our distribution correct? If we tried to reach clients through the media, was there enough coverage in either publicity or advertising?
- Did the right people, in the quantities desired, receive our message?
- How many of the people who received our message understood it? Did it increase knowledge, awareness, and understanding?
- Did anyone change their opinions and attitudes and therefore change their behavior as we wished?
- Are we obtaining our goals or solving our problems?
- As a result of the overall activity, is the individual attorney or firm getting what they really want?

To get at the answers to each of these questions requires different kinds of survey devices and questions. Various research techniques, discussed elsewhere in this book, will range from focus groups to telephone surveys.

IMPORTANCE OF CLEAR OBJECTIVES

Since evaluations are closely tied to objectives, the clearer those objectives, the more measurable they'll be and the more successful the attorney will be in achieving them.

For example, an attorney practicing in real estate may have a business development program goal of "increasing work from commercial developers." An evaluation to see if this goal was met may take the form of simply "yes" or "no" based on number of clients or gross fee income. This is not a satisfactory answer because it does not tell the attorney which components of the business development program are causing the success or failure. It also does not compare the fee income to the cost of obtaining that income.

A better objective would be something like this: "Increase profit through increased volume of contract reviews for commercial developers."

This objective is more on target, but the evaluation will be of more value if we clarify:

- *Increase profits.* By how much? Express this in percentages or dollars. Profits are related to careful budgeting so the costs necessary to carry out efforts to increase volume of contract reviews is important. Evaluation should measure both attorney time and money spent on the activity.
- *Increase volume.* By how much? This is usually expressed in terms of dollars or percentages. Effective evaluation cannot be undertaken unless a quantity can be identified.
- *Undertake contract reviews.* What type? Contract reviews can vary tremendously in complexity. Identification of more specific types such as "developments of more than *X* acres or *X* dollars" is helpful.
- *Establish time horizons.* Over what period of time should this program be conducted, and when should results be expected? Evaluation can show exactly the calendar dates when activities took place, which can then be compared to projected dates.

Evaluations ask questions related to goals with answers usually expressed in terms of numbers of degrees. The answer to the big question ("Are we obtaining our financial and personal goals?") can be evaluated by quantitative analysis of fee incomes and amount of profits and qualitative analysis of attorney satisfaction.

But effectiveness of programs to reach these overall goals can be obtained by evaluating the small steps enroute to that goal. Here are typical activities that can be evaluated and common methods to do so:

ADVERTISEMENTS

- Number of people who saw the ad. Measure by asking print media for circulation or readership rates, broadcast media for Arbitron ratings or audience share.
- Number of responses by telephone, by mail, by "drop in." Measure by tallying responses by category as they occur.
- Quality of responses. Measure by demographic study of respondents, fee income analysis of new clients resulting from advertisements.

ATTORNEY-SPONSORED SOCIAL EVENTS

- Number of attendees. Measure by tally of respondents versus actual attendees.
- Follow-up activities by attorney. Measure by survey of attorneys regarding number contacted and subsequent action.
- Quality of attendees. Measure by review of attendance list for titles and organizations.
- Effectiveness. Measure by number of valuable leads generated.

CLIENT RETENTION

- Number retained over period of time. Measure by client analysis of length of service, frequency of service, and gross fee income.

DIRECT MAIL ITEMS (REQUIRING ACTION ON THE PART OF RECIPIENT)

- Number of responses by telephone, by mail, by "drop in."

INFORMATIONAL ITEMS (ANNOUNCEMENTS, BROCHURES, NEWSLETTERS)

- Number distributed. Measure by tally of distribution list.
- Penetration (if mailed). Measure by counting mail returns.
- Quality of audience. Measure by checking quality of mailing list by title and organization.
- Degree of increase of reader understanding. Measure by tallying requests for more information or by sample phone survey of recipients. Measure by survey of firm attorneys for references by recipients to information.

PERSONAL MARKETING

- Number of contacts at target markets. Measure by survey of attorneys, audit of "client contact" sheets.
- Quality of relationships. Measure by client retention and fee analysis.

PRO BONO WORK

- Satisfaction of attorneys performing the work. Measure by survey of attorneys.
- Degree of effectiveness. Measure by client analysis and referrals.

PUBLICITY

- Number of news releases written and distributed. Measure by tallying number of releases by subject.
- Number of releases used by media and placement in media (used prominently or "buried"?) Measure by tallying column inches or broadcast time, with identification of prominence.
- Recall by readers or viewers. Measure by survey of attorneys for references from clients, colleagues, others.
- Value of publicity. Measure by calculating equivalent cost of advertising space (although publicity has greater value than similar advertising because of implied editorial endorsement).

REFERRALS

- Number of referrals. Measure by client analysis as to source of new business.
- Rate of referrals. Measure by survey of attorneys and comparisons to another time period.

SEMINARS, VIP FORUMS

- Effectiveness. Measure by tally of requests for additional information and by responses from attendees.

SPEECHES

- Size of audience reached. Measure by tally of number of speeches given and number of attendees.
- Quality of audience. Measure by analysis of demographics of audience.

- Effectiveness. Measure by tally of referrals and direct client calls. Measure by number of subsequent speaking invitations.

STAFF SERVICES

- Quality and effectiveness. Measure by tally of number of complaints/compliments received.

In every situation, evaluation can be used to compare the actual time required and costs (both in terms of attorney time and out-of-pocket expenses) budgeted for the event.

Attorneys should note that the measurement of a certain activity may not be a judge of its effectiveness. Quantities of news releases cannot be a substitute for changes in knowledge, opinions, or behaviors!

CAUSE AND EFFECTS

While evaluation is essentially to give feedback on the effectiveness of marketing activities, caution must be exercised in jumping to conclusions as to the causes of those results (or lack thereof).

The success of most business development programs cannot be attributed to one activity. Every program that meets objectives is usually the result of several concurrent and complementary activities. Additional work from an existing client comes because of good work performed in the past and a warm relationship with the attorney and staff doing the work. New business may result from a client seeing a well-located storefront office and seeing an advertisement in the Yellow Pages at precisely the time when they needed help.

But even information on these interrelated factors can be sorted out through client surveys and research (see discussion on these topics in Chapters 7, 8, 9, and 10).

The important issue is to understand that effective future programs are built on a foundation of good information about the past. Effective evaluations are continuous and central to the business development process. The attorney who sets clear goals and carries out meaningful evaluations will have the facts necessary to build a long-term successful practice.

Editor's Note: For a complete list of factors affecting the successful marketing of an attorney, see Appendix 1, "When Practice Development Doesn't Work."

Chapter 34
High Impact Marketing: Techniques to Get Quick Results and Build Support for a Long-Range Program

SUMMARY

Because marketing is by definition an effort that takes time, frustration grows and interest often wanes among attorneys. Typical first steps undertaken by attorneys are exactly those that take long and bring few immediate results. There are several marketing activities that require little time and can bring immediate results. If appropriate initial actions are taken, internal support for other longer-range activities grows.

The chapter discusses

- the importance of getting quick results when beginning a new marketing program.
- the three typical marketing activities to avoid at the beginning of any coherent program.
- 16 specific activities that can result in immediate positive results for a new marketing effort.

Internal support for business development efforts is essential. But all too often, initial enthusiasm for a significant effort drops as soon as the marketing program begins to consume a lot of time and bring few immediate results. This is a problem that plagues many attorneys and marketing directors who are charged with the responsibility of building a successful program.

One method that ensures continued support for the business development effort is to plan and carry out a few activities that produce quick results and bring initial success as a marketing program gets underway.

There is no doubt that business development is a lengthy process, with results often less than tangible. Many marketing activities have paybacks that are two or three years down the road or even longer (see Chapter 38 on marketing timetables). So even the strongest believer in marketing is hard pressed to justify six months of time and expense with nothing to show for it.

High-impact marketing is designed to make things happen, quickly. It is not a knee-jerk action to look busy but an approach to marketing that brings some immediate—albeit modest—successes. It mixes activities aimed at both short-term and long-term objectives so that the marketers themselves, as well as their partners and associates, can see that the process does indeed work.

GETTING QUICK RESULTS

So what must an attorney do to achieve high impact? Here are three methods that have worked for attorneys:

- An attorney in a small firm scheduled a meeting in a client's office to ask "How am I doing?" The client is gratified to be asked and the attorney receives candid feedback which the attorney shares with his partners.
- An attorney in a small firm performed an analysis of recent legislation affecting his clients, developers of mobile home parks. Among other things, the analysis informed the industry of future trends in government regulation, allowing individual businesses to plan ahead. He sent a copy of the document to a well-read mobile home industry trade magazine. The magazine editor called, saying he liked the public service angle of the article and intends to publish it in the next month's issue.
- Another small firm scheduled a private luncheon, inviting several clients to meet with another of the firm's clients, the CEO of an area high-technology firm that just received $7 million in venture capital. The law firm received exceptionally warm thank you notes from the clients, expressing appreciation to learn about the CEO's future plans.

What do all these activities have in common? They are all marketing activities that resulted in attorneys feeling good about themselves and marketing in general. Each activity is client-focused. The attorneys conducting them were not engaged in "selling" and did not ask clients for anything except a little of their time. Each activity fit the criteria important for high impact and effective marketing:

- It required relatively little attorney time to plan and execute.
- The out-of-pocket costs to carry out the activity were small (or nonexistent).
- The results were immediate.

INITIAL ACTIVITIES TO AVOID

There are three common mistakes made by attorneys and firms at the onset of a marketing program. In their eagerness to "get something going" and to have tangible results, attorneys will eagerly embark on efforts to (1) produce a brochure, (2) start a newsletter, or (3) get some publicity. All three efforts are fraught with problems if attempted as the first activities! The attorneys involved in them are destined for frustration and (perhaps) failure.

Brochures are time consuming and costly. Additionally, the process to write and produce them can be internally divisive. Brochures have their place in comprehensive marketing programs, but they are ill suited to be the first activity on the agenda. Law firms have been known to take *two years* to write, design, and print a brochure, during which time the attorneys have lost enthusiasm for marketing and resorted to individual (and often misdirected) efforts. See Chapters 55, 56, and 57 on brochure production and distribution.

Newsletters are also time consuming to produce. An estimated 20 percent of all newsletters, started with enthusiasm and filled with information, never publish a second issue. Sixty-five percent of newsletters never reach the tenth issue. Why? Because the people involved grossly underestimate the time required to produce one. Chapters 61 and 62 discuss the production and distribution of client newsletters.

Another common mistake is to define marketing as "getting some publicity." While a low-keyed, focused effort to attract attention through the news media can be effective, the results are rarely the "front page news" that some attorneys think they deserve. The news media generally ignore attorneys unless there is a celebrity client, a spectacular lawsuit, or a megamerger. Therefore, it is difficult to make a big splash in the media, and publicity efforts often go unrewarded. Chapters 63, 64, and 65 discuss the entire issue of media relations.

USEFUL ACTIVITIES

In addition to the examples listed at the beginning of this chapter, here are some examples of high-impact activities that have proven to be of value to attorneys and firms (details on all of these activities are explained elsewhere in this book; see the index for specific pages).

- Give everyone (attorneys and key staff) a Marketing Binder. This simple act dramatizes to all that they will play a role in the total program. The binder will eventually be filled with the firm plan, attorney plan, marketing update information, general "tips" copied from other sources, etc.

- Do a client/services grid (see Chapter 49, Figure 49-2, for explanation of this activity). This activity takes only a few hours and quickly demonstrates areas of potential new business. It can also suggest new areas where the attorneys could capture additional fees already being spent on other attorneys by their clients. The services grid quickly focuses attorney attention on actions likely to bring quick returns.
- Have the person primarily responsible for marketing do a *brief* (20-minute) individual interview with attorneys in the firm to determine their general attitude toward marketing. Identify each person in terms of the support they are likely to lend to the efforts. Subsequent marketing efforts can be developed that are in concert with prevailing internal attitudes.
- Obtain a data base software program to collect information on the firm's personnel, clients, and new business prospects. This will provide useful marketing information to be presented quickly to attorneys.
- If the firm places announcements in bar publications and other magazines, ask a graphic designer to upgrade the firm's tombstone advertisements. Improvement of graphics instantly creates a more contemporary, sophisticated image. This can be done without changing the firm's logotypes and letterhead (redesigning letterhead is a major effort; do not make this an initial effort!).
- If one does not exist, prepare a firm fact sheet. Avoid trying to describe the firm in terms of feelings, attitudes, and ideals. Simply state what the firm does, what it has done, and the benefits to the clients. Update an existing fact sheet with improved graphics and laser printing (a graphic designer can do wonders for $500).
- Along these same lines, collect resumes of all attorneys and have them formatted consistently and then printed out on a laser printer. The enhancement will be impressive and immediately give everyone a feeling of high-quality professionalism and unity of purpose.
- When new clients are obtained, find out the process by which they came to know and hire the firm. Sometimes this can be done casually at a partner's meeting. This question could be asked about each file—the answers would show a trend to everyone in the firm that would be of great interest!
- Build on success. Every firm has conducted some sort of marketing in the past. Therefore, a "new" program should always begin by building on past successes. Ask senior partners and others what has worked in the past. Then make an effort to do more of it.
- Bring in a consultant familiar with business development for attorneys and invite all professional staff to a half-day seminar. Ask the consultant to instruct on trends in legal marketing and "how to get started."

- Make sure that marketing is a regular agenda item for attorney and staff meetings.
- If there is an internal newsletter, make sure that some marketing news appears in each issue, even if it is only a "how-to" marketing tip. Identify positive steps forward in a program, no matter how small.
- If there is an existing marketing program that is not moving forward, analyze what activities should be happening. Then break down these activities into smaller steps (the more the better) and assign specific timetables for the completion of each step.
- Draft a sample "welcome" letter to new clients and make sure that the appropriate attorneys send it out as necessary.
- Analyze the firm's community involvement practices and develop a specific program of membership and involvement that is oriented toward business development. Ensure that attorneys become active in the organization (membership by itself is not marketing!).
- Bring in a training consultant to discuss with the office staff everything from telephone techniques to client confidences. Impress upon staff the importance of "customer service."

In sum, an approach to marketing that gets quick results helps attorneys in two ways. Their clients will be positively affected in ways that result in immediate new business or at minimum good feelings and strengthened relationships. The second benefit is internal support for the attorney's marketing efforts which will ensure that proposals for future efforts are well received!

Chapter 35
How Much to Spend: Methods and Guidelines for Setting the Marketing Budget

SUMMARY

Establishing and controlling practical marketing budgets is essential to the financial health and ultimate success of the attorney. A "balanced" budget, that is, one that addresses various marketing issues and contains a variety of marketing activities, is required for the most effective long-range results. There are four methods commonly used by attorneys to establish marketing budgets.

This chapter discusses

- general guidelines for allocation of money and time to the marketing effort.
- achieving a balance in marketing between satisfying the needs of existing clients ("the best source of new business") and undertaking efforts to get new work.
- the importance of spending equal amounts of time and money in both direct and indirect marketing efforts.
- the best methods to determine the budget size.
- setting budget size based on four methods: percentage of fees, competitive necessity, objectives, or all you can afford.

Enlightened attorneys are developing a formal procedure for establishing client-focused marketing budgets. Individual attorneys, whether sole practitioners or operating within the context of a megafirm, are realizing the value of having clearly defined, measurable costs of marketing. The budget needs to be developed and implemented if the total business plan of the firm—no matter how small or how large—is to succeed.

Sometimes the pressure to develop budgets comes from the firm's own financial people who want a better handle on marketing costs. In larger firms where there is a marketing director or coordinator responsible for a budget, this person will want an accurate and realistic budget which can be monitored and measured against preset objectives (this also prevents "dumping," a common practice of attorneys to charge to the marketing budget those expenses not clearly assignable to any other particular budget).

The most effective marketing budgets reflect a blance between low-level efforts and those that require more energy. Good budgets lay out programs that devote attorney resources to the "low-hanging fruit" or work that is easy to get. This is usually work from existing clients. But good budgets also lay out programs for obtaining work that is harder to obtain but necessary for long-term practice growth. This easy-to-get versus hard-to-get approach to marketing is explained more clearly in Chapter 3, discussing the effort grid, which illustrates the degree of effort required for attorneys to build their practice.

BALANCING THE BUDGET

Marketing budgets should be based on the 40/40/20 guideline of budget development. These are percentages of marketing targets or segments. Attorneys should plan to

- Spend 40 percent of a marketing budget "selling" existing services to existing (or recent past) clients, that is, the easiest "new work" to obtain.
- Spend 40 percent of a marketing budget "selling" existing services to new clients or new services to old clients, that is, new work that is more difficult to get.
- Spend 20 percent of a marketing budget "selling" new services to new clients, that is, the work that is hardest to get.

If business in any one area falls off a little, the remaining business generated from the split marketing effort will continue to account for at least some of the attorney's business.

Most marketing efforts are both client-focused and aimed at new clients. For example, a seminar for clients on a tax issue may be designed only for clients, but attorneys will often use the opportunity to invite nonclients. Also, they will hope (and maybe actively encourage) their clients to make referrals. Therefore, the client-focused seminar has an indirect and larger benefit for business development.

Other activities that appear to be nonclient-focused also have this dual benefit. A speech to a Rotary Club is a client-focused activity even if there are no clients in the audience. How can this be? Because any activity that causes the attorney to be recognized as an authority on a topic reinforces existing client relationships. The effort enables the attorney to hone research and speaking skills; news coverage or word-of-mouth publicity resulting from the speech will impress existing clients and perhaps remind past clients of the attorney's continued work in a certain practice area.

In the marketing budgets presented in the appendix (Appendices 3–7), there are line items that perform two and occasionally all three of these functions. For example, the cost of a $10,000 brochure that is distributed to both existing and potential clients could be allocated 40/40/20 or at a portion that uses the budgeter's best judgment. The important point is to recognize that a conscious effort needs to be spent in each area.

DIRECT VERSUS INDIRECT COSTS

Another general guideline for budget planning is to allocate one-half of the business development budget to direct marketing costs and the other half to indirect.

Direct marketing costs are those activities aimed at a specific client or known target for a specific kind of work. Examples are the effort of an attorney or firm to capture legal work in worker's compensation at the XYZ Manufacturing Company or, more broadly, to capture all employee-employer legal work at high-technology firms within 50 miles of the office (which includes the XYZ Company). Most but not all of the cost for this activity will be in attorney time. Direct marketing is the personal involvement of attorneys or firm administrators to capture the business through activities such as research, interviews, visitations, social events, and so on. It also includes brochures and other outside costs to produce items used for the specific target.

Indirect marketing costs are major marketing support activities, sometimes called public relations, that are of a more general nature, although they may be aimed at a specific target group. These activities involve both personal attorney time and impersonal components such as brochures or newsletters. In larger firms, indirect marketing is usually controlled by a marketing coordinator; in smaller firms, it is controlled by a partner or someone with appropriate interest and skills. Of the 50 percent spent for indirect marketing, a general guideline is that half will be in attorney and staff time to control and monitor the activities and the other half will be outside expenses such as public relations assistance, “image” advertising, memberships, entertainment, and so on.

CHOOSING THE RIGHT FORMULA FOR YOU

There are four generally accepted methods for attorneys to determine their business development budgets. In strict marketing terms, budgets can be set by one of four methods (which can be called “control” factors):

PERCENTAGE-OF-FEES METHOD

Attorneys can set aside the appropriate funds for the business development by using the percentages described. The process to determine this is very simple.

An attorney or firm has $1 million in fees (or projects $1 million in fees) in a year, can spend, say, $125,000 or $12\frac{1}{2}$ percent. This method is by far the most popular, as it uses a fixed percentage of the previous year’s fee (or at least an average of the past several years). The main advantage of this method is that the expenditures are directly related to funds available—the more fees collected, the more dollars available for promotion.

The disadvantage is that this method is illogical, because it assumes that business development budgets can be set on the basis of past income or, in other words, that the budgets are the result of income rather than the cause. There is little room for flexibility, plus an attorney or firm may underspend when the potential is great and overspend when the potential is low.

A variation of this method that often makes more sense is to determine budgets based on anticipated fee income, recognizing that business development precedes rather than follows income.

Recent studies have shown that 44 percent of advertisers of nonconsumer goods used the percentage fees (on sales) method. Of those, 28 percent based budgets on anticipated income and 16 percent on past income.

COMPETITIVE NECESSITY

Another method frequently used by attorneys is to set a budget based on the amount of real or perceived activity of the competition. Essentially, this boils down to matching or exceeding a level of activity that others seem to be doing.

This method is fraught with problems. At best it is risky, smacking of throwing dollars at a problem merely because "the other guys are doing it." This method also assumes that one attorney's objectives in business development are the same as the competitors', which is not a valid assumption. Plus, the amount of spending by the competition is very difficult to find out and can only be estimated. The dollars spent then are based on results seen from the competition and a general effort to achieve the same results. A further disadvantage is that an attorney can react only *after* the competition has developed a program and the results are seen.

Competitive analysis should rarely be the sole basis for determining business development budgets.

BUDGETS BY OBJECTIVE

The objective method is a process of setting a specific goal and then allocating money to obtain it. For attorneys, the objective is usually defined in terms of a percentage of new business from existing clients (or recent past clients) or in terms of a number of new contacts within a new client group. Then a determination of how much money will be necessary to achieve these goals is made. If the cost is greater than the money available, either the objectives must be scaled down or additional funds must be found.

Sometimes this method is called the "whatever-it-takes-to-get-there" method.

ALL YOU CAN AFFORD

Another method is to set aside profit or surplus over expenses. This amount can vary considerably in a short period of time. This approach is by definition the "affordable approach," which means that marketing costs will be appropriated after all other unavoidable investments and expenses have been allocated, including partner bonuses, and so on. This rule ensures that firms with limited resources are not wasting money.

On the other hand, experience has shown that firms embracing this approach consider marketing to be a discretionary budget item and therefore the first expense to be reduced when revenue goes down. The wisdom of this approach is usually suspect, because the lack of marketing may have caused the revenue to go down in the first place!

CHAPTER 36
What Things Cost: A Framework for a Basic Marketing Budget

SUMMARY

The amount of money and time spent on marketing by attorneys depends on the type of law practiced and the size of the organization to which the attorney belongs. The costs of marketing must be measured not only in out-of-pocket expenses, but also in lost revenue if the attorney spends time marketing that could otherwise be billable. "Lost revenue" can be a major factor in marketing budgets. Accurate timekeeping of these costs is important to measure effectiveness of a marketing program.

The chapter discusses

- time and money required by attorneys in various types of practices to launch and carry out an effective marketing program.
- variables in setting marketing budgets and how to account for them.
- setting up the framework for a basic marketing budget.
- accounting for actual cost of attorney and staff time spent on marketing.

An essential part of any attorney business development is a budget established exclusively for this purpose. Two questions continually arise in discussing budgets: What items are included in marketing? How much should I spend on them?

These questions are highly intertwined. One research study says attorneys—on an average—spend 1 percent of their gross fees for marketing. Another survey says that individuals and firms of fewer than 20 attorneys should devote 25 percent of gross fees to business development. Why the huge discrepancy?

The difference can lie in the type of practice. Attorneys in consumer or "retail" law require more marketing effort to remain competitive, since by definition their practices are oriented more toward transactions than to relationships. But a greater reason for the difference most likely lies in the accounting.

The first budget percentage is way too low, and includes only hard, out-of-pocket costs for things like brochure design and printing. At the same time, everything else that legitimately belongs in the attorney marketing budget is put somewhere else, probably into a catch-all budget item called "overhead." The second budget guideline is way too high and includes all attorney time (at billable rates) that is not billed to administration or to clients. It also includes things like interior office plant services and virtually every expense account item not rebilled to clients.

Assigning accurate costs and expenses to a business development budget is important to monitor the program and keep it on track. It enables the attorney to judge if they are doing too little or too much in the business development area.

In various reports of research frequently quoted in bar journals and other media regarding business development for attorneys, recommended budgets are usually presented in terms of a Percent of Gross Fees. They will range from as high as 25 percent for a firm of five attorneys to as low as four percent for a large firm of more than 200 attorneys.

But figures like these are meaningless unless specific details of the costs are stated. Costs are both internal (attorney and staff time) and external (out-of-pocket money paid to others for goods and services). Only by looking at both internal and external costs can a true picture of marketing budgets be obtained.

COST GUIDELINES

The cost of business development can be divided into two categories of *time* and *out-of-pocket*. Budgets by definition identify line item costs, both in terms of attorney time and out-of-pocket expenses. Each line item is therefore an action item of a marketing plan, with a cost assigned to it.

Figure 36-1 identifies average business development expenses for law firms. The figure differentiates between firms that base their business on transactions vs. those that base their business on relationships. The marketing costs for the transactional attorney are generally greater, due to the effort required to bring in a large amount of clients and separate legal matters. A

Practice Based on Steady Stream of Transactions.

Firm Size	Gross Fees for Practice Develop. (total)	Out-of-Pocket Expenses*	Attorney/Staff Expense**
2–10	19%	6%	15%
10–25	16%	4%	12%
25+	10%	2%	8%

Practice Based on Long-Term Relationships

Firm Size	Gross Fees for Practice Develop. (total)	Out-of-Pocket Expenses*	Attorney/Staff Expense**
0–20	11%	3%	8%
20–75	9%	3%	6%
75–150	7%	2%	5%
150+	4%	1%	3%

*Out-of-pocket expenses are those paid to others for goods and services.

**Represents attorney time calculated at billable rates and non-timekeeping staff time at cost.

Figure 36–1 Average Business Development Expenses for Law Firms. These costs are for an on-going and active program. Start-up of a new program generally takes 5 percent more in the first year.

significant amount of the additional cost comes in direct promotion such as advertising expenses.

PREDICTING COSTS

While the costs of various business development activities are important to know before beginning, they are tough to predict. There can be tremendous variation in time and expenses. The overriding guideline is to make sure—in the end—it is accurately accounted for.

Attorneys know very well that there are many variables that affect the cost of their services. Likewise, guidelines on the cost of training, brochures, newsletters, and seminars can vary widely, depending on many factors. If a client asks an attorney "How much will probate cost?"—a natural question—the answer is always couched in terms that define a scope of work, level of quality of end product, and amount of expected time to complete, providing certain criteria are present and unforeseen circumstances do not significantly change the situation during the course of work. In other words, the cost can be estimated beforehand but can change as the work progresses. Marketing costs are no different.

ACCOUNTING FOR MARKETING TIME

The hidden expense in marketing is the cost of attorney time or, more important, the loss of revenue that results from it. So when attorneys are budgeting time for marketing, they must clearly realize the value of this "hidden" cost. They must also establish strict definitions of what is chargeable to the marketing budget and what is not. This prevents attorneys charging hours and expenses to the budget for items that do not belong there.

To calculate marketing budgets, attorneys can account for time

- at its direct labor cost, which is the *actual cost per hour* to the firm of the individual. This will include payroll burden of taxes and benefits, as well as pro-rated overhead expense.
- at the billable rate, which will reflect the *loss of revenue* to the firm rather than the actual cost.

Either method is fine, as long as everyone understands which approach is being taken. Most attorneys prefer the loss of revenue method, although this results in an artificially high "cost" of marketing. On the other hand, it is a realistic number. One $100-hour spent on marketing and not spent on billable time is clearly a "cost" of marketing.

Several of the marketing plans and budgets in the appendix to this book assume that the attorney is capable of billing and collecting 2,000 hours annually and that the amount of hours devoted to marketing is subtracted from that total. In other words, an attorney devoting 15 percent of time to marketing will have an annual budget of 1,700 billable hours.

There are other ways that attorneys can budget for marketing hours. Some firms simply add the hours to the attorney's billable goal for the year. So in the example, the attorney must charge 2,300 hours annually, 2,000 to clients and 300 to marketing. A variation of this is to split the marketing time half and half, in which the attorney is assigned 300 marketing hours, but allowed to reduce the billable budget by 150 hours.

TRUE COST OF STAFF AND ATTORNEYS

Timekeepers (attorneys and staff) can use any of these methods. To calculate cost for nontimekeepers, it is most correct to use the base salary and divide it by 2,100, which represents the generally accepted number of hours a person is employed during the year. (When vacations, holidays, and sick days are taken into account, the actual number of working hours in a year for clerical and administrative staff is closer to 1,500). A $45,000-a-year administrative person costs $21.42 per hour. A $25,000-a-year secretary costs $11.90 per hour.

Also for consistency and accuracy, the sample marketing plans in this book account for expenses at the cost of the portion of expenses used in marketing (i.e., box seats to the professional sports team that are used half of the time by the firm's own attorneys are not charged 100 percent to marketing).

Attorneys can use the budgets in the appendix as guidelines for their own planning, but it is unlikely that any plan is entirely correct for any situation.

CHAPTER 37
Budget Items: What to Include in Marketing Costs

SUMMARY

Many attorneys believe that they are spending adequately on marketing because their marketing budgets are high. In actuality, many nonmarketing items are often included, resulting in artificially high and inaccurate numbers. Charges against marketing budgets must be limited to those items that are truly related to business development.

This chapter discusses

- why attorney marketing budgets are often "inflated" and misleading.
- those items to include and items to exclude from marketing budgets.

In the appendix to this book are typical marketing plans that clearly identify the costs associated with specific items of a business development program. These costs represent normal and expected expenditures for attorneys in various situations.

These budgets are of interest in what they include as well as what they do not. That's because so often attorneys include items in marketing budgets which do not belong there.

It is important to analyze current marketing costs to determine the level of future activities. In a well-known case history, one group of attorneys analyzed their budget and determined they were already spending 14 percent of gross fees in marketing. They therefore felt they were making adequate efforts. In reality, their budget was very misleading because it included everything from birthday parties for the staff to subscriptions for magazines in the waiting room. Attorneys may choose to put all these things in the "marketing" budget, but what is actually represented should be understood.

Here are recommendations of what should and what should not be included in business development budgets.

WHAT BUDGETS SHOULD INCLUDE

ATTORNEY, PROFESSIONAL, AND SUPPORT STAFF COSTS

Nonadministrative, nonbillable time for activities devoted to the broad range of business development activities as discussed in this book. This includes attorney time for speeeches or article writing to client or potential client and referral audiences, including other attorneys. Other costs are time devoted to the following:

- Development of internal consensus and preparation of marketing plans
- Client surveys and new market research
- Certain types of pro bono work
- Membership activities during business hours

OVERHEAD COSTS, ADMINISTRATION

- Business development salaries and expenses
- Business development overhead portion (rent)
- Travel and entertainment expenses on behalf of clients
- Storage costs of business development materials (brochures, etc.)
- Internal newsletters and other employee information costs
- Employee relations costs, such as parties, gifts, bonuses related to building morale, and increasing productivity
- Cost of attorney and administrative time devoted to employee training and communication

DEPARTMENT HARD COSTS

- Capital expenses used exclusively for business development (computer software, dedicated mail list management, etc.)
- Depreciation of equipment devoted solely to business development

PRACTICE DEVELOPMENT ACTIVITIES

- Cost of seminars, including related printed materials, meals, room, and equipment rentals
- Cost of attorney-sponsored socials, such as client lunches, open houses, holiday parties, and so on
- The portion of the cost of attorney retreats that is devoted to business development
- Contributions, donations of both money and time
- Scholarships to students of any kind (law school and other)
- Association, membership dues including chambers of commerce, economic development groups, trade groups, social clubs
- Tickets to spectator events, used for client goodwill
- Affinity marketing costs (see Chapter 76 for an explanation of affinity marketing)

PRACTICE DEVELOPMENT MATERIALS

- Direct mail to clients, including newsletters, fact sheets, updates, briefs, holiday greeting cards, announcements, invitations, notes and all noncase specific and nonbillable correspondence, and postage/handling related to same
- Gifts to clients
- Subscriptions to periodicals and magazines used for client/market research or for general business development purposes, that is, client-centered publications (trade magazines), general business publications (*The Wall Street Journal, Business Week,* etc.), and general media (local newspapers).
- Cost of design and printing of brochures and other materials developed to provide information to clients at no charge, such as firm information sheets, recruiting brochures, fact sheets, attorney biographies, practice group descriptions, and so on
- Cost of reprints of any article or speech for use for nonlaw audiences
- Outside services purchased to support the marketing effort
- Fees and expenses paid to outside consultants for services such as strategy development, sales training, public relations, advertising, and graphic design
- Media space and time costs for all product and service advertising including “tombstone” advertising, Yellow Page listings, and advertising. “Image” advertising in programs, directories, and yearbooks
- Client research, market research

- Cost of design of letterhead, business cards (but not including cost of printing)
- Media clipping services

Frequently, many items get placed into marketing budgets that do not belong there. An attorney or firm may elect to call these items marketing expenses, but it should be clearly understood by all that they can artificially inflate the budget.

BUDGETS SHOULD NOT INCLUDE

- Subscriptions to practice-centered media such as bar journals, *National Law Journal, American Lawyer, Law Practice Management*
- Noncapital expenses, office supplies
- Capital expenses of computers, printers, software used by business development staff but also by others for general purposes
- Cost of printing letterhead, business cards, and so on
- Office artwork and signage (interior and exterior)

Chapter 38
The Marketing Timetable: Why It Takes So Long to Get Anything Done

SUMMARY

The time required to perform marketing activities is usually greater than expected. Further, the completion of the marketing activity does not mean that marketing is successful, because results from the activity will take even longer to return. With few exceptions, most marketing activities take weeks to complete and may take months to produce results.

This chapter discusses

- factors affecting the length of time to accomplish marketing tasks.
- the time to complete the most common marketing activities undertaken by attorneys.
- the results and "payback period" that can be expected from many of the same marketing activities.

Timetables are probably the most easily understood yet most likely error-filled elements of marketing plans. That's because most attorneys, unaccustomed to marketing, will severely underestimate the time required to get things done.

Attorneys realize that quick resolution to many complex legal problems is not possible. They understand that things take time to complete. Nevertheless, it is amazing how frequently attorneys will embrace a marketing plan, create strong goals, develop reasonable tactics, and estimate accurate costs. Yet they will create totally unreasonable expectations as to when it will all be accomplished.

FACTORS AFFECTING TIMETABLES

The skills and attitudes of the participants determine the speed at which plans get carried out. This applies, of course, to most human endeavors but is especially true in business development activities for attorneys. If the attorney marketing skills are limited and the interest is low, very few if any successful activities will be completed. On the other hand, a marketing program led by a skilled attorney, capable administrator, or experienced consultant and supported by enthusiastic colleagues and staff can provide marvelous results for all concerned.

The attorney's desire to control costs and reduce expenses is a common limitation to marketing. But these factors are frequently a disguise for lack of interest. They are also indicative of an attorney or firm who doesn't understand business development as not a *cost* item but rather an *investment* in the future.

The most common limitation is availability of attorney time. This, of course, is the attorney's inventory—the product with value. It is rationed carefully, and hours devoted to marketing may be taken away from billable time or from personal lives. Attorneys do not willingly let go of billable hours for the sake of marketing or any other reason if they feel they will not be compensated for nonbillable activity. In many cases, the time devoted to marketing is clearly lost revenue to the firm. An attorney billing $100 an hour, devoting only two hours a week to marketing, "costs" a firm roughly $10,000 annually. No wonder this is a limiting factor not only for the firm, but for the individual attorney who may receive less favorable reviews for recording fewer billable hours.

TIMETABLE GUIDELINES

The following list provides a general guideline on the time required to accomplish specific activities. These timetables are established for a 15-member firm practicing in two or three major areas of the law (similar to the firm described in Appendix 5).

The "time to complete" for these activities is based on an assumption that the activity occurs within the framework of a well-planned marketing program. This means that each activity is launched from a foundation of internal consensus, direction, and communication. For example, a brochure can be written and produced within two months if consensus is already achieved. If not, the process can take much longer. Therefore, the times listed are realistic only within a generally supported and reasonably well-functioning marketing program.

Specific Activity	Time to Complete	
Developing a plan	12–17	weeks total
Internal analysis	3–4	weeks
Internal consensus	4–6	weeks
Writing the plan	2	weeks
Revisions and agreements	3–5	weeks
Establishing a new graphic identity	8–14	weeks total
Selection of designer	1–2	weeks
Designer research	1	week
Initial concepts	1	week
Concept reviews	1–2	weeks
Artwork and approvals	1–2	weeks
Applications and approvals	2–3	weeks
Artwork production	1–3	weeks
In-house newsletters	8–11	weeks total (after first issue completed)
Concept development (first issue only)	2–4	weeks
Layout and format (first issue only)	1–2	weeks
Content development, story ideas	1–2	weeks
Story drafts	1–2	weeks
Initial layout	1	week
Final design and final text drafts	1–2	weeks
Photography, illustrations	1	week
Mechanical artwork preparation	1	week
Final approvals	1	week
Printing	1	week
Client newsletters	9–15	weeks total (after first issue completed)
Concept development (first issue only)	3–6	weeks
Layout and format (first issue only)	2–3	weeks
Content development, story ideas	1–2	weeks
Story drafts	2–4	weeks

Specific Activity	Time to Complete
Initial layout	1 week
Final design and final text drafts	1–3 weeks
Photography, illustrations	1–2 weeks
Mechanical artwork preparation	1 week
Final approvals	1 week
Printing	1 week
Advertising program	8–35 weeks total
(Time required for each advertising type, i.e., recruiting, "image," Yellow Pages)	
Concept development	1–2 weeks
Copy writing	1–2 weeks
Photography, illustrations	1–2 weeks
Layout revisions and approvals	1–2 weeks
Mechanical artwork preparation	1 week
Final approvals	1 week
Media insertions	1 week
Media appearance	
Daily publications	1 week
Weekly publications	3–5 weeks
Monthly publications	10–24 weeks
Brochures	13–25 weeks total
Concept development	1–2 weeks
Rough designs and text draft 1	2–4 weeks
Schematic designs and text draft 2	2–4 weeks
Final design and final text draft	3–5 weeks
Photography, illustrations	1–3 weeks
Mechanical artwork preparation	1–2 weeks
Final approvals	1–2 weeks
Printing	2–3 weeks
News releases	4–21 weeks total
Topic selection	1 week
Drafts and revisions	1 week
Final approvals and distribution	1 week
Media appearance	
Daily publications	1–3 + weeks
Weekly publications	2–5 + weeks
Monthly publications	6–18+ weeks
Publicity placements	6–32+ weeks total
Topic selection	1 week
Editor contacts	1–4 weeks
Drafts and revisions or interviews	2–8 weeks
Final approvals	1 week
Media appearance	
Daily publications	1–3 + weeks
Weekly publications	2–5 + weeks
Monthly publications	6–18+ weeks

Specific Activity	Time to Complete
Reprints	3 weeks total
Selection of original materials	1 week
Layout and pasteup of material	1 week
Printing	1 week
Media relations programs	5–9 + weeks total
Topic selection	1 week
Editor contacts	3–4 weeks
Media appearance	
Daily publications	1+ weeks
Weekly publications	2+ weeks
Monthly publications	4+ weeks
Speeches	12–14+ weeks total
Topic selection	1 week
Identification of appropriate forums	1–2 weeks
First draft of "all-purpose" speech	2–3 weeks
Drafts, revisions	2 weeks
Speaking opportunities	6+ weeks
Seminars and forums	20–36 weeks total
Topic selection	1–2 weeks
Concept and planning meetings	2–5 weeks
Operations plan	2–3 weeks
Content development	6–8 weeks
Preparation of invitation list	1–2 weeks
Design of invitations	2–4 weeks
Preparation of training materials	4–8 weeks
Logistical arrangements	1–2 weeks
Event and follow-up	1–2 weeks
Effective volunteering program	13–22+ weeks total
Concept, agreement on focus and intent	2–3 weeks
Development of selection criteria	1–2 weeks
Selection of groups to assist	3–5 weeks
Approval of written plan (annually)	1–2 weeks
Implementation for individuals	6–10+ weeks
Effective contribution program	8–13+ weeks total
Concept, agreement on focus and intent	2–3 weeks
Development of selection criteria	1–2 weeks
Selection of groups to assist	3–5 weeks
Approval of written plan (annually)	1–2 weeks
Implementation	1+ weeks
Affinity marketing program	28–42 weeks total
Concept, agreement on focus and intent	2–3 weeks
Selection of group or event	2–5 weeks
Writing of operations plan	3–5 weeks

Specific Activity	Time to Complete
Content development	6–8 weeks
Preparation of promotional materials	6–8 weeks
Logistical arrangements	7–10 weeks
Event and follow-up	2–3 weeks
Attorney-sponsored social events	8–15 weeks total
Event selection	1 week
Planning meetings	1–2 weeks
Operations plan	1–2 weeks
Preparation of invitation list	1–2 weeks
Design of invitations	2–4 weeks
Logistical arrangements	1–2 weeks
Event and follow-up	1–2 weeks

WHEN TO EXPECT RESULTS

Some of these marketing activities provide immediate, tangible results, such as a television advertisement that generates 15 responses from potential clients within one week. Other activities result in meaningful benefits only after months, such as a consistent media relations campaign to establish oneself as an "informed source."

It is helpful for attorneys to understand that very few marketing activities have immediate results. Further, a single marketing activity is rarely responsible for marketing success. Typically, many activities over time provide a total package of service and product delivery that results for the totally satisfied client.

Here is a list of specific activities, expected results, and a projection of when an ultimate payback can be expected.

Activity	Expected Results and Payback Period
Developing a plan	Results in internal understanding of overall marketing effort, focused efforts, coordination of activities, budget control, and realistic timetable. Payback in immediate internal agreement in both short-term and long-term coordination of marketing activities, saving time and money.
New graphic identity	Results in consistent image and name recognition and reinforcement. Creates impression that firm is contemporary, "on top of things." Payback in instant internal attitude improvement, midterm client perception change.
In-house newsletters	Results in understanding of importance of marketing in firm growth and stability. Payback in immediate improvement of internal communcation. Long-term service/quality improvement.

Activity	Expected Results and Payback Period
Personnel development	Results in gradual improvement in service skills. Payback in long-term service/quality improvement.
Client newsletters	Results in name recognition and perception as knowledgeable on topics. Of value when done consistently for a year or more. Payback in long-term credibility and possible cross-selling of new services to existing clients.
Advertising program	Results in visibility and informing public of services, events. Payback depends on dollars spent. Generally, midterm response for consumer-oriented advertisements, long-term payback for image advertising.
Brochures	Results in awareness of services and personnel. Builds image of credibility and stability. Payback is long term.
News releases	Results in awareness. Long-term payback if releases achieve consistent news media coverage.
Publicity placements, media relations	Results in building credibility and creates awareness. Long-term payback if placements are consistent. Payback time can be shortened with use of reprints of articles.
Speeches, seminars, forums	Results in building credibility. Can result in immediate inquiries for more information. Generally payback is long term as these activities supplement other programs to solidify existing clients relations.
Effective volunteering and contributions programs	Results in building of awareness and trust. Payback in long-term relationship development and improvement. Programs must be long term and consistent before any results are achieved.
Affinity marketing	Results in demonstration of creative community involvement. Builds and solidifies relationships. Creates name awareness. Long-term payback.
Attorney-sponsored socials	Results in development of relationships. Long-term payback. If events are "worked" for cross-selling, discussion of specific attorney skills, payback can be immediate.

PART 4

Implementation

Attorneys reading this book cover to cover have finally arrived at the part where all the theories, the assessment, and the planning come together. This fourth part of the book, dealing with implementation of specific marketing tactics, describes how the attorney and firm can carry out both internal and external activities needed for a complete and successful business development program.

This part lays out numerous specific actions, all of which are good ideas. All of them have been and are being used by attorneys. But not every one of these actions is right for every attorney. No attorney or firm will ever do all these things, nor should they. The only way an attorney can know which action is appropriate is to understand the conceptual and intellectual basis of business development programs described in earlier sections. Then sound decisions can be made regarding which steps to take in inaugurating or improving a marketing program.

CHAPTER 39
Applied Internal Marketing: Getting your Staff Involved

SUMMARY

Bringing marketing from the planning stage to actual implementation takes a united effort. To be most effective, the attorney's staff must fully understand the purpose of the program, must be informed of intended activities, and must continually see that the attorney thinks it important. An important element is to reward staff for their marketing activities.

This chapter discusses

- the importance of interactive, two-way communication between attorney and staff.
- methods of communicating to staff about marketing activities and their role in them.
- how to involve staff in marketing effectively.

> A medium-sized firm was in the highly competitive segment of law firms catering to business and professional clients. The firm had low staff turnover and high morale. Several staff members played a productive role in the firm's external marketing program.
>
> But this was not always the case. Six months prior, it experienced considerable staff and associate turnover. Temporary cash flow problems sometimes resulted from losing gambles on marginal contingency cases. Another problem was incorrect and late billings and time write-downs. As a result, staff morale was low.
>
> The firm administrator decided to tackle the problem head on. He began by instituting regular staff meetings at which he communicated management's concerns about the firm's service quality, scheduling, internal communications, work flow, and administrative details. He distributed agendas prior to the meetings. He provided summary memorandums afterward so that solutions to the problems and agreements reached would be confirmed and implemented. The meetings allowed, in fact encouraged, frank discussions of daily challenges.
>
> At first staff members were slow to comment during the meetings. But as trust was established, they began to talk more openly. The administrator was careful to let staff talk freely, inserting very few of his own comments.
>
> He also instituted a regular internal newsletter to keep attorneys, associates, and staff informed regarding successes and honors, personnel changes, and outside activities.
>
> To clients and observers, the changes in attitudes toward service quality and client relations were nearly phenomenal. The energy placed by the administrator into an internal marketing effort spilled into external marketing, so that the clients ended up much happier as well.
>
> As business improved, attorneys and staff discussed the firm's facilities in terms of production capabilities and appearances. Many of the staff and associates complained that the entrance and reception area were dark and drab and

did not project an image of which they could be proud. The partners agreed. The administrator kept careful notes and then outlined, for the entire firm, the appearance problems noted. Through a vote, attorneys and staff reached several conclusions.

With some rearranging and remodeling, the firm's new image was completed in time for an open house celebrating a milestone anniversary of the firm's founding. Even more importantly, encouraged by the success of the firm's new image, the staff began to exhibit more pride. This pride translated into increased expectations of themselves regarding their quality of work and client relations.

The internal marketing effort did not stop with the turnaround of the firm. The administrator continued to hold regular firm meetings, distribute newsletters, and planned several in-house development seminars. Additionally, he utilized the abilities of several employees in drawing up new internal and external marketing concepts and formulating an overall firm marketing plan.

PURPOSE, COMMUNICATION, AND ATTENTION

The principal distinction between internal and external marketing communications is more emphasis on interactive, two-way communications with the internal program. This happens by virtue of the frequency in which the attorney meets and works with the staff–the intended audience of the marketing effort. Internal marketing programs will succeed only if, in these frequent communications, attorneys pay heed to three basic areas: purpose, communication, and attention.

Purpose is important because these must be a real desire by the attorney conducting the internal marketing to achieve the maximum benefits possible. In the case study example, the administrator's purpose was to reverse a downward trend in service quality, morale, and income at his firm. That purpose guided him initially into holding regular staff meetings and regularly distributing newsletters.

Communication seems obvious, but it is often overlooked by the attorney who is just starting to think in terms of internal marketing. There must be a sharing of information between firm employees and the attorney regarding the internal marketing objectives. This sharing maintains consistency in all internal and external marketing efforts. For the case study of the firm described, the meetings and newsletters provided part of this communication. The administrator's open-door policy regarding feedback provided the rest.

The fact that an attorney or firm administrator is making an effort to reach his or her office target market does not have to be kept a secret. Staff generally appreciate knowing that their presence, opinions, and work output make a difference in the firm's success. Internal marketing actions will be interpreted by staff as a sign of interest in them on the part of the attorney. Open-door feedback policies are always a good idea.

Attention refers to the concentrated effort which must be placed on managing the internal marketing program. The attorney may choose to delegate some tasks, but must remain intimately involved in the management of the process to ensure that specific objectives are met and adherence to the vision remains constant.

ELEMENTS OF A SUCCESSFUL INTERNAL PROGRAM

Information must be collected, organized, and presented to all firm personnel, including staff and attorneys, from the onset of an internal marketing program. A firm meeting should include information regarding client analysis, firm capabilities, and competitive analysis. By hearing and seeing this information, staff and attorneys can judge for themselves the rationale behind all marketing efforts as well as the significance of their own roles within the process.

On a regular basis, specific recognition and acknowledgment of quantifiable achievements are extremely important so that all members of the firm (or in a small practice, all office staff) know how they are doing and will clearly understand what firm expectations are. An example of this might be telling the staff a particular client's reaction to the service received and rewarding the staff if that client feedback was positive.

One of the simplest and commonly overlooked methods to inform staff that an attorney values their input is to involve employees in client projects. This recommendation goes beyond paperwork—it means asking staff their opinions regarding how client business and relations should be handled. This also reinforces the concept of serving the client, not selling services. A sense of teamwork is a very important element of internal marketing.

Finally, a sense of pride can do wonders for an attorney's staff. If each person feels a sense of ownership and responsibility, if they each want whatever crosses their desk to be something of which they can be proud, the attorney will benefit. Staff responds with increased efficiency and effectiveness with regard to clients, quicker reaction time to client requests, and less duplication of effort throughout the office.

CHAPTER 40
The Attorney's Image: How It Affects Client Behavior

SUMMARY

The sum of all client perceptions constitutes an attorney's image. The image, whether accurate or not, affects virtually every activity in which the attorney and the firm engages. Successful marketing results when attorneys understand what factors affect image and respond accordingly—correcting the bad ones and improving the good ones.

This chapter discusses

- how an image is created.
- importance of an attorney's image and reality being the same.
- how images can be shaped and molded.
- the importance of having a unified image in all attorney activities, both personal and nonpersonal.

Because of the importance and prevalence of attorneys in American society, everyone has an opinion regarding them. The American Bar Association says that at any given time, 67 percent of Americans have hired an attorney for some reason, and that before they die, 92 percent of all Americans will have had some direct dealing with one. Most people, through personal experience, have already formed an opinion about attorneys and the profession.

Whether the image is good or bad is not the key issue. It is the realization that clients and the public have preconceived notions of the legal profession and the attorneys who practice in it. Legal services marketing must deal with these issues.

IMAGE VERSUS REALITY

An example of the importance of image with regard to marketing was illustrated by a very large American corporation. In the early days of the desktop computer marketing explosion, Exxon Corporation, looking at the success of many companies in the business machines area, launched an office products division. How did consumers respond? Not well. The typical response was, "What does an oil company know about computers?" Exxon was a reasonably competent corporation and had, even then, the technology to manufacture and market computers and related equipment. But its image as one type of company did not parlay well into a successful image in an entirely new area. Exxon failed because it did not lay the groundwork for establishing a reputation, or image, in computers.

A possible conflict that must be resolved is the difference between the external image of an attorney's practice and the internal reality. Every attorney has an image the moment he or she goes into practice; the key questions then are "Does this image reflect reality?" and "Is this image consistent with the attorney's desired image?"

The image (what clients and the public think) conveys information regarding the attorney's personality, services provided, quality of service, and client status. The attorney's marketing program must be consistent with a desired image and be developed in response to it.

UNIFIED IMAGE

People act on what they think is real or true (perceptions) without always checking all the facts. This brings many business owners and professionals, including lawyers, to realize the significance of a unified and consistent image. If perception is everything as far as the client is concerned, the attorney had better make sure that perception is on target.

A unified, consistent image serves two major purposes: It indicates a level of thought, organization, and commitment on the part of the attorney or firm behind it. It also makes the attorney or firm more memorable. If an attorney uses a letterhead which projects a different image from that of his or her business card, which is entirely distinct from the image projected by the attorney's office, and so forth, that attorney is making a statement. The statement is that his/her practice does not deserve the attention it would take to establish consistency. There is no consistent visual quality which immediately identifies the printed message with the attorney.

If the image is consistent and well thought out, it will in all likelihood be memorable. That's the desired result sought in all product advertising—that the message is remembered by the intended audience and presumably acted upon (i.e., the product is purchased). This same concept works for service providers as well. Isn't the page layout of *The Wall Street Journal* immediately recognizable on the newsstand or in the mailbox? The reason is its visual consistency. It doesn't change although the daily news is different every day. The same concept—consistency breeds recognition and recall—holds true for attorneys. An attorney or firm that wants to be remembered must have only one visual image projected through its stationery, business cards, physical facilities, and even personnel.

IMAGE OF THE LEGAL PROFESSION

The image of all attorneys plays an important role in the image of one attorney. If the public thinks of attorneys as litigation-oriented individuals taking a large portion of huge court settlements, this thinking, naive and narrow as it may be, affects clients' response to all attorneys.

Clients may see an individual attorney as being typical of the industry or profession. It is up to that individual attorney to assess how the client views the profession and make a decision whether that global perception is apropos to his or her individual practice image.

An attorney may view his or her practice as sensitive to clients' needs. Yet client analysis may demonstrate that the attorney's clients tend to think of all lawyers as aloof and insensitive. This perception will impact the way clients behave and therefore the way the attorney behaves. The attorney, in order to achieve success, must demonstrate to clients that their perception is without basis. The process of changing client perceptions can take time, but must receive a concentrated effort on the part of the attorney.

FACTORS INFLUENCING IMAGE

Factors influencing image may be identified in two distinct areas: personal and nonpersonal.

Personal factors affecting an attorney's image are those occurring in face-to-face situations. A checklist can be developed to evaluate how each factor impacts the desired image:

- Attorney language, attitude, mannerism
- Attorney wardrobe and general personal appearance
- Staff wardrobe, demeanor, and effectiveness
- Receptionist greetings and telephone techniques
- Office atmosphere: landscaping (indoor and out), office decor (art versus pictures), magazines, office layout, lighting, neighborhood, and parking
- Community relations activities
- Association memberships
- Awards (for whom? for what?)
- Types of clients, nature of their business and attorney work for them

Nonpersonal factors are those not directly involving the attorney or staff, but are secondhand factors such as printed materials. These are items where personal contact may be involved but usually where the item stands alone. These can also be called promotional tools. A checklist of nonpersonal factors can also be developed to evaluate impact on an attorney's image:

- Comments from referral agents
- Brochures and related supporting materials
- Direct-mail pieces, which are any sort of printed material sent out of the office, including regular correspondence
- Advertising
- Publicity and any published item

CHAPTER 41
The Reception Area as a Marketing Statement

SUMMARY

Consciously working to keep the reception area suitable for the clientele is important in terms of setting the tone for a relationship. Inconvenient arrangements will affect the perception of difficulty of doing business. Amenities clearly inappropriate will tell the client you don't care about them.

This chapter discusses

- the impact of first impressions.
- the major impact of minor factors.
- the details affecting client impressions.
- comfort and appearances for clients.

How convenient is the attorney's office for clients? What short of creature comforts does it offer? What sort of image does the office project? These questions and others like them are the essence of positioning strategy. They are marketing issues over which an attorney has a great deal of control.

A wealth of literature is available regarding firm or practice facility considerations. This information is often subdivided into such areas as choice of location, shared or joint tenant space, office layouts, computers and other office systems, library maintenance, and even lease negotiations. Yet very little has been written about the marketing-related issues of facilities.

Importantly, a client's perceptions can be dramatically impacted based on the ambience created by the attorney's office. Facilities make a profound marketing statement.

Designing and implementing a facility plan can be very affordable, if done correctly. If attorneys have a clear vision of the impact statement they want to make, a number of common (not to mention expensive) mistakes can be avoided. The attorney's office, including the reception area, conference room, and even exterior entrance, will always represent that attorney to clients. Physical facilities, therefore, deserve the same amount of attention that any other aspect of a planned marketing program would receive.

THE RECEPTION AREA SETS THE TONE

A potential client had learned of a unique approach to a land use legal problem practiced by an attorney he did not know. If the approach worked, it would substantially increase the value of the client's property. The potential client felt it critical to get a feel for the attorney's approach. Besides, he had some other legal situations he wanted to explore. He set an appointment to meet with the attorney.

The firm's office building was easy to reach in one of the buildings of a small office park. But no visitor parking was available near the door, so he was forced to park several rows of cars away, in the rain, of course.

Once inside the firm's office, he peered over a large counter down onto a receptionist who was busily answering telephone lines and responding to questions that occasionally came through on a loud speakerphone. The visitor waited more than a minute to introduce himself, meanwhile watching the receptionist answer calls and fold letters and statements into envelopes for mailing.

When the receptionist did greet him, she was very pleasant and offered a cup of coffee. He declined the coffee, seeing how busy she was and how it might disturb her routine. He took a seat on a low couch in the reception area facing the doorway and the receptionist.

The visitor was on time for the conference yet there was a wait of about ten minutes. The potential client glanced through his papers, made a couple of notes, then picked up one of the magazines on the cluttered coffee table, noting the outdated issues and dog-eared pages of periodicals which would be of little interest to someone in real estate development or any other business for that matter.

The meeting, once underway, was definitely pleasant and encouraging, yet the first impression lingered. At the conclusion the potential client agreed to consider the attorney's approach to the problem and attendant cost estimates and get back to the attorney.

> Following the meeting, he stopped in the reception area to thank the receptionist and to make some notes about the conference. While there he noted that firm employees left to get into cars parked close to the front door.
>
> The attorney was not given the land use matter to pursue nor did the potential client discuss any other legal matters, although not solely on the basis of the first impression. But that visit did form an image. The experiences told the prospective client several things about the firm. First, that the firm valued staff more than clients or at least with regard to parking convenience. Also, that staff members were required to perform a number of tasks under pressure (answer telephones, provide refreshments to guests, stuff envelopes). Finally, that client comfort was not valued (the low, uncomfortable couch facing the busy receptionist and door, the outdated and inappropriate reading material, the unnecessary wait).

THE RECEPTION AREA PERSONALITY

Firm reception area statements are not made by the furniture and wallpaper alone. These statements are made by the way a visitor is treated there. Take, for instance, the reception areas of large firms: some are formal, some are casual, some have expensive art, some are very plain. But almost all successful larger firms have one trait in common: the visitor is the most important person in that room. Parking, reading material, refreshments, and the front office personnel all convey that image very clearly. It makes no difference if the visitor is a major client with an appointment to see a senior partner or a walk-in seeking legal help outside the firm's practice emphasis. Visitors are cordially yet efficiently greeted and taken care of.

An entire office personality is created through the treatment of visitors. Are vendors which visit the office to check or repair office equipment immediately walked to the appropriate equipment? Or are they seated with their equipment boxes next to waiting clients? Are vendors allowed to stand and visit casually with the receptionist? How would either of these forms of protocol affect client perceptions regarding the firm? More important, is the behavior in keeping with client expectations and values?

RECEPTION AREA DECOR

A common reception area quandary is whether decor should be elaborate and plush or plain and spartan. The deciding factor in this is whether the practice image includes financial success or financial moderation. The attorneys must know what the client perceptions and expectations are.

Some clients think of legal services as part of their own image and so want to be treated as VIPs. Other clients perceive legal services as expensive but necessary and would rather not see their attorney "waste" money on elaborate decor. Clientele ultimately dictates reception area and even entire office decor.

Research shows that most clients prefer successful professionals, whether in the area of law, accounting, or health care. It is admittedly a fine line between opulence and a normal display of success. It is up to the individual attorney or firm to decide where that line falls. A typical observation of law offices on the modest side is that clients in those offices may be less than successful. As a rule, successful clients, after all, are generally better clients and also better referral sources. Staff and associates also take more pride in their work if they work in an environment that is a reward of success.

Chapter 42
Individual Offices: A Reflection of the Attorney's Style

SUMMARY

An attorney's personal office, especially the desk, can have a positive or negative impact on a client. Orderliness is important and projects a favorable image. A desk cluttered with files, periodicals, and other papers can cause clients to believe that the attorney can never find anything, handles confidential matters poorly, and wastes time in responding to inquiries.

This chapter discusses

- the importance of an orderly attorney desk and office.
- increased time efficiencies through good management of files and paperwork.
- office order and its effect on staff efficiency and effectiveness.
- formal versus informal style of office management.

> Jan frequently encouraged clients to visit her office to conduct business or discuss issues. As a sole practitioner, she generally found it easier to work there, where she could access files and random information in her library. She also did not like to visit clients' offices because of the time she had to spend packing and unpacking her briefcase. She never was sure which file to bring, and ultimately, she ended up taking everything. Also, it was implicit that client visits to her office were billable time.

Clients visiting Jan couldn't help but notice all the files, periodicals, and other papers on her desk and office tables, and some wondered how she ever found anything. Most had noticed that if they called her unexpectedly with a specific question regarding a particular matter, she would almost always have to return their call. Sometimes that return call didn't take place for up to an hour. After seeing her office, they realized it probably took Jan that long to locate the appropriate files.

Another concern for many of Jan's clients was that some of the paperwork on her desk lay perilously close to the guest chairs. A guest in Jan's office might easily glance over the papers and learn the nature of the business. Clients wondered if their confidential matters were really being held confidential.

Most of Jan's clients chose to continue utilizing Jan and accepted her disorganization as a "necessary evil"; they felt she was a good attorney and genuinely liked her. But two of Jan's major clients ended up hiring another lawyer because of their discomfort with her state of disorganization.

Jan lamented to her secretary after losing the two clients that she did not know what the problem was. They had told her they wanted an attorney who was more "on top of things," with a quicker response time to questions. Jan's secretary told her candidly that she needed to present a better office image. The secretary knew this was a problem for Jan because the clients had made off-the-cuff comments to her on their way out of the office.

Marking three days off her schedule the next week, rearranging appointments, and completing work ahead of time, Jan set out to organize. She and her secretary purchased new file cabinets and file folders and began to file client business forms, periodicals, newspapers clippings, and all the other loose papers. Jan also organized her computer files, backing up outdated files onto floppy disk for storage and keeping only current, relevant files on her hard disk.

Visiting clients noticed the difference immediately and complimented Jan on the change. She invited her two former clients back to her office to display the improvement and to ask them to consider her for future work. Although the former clients made no promises for the future, they were clearly impressed with Jan's resolve to improve her office.

THE ATTORNEY'S OFFICE

Orderliness comes more easily for some attorneys than others, but for anyone, keeping an office organized is easier than trying to bring order out of chaos. Clients expect attorneys to work efficiently when the time clock is running, and they certainly expect confidentiality.

Response time to unexpected questions is a key issue for lawyers. Some clients do not understand the importance of research and expect their attorneys automatically to know many of the answers to their questions. For an attorney to say to a client, "I need to finish something, but I will call you back within ten minutes," is acceptable to a client. That gives the attorney the time to access necessary files, peruse the information, and make some general recommendations, either for further research or abandonment of the issue. For an attorney to be asked the same question and tell the client, "I will call you back as soon as possible," and telephone with a response hours later is unacceptable. Clients will understand if the attorney is in a meeting and must wait to return a call, but a meeting is never an excuse for poor organization.

Orderliness helps staff to work more efficiently and effectively. Imagine the litigator, calling his office during a court break to ask an important question and the secretary being unable to find the answer because she cannot, in the given time frame, locate the correct file! The attorney's secretary should always have easy access to all office information for the benefit of the attorney and the ultimate benefit of the client.

STYLE

The attorney's particular style in terms of his or her office should meet that attorney's desired image and client expectations.

The archetypical formal office gives a closed impression through the traditional furniture placement. The desk, which tends to be large, relative to the space available, is placed to serve as a barrier between the lawyer and the visitor. Further, visitor seating is usually limited with only two upright or wingback chairs, relatively close together and close to the desk. Usually there is no end table or other place for the visitor to put coffee or papers. Consequently, only a small space on the desk, at best, is available for the visitor. This office is a power statement; it is domineering for the attorney and belittling for the client.

Another option, the reverse of the formal office style, is an informal style. This is possible even in the smallest of office spaces and often makes visitors feel more equal to the attorney than the formal style. The most notable feature is that there is nothing of substance between the visitor and the lawyer, most especially the desk. The desk might be against a wall, or in a large office, off to the side of the room. Attorney and visitor meet in facing chairs, possibly at a shared table or with an occasional table between them. There is ample space for files, coffee mugs, and other relevant paperwork for both.

The informal style works well if the attorney is comfortable in a casual setting with clients and visitors. It requires a higher level of self-esteem than the formal arrangement, since the attorney really is on an equal level with his or her visitor. There are times, though, when the formal style is more appropriate for the office. Some clients might expect a formal arrangement and be uncomfortable in anything but that. It would be up to the attorney in that case to make the client comfortable in the less casual setting or opt for more formality.

CHAPTER 43
Employee Communications: How to Make Them Most Effective

SUMMARY

An attorney's employees are deeply interested in their organization's plans for the future. Internal communication among all concerned is essential to create a unified group who understands the organization's objectives (both marketing and otherwise). The benefits are high morale and loyalty toward those objectives. Internal informational meetings, training programs, and newsletters play a critical role in this.

This chapter discusses

- what attorneys and employees want to know about their oganization.
- recommended standards for employee communication.
- several specific techniques that attorneys have used effectively to improve employee communication and, as a result, to improve their overall business development efforts.

Effective employee communication is two way—*downward* from top management to other professionals and support employees, and *upward* from employees and staff to the senior partners.

Current research shows that employees in all types of organizations report that they now get most of their useful information about their organizations from the "grapevine," but say they prefer getting it from their supervisors, meetings with management, and publications. Research conducted by firms involved in human resources and employee communications consistently points out the same needs in this area. Employees of every kind of organization—from a major manufacturer to a smaller retailer—respond similarly to survey questions.

Several other items of note from recent research on attorney/staff communications:

- Most employees (attorneys and staff alike) feel that they neither receive nor have the opportunity to send a great deal of information.

- Their primary need is for information related to their jobs.
- Employees generally enjoy good communication relationships with their immediate supervisors and co-workers.

Effective employees communication is involved in all four phases of employment:

1. *The start,* in which recruitment, advertising, interviews, orientation pamphlets, and meetings are used to attract, select, and indoctrinate new employees
2. *The work,* during which many face-to-face and printed communications provide instruction, news, and job-related information
3. *The rewards and recognition,* involving announcements, publicity, and special events concerning compensation, promotions, benefit programs, special events, and awards
4. *The termination or work interruption,* whether caused by mergers, lay-offs, elimination of positions, or dismissals of individuals

Employees are remarkably consistent in identifying the kinds of information they want to know. Figure 43-1 shows the result of a survey of

Subject	Percent "Very Interested"
Organizational plans for the future	95%
Productivity improvement	90
Personnel policies and practices	90
Job-related information	89
Job advancement opportunities	88
Effect of external events on my job	88
How my job fits into the organization	85
Operations outside of my department or division	85
How we are doing vs. the competition	83
Personnel changes and promotions	81
Organizational community involvement	81
Organizational stand on current issues	80
How the organization uses its profits	78
Advertising/promotional plans	77
Financial results	76
Human interest stories about other employees	70
Personal news (birthdays, anniversaries, etc.)	57

Figure 43-1 Information Employees Want from Employee Communications. From Cutlip, Center, Broom, *Effective Public Relations,* 6th ed., Prentice Hall, Englewood Cliffs, New Jersey.

1. Establish a formal, organized program of regular communications with all employees involving key information about the business and its effect on employees.
2. Establish regular, frequent, printed communication for all employees.
3. Encourage regular meetings between management and employees. At least twice a year, management should provide all employees with a review of the state of the business (from both corporate and local viewpoints), as well as discussion of management problems, goals, and outlook, plus what is expected from employees. Employee questions should be encouraged, with answers ideally being given at the meetings or through other communication channels as soon as practical.
4. Make effective use of the supervisory structure to provide for two-way communication. All supervisors should understand the importance of communicating key information to subordinate supervisors and to employees in their work groups. Top management should make sure that supervisors have a regular flow of information to discuss with their employees—weekly newsletters and regular meetings with all supervisors to exchange information are recommended. Also, supervisors have a responsibility to receive and transmit upward through organizational channels pertinent employee opinions, problem areas, and ideas for improvement.
5. Conduct periodic surveys to evaluate the effectiveness of employee communications and to provide direction for continuing improvements.

Figure 43-2 Recommended Standards for Employee Communication. From Cutlip, Center, Broom, *Effective Public Relations,* 6th ed., Prentice Hall, Englewood Cliffs, New Jersey.

employees in all kinds of business and professions. The responses apply as much to an attorney's office as they do to General Motors.

For attorneys to develop their own guidelines for total employees communications, a sample program is presented in Figure 43-2.

EFFECTIVE METHODS OF INTERNAL COMMUNICATION

Ongoing communication with everyone in the firm is essential to an effective marketing program. So "employee communication" refers to all people who work at the firm, from senior partner to mailroom clerk.

A tried-and-true, and effective, method of employee communications is meetings designed to include all employees. Some are designed only for attorneys, some for other professional staff, and some for support staff. Except for specific and confidential case matters, attorneys are encouraged to inform associates, other professionals, paralegals, and administrative and clerical staff—in short, everyone in the firm—about issues affecting the firm and the people who work there. Secretaries and very junior people will find the information of interest and long-range value to them.

FIRMWIDE MEETINGS

Firmwide meetings should be held on a quarterly basis. Meetings provide a simple way to communicate consistently throughout the firm information on policy decisions, significant news, developments, and new business successes. In addition, the quarterly meetings would demonstrate to everyone in the firm the importance of all levels of employment—from the senior partner to the newest law clerk. Increased cooperation will be the result.

The meeting should be conducted by the most senior active partner in the firm, demonstrating that the information is "straight from the top" and is important to senior management. The atmosphere for the meetings should be casual, although the attorneys will want to have notes and, in some cases, prepared remarks. Questions and answers should be encouraged.

It is important to schedule the meetings at a time and place where all attorneys and others can attend. Larger firms may need to schedule more than one meeting—7 A.M., 11:30 A.M., and 4:30 P.M. seem to be good times to catch busy attorneys but accommodate the clerical staff too. Two-way communication should be encouraged at the meetings.

DEPARTMENTWIDE MEETINGS

For larger firms, additional meetings on the department or section level are important. These are more frequent than the firmwide meetings, probably once a month. But like the firm meetings, the department gatherings are forums to encourage two-way communication and to inform everyone of the department's approach to new business, with specific activities described if appropriate. Recent successes in developing business contacts can be shared, and all staff can be encouraged to exchange ideas on prospective business. Colleagues can be updated on new business prospects, and departmental goals can be set. Information can be shared.

Several departments prefer to have their meetings during breakfast or lunch—sort of a brown-bag environment. To keep the meetings short and to the point, clear agendas should be established. Some firms have brought in "guest speakers" to these meetings for short (10–15 minutes) information presentations on current issues.

ALL-DEPARTMENT MEETINGS

To improve communication between departments, monthly meetings should be held with partner and associate representation from each section. Not every person in each department attends these meetings (then it would be a firmwide meeting!), but partners should attend every time, and associates' attendance might be rotated to keep them informed as appropriate. Again, a strict agenda but allowing for interchange and feedback is important.

FORMAL NEW EMPLOYEE ORIENTATION PROGRAM

Each attorney and organization around them has its own culture. New attorney and employee orientation is always required to ensure they embrace the overall goals and objectives of the organization.

The approach to "new employee training" will vary tremendously depending on the size and practice area of the firm. In larger firms, most employees are immediately trained in their specific job by a supervisor or another attorney. It usually works well that when a small number of new employees have been hired (usually fewer than five), these employees set aside a half-day for an orientation to the firm as a whole—meetings with the senior partners, discussions of the firm's history, goals and objectives, attitudes toward business development, client services, new practice areas, and so on.

Candid projections into the future are of tremendous interest to employees because, since it affects them directly, all employees find this kind of information to be of great interest. Turnover of nonprofessional staff can be a real problem in law firms. Usually, employees who quit will do so for reasons other than money or working conditions. It generally will relate to issues such as respect, attitude of fellow employees, and feeling of contribution to the organization. Employee communication programs can help to overcome these problems by creating a "we" feeling, especially among the clerical employees. Turnover can be reduced by efforts to ensure employee involvement in the firm, often by simple measures such as informing them of upcoming events and providing them with an opportunity to ask questions,

Any attorney office of two people or more needs a policy manual covering topics ranging from client confidences to dress codes. This manual should be distributed and gone over in detail. Other information of value is a style manual so that secretaries or anyone preparing their own written materials will confirm to the styles preferred by the whole firm, as well as to ensure quality and consistency in all the firm's written correspondence. Any sort of printed information about the firm—brochures, narratives on areas of emphasis, and key attorney biographies, should also be distributed.

ADMINISTRATIVE PERSONNEL MEETINGS

If most law firms did a survey of internal staff, they would probably be surprised at what they learned. Issues like communication, job appraisals, new staff recruitment, and work loads will often be raised by the administrative staff. The degree of interest apparent will determine the level of attention these issues require. At administrative personnel meetings, these issues and others should be discussed. Frequent topics involve such things as the efficiencies of new equipment, training programs, new policies, and other items. Any of these could be causing a loss of productivity at the clerical level that management may never know if they didn't ask.

The office manager or chief administrative officer should meet with the staff once a month to discuss issues of importance to them. These meetings are not as formal as department- or firmwide meetings, and the agenda is mostly set by the participants. If the staff is not accustomed to open communication and candor among all employees (staff and attorneys alike), then the first few meetings may need direction from the office manager to encourage discussion. But experience has shown that as soon as secretaries and others are encouraged to speak up, they will.

EMPLOYEE NEWSLETTERS

Frequent communication to employees is best in face-to-face situations, such as the meetings described. To supplement this effort, a regular communication vehicle has tremendous value for internal audiences. An internal newsletter is desirable for attorneys in firms of 15 total personnel or more. See the following chapter for a greater discussion of employee newsletters.

CHAPTER 44
Internal Newsletters: What To Say and How To Say It

SUMMARY

Newsletters to keep all members of an attorney organization informed can be very effective and essential to the marketing effort. In larger firms, up to four people need to be involved in producing successful newsletters. Design is not as important as content, but the newsletter must look professional and be "user friendly." It must be frequent to be effective. A smaller size to enable greater frequency is desirable.

This chapter discusses

- the correct way to set up internal staff and facilities to produce effective employee newsletters.
- the design and format of effective attorney newsletters.
- typical subject matter covered in internal newsletters.
- the easiest and most efficient means to gather materials for inclusion in the newsletters.
- recommendations on writing style, size, frequency, costs, and distribution.

Two-way communication with employees is always better than one way. Two-way communication through the meeting process enables attorneys to develop relationships and receive feedback from other attorneys and employees of the firm. Open, honest communication is truly valuable.

To supplement two-way communications through meetings (and in some cases to replace it, due to time constraints) attorneys have found an internal newsletter to be worthwhile. They can be useful by firms as small as ten, including all attorneys and staff.

Their value lies almost solely in the information they contain. Staff are very clear about what they want from employee communications (see preceding chapter), and the newsletters that provide this will be successful and worth the effort.

WHO SHOULD BE INVOLVED

It doesn't matter if the attorney's firm is small or large—the approach to management of the newsletter and development of its content is the same. Four groups of individuals are involved:

- The *editorial board,* which sets guidelines and makes policy decisions regarding content and general operating conditions (budget, etc). In most firms, this would be equivalent to the management committee.
- The *editor,* who decides content, has the authority to approve each issue before printing, and interprets the editorial board's policies and guidelines. For attorney firms, this person is most likely the managing partner.
- The *managing editor,* who is responsible for writing, editing, and producing the newsletter. This person prepares the content and assembles all information from other sources. This person may be a person designated as marketing coordinator or a good administrative assistant. It may even be an employee from another department with a journalism

background or strong interest in the subject. In many businesses this is handled by the "personnel" department.

- The *production editor,* who manages the printing and distribution of the newsletter. In many larger law firms, this can be delegated to a mailroom person. Often the managing editor also performs this role.

DESIGN AND FORMAT

The basic "look" of the newsletter will not change from issue to issue. With the technology of desktop publishing and even sophisticated word processing systems, an attractive design for a newsletter can be done in-house. The design elements to be decided are a masthead, column widths, and type sizes. If the newsletter is produced on computers and the capability exists, then a choice of typefaces can be made.

The complexity of design is an individual decision, but the key is to keep it simple. A masthead with the newsletter name should constitute about one quarter of the top of the front page. A two- or three-column format can be used, but creating columns often requires more production time and may not be worth the effort. To develop the initial design and format, attorneys should ask a graphic designer to assist them. The cost for this service is usually less than $500 and in most cases well worth it.

CONTENT

Prior to the first issue, comprehensive guidelines for content need to be established. This is the job of the editorial board. Day-to-day decisions regarding content will be based on these guidelines and left to the editor and managing editor.

In general, content will be similar to that of employee meetings: information on policy decisions, significant news, developments, and new business successes. Other content issues that naturally find their way into employee newsletters are personal events such as weddings and the birth of children; however, these "news" items are actually of minor interest, and no major effort should be put into reporting them.

Confidentiality of internal matters is always an issue with attorneys. Good communication with staff stresses the importance of client confidences. Attorneys should be aware that internal newsletters may be read by others outside the firm, such as spouses.

The editor/writer should be a person who has knowledge of all the various departments within the attorney's organization. For newsletter writing purposes, this is a person who can be described as "knowing a little bit about everything, but not necessarily a whole lot about anything."

The point of the newsletter is to provide a wide variety of information but not necessarily lots of detail on issues of importance to the firm. Following the editorial approach of newspapers like *USA Today,* the newsletter will be of greatest interest if it touches on many subjects, but provides only brief details. If more information is required, the reader needs to go to other sources. Based on this premise, a two-page newsletter (single sheet, front and back) published twice a month could easily contain seven to ten news stories.

Here is a sampling of typical items that could be found in a good internal newsletter for attorney offices:

Product Liability Group to Handle Widget Corp. Announcement of retainer agreement with local company, describing in general the firm's anticipated work for them.

Wills/Probate Work Changing. Small feature article on the work of one department and a percentage of change over the same period last year and why.

Management Committee to Complete Compensation Policy Review. Update on policy review and anticipation of when it will be completed and information presented to attorneys.

Seminar on Insurance Defense Planned. Information about future seminar for clients sponsored by the insurance department.

Tax Department Laser Printer Working Well. New equipment story, discussing improved image of firm through improved quality of correspondence, and so on.

Office Procedures. A periodic reminder of office policies and procedures. "Don't forget to charge photocopies to the appropriate account." "Our receptionist needs to know your personal schedules—please keep her informed so she can handle your calls better." "The building manager tells us the front doors will be locked at 5:30 P.M. instead of 6 P.M."

Secretarial Tips. A regular feature on four or five common mistakes gathered from secretarial manuals and personal experience.

Personnel News. Another standard feature on new attorneys and others joining the staff, other information about people leaving the firm, a small change in the firm's retirement plan, and so on.

Odds and Ends. Regular feature of interest to employees, ranging from new babies to private accomplishments of attorneys, employees, and their families (keeping in mind that this kind of information is ultimately of little interest to employees).

HOW TO PRODUCE INTERNAL NEWSLETTERS

From a practical point of view, employee newsletters must meet two criteria or they will fail: they must be easy to produce, and they must be frequent. Both of these are relative statements. What is "easy" to one person may be overwhelming to another, and "frequent" may mean once a week to a managing partner but once a quarter to somebody else.

What follows is a description of the easiest and most practical process to produce internal newsletters for attorneys. The emphasis is to set up the process correctly in the beginning to ensure that it works well within the organization and then to allow the focus to be on the content. Too often, the form of the newsletter or production issues draw resources away from content, and the overall objective of the process is lost. A simple design and a nontechnical approach to the writing and production is recommended.

HOW TO GATHER AND WRITE THE NEWS

The editor doesn't have to do all the work. A good one will delegate responsibility and ask others in the firm for assistance. Typically, each newsletter has some standard features, such as the "Secretarial Tips" and "Personnel Changes." Logically, the office manager and person in charge of staff will have the responsibility to provide that kind of information in each issue.

Other sources of "news" should be regular contact persons in each department who, depending on the size of the firm, will most likely be the senior attorney and an administrative person.

The editor should also attend those meetings of staff and attorneys where matters of broad interest are discussed to learn information and report as appropriate on various items of interest to the entire firm and remind those involved of responsibilities.

The writing style should be breezy, avoiding legalese and complicated statements. A standard approach is to write to the eighth grade level.

Of critical importance will be the process of obtaining approvals for information in the newsletter. In most law firms, approvals of information to be released to the public (which is what happens in a newsletter) takes a tremendous amount of time. Obviously, if a ponderous review process is set up for each newsletter, one of two things will happen: it will consume too much valuable attorney time, or the content of the newsletter will slip into low-level, common knowledge items of little interest or value to the readers.

Therefore, all the people involved must place a good deal of trust in communication with each other, so that information is gathered and written at a level and in such a way that it does not require critical approval processes yet provides substance for the readers.

Obtaining this balance is not easy, and it is often through the trial-and-error process that a compatible arrangement is found. If a firm culture is based on open, candid communication and good judgment is shown by the people involved, then approvals are usually not a problem.

HOW MUCH IT WILL COST

A 50-person law firm with one office can prepare a newsletter every two weeks at the combined estimated "cost" of 16 workerhours for each issue. Average time requirements look like this:

- Establishing editorial content, one hour each by editor and managing editor
- Gathering facts, writing stories, eight hours by editor
- Obtaining approvals, editing and subsequent approvals, one hour by managing editor, two hours by editor
- Production, two hours by editor

Actual out-of-pocket costs, after start-up design fees are paid, should be less than $200 per issue (don't assume that these same "costs" apply to external or client newsletters!).

SIZE AND FREQUENCY

The size of the newsletter and the frequency of its arrival on employees desks are related. The ideal combination of size and frequency is one $8\frac{1}{2}$-inch by 11-inch sheet, two sided, every two weeks. Some firms are much more frequent, even daily.

A small size and relatively high frequency makes the communication process part of the office routine. It becomes a priority and part of the job descriptions of the editors. With the right content, it establishes an atmosphere of open communication which builds a spirit to teamwork among attorneys and employees alike.

DISTRIBUTION

How to get the printed word to the intended audience is relatively easy. Distribution will most likely occur through intercompany mail. Mailing labels are recommended in larger offices; handwritten names on the top of each issue are acceptable in smaller offices. The important issue is to ensure that each employee personally receives the newsletter. Merely putting a stack of them in the coffee room or at a receptionist area is not acceptable.

In firms that have multiple offices, the newsletter should be sent next-day delivery for immediate distribution. Some firms who have adopted the two-week publication schedule and have payday twice a month attach the newsletter to paychecks.

CHAPTER 45
The Attorney's Personal Involvement in External Marketing

SUMMARY

By having a simple plan to follow, client development (sales) is not something to fear. By adopting techniques used by other professionals to sell services to businesses, attorneys can effectively reach their intended audiences—business, government, other attorneys, and the general public alike. Effective plans emphasize preparation—not silver tongues.

This chapter discusses

- prospecting to identity potential clients.
- preparation—learning about client background and needs.
- approach—getting the client's attention directed favorably toward you.
- presentation—letting them discover they need you.
- objections—why the prospective client wants to use your services.
- client engagement—closing the sale, asking for the business.
- follow-up—seeing that the clients get what they need.

No matter how comprehensive or insightful a firm's external marketing program may be, it ultimately is up to the individual attorney to make his or her own practice grow and prosper. Some benefits for the individual practice may be reaped from a firm program, but many specific needs and situations will go unsatisfied. Therefore it is crucial for the individual attorney to have a personal commitment and to follow through with a personal plan of action.

The individual facets of the attorney's personal marketing program can and should be many. Individual efforts are part of the total marketing package. Attorney training is important because it develops skills—rarely taught in law school—to carry out marketing as an integral part of the daily practice.

In a situation common to many attorneys who are part of a firm, becoming a "rainmaker" is the inside track to partnership. The best approach to rainmaking is to write a personal marketing plan and to have it approved. Good plans cite specific objectives and the specific activities required to achieve them.

So attorneys write a plan and go through what they feel are all the right motions. They join clubs and attend client trade meetings. They write articles for trade journals. They take prospective clients to lunch. Yet, the attorneys do not get any new clients. What often happens is that the attorneys are not comfortable meeting people with the purpose of developing those acquaintances into new clients. In fact, although they realize its significance, many attorneys have a great deal of anxiety about rainmaking techniques. They can learn much from applying some of the basic "sales" techniques commonly used in business and industry.

BUSINESS DEVELOPMENT EFFORTS ARE UNIVERSAL

A business development effort is necessary for the business of widgets as well as legal services. The major difference between product and professional services business development is that with professional services, the "developer" also performs the service. That is, the seller is the doer.

In his or her own practice development effort, the attorney should be careful to deal with the potential client's decision maker, be that the CEO or client principal. Others may have significant input, but only that decision maker will have the final say. The attorney's relationship with that person will set the tone for the ongoing attorney-client relationship.

The attorney must sell benefits, not legal services. In this vein, Peter Revlon once said that his factories made cosmetics while the stores sold hope. The same might be said of Kodak, which manufactures film, but sells memories. The attorney may produce wills, estate planning, or litigation services, but must be sure to sell peace of mind or financial security or whatever solution the situation at hand requires.

SEVEN STEPS TO BUSINESS DEVELOPMENT SUCCESS

Seven steps constitute the total business development effort. Together they form the circle of activities necessary for successful legal services marketing. Those steps are prospecting, preparation, approach, presentation, objections, client engagement, and follow-up.

1. *Prospecting* is locating and evaluating potential clients. This is possible because of an understanding of what types of clients are wanted and where those clients exist (see Chapters 13 through 18). Evaluating those potential clients involves discerning whether a client can benefit from the attorney's legal services, taking into account the extent of legal services required in volume and whether that client is in a position to pay the commensurate fees.

2. *Preparation* for business development calls for the same mind-set as preparation for, say, litigation or negotiation. The attorney must study the needs of the prospective clients carefully, developing a keen understanding regarding that market.

3. *Approach* means getting the prospective client's attention, letting that person know what the attorney does and how that can be of benefit to a particular situation. One of the simplest ways to accomplish this is for the attorney simply to pay attention to that potential client. This means asking questions and demonstrating interest and knowledge regarding his or her concerns.

4. The *presentation* is the actual proposal. It is the attorney's "pitch" for business. The attorney should practice this step until it becomes a very comfortable topic of conversation, whether formal or informal. The presentation must ask questions that show the potential client that the attorney understands his or her needs, is aware of potential problems, and can be very specific with regard to that client's industry and situation. Active listening techniques can be very important in this situation because the attorney must let that person know his or her professional capabilities in terms of the client's desired benefits. In other words, ask—don't tell.

5. *Objections* are the clients' concerns regarding the attorney's presentation. The attorney must expect objections to occur and anticipate their very nature. Responses to objections demonstrate the attorney's problem-solving ability. Objections are the prospective clients' way of stating the solutions they seek.

6. *Client engagement* is really just closing the deal and getting to the nature of the matter or issues. How does the attorney close and actually engage the client? By asking, "Can we start to work on your legal matter?" Nothing more should be said until the client responds. If the answer is positive, an agreement should be signed at once and a firm commitment should be formed on the part of the client (see Chapter 47). After the agreement and commitment are clearly underway, assure the client his or her choice is correct and appropriate. Then thank the client and excuse yourself. The attorney should try not to linger and visit with the client, perhaps providing that person with the opportunity for a change of heart.

7. *Follow-up* is the start of the next "sale." It is comprised of constant communication and consistent client feedback. The attorney should ask the client regularly if he or she is satisfied and if there are any other needs which remain unmet. An attorney's best source of new clients is referrals from existing clients, so if the client is satisfied, it is appropriate for the attorney to ask for referral possibilities tastefully. If clients' expectations are being met by the attorney, they will usually happily oblige.

ETHICS CONSIDERATIONS

Possible ethical issues must always be considered. In most jurisdictions, direct personal solicitation is not permitted. However, local bar rules and practices will vary. Before you commence direct personal selling activities, check with your local bar's rules as to what is acceptable (see also chapter 52).

CHAPTER 46
Client-Centered Proposals and Presentations

SUMMARY

Proposals and presentations are becoming ever more important and not just for corporate transactional engagements. The key is to make the presentations client-centered. The most successful proposals do not emphasize the attorney or firm but stress an understanding of the client's needs.

This chapter discusses

- basic elements of proposals/presentations.
- how to assess client needs.
- the structure of written proposal.
- oral presentation techniques.

Proposals and presentations are quite significant in the individual attorney's marketing plan, as part of its conceptualization as well as its implementation. Each makes a statement about the attorney's image. A well-researched, neatly prepared proposal submitted on attorney or firm stationery speaks volumes to the client about the value the attorney is placing on that person's work.

The same is true of presentations. A well-rehearsed, smooth presentation demonstrates to the client that the attorney is conscientious. It grants the client a deserved position of importance in the process.

ASSESSMENT AND THE FIRST INTERVIEW

The first step in the written presentation process is assessment. One part is secondary research, the use of existing formal and informal sources to learn as much as possible about the prospective client, his or her particular situation, and related industries. The attorney should focus particularly on the client's customers and their prospects as well as industry prospects. (This information can be accessed through computer programs such as Nexis, Dialog, CompuServe, and other similar data services as well as through the local library.)

Next, having gathered an overview of the client and his or her industry, the attorney must focus on the unique individual legal situation. What other matters have the client been involved in, both past and present? (Lexis, Westlaw, Legal Resource, and similar services can provide this information.) If the attorney's office does not have easy access to this information, law school libraries often provide resources which, for a fee, can provide the necessary data.

While the attorney is checking the potential client's legal background, the attorney should also check the general legal background of the industry for an overview of client industry issues.

Having completed this research, the attorney is ready for a first interview. The purpose of this interview is actually a continuation of the assessment process. To this end, the attorney must ask questions to determine specific needs while focusing on client objectives. The attorney should also ask questions regarding the preferred manner of the attorney-client relationship, including type and frequency of communications (like status or progress reports). Relationship style will have a direct bearing on the attorney's matter administration.

One important aspect of the first interview is to determine if in fact there is a fit between attorney and client. In the final analysis, clients hire attorneys, not firms.

THE WRITTEN PROPOSAL

Following the initial interview, the attorney should go over in detail all of the information gathered. As a result of this the attorney's research will be tailored according to client feedback provided in that interview. Client perceptions are more important than trend analyses or historical data in establishing an attorney-client relationship!

The written proposal should be divided into sections, which should be named and noticeably headlined. These sections should include objectives, qualifications, scope and direction, methodology, fees, and expenses and benefits. Section names may vary according to clients, or even additional sections may be necessary in some situations.

The *objectives* section must state an understanding of the client's objectives for the matter. This is much more important than stating attorney objectives because it demonstrates the attorney's understanding of the client's situation.

The *qualifications* section should restate the specific qualifications that will be applicable to this particular matter. If the proposal is for a long-term counsel relationship, the proposal should state situation-specific qualifications which are applicable to the client, their industry, and their particular challenges. If conflicts and confidentiality are issues, information regarding these areas should be noted here. A sample listing of similar clients and similar matters may also be included. References may also be listed in the qualifications section.

Next, the *scope and direction* section must state the attorney's relationship to the matter, specifically spelling out how it will managed. One of the key elements of this section will be a demonstration of matter management techniques as well as the general breadth and depth of the attorney's relationship involvement.

The *methodology* section should be in outline form. It essentially is a step-by-step script which a client may follow to see exactly how the attorney will approach the matter. What is the first process the attorney will undertake and what will it entail? What is the next process, and so forth. If at all possible, the attorney can also provide a projected time line to give the client an indication of the amount of time and detail required by each step.

The *fees and expenses* section should be accurate, but brief. By reading this, the client should understand the attorney's basis for fees, whether hourly or value based.

The final section, *benefits,* should restate the anticipated results of the attorney-client relationship and if at all possible, the monetary value of successful completion of the matter. This stated monetary value is more important in a transactional matter than in the case of ongoing counsel. In the case of the latter, the attorney can only cite the importance of having ongoing counsel relationship because of the opportunity it provides to better understand client needs and objectives.

ORAL PRESENTATIONS

The first rule in successful oral presentations is to write out an agenda regarding the purpose of the encounter as derived from the assessment process. Included in this agenda should be all items to be discussed during the course of the meeting.

If more than one attorney will be making the presentation, each attorney should speak regarding his or her own area of expertise. Rehearsal is extremely important and valuable for attorney teams as well as for a solo presentation.

As with the first interview, the attorney should be careful to ask questions rather than dominate the client with nonstop talk. The attorney can ask if the proposal reflects an understanding of client needs and answers client concerns for information. This is a point where the attorney can get the client to agree that the proposal is responsive to their information needs.

Experienced negotiators know that the art of negotiating is simply a matter of asking a series of questions so that client needs can be matched with attorney requirements.

In closing the presentation, specific questions can be asked: When does the client want to start? Should the attorney proceed with the research? Should the attorney draw up the retainer agreement? The attorney must be careful to let the client have the last word. His or her response should end the meeting (see also Chapter 47).

Here is a summary checklist for attorney presentations. This works for get-acquainted meetings as well as specific work proposals:

1. *Prepare an agenda.* Hand it out in advance of the meeting so that all participants know what to expect.
2. *Do advance research.* Ask the company or potential client about the composition of the group, their previous experience with outside counsel, their individual interests and particular needs. Get all their names in advance, with biographies if possible. Ask "If I had one thing to say, what would it be?" Try to learn in advance what questions the group will ask.
3. *Focus your presentation on real needs.* Most groups want to know "What's in this for me? How can I use this information?" Tell them how your services differ from others, and describe what an attorney can do for them. Be really clear about this.
4. *Emphasize your help to protect them.* This is an overriding issue among all clients. Tell them your role in this.
5. *Illustrate what you do through anecdotes.* Make these numerous and short: "This was the situation. Here's what I did. Here's what the client did." Be careful that your stories do not run counter to the normal way that the person or organization operates. Tell four or five, or tell none. If you only tell one or two, they'll think you only work in one or two ways.

6. *Rehearse.* Especially if more than one attorney is involved, a dry run through the presentation is essential. Just as actors must perform a dress rehearsal, so too must attorneys prepare for their stage performance.
7. *Follow up with personal phone calls.* Ask individuals in the meeting about their specific areas of interest, so that you can send them information or share experiences. In a group, they'll tend to all agree on something; when you talk to the individuals, you'll get much better information on their specific needs.
8. *Distribute materials.* A "leave behind" is important. At minimum, leave your business card and a brochure/packet of information. Put each participant's name on the packet of materials to be distributed. For those who do not attend, leave the packets with the office secretary.

CHAPTER 47
Client Engagement Methods to Build Better Client Relationships

SUMMARY

The client engagement process, if client centered, can be a positive experience. Establishing both client and attorney expectations can lead to better relationships. Avoiding surprises will build trust rather than animosity. The focus of client engagement is on the two most sensitive issues—money and invoicing procedures.

This chapter discusses

- establishing new client policies of engagement.
- setting the business tone of the client relationship that works best for both client and attorney.
- simple techniques to avoid later billing disputes.

If there is one issue that causes the most stress among attorneys and clients alike, it is money. Attorneys send invoices that ask for it and clients are expected to pay the invoices promptly. It doesn't always work out that way.

Here's a case history of an attorney who had cash flow problems and how she was able to handle them.

> The attorney had a high proportion of clients who were slow to pay the bills sent them. Both monthly statements and trust account balances often seemed to be ignored by clients. Finally, in desperation, she asked one of her clients about the problem.
>
> While this client was one of those slow to pay and who had not kept a trust account at a satisfactory level, the person was a longtime acquaintance and the attorney felt comfortable asking him this.
>
> The client said he didn't see any reason to pay monthly since the matter was going to take several months to complete. Further, he thought the trust account statement merely reflected funds which were deposited on his behalf when received by the attorney, but he assumed they were sent from the other party in the transaction.
>
> The attorney realized that she had taken for granted a client understanding her billing practices. She had never clearly established what her expectations were or asked clients what theirs might be.

ESTABLISHING POLICIES WITH NEW CLIENTS

Misunderstandings regarding attorney billing practices are all too frequent. In most cases, it is because the client does not receive an adequate explanation of all the terms of engagement. Why? Many attorneys are very reluctant to discuss payment conditions with clients, especially new clients.

Too many attorneys are interested in getting the client in the door at all costs. After the new client and the attorney discuss in some detail the specific problem which needs attention, the attorney must quote or at least paraphrase his or her understanding of the client's need and ask for the client's confirmation.

If the attorney and client have the requisite mutual understanding, it is then time to formalize the relationship. The attorney needs to come to a verbal understanding with the client regarding the client's spending limits or at least a range of costs. Probable causes of cost variables must be specifically identified.

The basis for costs needs to be outlined in some detail. The attorney should start with the lead attorney's hourly rate. This should be followed by an explanation of the probable roles of other attorneys or staff involvement and related costs. If outsiders, such as researchers, investigators, or accountants, become necessary, the attorney should explain their roles and the effect on costs.

If the attorney chooses an alternative billing method other than hourly rates, the total fees and expenses should be discussed and agreed upon. If there is more than one possible figure, such as possible shared contingency or other arrangement, it needs to be specifically spelled out.

The frequency or intervals of billing options should be discussed next, with regard to the matter at hand. Many clients prefer to be billed on a regular monthly basis and appreciate the receipt of a statement well before the tenth of the month in order to calculate their payables due for the month. Other billing interval options are possible, including, although not used very often, a one-time billing. The attorney and client must agree which option is appropriate and make sure that agreement is clearly understood by both.

The attorney should review the billing format options available to the client. For example, some clients prefer detailed bills and want to know the amount of time, by attorney, expended in any given activity. Other clients only care about the total expenditure in a given billing period.

The client must understand how much advance retainer is required, if any, to initiate work. If the attorney requires trust account deposits to cover anticipated expenses or to maintain a balance to cover fees, he or she must explain this to the client during the engagement process. Often, less sophisticated clients do not understand the significance of a trust account.

All of the applicable conditions must be committed to writing by the attorney on a standardized form or in a personal letter to the client.

Finally, the attorney should review the written conditions one last time with the client before work commences. This is particularly important for new clients but also important for existing clients.

In the appendix to this book are forms that provide examples of appropriate client engagement methods. The forms are the

- Acknowledgment Letter
- Contingent Fee Retainer Agreement
- Attorney Employment and Fee Agreement (General)
- Attorney Employment and Fee Agreement (Limited)

Chapter 48
Communicating the Bill to the Client

SUMMARY

The most critical, sensitive, and often the most frequent communication from the attorney to the client is the bill. It is vital that the billing meet the clients' expectations and be presented professionally and error free. The billing may inadvertently reflect the quality of legal work.

This chapter discusses

- client perceptions based on billing.
- client expectations of billing.
- the importance of a billing protocol for each client based on client engagement documents.
- checklist for attorney and staff bill preparation.

> An attorney's client seemed to be particularly distrustful of the quality of legal service he was receiving. The attorney had the feeling that the client was constantly checking to see if he was doing the work correctly and providing appropriate counsel. The attorney did not think he was being unduly paranoid. The client often asked about a point of law or cited a similar circumstance that he had "heard about."
>
> Finally, the attorney decided to ask the client outright why he did not seem to be comfortable relying on him. The attorney was in for a surprise! The client was more candid than he expected and more than the attorney felt he would have been if their roles had been reversed.
>
> First, the client admitted that he originally relied on the attorney totally. His reputation was excellent and several of his other clients had recommended him. The client said that billing was the problem and to a lesser extent, correspondence.
>
> Specifically, the client thought the billing was not as he understood it would be. It was often sloppy with frequent typing errors and printed on sometimes wrinkled or smudged paper. Even though the attorney had discussed several options with the client in terms of billing periods and amounts of detail, their consensus on an option was not what the client received. Each bill seemed to the client to be vague. When time expenditure was listed, several different rates were evident with only initials for reference. The description of the activity made little sense to the client. Further, the client had no idea what had determined the varying hourly rate.
>
> The attorney learned a great deal from this experience. He immediately explained to the client the nature and function of billing amounts, initials, and descriptions. He promised to produce bills which could be easily understood by the client and which would be more acceptable in terms of appearance.

ESTABLISHING A BILLING PROTOCOL

In a multi-attorney situation, the lead attorney is ultimately responsible for checking and approving the billing to each client. This attorney's job is to examine each invoice carefully to ensure the manner, frequency, and form are exactly as decided upon in the initial engagement agreement.

The appearance of the billing is as important as the amount. Lack of attention to that detail can result in a considerable amount of client upset and distrust. If the billing is not closely watched by the attorney, the client may doubt the competency of the legal work itself, particularly the work performed by the attorney's staff.

After a new client is engaged and the first bill has been sent, the attorney should telephone or visit the client to sound out possible concerns or confusion. In this way all future bills can meet client expectations and any billing problems can be eliminated before they really begin.

Administrative staff should understand the importance of the billing procedure as well as its delicate nature with regard to its role in client satisfaction. A checklist can be developed to help staff understand exactly what is expected of them:

1. Was the engagement promise regarding billing followed exactly?
2. Had the bill been recorded in the attorney's records?
3. Is the work description adequate and appropriate for the lay client?
4. Is the relevant personnel description appropriate for this client?
5. Is the work for period billed or matter involved submitted on a form clearly labeled "Invoice" that is distinctly different from correspondence?
6. Is the monthly statement of account which indicates the history of payments and charges for trust account and services clearly marked as such?
7. Does the physical appearance conform to standards?
   a. Is typing legible?
   b. Is the bill error free?
   c. Is the paper perfect, flat, and clean?
8. Has the "lead" or "billing" attorney reviewed the bill?
9. If this is the first bill to a new client or a large sum to be paid in full, has the attorney signed a thank you note to be sent when the client pays the bill?

Billing is the most carefully scrutinized of all written communications to the client.

Chapter 49
Cross-Selling Attorney and Firm Services: The Easiest Method to Increase Revenue

SUMMARY

Cross-selling, the process of selling existing clients additional services, is probably the easiest avenue for business development. Many attorneys do not utilize the technique either through fear of losing "their client" in the process or fear of offending the client. Both sole practitioners and members of a firm can successfully get additional business through cross-selling.

This chapter discusses

- how to tell the client about other legal services.
- the business development value of cross-selling.
- dealing with the client handoff.
- setting up a client/service grid.
- cross-selling to build referrals.

A sole practitioner in a fairly competitive midsized market primarily served clients' tax law matters. Many of his clients were referred to him by accountants and financial service organizations as a result of his reputation. But the attorney also had acquired a level of expertise in commercial real estate transactions and felt this practice area was underutilized by his clients.

He wondered why his small-business clients did not ask him to help them with their other legal needs and was disappointed when he discovered they were seeking counsel from other attorneys. The attorney felt his service to clients was very good and clients seemed to be very satisified.

One small-business client with whom he had a longtime relationship stopped by one day to drop off some tax and financial papers. The attorney asked the client to stay a few minutes. Over coffee, the attorney asked the client if he minded sharing his reasons for not using the attorney's services in matters related to business law.

The client seemed genuinely surprised! He told the attorney that he did not realize the attorney wanted to practice in anything but tax-related areas. His only reason for using another attorney is that he thought the first attorney did not want the work.

The attorney realized this misconception regarding his practice probably was shared by most of his other clients. That afternoon he drafted a letter, to be sent to all his clients, describing typical small-business legal needs and his unique ability to respond to them. He cited recent seminars and training opportunities to develop his ability in this area.

The attorney mailed the letters and marked on his calendar to mention the subject during each client's next visit. Over the next year, his small-business counsel blossomed as he had hoped it might. He continued vigorous efforts to let clients know all of his capabilities, beyond the matters he was currently handling.

LETTING THE CLIENT KNOW

Attorneys often take for granted that their clients understand their practice or firm as well as they do. They do not take the time to make sure the client is aware of the entire range of practice area capabilities. But unless they are told by an attorney or read a firm brochure, clients often do not have a realistic image of what their present attorney or firm's capabilities might be.

Cross-selling is simply letting clients know what else the attorney or firm can do for them. It is making sure that the broad range of legal services offered are fully understood and easily retained by each client. (See Figure 49-1.)

Many firms have found that cross-selling is the biggest single source of new business. It exceeds referrals and community activities. Some firms have even suggested that as a source, the positive results of cross-selling are more profitable than all other sources of business combined!

Cross-selling is nothing more than the process of making sure *all* client legal problems are solved by selling others in the practice to the client. Cross-selling works best if the *clients'* best interests are kept in mind. In other words, instead of spending a lot of effort to make sure all the attorneys are busy, the attorney needs to look out for the clients' needs.

Cross-selling involves one attorney talking about another. It is easier

TABLE 49-1 Client/Services Grid

A detailed review of *practice areas* provided to *specific clients* quickly reveals areas of potential cross-selling. The more detail of services listed, the more information will be revealed to the attorney.

PRACTICE AREAS

CLIENTS	Real Estate Transaction	Tax and Employee Benefits	Comm'l Litigation	Wills & Estate Planning	Land use	Business and Corporate	Labor	Domestic Relations	Merger/Acquisition	Personal Bankruptcy	Telecommunications	Environmental	Construction
John Doe													
Jane Jones													
Acme Mfg.													
Widget Dist.													
Smith Builders													
Harry Smith													
Bob's Supply													
First Local Bank													

to talk about the benefits another lawyer can deliver and to talk about the problems they can solve than it is to talk about ourselves. Further, as is equally obvious, it is better received by the client than a blatantly self-aggrandizing position.

One reason, if not the biggest, that attorneys have a hard time instituting a cross-selling mode is the fear that clients they introduce to another attorney, completely apart from differing practice areas, will be lost as "their" client to the second attorney. While there is no doubt that this can happen, most of the attorney's fears are unfounded. First, if the attorney's relationship is truly solid, it will not be jeopardized by introducing the client to someone else for specialized help. Second, the attorney will actually solidify the relationship by looking out for the client's best interests.

When the introduction is made, the attorney should make it clear to the client and the other attorney that a strong interest in the clients' affairs will be maintained. The attorney will follow up to make sure the problem at hand is solved to everyone's satisfaction. The attorney should go beyond words by maintaining verbal and written communications with the client and attorney.

These principles apply equally to attorneys within megafirms, small firms, or sole practitioners. The sole practitioner may suffer from the most paranoia, but is probably no more justified than the lawyer in a megafirm worrying about making a billable hour requirement for the year.

HOW TO CROSS-SELL EFFECTIVELY

Certain axioms of effective cross-selling will work in any situation in which an attorney practices—in a group of sole practitioners sharing space, in both formal and informal networks, in affiliations, or in megafirms. Here are four proven methods that have helped the cross-selling efforts:

1. *Internal advance sheets* that list matters, clients, and current legal issues. Advance sheets are frequently read, whereas memos sometimes are not.
2. *All-attorney memos on new matters.* Some firms do this routinely for all new activities, beyond conflict-checking procedures.
3. *Attorney meetings.* In addition to methods 1 and 2, regular attorney meetings can be held to describe new statute or case law and its significance for clients. This raises other attorneys' sensitivities to issues of their area. The meetings are chaired on a rotating basis by different attorneys, departments, or sections. The structure and time slot for these meetings will vary according to situational traditions, but monthly lunches have worked well for some firms.
4. *The client/services grid.* The format has of itself raised awareness in many groups of attorneys of cross-selling opportunities.

Nearly all attorneys, regardless of their practice area, either receive or give frequent referrals to other lawyers. Some lawyers have said that nearly 80 percent of their referrals are from other attorneys!

Cross-selling has its roots in the client-focus theory. If the attorney is mindful and truly understands his or her client's needs, the client should be informed of additional attorney or firm services as soon as a need for such a service becomes apparent. The attorney should be that much in touch with his or her clients' needs!

CHAPTER 50
Legal Audits to Identify Client Needs

SUMMARY

Conducting audits, whether simple or complex, can be an important service to clients. Often the audit will identify needs previously unknown to the client. The practice of preventative law is an obligation under Canon 21. By providing this service an attorney can capture and retain the right kind of clients.

This chapter discusses

- the basics of business legal audits.
- the value of personal legal audits.
- dealing with the general client perception of preventative law.
- how to identify present and future needs of clients efficiently.

A large metropolitan law firm was asked by one of its corporate clients to conduct a legal audit. Corporate general counsel wanted to know in what areas they might be susceptible to litigation and in what areas they were on solid ground. Since the firm had worked with this client for a number of years and valued its relationship, a flat fee to cover time and expenses was negotiated for the service.

The firm principal who was the client's primary contact suggested that the legal audit begin with a survey of the corporation's key managers. The survey was in the form of a questionnaire, containing four general areas: work products, administration and finances, marketing and client services, and general matters. Each area contained subcategories with very specific questions.

The questionnaire was designed to assess exactly how much managers and employees really knew about company policies and procedures, and to determine the extent to which that protocol was being followed. Managers were asked to complete the survey forms and return them by a two-week deadline. Emphasis on the importance of the questionnaire came from the corporate CEO, who wholeheartedly endorsed the project. All of the managers complied.

The results pinpointed a number of sensitive areas of which general counsel had previously been unaware. Responses were examined carefully and combined with all other responses to form general issues of concern.

As a result of the legal audit, the law firm was retained by the corporation to beef up legal protection in some areas and to correct problems in others. The decision by the firm to ask only a small fee for the audit paid off, as the corporation spent a great deal more on services resulting from the outcome of the audit.

WHEN TO PERFORM LEGAL AUDITS

Legal audits make good sense not only for megacorporations but also for private individuals. In today's litigious society, many entities require legal advice and service but are unaware of their need. Legal audits help those organizations and individuals to demystify their own legal requirements and to seek expertise regarding their disposition. Unfortunately for those organizations and people who have never had any sort of relationship with the legal profession, they may initially be very hesitant to agree on its obvious benefits.

Legal audits are every bit as important as financial audits. In this sense, attorneys play essentially the same roles as accountants in the process. The attorney is an outsider looking in at the process and so is more able to detect objectively where help is needed. This service is a preventative measure which helps to ensure that future legal problems, including litigation, are avoided.

CORPORATE LEGAL AUDITS

According to a managing partner and associate from Gammon & Grange in Washington, D.C., who authored an article regarding the legal audit process for *Preventative Law Reporter,* corporate legal audits must contain 13 categories:

1. General information
2. Governance
3. Organization purposes
4. Business practices

5. Financial information
6. Books and records
7. Property information
8. Employee and labor relations
9. Officers, directors, and management
10. Licenses and other regulatory requirements
11. Tax-exempt status
12. Charitable solicitation activities
13. Antitrust, copyright, and trademark

The corporate legal audit form can be adapted to suit the needs of the corporation and situation. A basic outline which can be followed would include an general introduction, introductions for each category (or department) audit, specific questions, and a conclusion.

The general introduction must explain the purpose of the audit and convey potential benefits to the readers. If the audit is receiving the support of high-end management, endorsements can be noted in this section. The respondent must be convinced that his or her answers are integral pieces to the entire puzzle and so must be genuinely insightful.

The introductions to each category audit must explain the purpose of that category's existence. It is important for the attorney drafting such a questionnaire to speak in the vernacular of the reader, not in legalese. The respondent must not only accept the value of each area as a separate entity, he or she must be committed to seeking the truth regarding it.

Specific questions are situation specific, meaning they inevitably will be different for each corporation using the legal audit process. Some examples of questions might be

> Are you aware of any contributions made by corporate personnel on behalf of the corporation to political, philanthropic, or social service causes?

or

> On what basis are customers granted discounts?

and

> Does the above discount formula ever vary?

As many as 100 very specific questions might be asked. It is appropriate to grant a reasonable amount of time, depending on the number and complexity of the questions, for the respondents to complete and return the questionnaire.

The final, general conclusion should thank the respondent for his or her time and contribution to the legal audit. It should restate the purpose of the project and let respondents know how, when, or even if they will be able to access result.

THE SMALL-SCALE LEGAL AUDIT

Small-scale legal audits are much simpler than corporate legal audits to draft, conduct, and assess results. Because the number of individuals involved is substantially less (in fact, oftentimes only one person is involved), the small-scale legal audit can be very comprehensive, very explicit, much less expensive to conduct, and conducted with greater frequency.

New businesses find legal audits particularly helpful in ascertaining exactly what their future legal needs might entail. By knowing this at an early stage, they can budget and plan appropriately. A legal audit for a small business might recommend investigation of areas related to public offerings, if such an event is likely. There are many other areas of need regarding small and new businesses.

A legal audit conducted for an individual can also help that person to budget and plan for future legal expenses. Such an audit might uncover the need for a new will, which in turn can be provided by the attorney. Other needs might include property holdings, trust accounts, or real estate and other investments.

CONVINCING THE CLIENT OF THE VALUE

Very rarely will a client seek out a legal audit. It is up to the attorney to convince the client that such a program is appropriate, cost effective, and an essential part of the planning process. Comparison to the need for financial audits might be helpful, as the value of those is widely known and accepted.

The legal audit should be packaged as a preventive measure which can actually prevent or at least mitigate many legal needs before they occur. Although this may decrease the amount of work required by the attorney in the short run, it increases overall attorney efficiency (not to mention client satisfaction) and may allow attorneys more time to seek other new clients.

BIBLIOGRAPHY

The Preventative Lawyer (available from the University of Denver College of Law, 7039 E. 18th Street, Denver, CO 80220).

Chapter 51
Proactive External Marketing: Why Attorneys Must Do It

SUMMARY

Changes in the legal profession are forcing attorneys to engage in smarter and more agressive marketing activities. Attorneys, if they wish to continue the successful practice of law, have no choice but to rethink their current practice-development activities, then thoroughly plan and implement intelligent and effective programs to retain old clients and gain new ones.

This chapter discusses

- external factors affecting the way attorneys will manage their practices in the future.
- increased public interest in attorney and legal activities, forcing attorneys to learn how to handle public relations problems effectively not only for themselves but for their clients as well.
- the control and delivery of printed messages to a selected audience through means of effective advertising and literature distribution.

"Doing good work" is the ultimate business development activity, but there are many solid reasons why this fundamental aspect of the legal practice is no longer sufficient to retain existing clients and gain new ones.

External factors, beyond the attorney's control, are requiring no small effort to retain clients and to obtain new ones to replace the old that will inevitably fall away.

Efforts directed to the external audience are important for one simple fact: There is increasing competition among law firms for clients. The legal practice pie is growing, but the group of people who want a share of it is growing faster. This means that everyone will either have less or will take more than their share.

Other factors build pressure on attorneys to engage in more extensive external marketing activities. One is a prevalent negative image of attorneys and the legal professional in general. Another is that clients will drift away because of less than warm relationships and/or continual actions by the attorney that result in anxiety or mistrust of the work being done for them.

At the same time, there is a growing interest on the part of the public and the media in legal matters. As the media become more aggressive and the public demands inquiry into everything, the attorney cannot practice in isolation or assume that communication with the public and the media will be unnecessary.

In general, communication problems are being created for attorneys due to the increasing complexity of the legal process and the spiraling costs of litigation. High legal fees and large settlements always make news. The attorney and their client are forced to talk about them—to each other as well as the public!

External activity is growing simple because everyone else is doing something too. In short, the competition is everywhere. Advertising for legal services will grow in quantity and scope.

It has taken a good two-thirds of this book on business development to arrive at the point where external action begins. Is this indicative of the process? You bet it is!

GETTING THE MESSAGE OUT

"Get the right message to the right people at the right time." That's the secret of success in any business. The following chapters discuss methods for attorneys to establish and maintain as much control as possible over all messages that are delivered to the selected audience.

There should be no doubt that attorneys must continually plan new marketing programs, revise old ones, and then implement intelligent and effective activities to be successful. The development of the "right message" is a complex process all by itself, requiring the analysis and consensus described earlier in this book. The "right people" are the clients (past and present), potential clients, and referrals so important as sources of new business. And the "right time" is a key part of any communication effort, that is, a message delivered to a person at the moment when he or she need or want it.

The proactive external marketing described here is carried out through advertising, literature distribution, publicity, speeches, personal contacts, community involvement, and many other activities. Attorneys are good on developing ideas for marketing, and they generally know what to say. But they are usually weakest on the delivery system, or the distribution of proactive marketing processes to the market.

Of the three components of the communication process—content, production, and distribution—it is this third and last component that invariably receives the least attention from attorneys. Just like the proverbial chain with the weak link, the best written newsletter, for example, has absolutely no value if it is not delivered correctly or on time.

Attorneys will write strong speeches, spend much money on beautiful brochures, achieve good publicity, and develop excellent advertising programs, and then in the end will fail to carry through with the delivery in an effective way. This final process of delivering messages is critical for ultimate success.

CHAPTER 52
Ethical Considerations: Advertising and Solicitation Within Professional Limits

SUMMARY

Attorneys are guided by codes of professional responsibility related to the promotion of their legal practice. Every local jurisdiction has adopted guidelines which must be rigorously followed. Inappropriate advertising may not only violate the codes, but also will create unrealistic expectations among clients and ultimately harm overall practice-development efforts.

This chapter discusses

- guidelines for attorney marketing activities so as not to violate ethical standards.
- appropriate use of language and information on letterhead and promotional materials.

When attorneys prepare a business development program that involves anything related to marketing communications, there is legitimate concern that the programs and activities adhere to professional responsibility codes and other regulations. Virtually all jurisdictions give significant attention to issues involving advertising, solicitation, and other promotional efforts. There are two basic restrictions to attorney advertising: one involves direct solicitation; the other forbids attorneys from calling themselves specialists unless they practice in a jurisdiction where there is a system for designating or licensing specialists. The appropriate language is that an attorney "emphasizes land use (or whatever)." To "specialize in land use" implies some sort of formal training that may or may not exist.

Restrictions on advertising are usually combined with guidelines on publicity, solicitation, and promotion. They are discussed in professional codes of the jurisdictions. But the U.S. Supreme Court has continually stopped attempts by bar officials to block attorneys from seeking new clients through advertisements and other written communications. In the landmark 1988 decision that affected bar guidelines in 24 states, it held that *Shapero* v. *Kentucky Bar Association*—that state's ban on targeted direct-mail solicitation of clients—violated the First Amendment.

It is obvious that an attorney cannot make any false or misleading statement. But this basic concept brings about the most criticism of attorney advertising. Critics argue that it is virtually impossible to tout legal services without making promises for or overstating the quality of the services performed.

Creating unreasonable expectations is not only wrong but is also poor marketing. Additionally, it is wrong to state or imply that the attorney handles matters in a particular practice area when in fact the attorney routinely refers such matters to others. An attorney may not claim experience when it doesn't exist. The attorney may not convey an impression that he or she is in a position to influence any court or other public body improperly.

- Direct solicitation is not appropriate. (Direct *personal* solicitation is almost uniformly banned. Direct-*mail* solicitation is also banned in many jurisdictions. Even items such as holiday greeting cards to nonclients may be prohibited.)
- Communication should not be false or misleading about the attorney or services. "Communication" includes statements both oral and written or through any other means of expression.
- Communication should not
  - misrepresent facts or laws.
  - omit facts that make a statement misleading.
  - make misleading statements causing unjustified expectations.
  - state or imply that results can be achieved by means that violate disciplinary rules or applicable laws.
  - compare services with another attorney.
  - state or imply that matters are handled which are actually referred to others.
  - state or imply that experience at handling specific matters exists when in fact it does not.
  - convey the impression that the attorney can influence a court, public body, or other office.
- Copies of all written promotional communication and recordings of all broadcast promotions should be kept for a year, along with records of where, when, and how the communication was used.
- An advertisement should be identified as such, unless it is obvious that it is a paid promotion.
- All advertisements should clearly identify the name and office address of the attorney or firm whose services are being offered.
- Publicity, as different from advertising, should not be obtained through purchase or any other kind of compensation directly to the media.

Figure 52-1 Ethical Considerations for Attorney Marketing Activities

- Information on printed materials should not violate any of the guidelines listed in Figure 52-1. This includes language on materials such as announcements, office signs, letterheads, telephone directory listings, legal directory listings, or other professional notices.
- An attorney can be "Of Counsel" on a letterhead only if he or she has a continuing professional relationship other than as a partner or associate.
- An attorney can be "General Counsel" only if he or she devotes a substantial amount of professional time representing clients.
- An attorney should not practice under a name that makes the identity of the attorney unclear.
- Trade names ("The Attorney Group" or "Southside Attorneys, Inc.") are generally acceptable, as long as they do not imply an false association with a government agency or public or charitable organization.
- Attorneys should identify who is qualified to practice in various jurisdictions, particularly when there are multiple offices.

In addition, most jurisdictions have specific rules regarding the use of names of attorneys no longer practicing in the firm. Local codes should therefore be checked carefully before preparing any kind of printed materials.

Figure 52-2 Ethical Guidelines for Attorney Printed Materials

Some individual jurisdictions also have specific guidelines on identification of solicitations or promotions if there is any doubt that the reader or viewer may be confused, even to the point of specifying the size of the word "advertisement" that must appear on all printed materials.

Figures 52-1 and 52-2 are checklists for attorneys to review when carrying out promotional activities and printing brochures, letterhead, and so on. For specific guidelines, attorneys should consult the codes of professional responsibility for their local jurisdictions.

Chapter 53
Printed Materials: Consistent Graphic Standards Enhance Professional Appearance

SUMMARY

The quality of printed materials says much about an attorney and law firm. A consistent use of good graphic design, applied to all documents and materials carrying the attorney's name, communicates a professional image. Logos and logotypes, type styles, paper, ink colors, and other items all play a role in the attorney's image.

This chapter discusses

- the role of good graphic design in the marketing process.
- the effect of graphic design elements on clients' perceptions of an attorney.
- use of desktop publishing by individual attorneys.

Most attorneys are surprised when they realize the large number of printed materials that carry the firm name on them and therefore reflect the firm's image. Every attorney has business cards and letterhead with some sort of typeface and color of ink and paper representing his or her name. But there are many other items where the name of the attorney or firm is represented: outdoor signage, brochures, invoices, internal memos, transmittal slips, note papers, binders, fax transmittals, notebooks, and many more.

Therefore, establishing standards for graphic design is desirable to achieve a professional presentation of the firm name whenever and wherever it appears. The purpose is not only to cause instant recognition of the sender by the receiver, but also to reflect a high quality and consistent image at all times.

When establishing graphics standards, it is helpful to think of graphic design as a language. It has a vocabulary that includes color, type, paper, grids, size, layout, photos, illustration, graphic devices, and printing techniques. By combining the various elements effectively, an attorney creates appropriate and powerful communication and a common unified presentation.

LOGOS AND LOGOTYPES

Logos are symbols or marks that identify a company or organization. Most attorneys prefer the use of logotypes, simply the attorney's name printed in a certain typeface. In both cases, the design elements are presented in a certain relationship of words and lines to each other. The logo (if there is one), typeface, and colors work together to create the visual impact desired.

TYPE STYLES

There are hundreds of different typefaces. Through historical association and exposure to type, the average person is conditioned to respond and feel differently about each face. Although this response can be strong or subtle, type plays an important role in the reader's reaction to a printed piece and therefore the attorney who produced it.

For example, if an attorney selected a typeface called Goudy Oldstyle, it would convey an elegant, sophisticated image. This typeface is highly legible, is widely available, and comes in a variety of weights and forms.

Most typefaces come in variations, such as light, bold, and italic. The variations can all be used to allow variety but at the same time maintain visual organization to printed communication.

Although one typeface is always recommended for official communications, other typefaces can be used when the printed piece calls for variety. For example, the type styles shown in Figure 53-1 provide some variety and will look nice when used in conjunction with Goudy Oldstyle.

COLORS

Most attorneys prefer black on their stationery. But in printing newsletters, announcements, brochures, and other materials, other colors can be used. It is important to choose colors that are designed to provide a wide variety of color selections for the particular needs of a printed piece but at the same time establish a color harmony throughout all communications.

PAPER

The use of appropriate paper is probably the most overlooked opportunity for attorneys to make a powerful impression on clients and other alike. For relatively little extra cost, the impact of high-quality paper is generally worth it. Most attorneys choose white paper, but papers that are cream or ivory can be of value. Like type style, each of these creates a different impression.

Paper also comes in various weights, measured usually in pounds. Standard photocopier paper is 24 pound, although some with a lighter "feel" will be 20 pound. Most letterhead is printed on 24-pound paper, but with a texture added. The point here is to realize that there are numerous options, and a few minutes with a knowledgeable printer or graphic designer choosing a good-quality paper is time well spent.

GRIDS

A grid is a way of organizing a page so that information can be easily placed in a consistent and structured manner. A grid divides a page into units which are the basis for determining the layout. A typical grid will be

Goudy Oldstyle roman with small caps (14 point)

ABCDEFGHIJKLMNOPQRSTUVWXYZ
abcdefghijklmnopqrstuvwxyz.,:;
1234567890 - —()[]"*‡«»#?¿!¡&%$¢

8/10

A type family is a collection of typefaces that are variations of one basic style of alphabet. The usual design components of a type family are roman, italic, and bold.

Helvetica light (14 point)

ABCDEFGHIJKLMNOPQRSTUVWXYZ
abcdefghijklmnopqrstuvwxyz.,:;
1234567890 ()[]- —"*?!&%$¢

8/10

A type family is a collection of typefaces that are variations of one basic style of alphabet. The usual design components of a type family are roman, italic, and bold.

Times Roman with small caps (14 point)

ABCDEFGHIJKLMNOPQRSTUVWXYZ
abcdefghijklmnopqrstuvwxyz.,:;
1234567890 - —()[]"*‡«»#?¿!¡&%$¢

8/10

A type family is a collection of typefaces that are variations of one basic style of alphabet. The usual design components of a type family are roman, italic, and bold.

Century Expanded roman with small caps (14 point)

ABCDEFGHIJKLMNOPQRSTUVWXYZ
abcdefghijklmnopqrstuvwxyz.,:;
1234567890 - —()[]"*‡«»#?¿!¡&%$¢

8/10

A type family is a collection of typefaces that are variations of one basic style of alphabet. The usual design components of a type family are roman, italic, and bold.

Figure 53-1 Typeface Examples.

Garamond No. 3 roman with small caps (14 point)
ABCDEFGHIJKLMNOPQRSTUVWXYZ
abcdefghijklmnopqrstuvwxyz.,:;
1234567890 - —()[]''*‡«»#?¿!¡&%$¢

8/10

A type family is a collection of typefaces that are variations of one basic style of alphabet. The usual design components of a type family are roman, italic, and bold.

Figure 53-1 Continued.

based on a rectangular module. The most common page size is $8\frac{1}{2}$-inch by 11-inch and the grids will typically be in the same ratio. Documents of other sizes work well using the grid concept. The 4-inch by 9-inch horizontal and vertical formats are functional sizes for self-mailers and inserts into standard envelopes. The same square grid is applied to these sized pieces.

A grid should be designed to guide the layout of every printed piece. The use of the same grid from piece to piece will contribute immeasurably to the continuity of an organization's presentation. A basic grid format is provided in Figure 53-2.

GRAPHIC DEVICES

Graphic devices such as bars and rules can be used to add emphasis and interest. They should, however, be used sparingly and should have a communication function rather than simply being decorative.

DESKTOP PUBLISHING

Desktop publishing software gives an attorney great opportunity to reduce outside design expenses. But it also may cause attorneys to spend enormous amounts of time creating documents that may or may not look better than other options.

Both individual attorneys and firms can become enamored with the technology of desktop publishing, with the intentions to increase efficiency and save money. In reality, a downturn in staff and administrative productivity can easily occur. Most attorneys now use some form of computers for

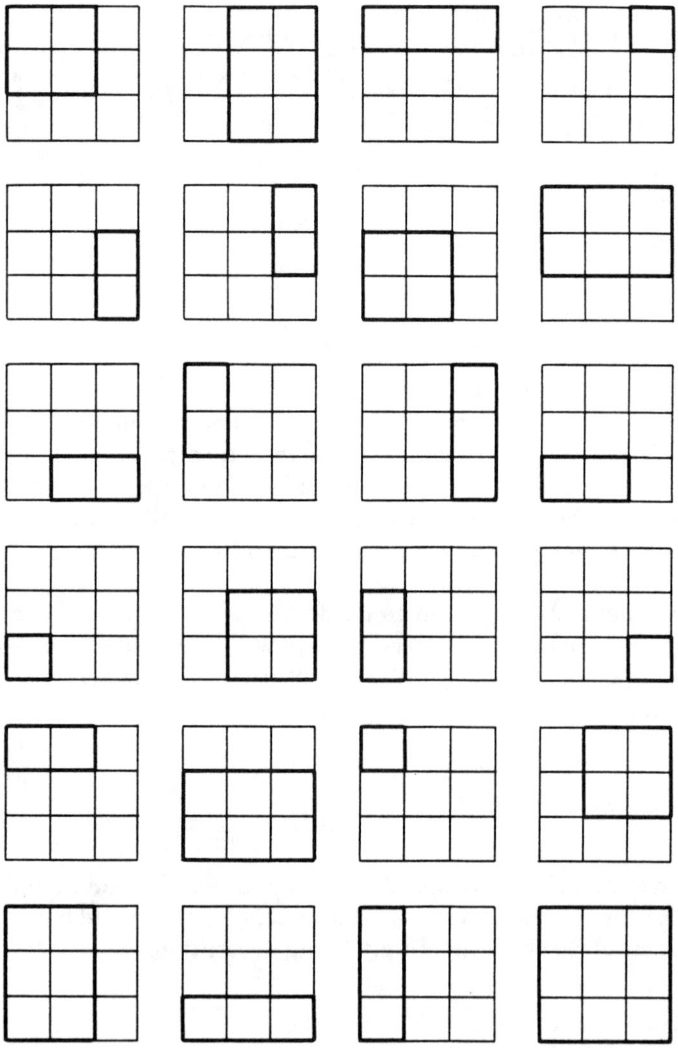

Figure 53-2 Grid Format. Using a grid format, all design elements (type, photos, artwork, etc.) are organized to allow the flexibility to help make designing easy and more effective, never boring or repetitious. Type, photos, and design elements should align with the grid. Column widths should be in multiples of the grid modules.

word processing. This is almost mandatory in today's business environment. However, as word processors get more and more elaborate and allow users to enter the world of desktop publishing, the user can go astray. Desktop publishing is best left to the outside experts, or in the case of very large firms, left to one individual who uses it daily and becomes proficient.

Chapter 54
Writing for Results: Speaking the Language of Your Audience

SUMMARY

Attorneys write for a living, but they must shift gears when writing for business-development purposes. Promotional materials must be written from the reader's viewpoint, emphasizing significance of the facts and benefits to the audience.

This chapter discusses

- importance of addressing the reader's needs and interests.
- how to ensure that facts about an attorney or practice are translated into benefits for the reader.
- a formula to analyze written materials to ensure clarity of context and subsequent understanding.

Attorneys write. This activity is integral to the practice of law: briefs, reports, analyses, and correspondence of all kinds.

When the attorney writes for marketing purposes, the activity requires a different approach, one that is oriented toward a nonattorney audience whose interests and "language" are far different from the attorney's. Even attorneys writing to other attorneys should use nonlegal approaches to the prose.

Written materials generated by attorneys in the normal course of practicing law are almost always prepared to inform and persuade. The attorney writes knowing that the recipient of the message—be it a court, colleague, or client—will read it.

But this is not the case in marketing. People do not have to read many marketing-oriented materials produced by attorneys. People voluntarily read things for two reasons:

1. They will enjoy the process.
2. They think they will learn something from it.

It is safe to assume that potential readers, upon seeing a brochure, newsletter, or other "optional" message from an attorney, will be inclined to read it only if one or both of the two reasons are present. Therefore, the attorney needs to write with this approach in mind.

For instance, consider an attorney's brochure from the potential client's viewpoint. It is nice to think that the reader will voluntarily pick up the brochure in search of general information about an attorney or firm. In reality, brochures are used almost always by clients or potential clients for specific information at a specific time. The most effective brochures are therefore those that can address a client's needs as clearly and directly as possible. Brochures are most useful when they provide valuable information, written in clear, concise, and easily understandable language.

FACTS VERSUS MEANING

The minds of attorneys, like their libraries, are storehouses of facts. The client-focused attorney succeeds in marketing communication when he or she can sort through those facts, select the relevant ones to pass on to clients, and then translate or assign meaning to them. When writing for marketing purposes, attorneys can check the communication value of their prose in this way:

1. Periodically, review two or three sentences for their factual content.
2. Then look elsewhere in the same paragraph for some sort of interpretation of the facts or a description of their significance. "What does this mean to me?" is always the question in the reader's mind. The attorney's job is to make sure the answer is always clear.

Since a common writing activity for attorneys in marketing is the drafting of brochure copy or firm descriptions, extra care must be taken to ensure the text has meaning for the reader.

One successful approach is to address the attorney's capabilities in terms of legal activity and problems solved, rather than merely naming practice areas. The reality is that clients generally don't care about legal terms; all they want is their immediate and specific problem solved.

FEATURES VERSUS BENEFIT

A second approach equally important to the text of the brochure is to establish "features" of the attorney, department, or firm and link them closely with "benefits" to the audience.

Students of advertising learn this from their college professors in Copy Writing 101. In a typical exam, students are asked to write a headline and text for an advertisement of a new lawn mower, based on a set of facts provided. Invariably, students use a new *feature* of the lawn mower—its 3.5-horsepower engine—in the headline. These students fail the exam because what is really important is what this engine means to the potential customer, or the *benefit*. In this case, the significance of a 3.5-horsepower engine is faster, more efficient lawn mowing. So for attorneys to write for marketing purposes, they must simply take the "features versus benefits" approach to copy writing.

Here are some examples where typical features of attorneys and firms are linked with benefits to the clients. How many of these "features" of attorneys and firms have been written without the benefits that follow? Many attorneys might say the benefits are obvious. Not so, as research into reader response will attest. The only opinions that matter are those of the potential clients.

Feature (of the attorney or firm). The attorney/firm has a long history of providing business and litigation service to many business enterprises, institutions, and individuals.

Benefit (to the client or potential). The client can have confidence in the attorney/firm's experience to handle a broad array of legal needs.

Feature. The attorney/firm is sophisticated and contemporary, employing new ideas, concepts, and methods in the practice of law.

Benefit. Clients can have confidence in the attorney/firm's abilities to arrive at contemporary legal solutions in a modern business environment.

Feature. The attorney/firm is strong in litigation, but at the same time frequently negotiates, mediates, and arbitrates.

Benefit. The attorney/firm seeks alternative solutions of real value for clients.

Feature. The attorney/firm has and will continue to tackle aggressively more complex, sophisticated areas of law.

Benefit. The attorney/firm has the experience and skill to assist and advise in complex legal issues.

Feature. The attorney/firm understands the broad context in which the client operates and offers counsel and legal services to fit that context.

Benefit. Services and results will mesh with the client's organizational objectives.

Feature. (in larger firms only): A good deal of camaraderie and social cohesion is present within the firm.

Benefit. Services are provided in a friendly, noncompetitive way. The attorneys are easy to work with.

Feature (in larger firms only). Teams of attorneys, assembled to handle complex projects, work well together in creative, innovative ways.

Benefit. Solutions for clients of complex problems can be achieved creatively and—as a result—cost effectively.

Feature. The attorney/firm is located in (city), providing services in the (geographical location).

Benefit. Legal needs can be met in the (geographical location).

Feature. The attorney/firm utilizes state-of-the-art technology in research and administrative matters.

Benefit. The attorney/firm provides superior, cost-efficient legal services.

KEEPING IT SIMPLE

Besides looking for meaning in text, good writers pay attention to the overall difficulty of the words. One way to measure difficulty is through various formulas, one of which is presented in Figure 54-1, the Gunning Fog Index.

The Gunning Fog Index helps you estimate the years of schooling needed to read a written passage with ease. Here's how to do it:

1. Select a sample of writing 100–125 words long. Put down the number of words in each sentence in the sample, then the total. Divide the total number of words by the number of sentences to get the average sentence length. (In counting sentences, treat independent clauses as separate sentences. "I came, I saw, I conquered" counts as three sentences.)
2. Count each word of three syllables or more. *Don't* count
   a. words made by combining short words, e.g., butterfly,
   b. words made into three syllables be adding "-ed" or "-es,"
   c. words that begin with a capital letter,
   d. the first word in any sentence.
3. Add 1 and 2 (*average sentence length* plus the *percentage of long words*). Multiply the sum by the factor of 4 Ignore the digits that follow the decimal point.

The resulting number is the Fog index: The years of schooling needed to understand the writing tested *with ease.* Because few people have over 17 year's schooling, any passage above 17 gets a Fog Index of "17 plus." A score of 16 or higher means only a graduate student could read the copy with ease. At the other end of the spectrum, a 9 means a ninth grader could understand. *Business Week* averages 10. The Gettysburg Address is 10. *Time* and *Newsweek* average 11.

Figure 54-1 The Gunning Fog Index. From *The Technique of Clear Writing,* by Robert Gunning (New York: McGraw-Hill, rev. ed. 1968). Used with permission. "Fog Index" is a service mark of Gunning-Mueller Clear Writing Institute, Inc., Santa Barbara, California.

Writing to the proverbial eighth-grade level is not an insult to readers or "talking down" to them. Writing simply and clearly is actually a courtesy, enabling the reader to understand quickly and easily what is being said.

CHAPTER 55
An Orientation to Producing a Brochure: The Toughest Marketing Project an Attorney Will Ever Undertake

NOTE: If the reader is considering a brochure as the first step in a marketing program and has turned to this chapter before reading either the introduction to this book or reading Chapter 29, "Getting Started," please go back and read those materials. They explain, among other issues, that brochures are valuable tools to supplement attorney marketing programs, but are not recommended as the first step!

SUMMARY

Brochures are powerful devices to summarize in writing and design an attorney or firm. But, to be effective, they must be viewed for what they are: a small piece of the attoney's total marketing program. To write a brochure successfully, the attorney must undertake a comprehensive approach to production. A common flaw in most attorney brochures is their lack of focus and clarity of language to leave a strong impression in the minds of readers.

This chapter discusses

- the role of brochures in the attorney's total marketing program.
- how to resolve internal disagreements on the importance of brochures and how to get them produced.
- the "internal" benefits of the brochure preparation process.
- the seven steps to brochure production.
- the four objectives that effective brochures can accomplish.

A brochure is not a goal by itself—it is a means to another end. Brochures usually strive to provide full and accurate information about an attorney or a firm, leading to opportunities for additional practice.

Brochures project an image, conveyed not only through design features but also through content, organization, and flow. They are powerful devices to tell the attorney's story, document achievements, and showcase capability.

Brochures and other marketing tools such as seminars and newsletters do not alone sell a potential client on an attorney or firm. They are the kind of things that are important in their absence. They are a piece of a total program that helps develop new clients and generate more work from existing clients, (See Figure 55-1.)

Figure 55-1 Sample Brochures. Here are examples of brochures produced by attorneys. The best brochures are those with a single purpose, easy-to-read writing style, and professional graphics.

VALUE TO ATTORNEYS

Brochures have other useful purposes, not the least of which is internal. Many times, the process of writing the brochure has provided immeasurable benefits to individuals and groups of attorneys. It forces them to articulate their thoughts on their current and future practice of law.

As with other forms of promotion, brochures are of value for the client-focused attorney in reinforcement for existing clients, prompting the "That's my attorney" response. Brochures are useful in recruiting and in helping to develop the firm's identity. But if the process is not handled correctly, brochures can be costly to produce both in terms of attorney time and outside expense for writers, graphic designers, and printers.

SUCCESSFUL APPROACH

Here are the seven steps to preparing the text for an attorney brochure (see following chapter for information on brochure production). Because of the unique needs of attorneys, this method works best:

1. Decide that the objective of the brochure is clear. This is a decision of the managing partner or management committee.
2. Decide the firm's self-perception. This information may already be available from earlier firm analyses. If not, it can be obtained through interviews of key partners, associates, and staff. Remember that all levels within the firm have a stake in the success of the brochure and other marketing activities.
3. Decide the firm's *desired* image through interviews with managing partner and other key attorneys in leadership positions.
4. Decide the firm's desired target audience and specific targets by name. Ensure that these targets mesh with individual practice area objectives.
5. Interview the target audience to learn, not only of their legal and regulatory problems, but also of the concerns in their lives and business outside the legal arena. Questions should uncover legislative (both federal and state) actions that are real or pending.
6. Present findings to the managing partner, then to the business development committee. From their responses, strategy recommendations can be developed that address client concerns in the brochure.
7. Write the brochure text to address client needs, both current and future. Minimize attorney "I" or "we" usage and demonstrate focus on reader by using "you."

TEXT WRITING DILEMMA

A tough issue that brochure teams face is this: Does a brochure, created for business development and marketing, represent the firm as it is? Or does it represent the firm as it wants to be? Most firms use brochures for dual purposes—to describe the firm as it presently exists and to position the firm for other services as well. Of course no firm can misrepresent itself. Yet, for example, do a few real estate contract reviews qualify the firm to claim it offers land use planning services? Aggressive staff will assert that it does. Conservative partners will be uncomfortable, finding the statement of these services indefensible. Yet the firm wants more land use and real estate work. To list or not? Discussion on this issue will reach fundamental levels of vision, direction, and growth.

Once issues of substance are resolved, the actual copywriting and design are easy.

SINGLE PURPOSE

The best brochures are those where everyone involved understands the brochure's *single purpose,* that is, the brochure does not try to do too much. In other words, a law firm brochure will generally have one of four purposes:

1. To introduce the attorneys and their particular skills and areas of emphasis
2. To identify the firm's services, providing sufficient detail so that new clients can fully understand the scope of the firm and existing clients can be "cross-sold" additional services
3. To describe the special character of the firm
4. To describe the benefits the law firm offers in a specific area of legal practice

It may be easy to say "My brochure does all these things." But there is an old axiom of advertising that says "Everything emphasized equals nothing emphasized." In other words, the *narrower the purpose of the brochure, the more effective it will be.*

Multipurposes can sometimes be addressed by designing brochures in component parts. Various pieces can be assembled or arranged to meet several objectives. An example is a "basic" brochure with a pocket in which other information can be placed. The "basic" may fulfill the purpose of describing the scope of the firm's services, with pocket inserts that describe the firm's services in detail. Another insert may introduce the attorneys and their areas of emphasis.

As the brochure production process is underway, attorneys should frequently ask themselves: What is the purpose of this brochure? In doing so, they'll stay narrowly focused and avoid the "everything emphasized equals nothing" flaw regularly seen in many brochures.

RESPONDING TO CLIENT'S INTERESTS

The final word on brochures is this: Brochures and the information in them are of most value, according to survey results of recipients, if they highlight three things: (1) the specific area of expertise of the attorney(s), (2) the outcome of cases, and (3) the success rate with certain types of cases. Brochures are also most effective when accompanied by a capability statement that responds directly to that client's particular legal need.

It's hard to resist writing "everything to everyone" but the more carefully focused, rifle-shot versus shotgun approach to brochure writing is the better solution.

CHAPTER 56
Brochure Production: Understanding Costs and the Production Process

SUMMARY

When producing a brochure or similar promotional piece, attorneys need to understand some of the basics of print production and the impact of each on the total cost of the project. Attorneys usually will take a crack at writing their own brochure (often a big mistake!), but they always need to go outside for design and printing. Awareness of printing terms and designer's graphic devices helps those responsible for the process to be more effective and avoid costly errors.

This chapter discusses

- brochure writing, design, and printing costs.
- content and design elements of the brochure.
- practical tips for attorneys during the brochure production process.

PHOTOGRAPHY/ARTWORK

Being document oriented, attorneys will focus on the text of a brochure rather than other elements such as photography and illustrations. But these other elements can say as much about a firm as the most eloquent prose.

Pictures, graphs, charts, and other types of illustrations can shorten required reading time and improve comprehension. The eyes of readers generally look to photos or illustrations first, headlines second, captions or "callouts" third, and text last. Therefore, the messages delivered by these other elements are often just as important as the text itself!

In most attorney brochures, the text is frequently accompanied by photographs. When using photography or other artwork, remember the rule that every good designer and art director lives by: It is better to use no photo at all than to use one of less than the highest quality.

Good photography is both dynamic and dramatic, designed and printed to get attention. But to be effective, it must also be substantive and document the attorney's capability.

Photography can be misused to satisfy oversized egos. A common mistake is to use a photograph of a firm member in the body of the brochure, making the entire brochure an embarrassment to the firm as soon as one of those pictured depart. Identifiable photos are better used on brochure inserts, if at all.

Because photography is such a strong medium for projecting an attorney's image, a good photographer can help translate the attorney and the firm into visual images. The skills a good photographer will have include understanding communication and attorney capability as well as photography.

COSTS

How much does a brochure cost? This is like asking: "How much does it cost to defend a client in court?" The answer is never simple, nor can it really be known at the beginning of the project. Brochures can cost as little as $500, whereas some law firms spend $35,000 and more on a single brochure.

These dollars represent the out-of-pocket costs paid by the attorney to someone else (consultants, writers, typesetters, photographers, illustrators, and printers). There is a hidden cost of brochures in attorney time, depending, of course, on how much "hands-on" work the attorney feels is required. Estimates of brochure costs should also account for attorney time, which like the outside costs can vary from 3 hours to 300.

So how much do brochures cost? It depends on the following factors:

Preplanning. How much has been done? Has a concept been selected? Does the attorney have a design already in mind? Have the contents been selected? Are decisions made regarding all the variables listed here? The cost here is for a consultant to help the attorney arrive at decisions. Costs can be entirely internal or can be developed with the assistance of an outside consultant. Expenses vary tremendously, because consultants will charge hourly rates ranging from $40 to $100 per hour. Time required could be up to 20 hours, or $2,000.

Writing. This depends on the degree of internal consensus and direction that exists. The creation of the text will prompt many substantive issues that need to be resolved beforehand. Writing is relatively swift if attorney agreement is also reached on the brochure's (1) message theme and (2) prose style. Message refers to the single purpose of the brochure; style refers to variables such as formal/casual, first person/third person, and so on. Descriptive brochures should be limited to 250–400 words of general information. Additional text on specific services, practice groups, and so on is a function of brochure size. Attorneys may write the brochure themselves or hire consultants. Time required for 250–400 words is about ten hours. Freelance writers charge $75–100 per hour.

Design. Graphic unity of all printed materials within the attorney's office is important. The brochure is not independent of letterhead, résumés, invoices, and all other printed materials. A graphic designer *must* be involved in the brochure production process. He or she will prepare a design concept, work with the copy writer to assure that text and design work together, and will manage the printer to maintain quality. Good designers will charge up to $100 per hour. An average is $75 per hour for concept and design and $50 for preparation of mechanical artwork and printing management. Prepare to pay a minimum of $1,000 for good design work. Brochures that are larger, use color, require various die cuts, and have unusual folds all require additional time to plan and produce. A general guideline is that the designer will require approximately 20 percent of the total brochure cost.

Photography. Good professional photography can cost $800–1,500 per day. Depending on location, a good photographer can usually be found at the lower end of that range.

Other artwork. Illustrations of a quality appropriate for most law firm brochures will cost at least $300. If a single artist is doing several illustrations, then the cost per unit drops significantly. Like all artists, illustrators vary in style and quality. The amount of detail requires more time, therefore higher costs.

Mechanical art and author's corrections. Once all the components of a brochure are assembled and approvals are obtained for copy and preliminary design, the designer will send final copy revisions to the typesetter and begin the preparation of mechanical art. The designer will seek approval of the finished art before submitting it to the printer. Changes made on the designer's mechanical art are costly; even more expensive are author's (attorney) corrections made on the printer's proof (sometimes called blue line) submitted for final approval and sign-off immediately prior to printing. At the blue line stage of the process, even changing one word in a brochure can cost $250 in additional designer and printer fees!

Paper. Most attorneys are surprised when a designer or printer shows them the vast selection of papers available for brochures. Paper has many, many characteristics, most of which affect its price. Those variables most frequently encountered by attorneys are

- *Color.* Most attorney brochures are printed onto one color of paper. Multipage brochures can use different colors of paper for interesting effects. Another option is to "reverse" print, where ink covers all the paper, except for the textual areas. The color of the text is actually the color of the paper. To the untrained eye, this looks like two colors—for instance, black ink on white paper and, elsewhere, "white" ink on "black" paper. Generally, the selection of different colors of paper has little if any affect on cost.
- *Texture.* Great varieties exist, each one having a different "feel" and thereby giving a different "feel" to the attorney or firm described on it. Linen, gloss, bond, coated, and book are all words that describe the texture of paper. Coated paper is more expensive than uncoated; linen is more expensive than bond. Generally, the cost is minimal when put in perspective of the overall brochure budget.
- *Weight.* There are also dozens of different weights, described in technical terms such as 24-pound bond and 80-pound cover. Usually, the heavier the stock, the greater the cost. The impact of heavier paper (giving a feeling of "substance") is generally worth the small additional cost.

Number of colors of ink. The more used, the more the brochure costs. Many excellent brochures are produced using one color. One color of ink can be combined with colored paper and printed in various densities (called screens) to give the impression of several colors. Most attorney brochures use two colors, which provide opportunities to create a much greater variation of colors. If four colors are selected, printers can create unlimited additional ones. In the printer's world, there are four primary colors—black, yellow, magenta (near red), and cyan (near blue). These are combined on four-color presses to create all other colors. Using two colors instead of one increases costs slightly (sometimes less than $100). However, using four

Here are some well-tested tips on actual production of the brochure and related printed items.

- Centralize control of the process, preferably with a single person responsible for production of the brochure and related items.
- Understand that a brochure is not a single printed item. In its best form, a brochure is a series of items, usually components that can be organized into a presentation package.
- Realize that the brochure process will prompt substantial questions about the attorney/firm goals and internal structure. Also realize that the process of brochure production will raise seemingly unrelated issues such as compensation policies, because a total plan will involve use of the brochure after production. A comprehensive distribution plan involves attorney time which will take away from billable hours. Be prepared to address these clearly before beginning the process.
- Never forget that the client is the focus of the brochure—not the attorney or firm. If the text too frequently uses the first person or third person (I/we or they), the brochure is attorney focused. The use of the second person (you) guarantees that it is focused at the reader.
- Before writing text for the brochure, achieve consensus on features of the firm ("we have practice groups") and link them to benefits to the client ("which provide a depth of service").
- Accept the fact that less is more. Readers of general brochures will spend no more than two to three minutes reviewing them and accompaning information. Therefore lengthy expositions on any topic go unread. Let the details be tailored in accompanying correspondence.
- Strive for a marriage of design and text as early as possible in the copywriting process. Words that are approved on standard paper suddenly take a far different emphasis and meaning when designed into a brochure.
- In the development process, present to the complete partnership or managing committee the design and copy at two or three junctures along the way. This ensures adoption by the total firm upon completion.
- In general, it is advisable to bring in outside consultants who are knowledgeable in graphic design and text writing, as well as sensitive to the specific needs of law firms.

Figure 56-1 Brochure Production Checklist

colors usually means a different type and larger press must be used, which has a significant impact on costs.

Special effects: Embossing, die cutting, and foil stamping. Interesting brochures can be created using any or all of these effects.

- For prestige, *embossing and debossing* takes printing into a third dimension: depth. Paper is pressed between two molds, called dies, that sculpt its fibers. Images higher than the rest of the paper are embossed; images lower are debossed. To create this effect a die must be made. Costs depend on size. Embossing generally cannot be done for less than $500 at any size or quantity.

- *Die cutting* is the process of cutting the paper into irregular shapes such as pocket flaps on presentation folders or slots for business cards and so on. Most printers have commonly used dies. Brochures with designs calling for unusual cuts will require hand crafting of the die. Standard die cuts can add $300 or more to brochure. Custom dies will be over $500.
- *Foil stamping*. This is a popular technique for attorneys, because it adds immediate prestige and color to a printed piece. In this process, a small piece of color film is applied during the printing process. Again, costs will never be less than $300, no matter what quantity of brochure is printed. Foils usually cost $500 and more. Some foils will curl under the heat of laser printers. Check this!

Folds. Good designers can suggest to attorneys interesting ways to arrange information in a brochure so that it unfolds in a significant and effective way. The fibers in paper run in a parallel direction, so folds should not be against the fibers or the paper will "crack." Custom folds can cost up to $200 each depending on equipment required and so on.

Quantity. At less than 500 copies, the per copy cost of printing is high. There are significant price breaks at quantities between 500 and 2,000. Generally speaking, the per copy cost does not drop fast after 2,000 copies.

Chapter 57
Brochure Distribution: The Weakest Link in the Communication Chain

SUMMARY

Storage rooms are no place for brochures. The value of printed materials is dependent on their distribution. A comprehensive brochure distribution plan requires some attorney and staff time but not a burdensome amount.

This chapter discusses

- a practical distribution plan for brochures.
- who should receive firm brochures and the process for getting them to them.

Just as a thoughtful process precedes brochure production, so too must a comprehensive program follow it to ensure proper and effective use. Many excellent brochures are developed by attorneys, but their marketing value, for which ostensibly they were prepared, is severely diminished due to the lack of a comprehensive distribution program.

Along with potential new clients, existing clients should receive a copy. In firms, all attorneys and staff should be the first to receive the brochure so that the internal consensus and vision achieved is clearly explained and understood by the people who carry it out.

DISTRIBUTION PLAN

Here is a general recommendation that seems to work for most attorneys and law firms.

To be successful, this program requires the support of management, the resources of staff, and the motivation of individual attorneys.

The first two requirements can be controlled. The third requirement is more difficult to meet. This program, designed to consume minimal attorney time, nevertheless requires thought and action on the part of all attorneys and staff. Essentially, this program is an organized approach to get the right information to the right people in the right way at the right time.

The approach here is to identify as many individual audiences as possible, and tailor the distribution program to them. In the program described following, there are three sample cover letters attached to accompany mailed brochures, although there are 15 "audiences" identified in this discussion. All other cover letters will vary slightly from the first three. Since distributing a brochure can, in part, be considered direct mail, attorneys are well advised to know their audience so as to avoid the ethical issues involved with direct solicitation. To carry out this program, an attorney must

- Designate a single person as literature distribution coordinator. That person facilitates individual attorney action to deliver or mail the literature within the appropriate context. This action is an ongoing activity.
- Prepare generic conveyance letters and scripts for various situation.
- Have the coordinator meet with all practice group heads and/or attorneys to review the list of audiences and implement a course of action.

- To organize this, the coordinator will need to develop a data base of audiences with a "contact history."

The first step is to identify "audiences" important to the attorney or firm, then to determine who should send or deliver the brochure.

COMMUNICATION WITH ATTORNEYS AND STAFF

The first audience is always the firm's own timekeepers. The brochure is distributed by the managing partner and conveyed usually with a cover letter of some sort. An example is presented in Figure 57-1.

Another "audience" is the internal staff. A suggested letter to convey the brochure to them is presented in Figure 57-2.

A third audience is existing clients with various needs, not all of which have been met by the attorney or firm. This provides an opportunity to continue good client relations as well as present the potential for cross-selling. A sample letter is shown in Figure 57-3.

TO: Attorneys and Staff
FROM: Managing Partner

Our new firm brochure is now ready for use. While we all know our firm well, hardly a day goes by where one of us doesn't learn something new about another's area of practice. I feel this literature and the accompanying inserts can be valuable for us internally as well as for outsiders to know and understand who we are and what we do. I'd like you to take a few minutes to look over these materials.

We encourage you to use this literature in many ways. We have designated (name) as our literature distribution coordinator. She (he) will help you in your distribution of the brochure and other marketing needs. Our goal is to make the most effective presentation on behalf of the entire firm.

One "target" of the brochure is existing clients, many of whom use us for only a single type of service and use other law firms for services that we can readily provide. We hope to cross-sell our services. Another "target" is potential clients who request a specific service or are after general counsel.

In general, we feel that this literature helps to capture the spirit and strength of our firm. We have a strong philosophy and a solid approach to the practice of law that is unique among firms our size. Thank you for your role in it.

(Signed) Managing Partner

Figure 57-1 Brochure Conveyance Letter to Attorneys and Staff

TO: Firm Staff
FROM: Managing Partner

Our new firm literature is now ready for use. I'd like you to take a few minutes to read these materials and learn a little more about the firm for which you work. These materials can be valuable for us internally as well as with outsiders to know and understand who we are and what we do.

I feel this literature helps to capture our spirit and strength. We have a strong philosophy and a solid approach to the practice of law that is unique among firms our size.

Everyone who works for the firm plays a role in its success. Thank you for your hard work and loyalty.

(Signed) Managing Partner

Figure 57-2 Brochure Conveyance Letter to Staff

Other typical audiences for attorney brochures are these:

- Existing clients with specific needs not met by the attorney or firm
- Potential clients with general and known legal needs
- Potential clients with specific and known legal needs
- Attendees at firm-sponsored seminars and symposiums
- Other attorneys with general but unknown legal needs
- Other attorneys with specific but unknown legal needs
- Other attorneys with general and known legal needs
- Other attorneys with specific and known legal needs
- Financial advisors, other consultants, significant others, that is, referral sources
- Other attorneys as laterals
- Law schools
- Business editors

Distribution of the brochure should be from the individual attorney or the firm member with the closest affiliation. Distribution is easiest via mail, although more impact is obtained if the brochure is personally handed out. Because personal delivery may seem awkward to some attorneys, a script should be prepared for use. Language similar to that used in the sample letters is appropriate.

TO: Primary Contacts and Decision Makers at Existing Client Organizations
FROM: Lead Attorney

You know our firm and the work we have done for you over the years. It is a real pleasure for us to have clients such as you, and we appreciate the opportunity to be of service.

We feel we are a unique firm with a strong philosophy and approach to the practice of law. The enclosed literature and related materials clearly identify those areas of the law where we can provide valuable assistance. It's hard to capture the spirit and strength of a firm through print, but we feel that these materials reflect our firm very well.

> Our firm has grown and changed over the years. We provide a broad spectrum of legal services. In the past few years, our (city) office has grown tremendously, adding to our regional scope. Our business law services have expanded to many new areas.

Our clients often know some of the attorneys within our firm and use some of our services. At the same time, they may be unaware of our ability to meet their other legal needs.

Thank you again for your trust and confidence in us to meet your continuing legal needs.

Regards,

(Signed) Lead Attorney

Figure 57-3 Letter to Existing Clients

CHAPTER 58
To Advertise or Not: The Attorney's Decision to Buy Visibility

SUMMARY

Attorney advertising ranges from direct selling of services via television to subtle "tombstone" announcements in opera programs. The value to attorneys and to clients alike can be great. Advertising is generally expensive, but is necessary for transactional-based practices to attract business. Advertisements not only "sell" but can also impart valuable and useful information.

This chapter discusses

- the most common methods of attorney advertising.
- the value of advertising to attorney.
- the value of advertising to clients.
- the difference between "message" advertisements and "image" advertisements.
- the means to produce effective advertisements.

The decision following *Van O'Steen and Bates* v. *State Bar of Arizona* opened up virtually any kind of advertising method available—magazines, television, directories, direct mail. It also allowed the message to be as aggressive and direct as imaginable. Successful advertising is presented in words and pictures that appeal to and are understood by the client. Since there are so many options for the attorney to advertise, the kind of advertising undertaken and the message it contains depends heavily on who the attorney wants to talk to. Successful advertising of any kind is client focused, speaking to an audience in their language. Different media and different messages can effectively reach the corporate client, the senior citizen, young families buying their first house, or any other group the attorney wishes to reach.

COMMON METHODS OF ATTORNEY ADVERTISING

There is no single way to reach each audience. More than one approach is often used. Advertising for attorneys is commonly found in

1. the Yellow Pages.
2. directories.
3. public print media (local newspapers, trade journals, event programs, etc.).
4. public broadcast media (television and radio).

Advertising is paid space. The purchaser controls the message to as broad or as narrow an audience as desired. The style and content of attorney advertisements run from tombstone announcements of new partners on the newspaper business pages to the "divorce for $200" huckster-style television promotions on the late-night TV movie.

The opportunities for attorneys to advertise are almost limitless today. Significant time has passed since the 1977 *Bates* decision so that virtually any form is accepted or at least tolerated by local bars. In advertisements ranging from cable TV to classified advertisements in free neighborhood "shoppers," attorneys now advertise their services.

Since one goal of attorney business development programs is the attracting of attention, the competition to get attention is fierce. Advertising offers a controllable method of attracting it. Therefore, many attorneys are finding their advertising budgets also to be fierce. It's not uncommon for individual attorneys to spend up to 10 percent of their gross monthly income on advertising.

VALUE TO ATTORNEY

Consumer advocates laud attorney advertising because it provides attorneys with a means of informing people of their rights and opportunities under the law to obtain justice. Many attorneys themselves deplore advertising, thinking it at best an unprofessional activity that hurts the image of all attorneys and encourages unnecessary legal action.

But it is clear that advertising by attorneys has achieved a permanent place in the business development process, and virtually every attorney will advertise at one point or another in the development of his or her own practice.

Here is a list of the goals that advertising can accomplish for a law firm:

- Position the firm strongly in the marketplace, creating name recognition and perception of leadership.
- Identify firm with new services.
- Show that the firm is aggressive and growth oriented.
- Create image of competence and professionalism.
- Create loyalty through reinforcement of the firm name and services.
- Attract new attorneys, laterals, and associates.
- Attract new personnel, both professional and staff.
- Build goodwill and improve reputation.
- Reawaken interest of previous client.
- Create name and service awareness for referral sources.
- Attract new clients.

Advertising performs another function for the client-focused attorney. It tends to reinforce among existing clients that they have purchased the services of a reputable attorney and that future purchases are a "safe buy."

VALUE TO CLIENTS

Many attorneys can find comfort that advertising not only creates awareness of services among potential clients, but performs a public service as well. It can have instructional value, telling the public what to look for in legal services. It can tell clients the importance of communication between client and attorney, timely follow-up and open fee discussion.

USES BY ATTORNEYS

For attorneys practicing "retail" law, advertising is almost mandatory, due to fierce competition and the relative lack of loyalty among clients. Advertisements are usually found in the general-interest media, including the Yellow Pages. Typical examples are practice areas such as plaintiff personal injury, plaintiff medical malpractice, immigration law, divorce and other domestic relations, personal bankruptcy, and wills and estates. The content and form of the advertisements tend to be attention getting. Yellow Page advertising works work best when it lists all the services provided by the attorney.

Advertising for attorneys serving institutional or corporate clients will be more often found in directories, bulletins, or programs at cultural events. These advertisements tend to be discreet and inconspicuous. They will rarely list any direct services or benefits. They serve primarily the "reinforcement" function, and are intended to be viewed by existing clients.

The options to advertise are many for attorneys. With the proliferation of communication channels and the general trend toward specialization of messages, it is now possible for any advertiser to target a specific audience, defined as narrowly as demographic studies permit.

Even major business markets can be reached cost effectively through regional editions of major business media. When done well, advertising can provide both direct and indirect benefits for attorneys in most areas of the law.

PREPARING THE ADVERTISEMENT

Each form of advertising has its own advantages and disadvantages. Each has different methods of production and varying degrees of cost. But one thing they all have in common is their requirement for a single theme that is delivered in the message.

In the development of most advertisements, one of three themes will dominate the message: *price, quality,* and *service.* Presumably, before an attorney advertises, he or she has developed internal consensus and agreement that enables him or her to single out one of these three as the predominate message of their communications. The advertisements are merely an extension of this theme.

Naturally, most attorneys will say "I deliver on all three of those qualities." But really? Some attorney advertisements clearly deliver the message that they are less expensive than the competition. Advertisements that feature this message will usually mention fee or contingency. Advertisements that feature quality will often refer to the qualifications of the attorneys, their experience, and results. Those that feature service discuss issues such as quick response time, constant communication, and attorneys that are easy to work with.

While the legal practice of every attorney will offer degrees of all three qualities, it is important for one to dominate the attorney's advertising and all the other communication devices (in brochures, personal conversations, etc.). Remember the axiom in advertising, "Everything emphasized equals nothing emphasized." In advertisements that emphasize everything, the message gets garbled. Good attorney advertisements should follow this guideline too—pick one theme and go with it.

TYPES OF ADVERTISEMENTS

It is helpful for attorneys to think of advertising as falling into two general categories, which we call *message advertisements* and *image advertisements*.

Message advertisements deliver information about the attorney or firm's practice, often listing services, types of cases handled, and perhaps even a few qualifications of the practitioner(s). (Be aware of ethical considerations when listing qualifications in advertisements.)

Image advertisements always contain the attorney or firm name and may communicate some information, but they do not specifically sell legal services. Image advertisements are sometimes called identity advertisements, because they establish or reinforce a strong identification of the attorney or firm. Examples are advertisements that appear in opera bulletins to the effect of "John Jones, attorney-at-law, a lifetime member of the Millview Opera Association" or "Jones and Jones, celebrating our 100th anniversary of practicing law."

Image advertisements are often a statement of the attorney or firm's name, or a simple message not specifically related to the practice of law, that is, "Support Your Local Art Museum," a public service message of Jones and Jones, attorneys-at-law."

Both types of advertisements serve a valuable function. Their use depends greatly on the attorney sponsoring the advertisement, the intended audience, and the medium in which they appear. The level of advertising among attorneys is expanding rapidly, and the amount of money being spent is growing. Of the two general categories, message advertisements capture the vast majority of expenditures.

HOW TO CREATE

Essentially, there are three ways to produce advertisements:

1. Produce the advertisement in-house. This is possible for print advertisements only. The assistance of a graphic designer and a typesetter will usually be needed. The attorney will need personally to contract for the space or airtime at the media of choice.
2. Ask the media to produce it. Every newspaper, magazine, or broadcast station provides this service. The advertisement is usually designed to be used only in the media that produces it.
3. Hire an advertising agency to produce and place the advertisement. An agency will help develop the attorney's "message." They will also make sure the advertisement accurately reflects the firm's personality and services. They will ensure that the advertisement is appropriate for the intended audience. They will also handle all production and the buying of the media.

Each of these approaches can be very satisfactory. The ultimate success of the advertisement will depend on the attorney's selection of the right approach for the particular situation.

The next chapter discusses more detail on each of these three approaches to producing advertising.

CHAPTER 59
Producing Effective Advertising: Looking Good by Doing it Right

SUMMARY

Attorney advertising is most effective when produced by outside professionals. This is also the most costly approach. Few attorneys know that media provide "free" advertising services. Attorneys can maintain full control over their advertisements by doing it themselves, seeking limited outside assistance.

This chapter discusses

- the three methods attorneys can use to produce advertising.
- advantages and disadvantages of each.
- the most effective method to use.

Virtually every advertising program requires outside professional help. There are degrees to which the attorney can be involved in the process. Basically, it works in one of three ways:

1. At a minimum, *attorneys can produce an advertisement themselves,* using the services of a typesetter and designer to create a combination of logo, artwork, and text in the right sizes and proportions (this applies to print advertisements only; anything to be broadcast over radio or television definitely needs the work of a professional).
2. The chosen *media can provide creative and production services* to write and produce an advertisement that will be satisfactory.
3. However, attorneys will generally be more satisfied with the results if they work with an *advertising or public relations firm* and the advertising is integrated into a more comprehensive business development program.

Any of the three approaches will produce an advertisement. Whether the quality is good and the advertisement is effective may be a matter of opinion. Attorneys can produce good advertisements themselves, the media like to do their own work, and a good advertising or PR agency will do an outstanding job. Here are the pros and cons of each of these approaches.

DO IT YOURSELF

If an attorney chooses to produce an advertisement using only the services of a designer and typesetter, the attorney will get exactly what he or she wants, having absolute control over the development and outcome.

However, the overall quality may suffer without strong outside direction. Designers vary greatly in their ability, and some will have a strong influence over the outcome of the finished product, while others will function as a "pasteup" person and execute whatever the attorney wants. The typesetter will respond to the designer's wishes, providing the various type sizes, weights, and faces required.

Generally, this approach involves quite a bit of attorney time to compose the advertisement and manage the outside consultants. A working knowledge of the language of designers and typesetters is very useful. The cost varies considerably depending on the quality of design, but generally a designer will work to a budget, no matter how small it may be. Out-of-pocket costs can be tightly controlled with this direct relationship, although a hidden "cost" is the attorney's time to manage it.

LET THE MEDIA DO IT

With this approach, the attorney will relinquish much control of the final outcome but will be assured of on-time and within-budget delivery. The newspaper, magazine, TV station, and even the Yellow Pages will provide advertising production services.

The quality of the finished advertisement will be adequate but won't win awards. This is not to discredit the media, but merely a realization that their primary business is not the production of the advertisements but rather the publishing or broadcasting of them. Most media approach advertisement production with a competent but modest effort—simple design and straightforward messages—using their own in-house people.

In addition, the media will produce an advertisement for their own uses only. In other words, if an attorney wishes to buy space in several newspapers, the advertisement created for one cannot be used in another. This means that the advertisement will look different everywhere it appears. There will no continuity of design.

For the attorney, this approach is the least expensive of all, because the media in many cases will include their production costs in the price of the advertisement itself. There are exceptions to this, so the issues must be clearly discussed before any contracts are signed. The media usually give a discount to agencies or designers who produce the advertisement and purchase the space or time. An attorney buying the space or time directly without an agency involved will get no discount.

HIRE AN AGENCY

Advertising agencies exist because they provide a valuable service. They exist solely to help their clients sell their products and services. They get results for their clients and keep them satisfied, or they go out of business.

Therefore, an attorney can approach an established advertising agency with the confidence in knowing that they will be able to understand what the attorney wants and deliver a satisfactory product.

Just as there are attorneys who emphasize different areas of the law, most advertising agencies specialize in certain types of work. Because advertising for attorneys is a relatively new area, many good agencies do not have this experience, although they may have worked with other professional service firms such as accountants and medical service providers. Firms with this kind of experience are usually qualified to assist attorneys.

Another good source is public relations firms. PR firms will not promote their advertising services but most of them have been involved in helping their clients establish an image and developing some sort of visual representation for it. PR firms (as do advertising agencies) also have access to a wealth of freelance creative talent for use in design, photography, creative writing, and editing.

Most agencies offer complete services, including development of a message theme (if one has not been established) and suggestions for placement, size, frequency, and so on. The services of agencies are comprehensive. Independent designers, trained to create attractive graphics, may respond to specific requests to produce an advertisement by asking "What size do you want it? Will you be using photos? Where do you want it to appear?" But an agency, with a more comprehensive view, will ask "Why do you want to advertise? Have you considered other alternatives to reaching your audiences? Who is your audience?" Once the answers to these questions are resolved in concert with the agency, the actual design can begin.

The agency will handle all advertising issues and usually produce a high-quality product. The attorney will require little "hands-on" management of the project, except for approvals. The agency will charge for its services by asking for creative fees and reimbursement of expenses. The agency will also have income from the discount it receives from the media. When an agency purchases on the attorney's behalf, the agency is obligated to pay the media. For this service (and inherent risk), the agency bills the attorney at full rate and pays the media the discounted rate.

IMPORTANCE OF USING AN EXPERIENCED AGENCY

Attorneys are well advised to locate either advertising or public relations firms with *successful* experiences with other attorneys. Most established agencies will claim experience, simply because any advertising or PR firm in business for a few years will have come in contact with at least one attorney wanting some publicity, an advertisement, or a brochure. But not all experiences are good ones, so it will pay to check references. If any attorney selects the wrong agency to guide and direct a marketing program, the *entire practice development effort will be less than successful* and viewed with suspicion by colleagues.

In general, it is best for attorneys to spend the money up front and hire professionals to produce the advertisement. The cost of design and production is relatively small compared to the cost of the space or airtime in the media. It makes no sense to allocate thousands of dollars to buy advertising media and only a few (if any) to ensure that the advertisement is as effective as it can be.

Chapter 60
Choosing the Right Type of Advertising and Not Paying Too Much for It

SUMMARY

Most attorney advertising is printed or broadcast, although other methods to advertise are possible. Attorneys are improving their traditional "tombstones" by designing eye-catching display ads that appeal to the intended audience. Costs vary dramatically but can be held down by understanding the many variables involved such as size, number of colors, frequency, and location.

This chapter discusses

- the three types of *printed* advertisements: tombstones, classifieds, and displays.
- "advertorials," publicity you buy in the same manner you buy advertising.
- new options open to attorneys in *broadcast* advertising.
- effective use of "specialty" advertising.
- the cost of advertising and factors that affect it.

Attorneys are most familiar with *tombstones,* which they run frequently in bar journals and occasionally in other media to announce mergers, new partners and associates, the opening of a new office, and other activities. Tombstones are most frequently designed and produced by the media in which they appear. Rarely is any "creativity" put into tombstones, although a law firm can hire a designer or agency to create a more attractive tombstone that produces a stronger and usually more sophisticated impression of the firm. Once a tombstone format is selected, the attorney or firm should use the design consistently to remain distinctive and memorable to readers.

More and more, tombstones are being published in the general interest media to announce an attorney's involvement in a major business transaction. They are becoming much more accepted by even the most conservative law firm as a way to increase visibility.

Classified advertisements. have virtually no design or creative elements. They merely impart information in a format and location that by definition groups them together with hundreds of other advertisements that are similar in appearance. Classifieds are frequently used by attorneys for recruitment purposes. For business development purposes, they are of value only to attract clients with immediate problems, such as bankruptcy or motor vehicle violations. They are relatively inexpensive to purchase and easy to produce.

Display advertisement. is a broad term that can be used to describe an advertisement that is not a tombstone or a classified. Unlike the other two, they will have design elements and will most likely include the attorney's logo or logo type. They will have varying sizes and weights of type. They may use a picture or some other form of artwork.

Other than in the Yellow Pages, attorneys tend not to use display advertisements very much, although their use will no doubt continue to grow.

ADVERTORIALS

One form of advertising that is being used effectively by attorneys in the print media is "advertorials." They are a combination of an advertisement and an editorial, purchased and published usually in a regional business magazine. Advertorials are printed in a news story format, providing the credibility of a news story with the control of advertising. Advertorials allow the attorney to determine the message and placement, along with allowing sufficient space to explain a situation and present a significant message in a thoughtful presentation.

Reprints of advertorials are usually available through the publication, and are extremely useful as a promotional piece. Purchase of advertorial space and reprints is handled through the advertising sales office of the news media.

BROADCAST ADVERTISING

In the broadcast area, *radio* and particularly *television* are effective methods to increase client awareness of attorney services. Both of these can be effective, if the advertising is professionally produced and carefully selected.

Broadcast media can be as effective as print to reach various audiences. Radio and television stations have a large amount of information about their listeners and viewers, such as typical age, income level, and buying habits. Therefore, broadcast advertising can be as effective as print, enabling the attorney to aim advertising exactly at the intended audience.

In broadcast, both types of advertising are used by attorneys—message ads to encourage business development and image ads to create visibility and build goodwill. The message ads are typically sponsored by consumer-oriented attorneys; image ads tend to be created by attorneys and firms that aim at the corporate and institutional markets.

When criticism of attorney advertising comes, it usually centers on television. Television messages can range from the serious, which are generally well done, to the ridiculous. One advertising program in particular that was subject of much criticism was that of a Wisconsin attorney who was shown emerging from a lake to the tune of Tchaikovsky's "Swan Lake," his corpulent and hairy-chested torso adorned with necklaces, bracelets, and other jewelry.

"If you're in over your head because of bad debts or inflation, call the Legal Clinic and we'll take care of your problems. We'll get you through the bankruptcy for $200."

After giving his phone number he reaches down into the water and pulls up a 300-pound woman by the hair. "And here's the person who answers the telephone," he says.

In another situation, attorneys on television have promised to buy their clients a 10-speed bicycle if they don't win a drunk driving case for them.

These kind of advertisements can be called "effective" if the objective was to attract attention, because they did. If they were effective because they attracted new clients who were willing and capable of paying is something else.

SPECIALTY ADVERTISING

The term "specialty advertising" refers to a variety of items that carry the advertiser's name and sometimes the advertiser's address and a short sales message. The specialty is often (but not always) inexpensive and handed out free of charge to selected clients or others. Examples commonly used by attorneys range from coffee mugs, fountain pens, and desk sets to etched glassware, calendars, and key chains.

Specialties have the same purpose as other kinds of advertising. They are used to cause the attorney or firm to be remembered. Attorneys use them in various ways to remind the receiver of the attorney or firm's presence, goodwill, or practice area.

A distinct advantage of specialties is their long life. Printed advertisements are gone with the next issue; broadcast ads are gone in 30 or 60 seconds. Properly selected and distributed advertising specialties can be around a long time. They are extremely flexible. The attorney can select an expensive item for a few clients or referral sources or, if the audience justifies it, a very inexpensive item.

Two rules apply when attorneys select a specialty item: it must be of reasonably good quality, and it must be useful. A third and desirable criterion is that it has some significance for the law firm and the receiver.

This connection among attorney, advertising item, and receiver is often hard to achieve. Consequently, most advertising specialities fail to obtain direct results for attorneys. There can be some advantages to massive distribution of ballpoint pens for a domestic relations attorney. But the cost and effort associated with the activity generally does not return direct new business benefits.

Often, attorneys will purchase various items for internal purposes as much as external marketing. T-shirts and baseball caps for a firm team are great for company morale at a group picnic. Coffee cups and pens are popular with professionals and staff alike. Often, the low cost of various items makes it simply fun to have them around the office or distribute them to selected clients. However, the role of advertising specialties in a business development program will always remain relatively small.

COSTS

Because most attorneys approach advertising with great caution, they spend modestly. The paradox of good advertising is that to be effective, it must be very well produced (which costs money), it must be used extensively (which costs even more), and it must be consistent in design and appearance. Many attorneys have built successful practices on the basis of aggressive advertising. Anyone seriously considering advertising as the backbone of their business development program must be prepared for significant cash outlays.

A personal injury attorney in Boston recently spent 11 percent of the firm's $20 million in fee business for advertising space. The attorney was quoted as saying that an earlier advertising program, at approximately 3 percent of fees, did little good. "It must be significant to reap the benefits," he said. "A little bit does almost nothing."

Advertising expense is no small matter, and costs vary tremendously depending on circulation of the media. For instance, Yellow Page rates can range up to $150 a month for a one-inch box to more than $3,000 a month for a half-page advertisement, and many attorneys need to be in multiple phone books to ensure geographic coverage. Other kinds of print advertising (newspaper and magazine) can cost as little as $100, but generally go much higher. Television is more expensive yet. Production costs for a 30-second television spot can run from $5,000 to $50,000. Added to this is the cost of "airtime," which can run from $100 for a 30-second spot during midday to more than $5,000 for prime-time evening. And these are the local station costs! Network advertising can run 20 times as much.

Radio is probably the least used medium for attorney advertising. But in a cost-benefit analysis, it may be the best buy for attorneys seeking to reach the general consumer. Radio ads are relatively inexpensive to produce. A particular audience can be targeted fairly easy because of the great number of radio stations and the highly defined audiences they capture. Production costs for radio are generally less than both television and print media. If the attorney chooses to let the media produce the work, radio will offer the highest degree of satisfaction, compared to print or television media. Costs to broadcast a 30-second radio advertisement can be as low as $25, depending on frequency and time of day.

Advertorials will cost about the same as a full-page color advertisement, which can range from $3,000 to $7,000 in a regional business magazine. Through reprints of the advertorial (usually negotiated with the publication), this cost compares favorably with the production of an inexpensive brochure. However, the reprint is clearly not a "brochure" but can function effectively as a credibility-building communication device.

To check on specific rates for any media, a call to a sales representative will bring quick answers over the phone. The key variables in the print media are these:

- Size. The larger the advertisement, the more expensive it will be. The cost tends to increase exponentially.
- Number of colors. The more there are, the greater the cost. Most advertisements are one color (black); a second and third color can be added at a relatively modest cost; a fourth color usually requires a different printing process and equipment and therefore becomes significantly more expensive. If used, a fourth color generally permits an advertisement to be produced in full color, using photographs.
- Frequency. Generally, the more often an advertisement appears in print or on the air, the cheaper will be the cost per each insertion.
- Location or Time Slot. In print media, an advertiser can specify a particular location for the advertisement such as the inside front cover or can let the advertising production people place it anywhere they see fit. Requesting a specific placement costs more. In the broadcast media, a bulk of the cost is determined by the time slot specified. The more listeners or viewers as determined by the station's research, the greater the costs.

CHAPTER 61
Client Newsletters: Are They Worth the Effort?

SUMMARY

Client newsletters are an effective method of maintaining regular client contact. Their popularity with attorneys is growing, and they are proliferating because people everywhere demand specialized news, hence the tremendous amount of special-interest publications. Successful newsletters require equal attention to content, production, and distribution.

This chapter discusses

- role of newsletters in attracting and retaining clients.
- three methods to produce newsletters.
- sources of information for newsletters.
- standards for effective content and high-quality appearance.
- recommended frequencies.

Attorney newsletters are best when they contain specialized information, presenting timely information to people who can use it and benefit from it. Newsletters can make an attorney stand out from the crowd and demonstrate his or her client focus. They can help attorneys establish themselves in an area of practice for which they are relatively unknown but in which they have genuine expertise.

To produce and deliver a newsletter and to have it achieve favorable results for the attorney, each of three links in the communication chain must be given equal status. The three links are *content, production,* and *distribution.* While attorneys will naturally focus on the content, each of the three is critical to overall success. Many firms are sadly surprised when they initiate a newsletter, putting tremendous energy into the content, only to discover later how much time is required to produce and distribute it!

NEWSLETTER OPTIONS

Individual attorneys have three choices of getting a newsletter to send to clients: They may

1. initiate their own newsletter.
2. participate in the preparation of one through their firm or department.
3. purchase a preprinted newsletter.

In this last option, the newsletter is purchased from an outside source. It contains information on general topics on a broad range of subjects, presumably of interest to a great number of readers. The attorneys or their firms simply add their own names and distribute it.

The first two options are discussed in detail below. Preprinted newsletters, because of their impersonal nature, are generally not too valuable for attorneys. They are useful for reminding a client (or potential client) that the attorney is actively practicing. Personalized methods of client contact, including direct mail of all sorts discussed elsewhere in this book, are much more effective.

CONTENT

There are essentially two kinds of newsletters—those presenting general ranges of issues and single-subject issues. Research has shown that individual attorneys have the best success with single-subject newsletters. They have greatest value to a narrow client group with narrow interests. But one of the greatest marketing benefits from general newsletters cannot be overlooked—cross-selling. An attorney who is well known as a land use attorney who produces newsletters solely on land use issues will have great success and build a strong reputation in this area. But very few people may ever know that the attorney is also skilled and experienced in other areas of the law. Newsletters can help to bridge this information gap.

Excellent sources of material for newsletters are internal memos and research work developed for a particular situation. Most attorneys, whether in larger firms or small, conduct research frequently; with extensive rewriting into simple English, it is ideal for client communication.

MAINTAINING READER INTEREST

A main challenge for any newsletter writer is to attract and hold reader interest. Brevity is critical to this, realizing that the newsletter will not be the last word on the issue.

Another method is writing articles in a style that allows for "callouts" and "subheads." They make the newsletter scanable, that is, with headlines that catch the eye. One in-house counsel, who receives no fewer than five unsolicited newsletters each week, says "I give these things 30 seconds each. If they don't have me by then, that's it."

An example of a "callout" is text alongside an article in a size 50 percent larger than the main text. If the article was on new tax legislation, the "callout" could say "This affects companies with profit sharing." That would catch the eye of any corporate treasurer!

Regarding other kinds of content, attorneys are cautioned to use sparingly personality features on individuals or information of personal activities. Yes, they give a flavor and personality to the firm, but they smack of self-aggrandizement and can easily irritate a client. The best advice is to stick to business to maintain reader interest.

Another effective method to hold reader interest and demonstrate attorney expertise is to develop a "point of view." This technique is used effectively in business management to initiate discussion and show leadership. Managers come to meetings or write memos espousing one point of view, instead of fence straddling and arriving at no decision.

A "point of view" can be taken in attorney newsletters on any number of subjects. Instead of taking an issue that is beaten to death in many publications, attorneys can delve into one aspect or creative element of the topic and draw conclusions. Of course, no attempt should be made to give legal advice in a newsletter. But the point here is that readers appreciate knowing the attorney position and beliefs on current issues.

PRODUCTION

The first issue of a newsletter, with a masthead and printed in newspaper-style columns—will require the services of a graphic designer or a good printer with graphic services. The newsletter design should conform to the existing graphic style of the firm. It should use the same type styles and colors of ink and paper in use for the firm letterhead, and so on.

Desktop publishing is growing in popularity, and it will soon find its way into more firms and ultimately onto lawyers' desks. One of the reasons for the growth in newsletters and publications of all sorts is the tremendous change in the graphic design and printing industry in recent years. Now, computer software with "templates" of newsletters is much easier to buy and use than ever before; therefore, costs have dropped and older methods such as typesetting and pasteup are no longer required for the quality of work usually needed in an attorney's newsletter.

A good printer can reproduce a quality newsletter directly from documents produced by a laser printer. Some offices with certain types of high-quality photocopiers can produce the newsletter in-house. Quality must be the deciding factor on final selection of method of production.

FREQUENCY

Newsletters should be prepared whenever there is something to say; some firms have a standard, easy-to-use format and have produced as many as two newsletters *a day*. More common is monthly or quarterly publication. Issues must be published at least three times a year. If this seems like too large a task then the project scope should be reevaluated. Three times a year is a minimum to maintain continuity.

Of most importance is to establish a comprehensive program at the outset that includes equal time devoted to production and distribution so that the newsletter not only looks good but also is delivered to the right people in a timely manner.

Quality must prevail. Conventional wisdom rings true here: "If you are not going to do it well, don't do it at all."

In sum, the experience of most law firms is that newsletters have their greatest value in two areas: in cross-selling and in combating the out-of-sight/out-of-mind problems for attorneys who have infrequent contact with existing or recent clients. Most attorneys and firms realize that in the end, newsletters will not bring in new business. They won't necessarily change buying decisions, but—like so many other of the client communications—will reinforce those who already bought, building and maintaining strong client relationships.

CHAPTER 62
Getting Your Newsletter Read (And Appreciated!)

SUMMARY

Good mailing list management is key to newsletter distribution. Personalized notes improve readership and effectiveness dramatically. Since the outward appearance of the newsletter in the mail can determine if it gets read or tossed, first-class delivery is generally worth the extra cost.

This chapter discusses

- data base management and its role in newsletter distribution.
- effective methods of distribution so that the newsletter gets to the intended reader.

If the attorney makes the effort to write and produce a good newsletter, every attempt must be made to get it into the hands of the people who will find the information of value. Ignoring this small detail can cause the whole effort to be wasted or in some cases even backfire.

For example, one law firm emphasizing municipal law mailed their quarterly newsletter to *all* their clients, referral sources, and friends. Since the newsletter was edited by one of the municipal law attorneys, it contained almost 80 percent information related to this practice area.

But the firm also had a significant number of clients who had no interest in municipal law, such as clients who were served by the firm's worker's compensation practice group. There were other types of clients too, including numerous small firms and individuals who were served on such matters as general corporate business, wills, probate, and estate matters.

When the newsletter was sent to the clients who were not involved with municipal law, the firm began to get negative feedback. The newsletter recipients were looking for "something of relevance to me or else my attorney would not have sent it." Finding nothing of interest, they expressed frustration that the firm wasted their time in sending the newsletter, plus questioned the firm's internal organization and control of external communications.

In situations where a firm develops a general-interest newsletter with several subjects in each issue, attorneys can express their client orientation by ensuring that each newsletter is accompanied with a personalized note drawing attention to something in it. A small note to the effect "I believe you will find the article on profit sharing on page three to be of interest" goes a long way to show personal attention to individual client needs.

THE RIGHT DISTRIBUTION METHOD

The preceding illustration points out the importance of good internal control of client communication. With the multitude of data base software programs available today, an attorney can sort clients and others by their interest area. From this can come a mailing list and labels that enable the attorney to mail specific information to specific people—the ultimate in target marketing!

Unless a firm is very large and there are data processing personnel on staff, mailing list management is best handled by outside vendors. There are companies that provide mailing lists, usually called direct-mail specialists or similar names, that are in business to provide mailing lists of all kinds. These preprepared lists can be purchased in label form, and are generally considered to be about 70 percent reliable (but this can vary, so ask when the list was last updated).

If the attorney prepares his or her own list of names, other companies who specialize in handling mailing lists can be of great assistance. These companies charge for setting up the mailing, printing labels, and making alterations to the list. Typical costs depend on location and service availability. They will range from $35–60 for a one-time-only setup fee, $0.20–0.30 per name added to the list, and $0.10–0.15 per existing name to make changes.

Professional mailing list companies can typically create numerous "fields" of data for each name. A field is a piece of information. A name of a person is a piece of information or a field. The person's title is another field, and so on. Other fields are their Standard Industrial Classification (SIC) Code, street address, city, and zip code. But the real value of the mailing list data base is apparent when other fields are established, such as type of business, area of interest, and legal needs. Almost any number of fields can be created.

This enables the attorney to generate a mailing list of people who meet certain criteria—for instance, all claims managers for insurance companies in New Jersey. A mailing list can easily be generated that contains all persons who have this title, work for this kind of company, and work in this state.

MAILING METHODS

Because the purpose of attorney newsletters is not only to communicate information but also to make a positive impression on recipients, the "package" the newsletter is delivered in is important. The options are a *self-mailer, individual wrapper,* or *standard envelope.*

Self-mailer usually means the newsletter has a place on it for label and stamp, is folded into letter size, and stapled or taped together. Wrappers are almost like envelopes but usually open on the ends. They are usually paper or clear plastic, and may have some sort of message printed on them. The standard number 10 (letter size) envelope is used for the $8\frac{1}{2}$-inch by 11-inch folded newsletter. Thicker newsletters should be mailed flat in larger envelopes.

Any of these three methods is acceptable, providing the newsletter arrives in good condition. Self-mailers are acceptable only if the paper is thick enough to withstand handling. Regardless of how they are wrapped, distribution of attorney newsletters should be via first-class mail. This ensures overnight delivery in many cities and delivery within two days in most.

Bulk mail can result in two-day same-city delivery. Anything beyond 20 miles will take considerably longer. The attraction of bulk mail is its reduced cost. But in the quantities involved for most attorney newsletters, the difference is minimal. Bulk mail permitting regulations change from time to time, so careful attention must be paid to post office regulations. Costs are about $100 for the annual permit. Each piece mailed by a profit-making organization is charged at roughly half the first-class rate. Because of other issues involved with bulk mail (buying an indicia stamp, getting the items into zip code order and bundled correctly, etc.), most law firms find first-class mail to be the better choice.

But perhaps the single greatest reason against using bulk mail is that many people simple toss out, unopened, any bulk material. This may mean that the newsletter never even gets into the hands of the intended receiver, let alone read!

Attorneys can perform a test mailing by addressing at least one newsletter to their home and another to themselves at the office. This will provide information on both delivery time and condition.

CHAPTER 63
Media Relations and the Double-Edged Sword Called Publicity

SUMMARY

"Doing good work" remains the best method of attracting new business, but "telling about it" is equally important today to achieve greater success. Telling about it via publicity is not a goal by itself; however, it is an effective method of attracting attention. It builds credibility more quickly than advertising and is considerably less costly.

This chapter discusses

- the role of the media and their interest in attorney activities.
- a basis of understanding of the news media and their interests and working environments.
- what publicity can and cannot do for an attorney.
- situations and events that are likely to generate media interest for attorneys.

If there is one topic likely to generate conflict within law firms of any size, it is publicity. Tensions occur not only between professional ethics and a pressure for exposure, but also between conservative partners adverse to any but the most traditional ways of business development and aggressive partners eager to promote the records of themselves and their firm.

Most attorneys and law firms want to increase their visibility, but carefully. Only with trepidation are publicity and its attendant "media relations" or active working with the media considered a viable means of business development.

Attorneys normally think of publicity as "getting some good press" for themselves or their firm. Publicity may occur as a result of mergers, naming of new partners, or the opening of a new office. Publicity may also involve a client or case matter. In this situation, the reporter with pencil and microphone may be encountered on the courthouse steps or, more frequently, will call the attorney's (or client's) office for comments. There are numerous situations where clients appreciate their legal counsel handling publicity-related issues for them, or at a minimum advising them in advance as to the publicity potential of the issue. Guidance from legal counsel on the handling of publicity can be of great help to clients.

"Good" publicity about an attorney or client can be useful for an attorney's business development program, but it never made any attorney successful. Publicity may be the result of success, never the cause of it.

Publicity is the publication or broadcast of information in the media. Some of it is desirable and sought after; some not. But in spite of its generally low value in business development, some publicity can have a surprisingly profound effect on an attorney and his her existing clients. Essentially, it reinforces positive client attitudes that the attorney is well known and respected for a particular aspect of the law.

MANAGING THE NEWS

The management of publicity by lawyers may be defined in both *proactive* and *reactive* terms. More and more, attorneys are becoming quite proactive to seek out the media purposefully to draw attention to a situation. But at other times, attorneys must be prepared to react and respond to inquiries about a situation that they would just as soon keep private.

In both forms of publicity, there is one element that makes attorneys extremely nervous: lack of control. In a profession where words are weighed heavily and text is redrafted to express precisely what is meant, the idea of presenting facts to someone else (a media person) for their rewriting is terrifying. There is little alternative to the process. It is no wonder then that individual attorneys are torn between the pros and cons of publicity. Most attorneys will know publicity for what it truly is—a double-edged sword.

ATTORNEYS MAKE NEWS

In the course of virtually every attorney's practice, there will be situations that are newsworthy. In some cases the attorney may actively seek publicity and in others will actively avoid it. The news items can involve the attorney, the firm, a practice area, a specific case, or a specific client. The action of the attorney to "manage" the news depends on the situation.

Here are typical situations where news media attention is possible. Some are topics suitable for news releases, some can be developed into feature articles, and some will result in front-page, high-visibility news:

- New attorneys joining the firm as associates or partners. Of particular interest are laterals.
- New services, usually coupled with the addition of a lateral.
- New literature, such as a report or analysis on a topic adapted for general distribution.
- Availability of a newsletter. Many firms create and distribute a regular newsletter. It can be offered to a selected audience via a news release (recommended to trade journals, narrow-circulation business publications, etc.). Those who request the newsletter are obvious new business potentials!
- New uses for existing services.
- Promotions, elections of attorneys, professional staff.
- Professional awards.
- Election of attorneys to positions of importance in professional groups, community activities, and so on.
- Anniversaries of the firm.
- Addition of new or unusual equipment.
- New or expanded facilities.
- Reports on conditions of an industry.
- Report of research and predictions of trends.
- Virtually any situation involving clients or cases that have attracted media attention before. (Media are particularly sensitive to "anniversaries" of landmark decisions, major litigations, and so on.)
- Any case that can have broader implications for the business community, set a precedent, or signal an economic trend.

One area where attorneys are encountering intense media interest is in any situation that involves subject matter that is "hot." Examples are topics such as abortion, drug use, automatic weapons, frozen embryos, leveraged buyouts, hostile takeovers, and the environment. Any attorney can also be guaranteed publicity, desired or not, when dealing with significant cases in these areas.

A common example of this is attorneys who deal with celebrities or famous personages. Any sort of activity—divorces, bankruptcy, lawsuits, and so on—is likely to attract media attention. Entertainment law attorneys are well aware of the importance of the media to their clients. In conducting any kind of litigation in the entertainment business, the attorney is always aware of how the case will appear in the media. They know that public perceptions created by the media are almost as important as how the case appears in court, because entertainers live and die through their images. The attorney can help or hinder an entertainer's career depending on how he or she deals with the media.

So when the news is handled correctly and the attorney and/or the client's name appears successfully and favorably in the media, the value is great. For the attorney, favorable exposure implies a third-party endorsement. The attorney is perceived at worst as honest and direct and at best as a credible, knowledgeable source sought out by the media for information. In either event, the attorney is a good source for legal counsel, demonstrating real legal expertise.

Chapter 64
Proactive Media Relations: Getting the Media to Pay Attention

SUMMARY

To achieve success in getting publicity, the attorney must know what the news media like to report and must offer story ideas to the media that are truly newsworthy. Effective methods to obtain publicity are to issue news releases, create "feature article" situations, and become an "informed source."

This chapter discusses

- effective methods to obtain favorable publicity.
- how to write a good news release.
- how to get an article published.
- methods to get quoted in the media and to create feature articles about yourself or your firm.

In discussions of business development, most attorneys will consider some sort of program that involves attracting attention to themselves and their work. It's commonly called publicity, with the word "good" implied before it. Attorneys see their peers mentioned in the media and, logically, seek recognition for their own accomplishments.

Advertising is frequently called the "space that you pay for." Good publicity, on the other hand, can be called the "space that you pray for."

The secret to obtaining publicity is to look at situations as a reporter, not an attorney. Reporters are interested in things their readers will find of interest, which may be different from what the attorney finds of interest.

There are two ways to obtain publicity: issue a news release, or seek out some sort of publicity placement. In both cases, the attorney can take steps to present accurate information in the correct format so as to be pleased with the outcome, keeping in mind that final control always rests in the hands of the media themselves.

NEWS RELEASE

A news release is a prepared story or statement, reproduced in quantity and sent to news media that may have an interest in the subject.

Distribution depends on the subject matter. A successful new trade agreement between a local manufacturer and an off-shore distributor is of interest to the local general-interest newspapers and regional business publications. At the same time, the merger of two 100-plus member firms from two major metropolitan cities 300 miles apart is of interest also to area radio and television stations, to national business publications, and to major trade journals (including the trade journals of major client groups of the firms).

News releases are relatively easy to prepare and distribute. The attorney can control the content and ensure the accuracy of all statements. Because of the great quantity of news releases received daily by any news media, the form of the release is important so that it is easy to read and be edited by the media.

Here is a checklist for a professionally prepared news release that will help its chances of getting noticed and used:

- Double spaced.
- Typed on one side of paper only.
- Headline to give editor quick indication of story contents.
- Includes who, what, where, and when. If appropriate, also includes the why and how.
- Has a name, date, and contact phone for more information.
- Written at eighth-grade level, avoiding jargon, citations, and so on.

TOPIC (4–5 words): ____________________

WHAT: ____________________

____

____

WHEN: ____________________

WHERE: ____________________

HOW: ____________________

____

____

WHO WAS/IS INVOLVED: ____________________

____

____

WHY IS THIS IMPORTANT? ____________________

____

____

____

FOR MORE INFORMATION, CONTACT:

Name ____________________ Phone __________

Organization ____________________

Address ____________________

____

Figure 64-1 Sample Fact Sheet.

A useful alternative to the news release is a fact sheet to provide information to the media. This lists the key relevant information in simple, declarative sentences. The media can write a story from the facts or call for more information. In many cases, the media prefer fact sheets because of the clarity of information that they provide. (See Figure 64-1.)

GETTING AN ARTICLE PUBLISHED

Writing an article and getting it published in the news media is a popular method by attorneys to attract favorable attention. For attorneys, these "feature" articles are normally sought in business publications on a topic related to some area of expertise. For example,

- An attorney who emphasizes franchise law can write an article about trends in franchising. It can be localized to a city or region and published in a business magazine or newspaper.
- An attorney who emphasizes admiralty law can write about new national legislation that will affect river traffic in fresh water ports. It would have great interest to commercial shippers of all kinds and thus be suitable for transportation trade journals.
- An attorney who emphasizes land use law can write about a recent annexation of land that demonstrates a creative use of the public involvement process. An article would be suitable for the opinion/editorial section of a local newspaper.

To get an article published, query an editor to determine interest in the subject; then prepare materials specifically (and usually exclusively) for that publication. A same proposal letter is shown in Figure 64-2.

Writing a story for publication is not hard, if the attorney follows a few simple rules.

1. Tell a story. Editors and readers like to read anecdotes. Humanize the situation as much as possible.
2. Explain the situation clearly and easily. The readership is usually not versed in the law and legal language. Write to the eighth-grade level. Keep sentences and paragraphs short.
3. Citations are not necessary; in fact, the article is usually better without them.
4. Write on a topic that is "hot." This means not only one that has popular interest, but also one that excites you and is well within your current expertise.
5. Since you are telling a story, write all at once. Avoid interruptions; then go back a day later and edit your essay.

As with news releases, the format is almost as important as the content. Make sure it is double spaced and the margins are wide.

Dear Editor:

I would like to write an article of interest to your readers. The subject matter is recent penny stock offerings of local start-up companies. Situations we've seen recently lead me to believe that many investors in this region are buying stocks, losing money, and not realizing they may be able to recover some of their losses through a lawsuit.

Here's what is happening:

> The public buys stock of a three-year-old company that has just gone public. The firm's prospectus shows three years of increasing sales and profits. Perhaps a broker recommends purchase. Soon, the stock price plummets to 10 percent of its former level.
>
> This kind of situation merits discussion with a securities lawyer. The laws of this state are strict regarding securities fraud and are designed to protect the investor. If the firm's prospectus was unclear or left out relevant information, these investors may be entitled to 100 percent of their money back.

We can provide you with several case histories that are a matter of public record. We can also tell you steps for the small investor to take to avoid these kind of investments.

I would be glad to author this article at no cost to you. I ask in return a byline and brief biographical sketch.

Regards,

(attorney signature)

Figure 64-2 Proposal for Attorney-Authored Article

GUEST EDITORIALS

Another proactive publicity opportunity is in "guest editorials." Most newspapers encourage what are essentially lengthy letters to the editor but give them prominent play. They will often include a photograph and biography of the author.

Attorneys can adapt the "attorney-authored article" letter to the news media to propose a guest editorial.

INFORMED SOURCE

A method of obtaining publicity that works well for attorneys is establishing themselves as informed sources. The news media inherently like informed sources. These people are quoted daily in major newspapers, particularly in political circles when dealing with sensitive matters. But the process works for attorneys wherever they work and in whatever business they handle.

Being identified as a good source of information on topics likely to be covered in the media builds confidence in existing clients ("That's my attorney being quoted there. She must know what she's talking about."). It also establishes name recognition among other potential clients. A third reason is the generation of referrals from other attorneys who become aware of a specific expertise through the media.

An attorney can inform writers, editors, and reporters of areas where the attorney has expertise. This can be done through letters or a phone call

Dear News Editor:

I've noticed that you and your staff frequently cover news stories dealing with land use issues. I was particularly interested in your recent coverage of our city's annexation attempt to the north and the controversy surrounding that process.

Although I wasn't involved in that specific issue, I have worked on numerous annexations. I could help put this in historical context for your reporters, as well as describe regional and national trends on this topic.

Here are some other topics I would be glad to provide information about

- land use planning. I recently helped Exurbia revise its growth limitations policies, in conjunction with local neighborhood input.
- annexation. We represented the owners of Mega Shopping Mall during the recent election that placed the mall inside the city limits of Exurbia.
- taxation rates and assessments districts. I am currently working with the board of directors of Hillside Recreation District to structure a new levy measure.
- zoning laws. The city of Millview has asked me to start litigation against an enterprise they say violated its laws.
- environmental issues as they relate to land use issues.

When someone from your organization calls, I will take the call immediately if at all possible. I understand the tight deadlines that frequently occur in your business and will provide you with as much as I accurately can in the time available. Please understand that client confidences or litigation underway may preclude me from providing you with details of specific situations.

Regards,

(signature)

Figure 64-3 Informed Source Letter to Media

every four months or so. The letter states that if the media are working on a story involving the attorney's areas of emphasis, then that attorney would be available to the reporter for background information, perspective, or comment (if possible) on a specific situation.

Becoming an informed source takes time, because the key to any successful media relationship is the building up of credibility. This process is useful for attorneys working in conservative firms or who themselves are cautious about media exposure yet at the same time realize the need for name recognition and acknowledgment of their expertise in specific areas.

For example, an attorney working in land use issues could write a personal note to local media, containing some of the ideas expressed in the sample letter in Figure 64-3.

In the course of the response, the attorney builds credibility by being available as promised and speaking concisely so that the reporter can reduce complex information into terms understandable by the general public.

It is helpful to remember that *nothing* is "off the record." The news media will always assert their freedom to print or broadcast information "the public has a right to know." On the other hand, providing background information and perspective on an issue is deeply appreciated by most reporters and builds credibility quickly.

This concept also is helpful if an attorney wishes to obtain visibility through television and radio talk shows. It is increasingly popular in all major cities to have weekly "ask a lawyer" radio talk shows. Also, many television stations seek out attorneys as guests, although this is usually done to discuss controversial issues and therefore should be approached with caution. Also, these shows are usually broadcast at a time when business clients are least likely to be watching. They can be effective, however, for attorneys seeking to reach the "retail" consumer market.

MEDIA LISTS

In all attempts at proactive media relations, a good list of the media and current editors is important. These can be assembled and maintained by a good administrative aide. Initial lists can be developed from several sources (Yellow Pages, library listings, etc.), although they will not have names of specific writers. Some law firms have found it cost efficient to hire a public relations firm to develop a list. This list will usually be accurate and comprehensive and can be easily updated internally. A good media list should include general interest local newspapers, regional business publications serving the community, regional offices of national business publications, legal trade journals, trade journals of major client groups, and local radio and television stations. College alumni publications (both undergraduate and law school) and "hometown" newspapers should also be included.

San Francisco Chronicle	*San Francisco: The Magazine*
San Francisco Examiner	*Forbes* (local office or writer)
Oakland Tribune	*Fortune* (local office or writer)
Oakland Business Monthly	*Business Week* (local office or writer)
San Francisco Business	*The Wall Street Journal* (local bureau office)
San Francisco Business Times	*Christian Science Monitor* (local office or writer)

Figure 64-4 San Francisco/Bay Area News Media

Figure 64-4 illustrates some of the major media in one metropolitan area. Depending on the news item, publicity about an attorney or firm could occur in any one of these media.

Chapter 65
Reactive Media Relations: What to Do When They Call You

SUMMARY

When media coverage is likely but not desired, the attorney is well advised to be prepared to respond to the media and even to initiate contact with them. The media are not always hostile but will print or broadcast information of interest to its audience. Since accuracy cannot always be ensured, the attorney can protect his or her interests through cooperation.

This chapter discusses

- options to handle situations where negative publicity is likely.
- what can happen to attorneys who ignore or are ill prepared to deal with media inquiries.
- how to prepare for media interviews.

Situations can develop for attorneys where publicity—either regarding their firms or their clients—is not desired but at the same time is likely. In these situations, attorneys rarely seek out the media to provide information.

Yet there may be good reason to do so or at least to make solid preparations to respond to queries from the outside.

The experience of many law firms has proven that certain steps enable an attorney to "manage" the news insofar as possible. While total control is never possible, there are actions to be taken that will mitigate negative publicity and subsequent damages to individuals, companies, or specific situations involving legal matters.

The argument is made that the public has a right to know information that will affect them or their lives. Because of the sensitive and confidential nature of their work, attorneys particularly may encounter situations where they must advise their clients to fulfill both moral as well as legal obligations to inform the public. So while this chapter discusses ways to avoid publicity, it must be understood that in some situations, the public's right to know supersedes the client's right to privacy. The attorney and the client may not like it, but preparing for the inevitable is always best.

PREPARING FOR BAD NEWS

Most attorneys are leery of publicity regarding a specific case, particularly litigation, and rightfully so. There is good reason for "not trying the case in the newspapers" due to possible libel issues, accusations of exerting undue influence, or creating an environment inappropriate for a fair trial. But with ever-increasing demand for news and exploding channels of communication to the public, attorneys should be prepared for publicity and exposure of many more of their transactions than perhaps they would care to have made public.

In the course of a complex legal situation, most attorneys will respond with the perfunctory "no comment" when asked about details of a situation. But it is naive to think that the news media will stop their queries at this point. The media will keep asking until they find a source who will provide information. It usually behooves attorneys then, given the constraints of the law and prudence in divulging privileged information, to cooperate with the news media.

A good example for many attorneys is to watch how their own corporate clients handle publicity, particularly "bad" news or something the client would just as soon keep quiet. Corporations, both public and private, have long realized that their interests are best served if they cooperate with the news media and make themselves the best source of accurate and credible information. It is generally understood that once the media decide to gather information on an event and to make that information public, the media will use whatever information it has. If a corporation decides to let someone else provide the "facts" to the media, chances are excellent that the corporation will not have its story told the way it would like.

RESPONSE OPTIONS

To handle any news story, attorneys can advise their clients (or themselves if the matter is internal) to pursue one of three courses of action when faced with "bad" news. Two of these are reactive and another is proactive (discussed in Chapters 63 and 64).

1. The first reactive mode is to *do nothing,* hoping the situation will not become public or, if it does, that it will pass quickly. At best, the attorneys or client will be forced to react to a situation for which they are unprepared.
2. Another reaction is to *take an active defense,* preparing for questions from the public and the media. This usually occurs after some information has been made public which has caused the public to have only partial information (leading to false conclusions) or incorrect information, all of which will require the attorney to explain the situation publicly. This communication may have to occur in a less than friendly environment, such as a public meeting or in a news article that gives major attention to the opposing party or critics.
3. The third option is to *take the offense,* becoming proactive in managing the flow of information. This is "getting out ahead" of the story to avoid a mode where the attorney or client seems defensive and reactionary.

If option 2 or 3 are selected, it behooves the attorney (or spokesperson) to rehearse anticipated situations. Just as an attorney anticipates questions in a courtroom, questions from the media can be predicted and responses prepared. Media spokesperson training is an area where training by professionals is not only possible but desirable for persons likely to be queried by the media and others.

MEDIA COOPERATION

The news media are not inherently hostile. They will respond to reason and truth. If an attorney cannot comment, it is best to explain why. Attorneys can demonstrate their willingness to cooperate with the media by offering to verify facts obtained from other sources. At worst, the attorney will be described in "neutral" terms, as opposed to appearing obstructive or hostile.

In a recent situation, internal "bad" news was mishandled by a law firm in a major West Coast city involved in a very difficult situation. The news media learned of the situation and obtained statements from a variety of sources both inside and outside of the firm. Because of a lack of preplanning, the firm was embarrassed by the impression created by the media exposure which subsequently eroded client confidence. Here's what happened:

The firm's 7-member executive committee decided abruptly to terminate 14 attorneys (including 8 partners and 1 of the named partners) along with 15 staff members. The remaining attorneys said that because of an erosion of the firm's primary client base, the firm was facing a decline in work and needed to pare down.

Subsequent news stories in the business media quoted attorneys on both sides giving different reasons for the departure, severely straining client and public confidence. It also tarnished the image of both groups because the conflicting statements left neutral members of the public confused and doubtful of the "truth" from any source.

The managing partner of the surviving firm was quoted as pointing to the departures as simply a "cost-cutting measure." The departing attorneys, obviously embarrassed by being fired, expressed total surprise. They were quoted as saying that "we were not unproductive" and that the surviving firm had released "only the community servants, the public spirited, and the dissenters."

In reality, the separation was good for both groups. The departing attorneys were able to form a new firm that emphasized their unique approach to the changing insurance defense market. The remaining firm was able to stress other areas of law as it wished, in this case, environmental litigation. Both messages—positive and helpful to all concerned—were lost in the barrage of charges and countercharges among both sides.

MANAGING THE NEWS

So whether they are preparing for inquiries on their own business (mergers, breakups, etc.) or on their client's business (sales, acquisitions, leveraged buyouts, bankruptcies, etc.), attorneys can prepare to handle media inquiries successfully by:

- preparing a list of anticipated questions and answers.
- identifying a single spokesperson; if not possible, then ensuring that all parties speaking on behalf of the firm or client have a unified message.
- making sure that all parties will not speculate or answer questions that probe "worst-case" scenarios.
- responding to all media calls unemotionally and with courtesy and honesty.
- emphasizing where possible the "positive" side of a situation, such as benefits to the community or to clients.
- in negative situations, releasing as many facts as possible as soon as possible. This generally shortens the media's interest in the story instead of dragging it out for a long period while "new information" comes to light.

- avoiding the use of humor or making light of any situation the media consider serious.
- making sure all information is shared internally as well as externally so that colleagues and staff do not read "new" news in the newspaper.

Chapter 66
Publicity Reprints: Extending the Message

SUMMARY

Reprints and distribution of good publicity provide an opportunity for attorneys to maximize attention and build credibility. The opportunity for practice development provided by reprints is often overlooked by attorneys.

This chapter discusses

- value of publicity reprints to attorneys.
- methods and costs to produce them.

Reprints are very useful as direct-mail and promotional items, lending credibility and prestige to attorneys and their practice. Publicity such as law review articles or an original article in a bar journal are very useful for referral purposes.

Almost any kind of favorable publicity is suitable for reprinting and distribution. Being published means that the information has value, or else the editor would not have printed it in the first place. Therefore, its distribution to clients and potential clients with the message "You may find this of use" is not as self-serving as it may first appear.

PRODUCING A REPRINT

Most publications have a reprint policy and welcome requests to have their materials reprinted. However, some publications will not allow reprints under any circumstances, but these publications are rare. Regardless, guidelines should be followed closely to avoid any violation of copyrights.

Some magazines provide their own reprint service (such as *Reader's Digest* and others) where they will compose a reprint in booklet form and print any quantity desired. The magazine will usually reprint the cover of the issue containing the article, plus the pages exactly as they appeared originally. This means that if there was an advertisement on the page, it will be included in the reprint. In some cases, specific arrangements can be made to have the reprint designed and laid out without unrelated materials.

Most publications will have some sort of written permission form, along with stipulations on how credit is to be given. The request for credit is usually satisfied with the words "reprinted with permission from the (date) issue of (name of publication)." If the material was not copyrighted by the publication (and usually it was not), then the attorney can simply add the copyright mark to make it so.

Most publications do not have their own reprint service. For those that do, the cost of reprints obtained from the original publisher will often be at least $1.00 each and usually more, depending on the number of pages and photos. The quality is usually excellent, however, since original materials are used.

Another method of obtaining reprints is to copy the article and photos as they appeared in the publication. The quality is usually not as good (since this is second-generation material), but it is satisfactory for an article that is all textual material. For a reprint that involves black-and-white photography, every effort should be made to obtain the original photos from the publication. In the case of color, it is mandatory. Although it is possible to reproduce black-and-white or color photos that have been printed in a magazine or newspaper, the results are rarely satisfactory.

REDESIGNING THE ORIGINAL LAYOUT

Once the materials have been obtained, the attorney can have the printer or a graphic designer reassemble the materials as they appeared in the publication. Invariably, there is a need to "cut and paste" so that the materials will fit into a desired format. Many articles run from a leading page on to several not-always-contiguous pages. For instance, if an attorney's article was published on six pages in a trade journal, it can probably be laid out onto three $8\frac{1}{2}$-inch by 11-inch pages. These pages can then be easily reprinted onto an 11-inch by 17-inch page, folded in half, providing a cover page and plenty of room for the original material.

It is entirely within moral or ethical bounds to rearrange the news story for reprinting onto a few pages so that it is easier to read. However, it is not acceptable to change the headlines or text in any way so as to change significantly the meaning or impact of the original material. It is allowable for the attorney to include his or her name and address on the reprints, usually on the back page.

The desired quality of the final product will determine how it should be printed. A nearby printer who specializes in speedy service and photocopying is usually satisfactory for reprints with black-and-white text and/or photography. If color photos are involved, then a higher-quality commercial printer will be required. It is generally a good idea to spend a few extra dollars on better quality paper, such as a glossy stock.

It is also very important that the paper be opaque so that, when printed on both sides with heavy black ink, none of the text can be seen through. In most circumstances, this means using at least a 24-pound text stock or a 60-pound cover stock. Printers are familiar with these terms.

For additional information on distribution or reprints, see information provided in Chapter 68.

CHAPTER 67
Building Trust: The Ultimate Solution to Business Development Problems

SUMMARY

Clients hire attorneys, not firms. When they look for attorneys, they'll first hire expertise and experience but quickly will want to work with someone they understand and trust. The attorney who has strong legal skills coupled with the ability to establish good relationships is destined for success.

This chapter discusses

- the role of developing personal relationships with clients.
- indirect services to clients that can solidify existing relationships and attract new business.
- the role of personal activities in the overall program of business development.

Attorneys develop legal expertise through years of law school. But the second element of the success equation—trust from the clients—requires personal, eye-to-eye contact between attorney and client. It develops naturally in the course of work but is improved greatly and to mutual advantage if the attorney endeavors to establish good relationships beyond the working environment through means other than the practice of law.

PERSONAL MARKETING EFFORTS

Personal relationships are invaluable to retain good clients and develop new ones. Brochures, announcements, and news article reprints will attract attention, but they will never cause a client or potential client to hire an attorney. Every job seeker knows that the résumé serves only to disqualify applicants. The hiring is always done after the personal interview is complete and the "chemistry" between employer and future employee is good. Therefore, for individual attorneys, personal relationships make the crucial difference.

A personal approach to marketing is carried out through two kinds of activities, both of which create understanding and trust: *indirect services* that provide information to clients (at no cost to the client) and those that establish a *personal context* for the client to better know the attorney.

Indirect services are those activities where the attorney's professional background can be utilized and services performed that benefit existing clients and potential ones. But an equal payoff is an increase in client awareness of the attorney's knowledge and skills and an improvement of personal relationships.

There are several types of indirect services, all discussed separately in following chapters. They involve gratis professional services such as seminars, speeches, and executive forums, provided for clients and others. They also involve membership in client business and trade groups, requiring active participation in the professional organizations associated with the attorney's clients and practice areas.

Another area of indirect service is professional volunteerism in nonprofit groups where the attorney's skills and background can be put to effective use. Activities such as "affinity marketing" and "adopting an emerging business" (see Chapters 75 and 76 describing these activities in detail) also utilize the attorney's skills to promote effectively the community and the people within it.

Personal activities create a certain degree of visibility among clients and the community. In participating, an attorney establishes and maintains personal relationships, and is seen in a different light by clients, referral sources, and others. Activities that fit this description are many. They include donations and nonprofessional vounteerism, such as charitable contribution programs, involving tax-deductible donations for charitable purposes. They can include attorney-sponsored social activities, such as open houses and holiday parties. They also include community-sponsored social activities, frequently pursued by attorneys and managed for maximum business development opportunities.

By understanding these concepts and adopting them into a personal marketing plan, attorneys have a much greater ability to meet both personal and client goals.

CHAPTER 68
Don't Let Them Get Away: How to Stay in Touch with Clients

SUMMARY

Regular and frequent communication with clients can go far to hold together the client-attorney relationship. Some of the communication can also be used effectively as a method of developing new business.

This chapter discusses

- the common methods of general attorney communication with clients, including status reports, announcements, and personal notes.
- the value of these to attorneys.
- an effective data base system to maintain good client contacts.

"Deluge your clients with paper" is an axiom of legal services today. Attorneys, along with accountants and other consultants, are well advised to maintain communication with clients through frequent messages. It will be a rare client who ever complains about receiving too much information from his or her attorney.

FIVE EFFECTIVE TECHNIQUES

No matter how many and how frequent are the communications, they are most successful when they are prepared in such a way so that the client sees the relevance (and perhaps benefit) to themselves. For instance, an attorney announcing a new office location may be justifiably proud of his new surroundings. But the client will only find this to be "good news" if he or she perceives improved service, easier access, free parking, or some other benefit. If an attorney informs a client of a new change in employment law, the client will only ask "How does this affect me?" The more immediate benefit to the client that the attorney can establish in the client's mind, the better will be the relationship.

Highly professional and acceptable means of communication are

- announcements.
- situational letters regarding new legislation, deadlines, and so on.
- status reports.
- general printed materials (such as brochures, etc.).
- personal note cards.

ANNOUNCEMENTS

A common and frequently used method of client communication is the printed announcement of a relocation of a law firm office, new associates, awards, personal achievements, and so on. Most announcements, whether of a new firm member, office location, award, or settlement of a special case, are presented to clients, to peers and to the general public in limited terms. Specifically, most announcements describe the who, what, when, and where.

But the most important fact is often missing—the why. The "why" is the benefit to the client, which is ultimately the most important aspect of the entire event. When preparing announcements, attorneys should write the facts, and then ask themselves: "Why is this important to my clients?" The answer to this question must be added to the announcement to gain maximum impact. The most effective attorney announcements of all kinds are those that provide enough details so that the recipient understands the significance of the announcement.

SITUATIONAL LETTERS

Situational letters are used by attorneys to describe upcoming deadlines for employers, new or pending legislation, and a host of other broad legal subjects. Letters are frequently generated by attorneys from their current work on specific situations. By generalizing the information and sending it to nonclients, attorneys show interest in the client's business and reminding them of the attorney's expertise in an area of law.

Situational letters are clearly a well-established and acknowledged method of client communication. They are usually well within the comfort zone of even the most conservative attorneys. At the same time, they are perhaps the most difficult method of client communication for attorneys. If there is a universal criticism, it rarely involves the content of the letter. Most are technically accurate and, upon close study, provide an astute analysis of a current situation.

Where they fail is in their form. Most letters are single spaced, long, and presented in a standard letter format. They will have a formal salutation, 10 to 15 long paragraphs, and the close. The writer assumes the receiver is prepared to read and understand a usually complex legal matter.

This is a classic situation where the form gets in the way of the content. Situational letters are received and understood much better when the information is organized into three levels—a headline, an executive summary, and the main text. In other words, if the receiver can only review the letter quickly, a headline will tell him or her the subject and general conclusion. If time permits, the receiver can get a quick working knowledge of the situation through the executive summary. Then, if necessary, the receiver can obtain a better understanding through the main text.

For a common example of information organized into levels, *The Wall Street Journal* publishes many "situational letters" every day. The only difference is that they are called news stories. *The Wall Street Journal*'s system of headline, subhead (or executive summary), and body text enables the reader to scan a large amount of text quickly for information of relevance.

STATUS REPORTS

Another form of a generally accepted but little used communication method with clients is the *status report*. These are defined as regular communication with existing clients about specific matters and action (or inaction) taken by the attorney on their behalf. These are usually made via letter (although fax machines are being used more frequently).

Attorneys almost always know what is happening on a case but, surprisingly, the client may not until a bill arrives. This is not the best way of informing a client of activity during the billing period.

Research published in national law journals indicates that, when asked to identify three areas where they were disappointed in their legal services, the largest percentage of individuals currently buying legal services said "lack of communication from my attorney regarding the status of my case."

The most successful individual attorneys are those whose clients hear from their attorney frequently regarding the status of their case. These are also the clients who are most loyal and voice little criticism upon payment of invoices. Communication can range from as little as a fax that says "Your motion was filed in superior court this morning at 9:45" to a formal cover letter describing current action, with attachments of documents submitted to the opposing counsel.

This is an area where the axiom "deluge your clients with paper" can be easily carried out. The alternative is a little less work for your administrative staff and a small savings on postage and copier paper. But the price can be a disgruntled client calling to find out "what's happening on my case."

Figures 68-1 and 68-2 are examples of typical status reports used frequently by client-focused attorneys.

Date

Name
Affiliation
Address
City

Re: ______________________________

Dear Name

On ____________, 19 _____, you retained this firm to ______________
____

The purpose of this letter is to give you a status report on the project you requested us to handle. Currently we are ______________________
____
____
____
____

If everything goes as planned, we expect to complete this matter within __________ [weeks] [months]. If we experience any delays that significantly alter these projections, we will let you know promptly.

If you have any questions, or would simply like to discuss any aspect of your project, please call at your convenience.

Sincerely,

____

Figure 68-1 Status Report to Client

Date file opened: ____________________

Last action and date: ____________________

____

Current Status: ____________________

____

____

____

Next scheduled activity: ____________________

____

____

____

Estimated timelines: ____________________

____

Next tickler date: ____________________

Additional information to client [optional]: ____________________

____

____

____

____

____

____

____

Figure 68-2 Quarterly Status Report

GENERAL PRINTED MATERIALS

Any time that a lawyer develops *general printed materials* such as brochures and individual biographies, an opportunity exists to communicate with current and potential clients. While most attorneys will doubt the value of sending brochures to existing clients, its value is strong.

Proof of this can be found in advertising research which notes that the highest readership of advertisements for new automobiles is from people who have recently purchased that particular automobile. The reason is that the buyer wishes to reaffirm the wisdom of his or her previous judgment and therefore seeks information reinforcing the decision.

Existing clients are also continually looking for reinforcement that they made (and are making) a good investment in an attorney. Therefore, information as contained in brochures, announcements of awards, notices of conclusions of large business transactions, and related events are usually welcomed by the existing client.

Earlier in this book—in Chapters 55 through 57—discussion takes place on the distribution of brochures to clients. A new brochure not only provides an attorney with an excellent opportunity to cross-sell existing clients but also reinforces the client awareness of attorney skills and experience.)

PERSONAL NOTES

Another opportunity for attorney communication with clients is through *personal notes*. Items sent can range from news articles on the client's area of business to an article on antique automobiles. The point is to demonstrate interest in the client's business and personal life.

One technique that makes the sending of personal notes very easy for attorneys is to print cards with the message "Thought you might find this of interest" which are suitable to clip to any item being sent. In many cases, these cards can be printed concurrently with business cards at little additional cost.

With a little direction from the attorney, virtually all five of these communication techniques (and any other the attorney thinks of) can be handled by a well-trained receptionist and a good mailing list. Once the attorney has devoted the time to prepare the content of the document, a minimum of attorney time should be necessary to build a stream of steady and varied communication to clients.

REGULAR CLIENT CONTACT SYSTEM

A system that works well for maintaining regular and systematic client contact is a data base for each client or referral name. This can be computerized or consist of an index card for each person.

Here's how a good system works for attorneys. (For this example, a system using index cards is explained, since it will work for every attorney. Attorneys with computers can easily create the same process electronically with current software.)

> Each client (by company or individual) is put on a separate card. Each client is evaluated to determine the interval between contacts, in absence of the client

themselves initiating some sort of contact. If determined that XYZ Corp. (a recent past client) should be contacted every four months, their name was put on a blue card and the staff put the card in the action file box "tickler" for four months from now. That way, the person responsible for relations with that client would be reminded to call on XYZ Corp. in four months. Likewise, all clients that should be contacted in four-month intervals would have their names put on blue cards for the staff to file accordingly.

Red cards signified monthly contacts; yellow meant alternate months; green meant semiannual; brown signified yearly intervals.

The staff is responsible for checking the tickler file and advising which clients were due for a call or check to see if there had been contact.

The cards themselves hold several pieces of information valuable to anyone doing the follow-up. When is the best time to contact the client? Morning, afternoon, evening? How should they be contacted—telephone, personal call, fax, letter? The cards indicated the date of the last "client retention" contact.

What was the nature of the contact—a social event, a business meeting, or other situation? Was it a specially arranged conference, at the client's location? At whose office? Was the contact by phone, in person, letter, or fax?

What subjects were discussed? Who initiated contact? What action was to be taken by both parties? When was follow-up action relative to the matter appropriate?

With the assistance of the staff, this simple system would enable an attorney to keep track of clients in order to initiate appropriate client retention contacts.

Chapter 69
The Care and Feeding of Referral Sources

SUMMARY

Never underestimate the power of referrals. They are frequently the best source of new business. Existing clients are the best referral sources. There are many others, and attorneys are well advised to carry out regular programs to develop referral sources.

This chapter discusses

- importance of referral sources to a total marketing program.
- methods to stay in touch with referral sources.
- how to demonstrate attorney expertise professionally to referrals.

Many articles and research reports have been published discussing the primary sources of new clients for law practices. Some studies indicate that over half of new clients come from direct referrals.

For example, a survey of 126 high-technology business people with an average of $5 million in sales and 50 employees chose their legal counsel in the following manner: 45 percent used a business acquaintance as a reference, 19 percent chose attorneys from their own study, 11 percent relied on the recommendation of their accountant, and 4 percent relied on their banker. Twenty-nine percent of the businesspeople found a lawyer from "other sources."

Other law practices rely heavily on attorney referrals as the result of conflicts, dockets, or experience and expertise. Yet many attorneys behave as if they had never seen those reports or do not believe the results apply to their practices. They make no organized effort to develop or maintain two-way communications with referral sources.

WHO THEY ARE

The most important and productive of all referral sources are existing clients (which, in the survey, is included in the category "business acquaintance"). This applies to nearly all types of practices as well as virtually all other professionals. What can be done to assure that clients will be active and productive sources? Obviously, attorneys need to make sure they have satisfied their clients' needs. Following that, there are a few other techniques which can be employed.

The attorney can go beyond the legal matter or business at hand to ensure that clients' personal, business, and professional objectives are met. This can be accomplished in several ways. The attorney can send news clippings and letters which contain information not only valuable to the client but also to remind them of the attorney's expertise.

To the extent that confidences are not being violated, the attorney can provide referral sources with business development leads for their situations. Most will go unacknowledged, but it is important that the attorney is consistent and ongoing with this process.

Attorneys must recognize and appreciate their clients. When a referral is received, the referring client should be recognized and personally thanked with an expression of appreciation. A thank you note, even more than a phone call, is a minimum. The note should be short, on personal note paper, and in no way should resemble a form letter. Handwritten notes are best, if clearly legible to the clients. Gifts may not be explicitly permissible by the attorney's individual bar jurisdiction. If a gift is within bar guidelines, it should be unique to that particular client while of modest value and a visible reminder of the giver. For example, a desk set or pen could be engraved, "With appreciation from Roger F. Smith" or some other appropriate wording.

Another form of recognition is to acknowledge client accomplishments, including those of their families. Again, handwritten congratulatory notes along with article clippings have tremendous impact.

OTHER SOURCES

Each practice will have its own composition of referral sources. Often ignored are some of the most potentially productive sources imaginable! Examples are financial service organizations such as commercial banks; savings and loan institutions; credit unions; and casualty, life, and health insurance agents.

Frequently overlooked are attorneys in other practice areas and other jurisdictions. Law school classmates and fellow alumni of other law firms are additional valuable sources usually not systematically developed.

Service and product suppliers to the attorney's office as well as client offices frequently seem to be neglected when listing referral sources. Suppliers are excellent because they often overhear when a possible client is seeking legal services as well as who is financially solid.

CENTERS OF INFLUENCE

Many attorneys, particularly those targeting business clients, have had success by actively marketing centers of influence. These may be accountants, bankers, and other attorneys who are influential in the profession and respected in the community. Additionally, individuals and groups influential to the decision process for the attorney's target audience should be included. For example, these can include the leadership of a trade association and the public and private leadership of a community such as the chamber of commerce and local government officials.

It is up to the attorney to go beyond building personal relationships to build recognition aggressively with centers of influence. To do this, an attorney might offer to participate in or lead a seminar focused on legal developments affecting these centers and their clients. At any rate, they should be included in mailing lists and treated as if they too were members of the attorney's target market.

Chapter 70
Attracting Attention Through Speeches, Forums, and Seminars

SUMMARY

Speeches, forums, and seminars can be extremely effective devices to maintain existing clients and attract new ones in exactly the areas of law the attorney enjoys. But in spite of their popularity, these activities are often mismanaged by attorneys, and opportunities for business development are missed. Solid advance planning and attention to all the details of the activities are necessary for success.

The chapter discusses

- the value to attorneys of high-visibility activities such as speeches, seminars, and forums.
- their role in the total practice development effort.
- suggestions on how to conduct them successfully.
- costs and time commitments related to these activities.

Client-focused attorneys who are cautious or skeptical about many business development activities will readily accept and understand the value of speeches, forums, and seminars. These activities usually are undertaken by attorneys who feel uncomfortable with most other forms of marketing activities. Speeches, forums, and seminars are professional; they are controllable; in most cases the attendees can be carefully selected. The activities demonstrate attorney knowledge. But more important, attorneys have been giving speeches, arranging forums, and conducting seminars for years. It is second only in popularity to entertainment as an accepted promotional activity.

Speeches by attorneys are made everyday, not only to courtroom juries but to Rotary Clubs, trade associations, alumni associations, and client groups. By training and inclination, attorneys are generally capable of giving a good speech. Rare is the attorney who will not accept an invitation to speak before a selected group. Speeches have been and no doubt will continue to be a powerful and effective means of gaining both visibility and credibility for attorneys.

Forums are attorney-sponsored meetings featuring one or more outside speakers. A limited number of guests with a strong interest in the subject are invited, and the speakers are usually well-known authorities. Forums generally last two to three hours and include a meal or social activity. They are a relatively new addition to the arsenal of attorney marketing tools. Forums are becoming increasingly developed and used for business development purposes.

Seminars are presentations by attorneys, wherein a selected audience is invited as guests of the attorneys for the purpose of informing or educating them on a topic of interest. Presumably, the attorney has developed a level of expertise in the subject that qualifies him or her to sponsor the activity. Attorney-sponsored seminars are usually no less than one-half day; they are more frequently all day and occasionally longer.

VALUE TO ATTORNEY

Several benefits to both attorneys and their clients are readily apparent from these activities.

Clearly, when clients are invited, they show the attorney's interest in the clients' welfare. They provide information that the client can use to avoid future legal problems or help solve current ones. They help maintain and build solid relationships, resulting in long-term retention of clients.

In seminars, clients and other attendees get a chance to observe the attorney and colleagues at work and to appraise their communication skills. They help clients evaluate the attorney's ability to speak persuasively. If the seminars are held in-house, they give attendees a chance to see the attorney's offices and equipment.

There can be immediate benefits from speeches and so on by having attendees at the event call the attorney regarding a new matter. If there is a program or synopsis of the event circulated among nonattendees, there can be additional calls from those who did not attend but saw the attorney's name listed as an authority on a subject. Attendees can refer their friends and business associates to the attorney.

There are other indirect benefits that attorneys say they gain from these kinds of activities. They enjoy the information exchange with an audience, alerting them to real-world concerns and potential problems on a given subject. Attorneys in seminars share ideas with their intellectual peers. Attorneys also benefit from their own work to prepare the materials, learning and organizing information in new ways. New research or study may even be needed.

Speeches, seminars, and forums, unless they are terribly mismanaged, will enhance the attorney or firm reputation. They will garner applause not only from those who attended but also from those who did not. In the promotion of the event, the attorneys will have drawn attention to their expertise and interest in a certain area of the law. Their credibility will be enhanced.

Another reward, even less tangible but significant, is the feeling of having educated, of having increased the level of legal awareness of others so that they can lead their lives and conduct their business in a more complete, satisfying manner. It is a feeling of genuine accomplishment.

ROLE IN MARKETING EFFORT

While they are generally accepted to be an excellent form of maintaining client relations and building new business, speeches, seminars, and forums alone cannot constitute a total marketing effort. They must be considered part of a larger program that includes many of the other process and techniques discussed in this book.

Here is what can happen if the activities take place in isolation, that is, without a larger marketing program wrapped around them:

- A speech on new tax law changes to a Rotary Club will fall on deaf ears because the audience was not carefully identified.
- A forum on worker's compensation for a firm hoping to attract work in this area will fail in its purpose when attendees perceive a shallow knowledge of the subject on the part of the firm.
- A seminar conceived by one or two attorneys will become a logistical nightmare without total internal support from other attorneys and staff.

In each of these situations, a comprehensive approach to marketing was missing, and the effort went awry. A good marketing plan would have identified audiences, indicating to the attorneys that not all Rotary Clubs are composed of business leaders interested in tax issues. A good plan would have avoided the worker's compensation miscue by limiting forums to those subjects on which the firm has a depth of experience. A good plan would have built internal consensus for all external efforts so that attorney marketing efforts would command the full support of internal staff.

In addition, speeches, forums, and seminars must meet these criteria to be successful. They must

1. serve a useful professional purpose, such as explaining tax laws, zoning changes, and so on.
2. relate to the attorney's competence.

3. be focused on a carefully chosen audience that is a likely source of continued business (such as existing clients).

COST AND TIME COMMITMENT

Each of these activities must be done well or not at all. Each one takes time and costs money, so the return on investment in terms of new and continuing business must be there. Besides a loss of billable time, there are also out-of-pocket costs for collateral materials, travel, room rentals, and so on that can be significant.

Since the time commitment of attorneys and their staff and the costs associated with speeches, forums, and seminars can be huge, there are several steps to minimize this. The first approach is to budget carefully. The activity should fit within the overall marketing plan. Therefore, it should have a budget assigned to it, defining both time and money.

While these activities can consume tremendous amounts of time during a short period, their impact on the attorney's total billable time for the year is relatively small. In a typical marketing plan (see samples in the appendix to this book), an attorney or a firm can budget X hours and X dollars for ten speeches throughout the year. If the hours allocated are 100, and the attorney spends ten hours preparing for, delivering, and following up on one speech, then he or she is within budget. This sort of preplanning enables attorneys at all levels to know they have management support for the activity and will not be penalized for "nonbillable" time.

There are two methods to reduce significantly the time required for these activities: (1) limit any speech, seminar, or forum to an area of expertise that is already well established by the attorney and (2) adapt existing internal materials to be used in the presentations.

VALUE IN BUILDING BUSINESS IN A NEW AREA OF THE LAW

Speeches and seminars should not be the primary method used to attract business in a new area of the law. There are other, more effective, methods, such as the hiring of laterals or negotiations with existing clients to expand services to them. The time required for preparation is too lengthy to justify the return. Further, since the opportunity to adapt existing materials is not present, considerable time will be spent in research and writing to develop collateral and supporting handouts.

Forums can be used to help establish an attorney within a new area of the law but this is a slow process. Once a new area of the law is selected, a total marketing program must be developed that involves both short-range and long-range activities to develop the credibility needed for success. Forums are one of those, but certainly not the only one.

COSPONSORSHIPS

Many speeches, seminars, and forums are designed for an attorney's own clients. Therefore, the attorney or firm normally is the sole sponsor of the activity. But in some cases, particularly when nonclients are invited, cosponsorship of the event with an appropriate group will reduce the attorney's time and cost while at the same time increasing credibility.

A good example is cosponsorship of an event for a special-interest group such as trade associations. If an attorney is heavily involved in real estate law, then a related group is a logical "partner." Many of the attorney's clients will already be members of the trade association. Also, other members of the group are the most likely potential clients the attorney could identify.

Besides offering the benefit of implied endorsement, cosponsors will take care of many of the logistics of the event. They will supply staff and volunteers to handle invitations, sign-ups, distribution of materials, and so on.

THE SUCCESSFUL SPEECH

Attorney speeches outside the courtroom generally fall into two categories: those about a specific (and sometimes narrow) aspect of the law and those that are general, usually about "the legal system today" or "the image of attorneys." Speeches on specific topics are more useful for business development; speeches on general topics are of value for building long-term credibility and visibility but usually do not have any immediate impact.

It is helpful for attorneys to be known as experts on a certain subject and to orient all speech-making opportunities around that topic. Audiences can then be selected based on their degree of interest in that topic. This results in the best payback for the attorney. Clearly, if the attorney discusses his or her own area of practice and expertise, then their own clients are most interested and an ideal audience. Speeches on "general topics" get delivered to "general audiences" and the response will probably be disappointing.

For example, a real estate attorney is well advised to speak to associations of realtors, developers, architects, civil engineers,, builders, property managers, and others in related fields. Figure 70-1 provides tips on giving a good speech.

- Write your own introduction. Send a short but complete résumé and a publicity-quality photograph to the sponsors for inclusion in their publicity materials. Carry another résumé to be read as your introduction.
- Select your audience carefully. Find out their knowledge level of your topic and interest in it.
- Prepare thoroughly. Research your audience to see who they will be, what they want, and what they need to know. Look up pertinent quotes, stories, and statistics. Prepare index cards or an outline.
- Practice. Give your speech in front of a mirror or video camera, into a tape recorder, to friends or family members.
- Arrive early to make sure the room is in order, microphone is in working order, and so on.
- Look impressive. Dress at least as well as your audience. Walk confidently to the podium. The first impression you make will flavor the opinions of those in the audience.
- Vary the presentation tools. Distribute professional-looking handouts; use videos or slides.
- Involve the audience. Ask them questions; have them distribute handouts.
- Tell stories. Anecdotes are interesting and very helpful to illustrate points.
- Cite cases sparingly. Citations are important in briefs, but they are distracting in speeches. However, you can make reference to the fact that many precedents exist.
- Use your hands. Gesture naturally, using gestures to underline a point.
- Avoid jargon. Don't use terms the audience may not know.
- Use humor. But don't use jokes, especially those that ridicule.
- Use handouts. Make sure that a summary, a checklist, or some sort of information is distributed to the audience. Make sure the attorney's name and phone number is on the material.
- Conclude strongly. Offer a summary, memorable point or warm statement. Don't forget a sincere thank you.

Figure 70-1 Giving a Good Speech

POWERFUL IMPACT OF FORUMS

The creation of a forum for discussion of an idea or legal issue has a potentially great value to clients, prospective clients, and others. It is one of the more effective activities an attorney can undertake for business-development purposes. Because of the serious issues they discuss, forums can legitimately make an impact on people's lives.

Forums are different from speeches because there is usually more than one speaker (although this is not always the case), the audience is small, and meaningful dialogue among presenters and audiences is encouraged. Forums differ from seminars in that they discuss ideas and concepts, whereas seminars more often fall into the "how-to" category or get into detail on narrow topics.

Forums are special events where only special people are invited. When they are small, those invited consider it an honor to be there. If the guest speaker has some sort of celebrity status, the invitees will consider it a privilege to have a private meeting with the speaker.

So what exactly is a forum? Here's an example. An attorney or firm practicing in real estate identifies 10 or 12 developers, both clients and potentials, as an ideal audience for a forum on real estate trends. The attorney arranges for a nationally known real estate developer to be brought in to meet with the local developers. The attorney agrees to pay all expenses and an honorarium to the speaker. The subject discussed is an aspect of development of interest to all. Preferably, the issue will have legal ramifications, but it may not.

In another example, an attorney wishes to expand his or her international trade practice. To command the greater attention of both clients and other area businesspeople engaged in import and export, the attorney arranges for a government trade expert from Washington, D.C., to meet with the local businesspeople.

The role of the attorney at the forum is simply to make all the arrangements and to ensure that the speaker addresses the interests of the attendees. The attorney has no role other than to coordinate all logistics and most likely to introduce the speaker. However, after the forum, the attorney can capitalize on relationships established in several ways by sending a summary of remarks at the forum to invited guests and others.

In the following case history, all these elements joined together to create a memorable event with significant impact for the participants.

> A large firm in a major metropolitan area battled with a number of other firms for the city's premiere clients. The number of firms and attorneys in this area decidedly outweighed client work, making competition fierce. This firm had a strategic plan and was very proactive in its client relations. However, the firm was not satisfied with solely providing competent work. It went beyond that to making its clients feel a sense of worth in their association with the firm.
>
> An international dignitary was slated to visit the firm's city as part of an unofficial tour. Sophisticated and astute, this dignitary avoided any appearances smacking of profit for private interests. But firm partners saw an opportunity to conduct a forum, using the visiting dignitary as its centerpiece. So

several partners made contacts, called in favors, and through no small effort managed to arrange a private dinner for the visitor. The dignitary agreed to attend and make a few remarks, providing that the appearance would be devoted to the philosophical and pragmatic discussion of world affairs as related to the city's interests.

The firm had only one month's notice before the dignitary's appearance. Engraved invitations were sent to key city and state officials as well as to the firm's more prominent clients and potential clients (who also happened to be top business executives). Arrangements were made and paid for by the firm to accommodate the dignitary and his entourage. The cost of the event was quickly rising, reaching a total close to $16,000.

But the end result was a smashing success. The dignitary's visit to the city was major local news. Publicity also resulted from the forum by inviting the editor of the local newspaper and providing him with a written transcript of the discussion immediately afterward.

As a result of the publicity and subsequent follow-up by the attorneys, the firm won several new clients and received several referrals. Anticipated revenues from new clients and referrals *during the first year* were expected to be more than ten times the cost of the dignitary's visit. Other law firms in the same city could only watch in awe and vow to leap at similar opportunities. But this law firm's principals were now confident in their lead, realizing that the proper mind-set, rather than any particular opportunity, was the key to their public relations and business-development dividends.

Tips on conducting a successful forum are shown in Figure 70-2.

- Begin by carefully identifying common interests of key clients and then looking for a forum topic of interest and value to them.
- Ensure that the letters of invitation and related materials are of the highest quality.
- Follow up the invitation with a personal call so that the guest understands the exclusivity of this event.
- Create a prestige and exclusive atmosphere for the forum by selecting an elegant setting for the event.
- Use every opportunity to publicize the forum speaker. Announce to the media when and where the speaker will be, allowing time for interviews either before or after the event. Note: Exclude media from the forum itself.
- Assist the speaker with handout materials, ensuring that the attorney's name is imprinted on them.
- Follow up the event with thank you notes to attendees.

Figure 70-2 Conducting A Successful Forum

ORGANIZING AND PRESENTING SEMINARS

There are few marketing activities that are more warmly embraced by attorneys than seminars. A survey by Professors Caryn Beck-Didley and Paul Buller of Utah State University noted that client clinics and seminars are the second most common form of attorney promotion (the first was loosely labeled "entertainment," presumably luncheons, sporting events, gifts, etc.). The use of clinics and seminars in marketing was consistently used by law firms of all sizes. Just over 43 percent of the large firms used seminars; almost 27 percent of the medium-sized firms and 16 percent of the small firms also used them (the professors defined a large firm as 40 or more attorneys, medium as 16 to 39, and small as fewer than 15 attorneys).

Seminars should not be undertaken by attorneys without a full understanding of the time and costs involved. Seminars are major efforts requiring enormous amounts of time to carry out correctly. That's why many firms seek cosponsorship of seminars with a trade association or other group.

Seminars, like forums, offer the advantage of the attorney controlling the topic and setting the audiences. In addition, the attorney can produce and hand out as much material as desired. Successful seminars, no matter what the topic and how small the audience, take time to prepare. It is not unreasonable for good seminars to require six months from conception to execution. For seminars conducted annually by attorneys and firms, a four-month preparation time is common. Logistical issues must be handled well in advance, such as reservation of a room and planning for meals, travel, equipment, and so on. Along with oral presentations, seminars generally require the development of a workbook of some sort. This takes considerable planning and organization.

The quantity and quality of the audience will vary greatly, depending on the attorney's selection and recruitment process. For the client-focused attorney who invites primarily clients and sponsors a seminar of specific interest to them, a response rate of 50 percent can be expected. This compares to expected returns of $\frac{1}{2}$ to 1 percent return of mass mailings to the general public of invitations to a seminar.

Figure 70-3 provides tips on conducting a successful seminar.

- Keep it small. Unless you have the resources of a large firm and can handle the logistics or 50 or more attendees, small groups are much more effective.
- Keep it educational. Pick a topic of current interest and present information that will help the attendees in their business.
- Avoid selling of services. A good seminar should not be a sales presentation. Too many "seminars" are sponsored by financial planners, investment counselors, and so on, whose primary motive is to sell a product or service to the attendee.

- Use existing materials. For handouts, don't try to reinvent the wheel. Use previously developed material whenever possible, such as internal analyses.
- Pay attention to details. Small things gone awry can disrupt the whole presentation. Extension cords must reach machines, extra bulbs must be present for slide projectors and overheads, sound systems must be "feedback free."
- Involve other attorneys. Best results can occur for cross-selling if other attorneys are present. Wide office participation brings benefits!
- Stay on time. Events that run late or compress certain topics to gain time are irritating and demonstrate poor preparations.
- Work the socials. Ensure that the seminar is wrapped around a social event or meal. Schedule attorneys to meet attendees.
- Ask for feedback. Hand out some sort of survey to be turned in at the end of the seminar that indicates attendee satisfaction.
- Follow up. This is expected and mandatory for effectiveness.

Figure 70-3 Conducting a Successful Seminar

RELATED PUBLICITY

One of the easiest methods of obtaining good visibility is to use the speech, seminar, or forum as the basis for publicity. The event itself may be worthy of a news article (as in the case of a celebrity presenter at an attorney-sponsored forum). The attorney can also use materials prepared for the event as the basis of a news article. If the speech or seminar is open to the public, the media will generally run a news item or at least a calendar listing of the event. Any of this publicity will lend credibility and visibility to the attorney and firm and should therefore be sought out with vigor.

CHAPTER 71
Client Professional and Trade Groups: A Road to Building Personal Relationships

SUMMARY

Membership in professional groups can improve relationships with existing clients as well as provide the opportunity to meet new ones. Careful selection of a group that personally appeals to the attorney as well as holds existing and potential clients is the best choice.

This chapter discusses

- why attorneys should and should not choose to join professional groups.
- types of groups suitable for joining to demonstrate attorney expertise.
- a method to avoid duplication of effort among attorneys from larger firms.

One often-overlooked and yet potentially valuable opportunity for an attorney to increase visibility among a chosen client group is through membership in some sort of client professional organization.

Membership in groups is a well-established tradition in American society. The nineteenth-century writer Howard Penn Hudson perceptively noted that the concept of a business or professional association is a highly civilized one. He wrote

> It calls for what people do least well, subordinating their self-interest to the betterment of all. And when members of the group are competitors, it seems an unnatural alliance that won't work. Yet it does, as the proliferation of associations demonstrates.

Whether through full membership, associate membership, or just regular attendance at meetings, an attorney can show an active interest in the client and his or her needs. The presence and participation of the attorney is proof that the attorney is client centered (as opposed to practice centered) and interested in the real-world issues in the client's day-to-day business dealings. Memberships can improve the attorney's overall knowledge of what is happening in their client's business in order to serve them better.

Virtually every type of business, institution, nonprofit organization, and type of profession has several trade groups affiliated with it. With careful selection and judicious use of time, an attorney can benefit tremendously from involvement in these groups.

There are basically four types of client organizations that attorneys can join.

- *Professional associations and societies* are established for individuals, such as the National Education Association and the American Society of Foresters.
- *Cause groups* are associations of individuals with a common interest or goal. Examples are the National Rifle Association or the Sierra Club.

- *Trade associations* are usually representatives from companies or organizations engaged in similar activities. Examples are the American Electronics Association or the McDonald's Franchise Owner's Association.
- *Producer associations* such as the American Dairy Association or the Western Wood Products Association represent the interests of their members to promote the sale of their products.

Labor attorneys may also find of interest the similar structure among organized labor. Unions represent individual workers, as in the International Brotherhood of Electrical Workers or the Screen Actors Guild. Although attorneys in most cases cannot join these groups, affiliation with them through associate memberships (if possible) and participation at group events can build relationships in ways not otherwise possible.

> One land use attorney had a mobile home park as a client, helping them prepare leases and resolve related conflicts. The attorney found this work interesting and became involved in the local mobile home park owner's association. Through monthly luncheon meetings and occasional volunteer work on committees, the attorney eventually became counsel to the trade association itself. He has also provided services to several other mobile home parks on various issues such as land use and zoning.
>
> This same attorney was retained by a sign manufacturing company as a client, helping with problems involving various sign ordinances in local jurisdictions. He was able to parlay his work and connections with the owner of one sign company to an opportunity to discuss the topic at a regular meeting of the trade association. The attorney later began to attend all association meetings, got to know other owners of sign companies, and has increased his client base because of it. The attorney also utilized some of the client-development techniques described elsewhere in this book, particularly by sending general communication to group members on legal issues of relevance to sign companies.

USING RESOURCES EFFECTIVELY

As with clubs that are joined for social reasons, involvement with a client professional group provides the opportunity to establish personal relationships that ultimately build trust and credibility. It also provides a network with a large amount of people in exactly the target area the attorney wants. When the attorney becomes involved in activities with the group, it shows leadership and commitment.

Frequently, this involvement also demonstrates professional ability when the attorney works with the group on a project outside the legal area. Association with some groups can also carry with it a certain amount of prestige.

Firms of even a few attorneys can benefit from use of a membership grid. By identifying desirable groups for membership and ensuring that the firm is represented within them, the attorneys will systematically avoid any duplication of effort and ensure that their time is used effectively. A membership grid works well for professional as well as social memberships. An example of a grid is shown in Figure 71-1.

The main disadvantage for attorneys is that memberships can be very time consuming. In addition, it is often hard to "stand out" among several competitors. There is no single solution to these obstacles other than to research carefully the groups in terms of members and activities to determine if involvement would be beneficial. The key is to make sure that a significant number of clients (or potentials) are involved.

It is also important that the attorney really want to do this. When marketing committees mandate membership in trade groups for all attorneys in a firm, the activity backfires to a certain degree because of the lack of enthusiasm of some attorneys to participate. The goals of this business-development activity are met through active involvement, not merely membership.

The attorney must therefore "work" the group. This means that the attorney seek out opportunities to work together with members. Examples would be to work on committees that are involved with (if available) labor relations, local/national liaisons, publicity, and special event coordination.

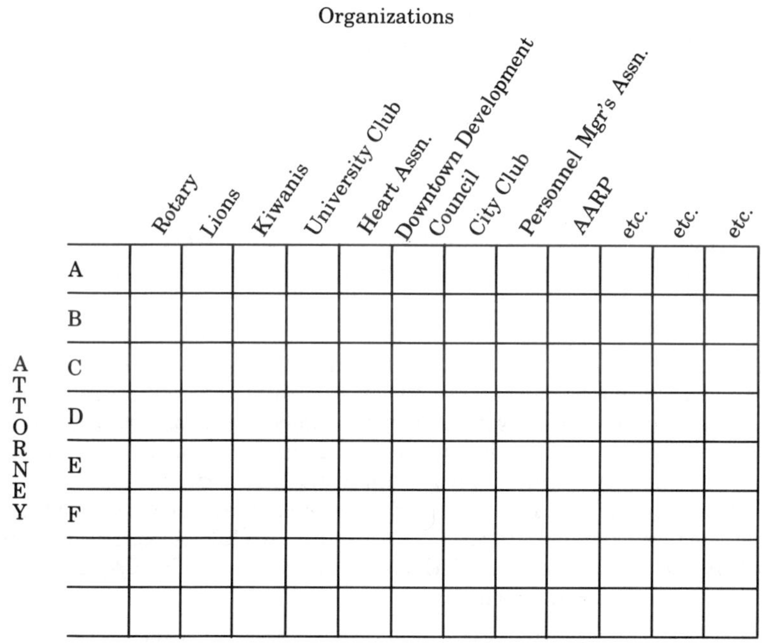

Figure 71-1 Membership Grid

Other active ways that any attorney can increase visibility quickly with a group is to develop and publicize case histories that describe the teamwork between attorneys and that trade group type. The attorney could request opportunities to present overall law firm capabilities to group members as a way of explaining what legal services can do for members of the trade group and increase the number of trade group members on lists to receive white papers and other attorney opinion pieces.

Because of the time commitment involved, these sort of memberships are of value only if the attorney (1) truly enjoys the area of law being practiced for this group and (2) truly enjoys the people he or she must work with in their day-to-day practice. If these criteria are met, then the activity becomes not only enjoyable but also successful in terms of building client relationships and establishing new ones.

Attorneys will also find their group membership successful if they look for these other characteristics of the group they are considering joining:

- The group has a membership that could be called prestigious.
- There is a good likelihood that in the future the attorney could assume top leadership in the organization.

(Being an active member or even a board member of a group is okay, but being the president or leader reaps greater benefits. Most attorneys can name the chairman of the Federal Reserve Board, but who are the board members? They may be equally powerful individuals, but their name recognition is nowhere near that of the leader.)

SENIOR CITIZEN LAW FIRM

One law firm in the southwest United States effectively used one of these forms of membership to their fullest advantage, primarily to develop a new client group.

> The firm had reached a plateau of 35 members and was at a crossroads because they foresaw no significant growth on the horizon in their general practice except through mergers, which the firm members did not perceive to offer any financial incentive. Following two weekend retreats in two consecutive months, the firm members agreed that growth could only occur through emphasis on limited areas of the law, concentrating their business development efforts among a few yet-to-be-selected target groups. Careful budgeting and projecting established that the firm's existing clients would provide adequate income to support new business efforts.
>
> The firm hired a marketing consultant to help with their analysis of future areas of the law and to gather information for decision making. Information

was obtained through interviews with attorneys to determine that any new business thrust would be compatible with existing attorney capability and, more important, would satisfy personal and professional needs.

Research was also conducted by analysis of the news media, interviews with financial consultants, reports from economic development groups, and others to develop facts on the social and economic future of the region.

The consultants were looking for a new business area that fit all the criteria established by the firm. They found it in what the lawyers soon referred to as "elder law."

Interviews with the attorneys had formed a pattern of solid expertise in areas such as wills and probate, inheritances, and trust funds. They also found a strong sensitivity among the firm members toward the senior market, and a genuine compassion for the plight of an aging population in issues such as lifestyles and health care.

The secondary research indicated that this was a probable growth area for the practice of law. A significantly aging population, due mostly to inmigration of retirees from other regions, was predicted. In interviews with leaders of local groups as diverse as chambers of commerce and Associated General Contractors, the research pointed to increasing concern and efforts to deal with an older population and their unique needs, ranging from buying habits to housing needs, from health care to insurance.

Once the interests of the attorneys were compared with population trends, it became clear to the firm that a practice serving older citizens was appropriate. But since the attorneys had done relatively little prior work in this area and only for isolated clients, they needed a coordinated business development program to enter this market.

They initiated research activities to understand this client group. They also continued research, which included subscriptions to senior citizen publications to stay aware of current issues. Those partners who were eligible joined the American Association of Retired Persons (AARP).

The primary method of introduction to this market was through trade group memberships. Specifically, the firm identified business and professional groups already serving this market, which included health care associations (especially nursing home associations), funeral home operator associations, and a committee of the local home builders association.

The attorneys then set about an organized program of active participation in each of these groups. They assigned two attorneys in the business group with a genuine interest to become associate members, and to become involved with various committees within the organization. In doing so, the attorneys became vitally aware of issues facing the senior market. Their membership in the groups enabled them to develop name recognition among the target audiences by capitalizing on opportunities to demonstrate their expertise in speeches, seminars, and related activities as appropriate.

In addition, firm attorneys sought out opportunities to reach the senior market through other methods outside of the trade group membership, such as donations to senior centers, volunteer work with "meals-on-wheels" groups, and limited pro bono legal services to nonprofit groups servicing senior needs.

With a year of a concentrated effort, the firm was well recognized in the city as the "senior citizen's friend," providing services not only to many individuals, but also to funeral home associations and several individual funeral homes in issues ranging from land use to construction liens.

Chapter 72
Making Those Contributions Yield a Good Return

SUMMARY

Virtually every attorney or firm makes contributions of some kind. Establishing guidelines for donations—no matter how small—can increase the benefit of the donation to both the recipient and the attorney. Methods are direct *donations* of cash to the organization's general fund or *sponsorship* of an advertisement or activity that in turn supports the group.

This chapter discusses

- effective disbursement of attorney resources (time and money).
- value of donating cash versus the value of donating resources.
- guidelines for a strong contribution policy.

For years, larger corporations have assigned professional managers to handle their charitable contribution programs. The requests are so many and the monies paid out so great that the task requires considerable attention. Some of the larger law firms are now beginning to do the same.

Attorneys and law firms are frequently sought out for charitable contributions. In larger firms, the requests are channeled through various individuals, sometimes reaching the executive committee level and sometimes paid out of department or sections budgets. In general, the activity is not well managed. Therein lies a missed opportunity for attorneys to help their overall business development efforts through a preplanned, effective charitable contribution program.

Requests for money come from many directions and there are obviously many forms that charity can take. But not all methods of community support are "cost effective" in the sense that they have a "return on investment" to the attorney in terms of goodwill and increased visibility.

It is understood that there does not have to be a "return" on every contribution. But it is possible for attorneys to manage their contributions, no matter how small, both to meet their personal needs and to support their business development effort.

ESTABLISHING POLICY GUIDELINES

Before any contribution of money can be made, it is very helpful to have a contribution policy in place. A good attorney policy defines the type of organizations suitable for assistance. It places a dollar "lid" on total contributions of the budget period. A policy helps screen out numerous miscellaneous requests. It saves attorney and staff time by immediately identifying a request for funding as appropriate or not.

Policy guidelines are relatively easy to establish and difficult to maintain. By definition they are guidelines, not budgets. As requests come in, contributions are each evaluated on an individual basis to see how they fit within the guidelines. Specific line-item donations are addressed in the firm's overall marketing budget.

Even though an executive committee may embrace the concept and adopt a strict policy, in reality there will always be exceptions. Each senior partner has his or her own "pet" charity, and donations will be made to the charity whether it makes good marketing sense or not.

A large law firm hired a consultant to evaluate the firm's charitable contributions over a period of ten years and to make recommendations for future activity. The consultant understood the firm to be oriented toward new business development. At the same time, the consultant knew that senior partners had a strong personal interest in education.

Based on his research, the consultant met with the five senior partners, recommending the deletion of more than 15 organizations, each one receiving a contribution from the firm totaling $56,000 during the past year alone. From the consultant's point of view, there was no legitimate reason for continued support of the various groups. However, in a review meeting with the partners, the contribution to each group was defended by an attorney who had a special interest in the group. Ultimately, all but two of the consultant's recommendations were rejected.

The point is that even the best policies and guidelines need room for individual interests. However, they force decisions to be made regarding donation policies, decisions which are of tremendous assistance to others within larger organizations when unsolicited requests come in for funding. Good policy guidelines save considerable time by allowing administrative personnel or a managing partner confidently to reject a request before any significant time is consumed reviewing it.

A contribution policy for an attorney or firm should adhere to the same general principles established for pro bono work. In other words, the contributions should be evaluated in terms of their ability to capture the attention and goodwill of clients and potential clients in the attorney's recognized areas of practice.

STRENGTH AND CONSISTENCY

There are two attributes of contribution programs—whether the donations are to the operating fund or to sponsor a specific activity—that should be present for overall success. They are *strength,* meaning that when a group is selected for support that the attorney's contributions be significant, and *consistency,* meaning that reliable, predictable funding of selected charities by an attorney leads to a greater impact for the program.

Some of the more successful attorney contribution programs are those that do not try to cover all the bases. They are relatively limited in their scope but deep in their penetration. This means that contributions are given to a relatively few programs and organizations but each of those is strongly supported. The decision of where to put the resources is difficult. But once the commitment is made, the resources concentrated on that one spot should be significant.

Consistency is the other major characteristic of successful contribution programs. Thoughtful, meaningful contribution programs are the offshoot of well-planned business development programs. Since both programs have long-term objectives, the best contribution programs are not flash-in-the-pan ideas. Too many law firms, having decided to contribute to a worthwhile cause, look for a charity that is "hot" this year and join hundreds of others making a donation. Long range, a more effective program is to adopt one or more charities and support them as strongly and as long as possible.

PUBLICITY

Publicity to make others aware of the attorney's donations to organizations can be worthwhile. Announcements or news releases drawing attention to the attorney's or firm's efforts, assuming they are significant, can reflect favorably on the donor and add to overall awareness and goodwill.

To achieve maximum benefit from the donation to build client goodwill, it is appropriate to send a letter to clients informing them of the contribution. Perhaps they can receive copies of the transmittal letter when the check is sent to the receiving group.

Publicity will also draw more requests for contributions. But those can easily be handled by establishing a standard response, either by phone or in letter form, that simply states the attorney or firm has budgeted only a certain amount for contributions in this year and that other requests that fit within the attorney's policy guidelines will be considered for next year. The person or agency requesting a donation will therefore indicate its seriousness by resubmitting a proposal for funding at a later date.

The strong, consistent approach to contributions results in a partnership being developed between attorney and recipient. This can provide significant benefits in terms of personal satisfaction and business development for years to come.

CASH DONATIONS

Contributions of cash to groups is a strong, simple statement that the attorney or firm believes in the organization and its goals. But why not try to focus these resources on organizations that are also in keeping with the attorney's own goals? As with pro bono, a great benefit for the client-focused attorney can be attained if this effort is carried out in concert with the attorney's business development objectives.

Certainly, some money will be donated without a connection to anything—simply because it represents the personal interests of the attorney. But a good contribution program is proactive. It seeks out opportunities where the donation would not only be of value and appreciated by the recipients but also provide increased visibility and goodwill among a previously identified target audience.

SPONSORSHIPS

Sponsorships are contributions to a group or organization which will use the money to carry out a specific activity. This differs from contributions to a "general operating fund" that the receiving organization can use for any variety of purpose it chooses. The opportunity for attorneys to build goodwill and publicity is great through sponsorships, providing they are carefully chosen. Particularly in the case of larger contributions, the benefit can be particularly effective if some sort of follow-through by the attorney occurs during the lifetime of the event.

Sponsorships can range from "buying" a park bench in a downtown redevelopment project to sponsoring an entire jazz concert. Activities where the attorney or firm is sponsoring the entire event are discussed in detail in Chapter 76, "Affinity Marketing."

Sponsorships for attorneys frequently take the form of participation with public broadcasting stations to obtain and broadcast various programs. While this activity is not strictly called advertising, it essentially is. The attorney's or firm's name appears at the beginning and end of the program, with a statement acknowledging their sponsorship. Only in rare cases is any substantive information provided about the firm and its areas of practice.

The value of this kind of sponsorship is remote for its potential marketing value. Like advertising, a great degree of money must be provided over a long haul to establish any significant name recognition for the firm. Also, this type of programming has a tremendous "me-too" element attached, since other professional firms do this quite frequently.

Another area of sponsorship is the purchase of advertising space in newspapers and magazines to encourage participation or recognition of a nonprofit organization. An example is a "salute to our local farmers" structured as a special section of a local newspaper or the running of an adverstisement in some sort of special-event program the group is sponsoring. In general, the costs are high for this kind of "support." The dollars spent often do more to support the newspaper or the printer than they do the organization and very little is received by the needy group.

Sponsorships in both broadcast and print media must be continual to have any significant impact. In addition, there are costs for design and production of the messages related to the sponsorship, although sometimes the media will produce the advertisement at no additional charge. But as with all media-produced advertisements, there are quality issues that must be addressed (see Chapters 58 through 60 on advertising for discussion of media-produced advertisements).

MATCHING GIFTS PROGRAM

One kind of contribution program that is being increasingly adopted by law firms is a matching gift program. This is modeled after those adopted by large corporations where the company simply matches the personal contributions of its employees, usually on a one-to-one basis.

Attorneys can include this in their own client-focused business development program by informing firm members that it matches all personal gifts to certain charities which of course are the charities the firm had already identified as appropriate for its own contribution purposes. This can have the impact of significantly increasing donations to a particular group.

One law firm wished to support a nonprofit music festival. The firm had contributed $5,000 annually to the festival for many years but was considering increasing its level of support. To draw attention to its past commitments, the law firm announced, through a series of print advertisements, that it would match, on a one-to-one basis, the contributions of any individuals. The firm also announced that its own historic level of support would continue unabated.

The result? Individual contributions increased to $3,500 that year, after averaging around $2,000 for the past few years. The law firm matched the $3,500, making its own total gift $8,500. The music festival was thrilled to have received a total of $12,000 in contributions, having averaged around $7,000 in previous years. The music group was so pleased with the law firm's matching gifts program that it took out advertisements subsequent to the festival thanking the firm for its past support.

Matching gifts also work effectively for donations to law schools. Through publicity at the law schools, it is useful as a recruiting device. Another innovative twist is to offer a matching program exclusively to clients, that is, the law firm says that it will match a client's contribution to any charity up to a certain limit.

CHAPTER 73
Effective Volunteering: Making Your "Free" Time Pay Off

SUMMARY

Changing social conditions are causing nonprofit groups to pursue attorneys more actively for assistance. Because attorneys tend to be joiners by nature, they can use their volunteer time to aid nonprofit groups while satisfying personal and professional goals. A common pitfall for aggressive attorneys is to take on too much responsibility and ultimately benefit no one.

This chapter discusses

- how the wise and effective use of contributions of attorney time in nonlegal capacities can fit into the total business development package.
- a process for selecting the "right" group.
- valuable types of in-kind contributions that attorneys can provide.

If a client-focused attorney or firm is looking to build goodwill among clients, a program of altruism can help accomplish this. Pro bono work, discussed in Chapter 74, is one method. Another is for the attorney to donate personal time to various charitable and civic improvement organizations. Virtually every attorney will engage in this practice to some degree during his or her career. Because of their background and training, attorneys are more sensitive to the political and social climate in which they operate. Therefore, they are more inclined to participate in community activities.

Americans in general volunteer a lot. A Gallup survey, sponsored by the Independent Sector, found that 84 million Americans did volunteer work, totaling 8.4 billion hours. The survey revealed that 47 percent of American adults volunteered over a one-year period in a structured setting. Thirty-one percent of these volunteer on a regular, active basis.

The opportunities to volunteer are vast. The pressure to do so is growing, caused by three trends: reduction of federal funding policies, reduction of government assistance programs, and increased expectations of the public for more services from voluntary organizations. In response to these trends, the agencies seek additional funding and increased volunteer time from private sources and individuals.

The nonprofit organizations can be expected to look toward attorneys more and more for assistance. Therefore, a planned program to respond to this demand is well advised.

DIFFERENCE FROM PRO BONO WORK

Community volunteering is different from pro bono work. Pro bono is legal service provided by an attorney acting as an attorney. But there are many charitable activities wherein attorneys are acting as concerned citizens of the community who just happen to be an attorney. Examples are when attorneys serve on a local school board or help a needy group on a fund-raising drive or plan a long-range strategy to recruit new members.

The difference is that pro bono work requires attorney training and competence; other kinds of altruism do not, although the attorney's intelligence and discipline will no doubt be of value to the group in various ways.

The donation of time to carefully selected nonprofit groups has the advantage of enabling the attorney to meet a large number of people in exactly the desired client group. The attorney also has the opportunity to demonstrate positive attributes of leadership, hard work, and dedication. By using their time effectively, the attorney can quickly generate awareness of their general professional abilities. The attorney can demonstrate good character, insightful thinking, and effectiveness while working on group activities such as the annual fund-raising auction and year-end "thank you" banquet.

Sometimes the return on this kind of activity can be very quick. While it takes a long time to build relationships, the needs of charitable and non-profit groups are often great and immediate. Therefore, the attorney can begin work immediately to demonstrate general skills.

The importance of establishing the credentials of the attorney in a nonlegal context cannot be underrated. Research has shown again and again that personal knowledge or personal referral is the primary basis for the purchase of legal services by the public. Therefore, getting to know people and establishing relationships builds a credibility and a trust that no amount of brochures or advertising can match. It is the greatest single activity for successful new business development. There is no experience like working shoulder to shoulder to build relationships!

CHOOSING THE RIGHT GROUP

To achieve maximum benefit for the client-focused attorney, the group chosen for services should be selected carefully. Its membership and activities must be of interest to the attorney. The group's goals and objectives must also be of interest and value to the attorney's clients or desired clients. As with groups joined for social reasons, it should be selected based on the visibility and prestige associated with the group.

Other criteria to consider in choosing the right group is an established pattern of leadership succession (so that leadership roles become open and available to newcomers) and the quality of the board of directors. Is there frequent turnover? Or is the board relatively stable without being do-nothings?

There are some disadvantages of active volunteerism. It takes time—perhaps up to ten hours a month during business hours and untold evenings and weekend hours. Leadership in some groups requires even more time commitments. Another disadvantage is that if the group is popular and useful for attorneys, it may also be hard to "stand out" among several competitors.

COMMUNITY INVOLVEMENT

While it may not seem readily apparent that some types of civic activism or community involvement will help an attorney's professional career, experience has shown that involvement is usually worth the effort. Involvement in activities from barbershop quartets to Little League coaching all place the attorney in social situations where relationships are established and, ultimately, sources of new business appear.

There is no way that an attorney can be effective and obtain benefits from a group in which he or she has only passing interest. Therefore, it is an error to join a social and community-improvement organization (examples: Rotary, Lions, Downtown clubs, etc.) unless the person has a deep interest in it. The important point is to recognize the possibility of business development through relationships established within the group.

Whether the group is a chamber of commerce or a neighborhood home owners association, the importance of getting involved is crucial. Many attorneys lend their names to letterhead as honorary board members or allow themselves to be elected or appointed to board positions or committee leadership, while they privately realize they cannot participate at a full level.

This can hurt the attorney in two ways: it implies that the individual does not live up to commitments or "keep his word." It also creates the impression that the attorney is spread too thin and is probably so busy that no new work could possibly be handled. Therefore, no referrals are forthcoming.

So it is better to concentrate resources on only a few worthwhile charities and organizations and to maintain an active presence therein!

IN-KIND CONTRIBUTIONS

Realizing that time is the most important commodity possessed by an attorney, methods are sought to establish and maintain community involvement and support without the direct time commitment so often required.

One method is through in-kind contributions, which are noncash methods of assistance but nevertheless deductible from taxes for the attorney. Examples are

- making photocopies for the group.
- allowing use of office machines and equipment.
- allowing use of office telephones in the evening for telethons.
- donating desks and other office furniture.
- allowing use of certain staff for office services, such as secretarial or research.

In-kind contributions are worth full value to the using organizations because their only other options are to purchase the goods or services on the open market.

Chapter 74
Pro Bono: How to Fit Your Volunteer Work into a Business-Development Program

SUMMARY

Pro bono work can have a marketing value for attorneys. The key is to work for individuals or groups whose success is of interest to existing clients or potential clients. If pro bono is undertaken as part of a business development program, then judicious publicity of the activity has additional value to the attorney.

This chapter discusses

- examples of effective pro bono work.
- importance of selecting a focus for the effort, that is, relating the work to the attorney's interests.
- how to attract attention and build additional goodwill as a result of pro bono work.

"I think it is only right that our attorneys donate some of their time for pro bono work in the community," says the senior partner of the firm. "It is a tradition of the legal profession to serve those who are unable to afford our services. It is a moral obligation."

"That's all good and well," counters another partner. "But the bar already has a program in place and we send a couple of associates over to help now and then. I think they stand in a booth at shopping centers or something and help people determine whether they need a lawyer or not. That's enough. We can't afford to have attorneys spending otherwise billable time working for free. If they have any extra time, they should be off looking for new business."

"Wait a minute," suggests a third partner. "Can't we find some way to make our pro bono services work for us in business development? It seems to me if we can find situations which provide a genuine community service but at the same time increase our attorney's visibility and credibility, then we are accomplishing both goals. Let's figure out some way to do that."

Professional services provided pro bono publico (Latin for "for the public good or welfare") by attorneys are not only of great value to those receiving them. If the type of work and the recipient are selected carefully, the work can also have great business-development value. This is a new concept just beginning to be understood by attorneys. In the foregoing narrative, it is the third partner that has hit upon the best program to satisfy both his partners' needs.

Pro bono services will never by themselves result in successful new business. But they have a legitimate role to play in a marketing plan. Their role will be established along side other volunteer work, club memberships, seminars, and contributions as being one of many efforts to comprise a comprehensive and successful business development program.

Pro bono work is ingrained in the tradition of attorneys and has now become a formal part of most bar associations. Most practicing members of the bar, at some point in their careers, will perform pro bono work. While some professions such as doctors may in effect donate some "free" services to the needy, there is no other program that begins to compare with the attorney pro bono work. All attorneys can be justifiably proud of their profession and this tradition of community service.

But while attorneys may embrace pro bono work, it is invariably unfocused and not coordinated within a marketing program. It will therefore have little direct value to the attorney. The needy will obtain legal services, and the attorney will "feel good about it." But there is a great potential for additional value to the attorney.

WHAT IS PRO BONO?

Pro bono work was defined in the previous chapter as professional legal services voluntarily provided to individuals or groups where the attorney's services are recognized and accepted as competent legal guidance. In pro bono work, attorneys provide professional counsel and services that require the unique training and expertise that only an attorney possesses.

Other volunteer work performed may draw on the attorney's unique skill and background, but it is not pro bono if the attorney is acting as an individual and not necessarily representing the legal profession. There are many kinds of community service and volunteer work where an attorney donates his or her time and energies that do not fit the definition of pro bono.

Much pro bono work is sponsored through a local or statewide bar association. But many attorneys and firms are finding they can obtain much greater benefits and aid the needy as well if they initiate a program on their own. This enables them to have greater control over the input and outcome of the effort and to maximize program benefits for all concerned. Good pro bono programs provide high-quality legal service to needy groups, improve attorney self-worth and fulfillment, and help business development efforts.

EXAMPLES OF PRO BONO WORK

Pro bono work has a tremendous value for society and is a boost to the overall image of the legal profession. It helps to dispel the myth that the profession is self-centered.

While attorneys themselves do most of the pro bono work, paralegals are also becoming involved in it. In New York, some of the larger firms release their paralegals for a certain number of hours per month to participate in social security hearings. For paralegals employed in business and corporate litigation, the opportunity to work one on one with clients and deal with "human issues" is usually most welcome.

Both attorneys and legal assistants of a Pittsburgh law firm have volunteered to work with the homeless, dealing with issues as varied as social security, family law (such as getting a temporary restraining order lifted), and welfare matters.

VALUE TO ATTORNEYS

There is little agreement among attorneys of the value of pro bono work for marketing purposes. The enthusiasm for it varies greatly. For the client-focused attorney, pro bono work can be incorporated into a business development program by actively seeking out opportunities that fit pro bono criteria.

Services are most frequently provided in areas such as unemployment compensation, custody cases, social security, and other matters related to welfare. Senior citizens receive a good deal of pro bono work. Service is typically provided through activities such as "law day," where attorneys will go to senior centers and offer no-obligation counseling in 30-minute sessions, and so on.

But of what value is this to an attorney or firm that emphasizes corporate law and insurance defense? Very little. Since the opportunities for pro bono work are virtually endless, a little thought and focus by the attorney can ensure that these efforts work to support and complement other business-development efforts.

SELECTING A FOCUS

An attorney or firm needs to identify individual or group goals (from the personal marketing plan or the firm marketing plan) and identify situations where pro bono work will support these efforts. Here is a listing of typical areas of attorney practice where pro bono work would support the marketing program:

- Admiralty law
- Personal injury
- Wills/probate
- Land use, real estate
- Landlord/tenant
- Debtor rights

While the immediate return on this investment may not always be present, the attorney will gain visibility and respect among many people who can be sources of work and referrals in the future. Judges, other attorneys, boards of directors, and individuals associated with these groups will all become aware of the work and will recognize the attorney's character and capabilities.

PUBLICITY OF PRO BONO WORK

Recalling our definition of good marketing ("doing good work and telling about it"), it follows that good efforts by an attorney or firm in the pro bono area can be used to draw favorable attention to a law firm. This can be done in various ways, ranging from tasteful tombstone advertisements in the general-interest media to mentions of the work in speeches and letters.

It is entirely appropriate for an attorney or firm to create an advertisement that says something to the affect of this:

> George J. Jones, attorney-at-law, is pleased to announce the completion of litigation work on behalf of the Westside Home for Unwed Mothers. The home will continue to provide shelter and counseling services at its present location on W. Main Street, following approval by the City to allow its conditional use permit. Mr. Jones, a land use attorney of the firm Johnson & Jones, provided legal counsel and services at no cost to the Westside Home.

An alternative is for the board of directors of the Westside Home to make the announcement. In either event, the tombstone adverstisement could be placed by the attorney in various publications where it would be seen by clients and potential clients who would value the land use and zoning abilities of the attorney. This kind of activity is a clear example of embracing two of the "six Ps" of marketing—publics and politics (see Chapter 1 for explanation of the six Ps of marketing).

The same language could also be used to issue a news release on the subject. The release must be written so that it is usuable by the media, that is, the "news" is not that the attorney helped Westside for free but that the shelter received the conditional use permit.

Publicity like this invariably results in additional requests from other groups for assistance. Depending on the attorney's or firm's ability to help, other opportunities can be considered. An appropriate way to say "no" is to simply state that the attorney or firm has budgeted a certain number of attorney hours for pro bono work and that the Westside Shelter consumed this amount. The attorney can then tell the inquirer to send a letter of request for services for next year and that it will be considered.

CHAPTER 75
A Unique Approach to Pro Bono: Adopting an Emerging Business

SUMMARY

A creative approach to pro bono work that can reap a multitude of benefits for an attorney or firm is participation in an "adopt an emerging business" program, cosponsored by others interested in economic development, such as a bank, utility, or government agency.

This chapter discusses

- an example of a successful "emerging business" program.
- benefits to attorneys of this kind of program.

Another marketing opportunity for attorneys is a program where an individual attorney or several attorneys from a law firm, often in conjunction with other consultants, "adopts" an emerging business. The firm provides pro bono services to the business for a specified period (usually one year).

The advantages to the attorney or firm of this program is that it concentrates pro bono efforts in one area, allowing for major impact and significant control over events. It can also result in high visibility and significant goodwill among program recipients and other supporters.

"Adoption" programs of emerging businesses are most effective when cosponsored by a government agency. Many cities, counties, or community groups will engage in activities to encourage the growth of emerging businesses. The U.S. government's Small Business Development Centers can put attorneys in contact with emerging businesses and will be a strong cosponsor of the activities. By participating in one of these programs, the attorney or firm will benefit from the goodwill created not only with the company being helped but also the goodwill within the sponsoring agencies.

ADOPTING A KNITTING COMPANY

Here is a case history of a 50-person law firm who participated in a statewide adopt-an-emerging-business program, sponsored by the governor's office of a western state.

> A regional office of a national accounting firm, a bank, and law firm chose to participate in their state's emerging business project. They "adopted" a company that would receive a year of free, coordinated services in the hope of aiding the state's overall economic development.
>
> Five years prior to "adoption," the company was started in a garage. Its products were knitted apparel, mostly made by local women in a small town of 4,000. The company manufactured "fleecewear," which it called a stylish cousin of the sweatshirt. The products came in pullover or cardigan styles and featured knitted decorative panels. They were commonly sold in resorts and boutiques at an average retail price of $42 to $60.
>
> The owners always believed their business had great growth potential. So when the governor's office announced the adoption program, the firm immediately applied along with 200 others.
>
> In the beginning, the owner had designed the first products as a way that women in an economically depressed section of the state could earn enough money to offset partially the cost of a knitting machine. She took the first garments to a local crafts fair, where they sold quickly.

Rapid Growth

> The owner formed a partnership with another woman and set up a business. Orders grew rapidly. Two years prior to adoption, they were selling 1,500 shirts per month. But at the time they applied to the governor's program, the firm was selling between 8,000 and 10,000 pieces in a month.
>
> The rapid growth left the partners uncomfortable with their business skills. One owner received business advice from her husband who ran three pizza parlors. The other owner had kept books for a family farm but neither felt equipped to run a business with annual sales approaching $1 million.

The bank, accounting firm, and law firm helped the partners build their business skills and solve business problems. The legal firm put together a lease for their plant and, together with the bank, helped refinance the business at a substantially better rate. The accounting firm helped the partners computerize the bookkeeping.

But most of all, the owners reported, it was "simply good to have counselors" to help with everyday problems such as how to set up an employee bonus system or how to deal with personnel problems.

Before being adopted, the partners discussed postponing any growth for a year while they learned more about running a large company. The owners feared getting overextended, so the consultants helped write a long-range business plan for safe, steady growth.

Specifically, the law firm assisted the company in several areas where small, growing businesses typically need legal help: form of entity, financing practices, and lease and other contractual agreements.

Attorney Participation

When the law firm became involved, they discovered the principals of the emerging company were in a partnership. The attorneys recommended the owners incorporate under subchapter S status, pointing out the issues to small-business owners of liability, responsibility for corporate debt, and tax consequences.

The attorneys helped negotiate the termination of an existing inventory purchase financing agreement. This financing arrangement was costly and was using up the capital needed to maintain operations and grow. Once free of the old arrangement, the company was able to pursue less expensive financing.

Because new businesses often are forced into accepting relatively expensive credit terms as a result of their lack of positive credit history, the attorneys moved the company out of its old financing agreement into a more conventional and less costly line of credit. The attorneys noted that although emerging small businesses can operate successfully on cash flow and a certain amount of high-cost credit, significant expansion usually requires a source of reasonable, conventional credit to avoid excessive cash flow drain.

The company held a month-to-month tenancy which either party could terminate on 30 days' notice. After determining the current facility would be adequate for several more years, the attorneys drafted a long-term lease which created greater stability for landlord and tenant and encouraged construction of tenant improvements.

The attorneys also reviewed insurance policies with their broker, consulted on employment law issues, and scrutinized their contracts with suppliers and personnel.

Benefits for Attorneys

The result of this activity was continual coverage in local and statewide newspapers on the innovative program. A major article in a statewide business magazine described the role of the attorneys in detail, along with that of the bank and the accountants. Since the program was initiated and cosponsored by the state governor's office, the state economic development agency continually praised the program in various forums, including department newsletters, public speaking events, and interagency memos. More direct benefits for the law firm included strengthening of relationships with individuals at the accounting firm and at the bank, which led to referrals for other business. In addition, the public information aspect of the program emphasized the role of attorneys to provide assistance in areas of financing and leasing. Other companies, realizing the value of this service, called the firm for assistance in this area.

This case history points out that, from a marketing perspective, the "adoption" approach to pro bono work can work well to supplement other business development activities. The key to a good program lies in ensuring that

- the program is well organized and sponsored by a credible organization or government agency.
- the company being adopted fits the market in which the attorneys wish to practice.
- the attorney regards the adopted company as a genuine client, performing high-quality, professional work.
- attorney staff understand the purpose of the legal work for the adopted company.
- appropriate publicity and recognition is undertaken either by the firm or other sponsors.
- good relationships and referrals from other consultants involved with the project are established.

CHAPTER 76
Affinity Marketing: Minimum Time, Maximum Impact

SUMMARY

Affinity marketing is an approach to business development wherein an attorney or firm provides significant assistance to a single nonprofit organization. It helps attorneys focus their contribution efforts for maximum impact and can provide solid business development benefits.

This chapter discusses

- the concept of affinity marketing.
- a case history of how it can work.
- criteria to select a suitable organization.
- typical costs and time commitments required for a successful program.

Here is a concept that works well for client-focused firms. Like many other of the activities described and recommended for attorneys in this book, this program—called affinity marketing—is designed not only to serve clients but also to attract attention to the firm.

Affinity marketing succeeds as an effective business development method because it satisfies two important criteria of most attorney marketing activity: that it be "professional" and that it be effective.

The concept involves attorney/firm support for a single nonprofit organization. The contribution is usually in the form of both money and attorney time. It differs from pro bono work in that the organization is not necessarily a social service group; it may exist to foster the arts, education, or the environment.

Affinity marketing can become close to sole sponsorship of an organization. To whatever degree it is carried out, it is effective because, within the selected group, the attorney/firm becomes extremely well known and visible. If handled correctly, the attorney develops a reputation for deep commitment to worthwhile charitable organizations, which develops trust and goodwill for the efforts.

To be most effective, the affinity marketing effort is directed toward an organization that is not only important to the attorney but also to a large portion of existing clients. Ideally, the effort involves the attorney's primary practice area, but not necessarily so. Here are some examples:

—For a land use attorney, affinity marketing could be directed toward a local zoning group.

—An attorney from a large firm that reaches for upscale consumers could support a local tennis, fencing, or swimming club.

—An environmental lawyer could support a Friends of the Earth program, providing a well-reasoned, balanced viewpoint.

—A lawyer emphasizing urban renewal law could sponsor a downtown, civic improvement club.

—A client-focused attorney could single out a specific performance of a dance group to provide total underwriting.

Care obviously needs to be given to the selection of the appropriate organization, in view of various political and social overtones connected with affiliation to a particular group. Nevertheless, with care, this activity can be carried out in a most effective manner.

CASE HISTORY OF AN EFFECTIVE PROGRAM

Here is an example of how affinity marketing can work.

> The second largest firm in a city of 200,000 was continually barraged by local nonprofit groups for donations. Historically, the firm scattered various amounts to a large assortment of worthwhile groups in the community, ranging from the region's public broadcasting radio station to a donation to the local 4-H club. The contribution program was not identified as a business-development activity; at the same time, donations of cash to the various groups totaled slightly over 1 percent of the firm's gross annual fee revenues, a relatively large amount of "expense" that lacked any sort of internal control. The list of organizations receiving money from the firm grew and diminished each year, depending on the whims of firm members. No single organization was supported significantly.
>
> Tighter controls over these costs was obviously needed, and the attorneys agreed in concept to a single-cause approach to contributions. "Favorite" charities would have to be abandoned.
>
> The firm agreed to a $20,000 amount as a sponsorship total. Because the firm sought major corporate work that could not be isolated to only one "group," organizations were identified for sponsorship that would attract the largest amount of attention among the broadest range of corporate clients.
>
> Research revealed that there was a strong local effort among prestigious civic organizations to attract more performing arts to the city. After considering several options, the firm agreed to sponsor a "Classical Pops Weekend" at a city park, which featured several symphony orchestras playing music made popular in movies and television. Classical music popular with children was played Saturday morning. In the afternoon there was classical music for seniors. Later in the afternoon was a program of contemporary classics. Into the evening was a "teenagers' classics," featuring themes from movies such as *Superman, Batman,* and *Star Trek,* with appropriate light shows and extra loud sound effects.
>
> A similar but slightly varied program was played on Sunday. Accompanying the music were food booths around the edge of the park, set up by local restaurants.
>
> Throughout the event, the name of the local firm was discreetly displayed and appropriate acknowledgment given by the various conductors. The firm's senior partners were present throughout the performances to introduce the programs.
>
> The actual contributions of the firm took the form of a "loaned" secretary, the payment of fees to a public relations consultant for graphic design and promo-

tional services, payment to printers and sign makers, and payments to the orchestras. Local arts groups, under whose umbrella the symphony played, paid for all other incidentals, including staging and related logistics.

The result was that for one week, the firm's name was prominently displayed and known throughout the community. But more important, it was clearly known among key corporate audiences.

VALUE TO ATTORNEYS

The benefits of affinity marketing for the sponsoring attorney or firm are many. If desired, the program can be conducted almost totally without the sponsor's direct involvement. Yet the sponsor will garner much praise and credit for the success of the organization's programs. The sponsor is also perceived as being truly community service oriented, without self-serving motives.

There are a few risks involved with affinity marketing. If the "wrong" group or event is chosen and the activities do not come off well, the attorney's image can be damaged. Another factor is the difficulty in finding a number of truly worthwhile organizations or "quality" events that are appropriate for this kind of program. At the same time, cost-effectiveness and benefit of these kinds of programs are often hard to quantify.

On the other hand, experience has shown that in terms of bang for the buck, attorneys have felt genuinely excited about affinity marketing activities. Their instincts have told them that the overall effort was more worthwhile than the usual and customary donation and contribution programs. Conducting affinity programs certainly shows community leadership and an innovative spirit!

SELECTION CRITERIA

Affinity marketing can be a very effective method of charitable contributions if the organization selected meets most or all of the following criteria:

1. Deals with a communitywide need that is of interest to a good number of the attorney's clients.
2. Lends itself to publicity, that is, have popular appeal and be "visible ."
3. Not be redundant or a piggyback on somebody else's program (to avoid a "me-too" image).
4. Have staff and operating funds of a level to carry out the programs and events developed for it (in other words, don't sponsor an organization that is operating on a shoestring budget).

Additional considerations are that the program be carried out in such a way as to require a minimum of attorney time and be of a nature that the attorney's contributions will have a major impact.

The process for an attorney to approach affinity marketing is to identify several local organizations that fit the criteria and are, of course, of personal interest to the attorney. Each organization is then sent a letter, explaining the attorney's program and offering help. The letter asks the organization to fill out an application and send additional information as they wish.

METHOD OF SUPPORT

If the attorney wishes, personal interviews can be made and from this can be selected an organization. Essentially, the attorney provides what the organization needs most: general funds for a special event, legal guidance on issues, office equipment, or perhaps the services of a marketing consultant or accountant to perform a special project.

The cost of a major program of this nature will vary, depending on the size of the community and impact desired. But for $10,000–15,000, a significant effort can be made, and resulting publicity and goodwill can be effectively used. Of course, costs can be much less, depending on the organization and degree of involvement desired.

The attractivenss of this approach to charitable contributions is that a major impact can be achieved in a small area. Military tacticians call this a "concentration of force." It can work well on the modern battlefield of practice development.

CHAPTER 77
Social Activities: Fitting Them into the Marketing Plan

SUMMARY

With a little forethought and planning, social activities can assist an attorney's overall business-development efforts. Both attorney-sponsored and community-sponsored events in which the attorney participates can build good relationships with existing and potential clients. But social activities have a value for the client-focused attorney only if the attorney truly enjoys them.

This chapter discusses

- the importance of establishing a clear purpose for attorney social activities.
- how to plan for and carry out a successful attorney open house.
- the value of joining and participating in community-sponsored social activities.

Most attorneys engage in social activities. Rare is the individual or firm that does not at some point entertain one or more clients in a social setting. Socials range from casual lunches to formal open houses, from an invitation to a sporting event to a holiday party for friends and spouses.

Attorney-sponsored social activities are those that are initiated, organized, and paid for by the attorney. They differ from community-sponsored social activities which are organized by someone else (and which are also valuable for marketing purposes). Attorney-sponsored social events are activities where clients, referral sources, and potential clients are invited. Examples include holiday parties, open houses, meet-the-new-partners receptions, fishing trips, golf tournaments, and so on.

ESTABLISHING A PURPOSE

Social activities are by definition designed to create an atmosphere of friendship, warmth, and goodwill. But the attorney can also gain more specific benefits by seizing the opportunity provided by social events to lead to future work. The key is to *define clearly the purpose of an event in terms related to business development.* If this is done correctly, planning for the event will include specific actions before, during, and after that more directly benefit the attorney.

> One 22-attorney firm held an "open house" each December in its penthouse offices. Clients, close friends, referral sources, and colleagues of the firm were invited, as well as their spouses and significant others. Formal invitations were sent a month in advance. Elaborate food and refreshments were catered by a nearby exclusive restaurant. It was always an elegant affair and about 200 people attended every year. A postevent review by the firm had everyone agreeing that the event was a "success."
>
> But was it? Each partner was well known to a few clients and during the two-hour event, each small group of clients, spouses, and the attorney talked to

each other. The firm associates, who had little client contact and therefore did not know them, talked to each other. Referral sources such as bankers and other community business leaders also spent most of the evening talking to each other, because each had little contact with more than one attorney and did not know other people at the firm.

A more careful postevent analysis by the attorneys revealed that little meaningful interaction occurred among attorneys and guests who did not previously know each other. Associates felt that they were cut off from meeting clients. Referrals talked with the attorney who invited them but met few other attorneys from the firm. In view of all this, the event could be called a failure because the attorneys missed opportunities to establish new relationships and impart new information about the firm and its services to the invited guests.

PLANNING AHEAD

In the foregoing example the firm had a purpose ("show appreciation to our clients and friends") but it was too short sighted and narrow. The same event, structured slightly differently, could have had a more meaningful objective such as "cross-sell partner services and introduce associates to clients." In doing so, specific actions could have been incorporated into the events. If these attorneys had stated more clearly their purpose beforehand, they would truly have had a "successful" event. A checklist for planning and carrying out a successful open house is presented in Figure 77-1.

While this checklist applies only to relatively formal attorney-sponsored social events, the principles underlying it are fundamental to all activities. Even fishing trips and spectator sports at which clients, referrals, and attorneys are mixing in a relaxed environment can be used to ensure that marketing information is provided by the attorneys to clients and others.

COMMUNITY-SPONSORED SOCIAL ACTIVITIES

Back in the old days of business development (i.e., prior to *Bates and O'Steen* v. *Arizona*), the single most popular activity for attorneys was club memberships and similar social activities. It was the days of Good Ol' Boy networks and country club marketing. It was easy and comfortable, and it worked. Those were the days when clients hired attorneys because of a personal relationship. That was all that was important. Trust was implicit.

Today, personal relationships remain at the heart of attorney practice development. The only difference is that in the total business development picture, these relationships are no longer sufficient to maintain and build a

- Establish a business-development purpose for the event and announce it to all attorneys. Impress upon attorneys and staff that the open house provides not only an opportunity for developing more personal relationships but for introducing clients to each other and to other attorneys.
- Announce the purpose of the open house in the invitation so that guests will anticipate the evening's agenda. This can be done by saying "The law firm of X, Y, & Z cordially invites you and your guest to an open house at (date, time, location) for the purpose of meeting our new partners and associates, recently added to increase our capabilities in the areas of corporate taxation and labor law. Please join us to celebrate this holiday season."
- Require an R.S.V.P. in the invitation (telephone is usually appropriate).
- Assign attorneys to be "greeters" at the door to direct the guests to the reception table. Rotate this assignment every half-hour or so.
- Prepare handwritten name tags and have a supply of blank ones for unexpected guests (try to have the same person handwrite all name tags).
- Ensure that specific attorneys are introduced to specific guests, depending on the guests' legal needs and the attorney's capabilities. A lead attorney can easily say to a good client: "Frank, I'd like you to meet Tom Johnson. He's in our tax department. You mentioned to me once that the new capital gains taxes were very confusing. Tom here does quite a bit of capital gains work."
- Even if no specific business relationship is known among attorneys and guests, ensure that each guest meets each attorney. Do not let cliques of attorneys, their friends, and spouses develop. Encourage attorneys (associates especially) to make self-introductions ("Hello, you must be a friend of the firm. We haven't met, but I am an attorney here. My name is . . .").
- Follow up with thank you notes to all guests, referring to at least one element of business discussion. This shows that the attorney is not only courteous but also sensitive to others' needs. It portrays a willingness to listen and an eagerness to assist as needed. What client could ask for more?

Figure 77-1 Planning For and Carrying Out a Successful Attorney Open House

successful practice. However, the concept they represent is fundamental to the attorney marketing effort.

Community-sponsored social activities will always be exactly what they are—opportunities to relax and enjoy other people in a completely nonbusiness environment. Activities range from attendance at ballet openings to neighborhood "block parties," from participating in a nonprofit telethon to joining a runner's club. The environment is a meeting hall and a golf course, a downtown opera house and a neighborhood storefront theater.

Many articles on marketing for attorneys discuss social activities as a route to effective networking and ultimately new clients. But as with formal club memberships, social activities have a value for the client-focused attorney only if the attorney truly enjoys the company he or she keeps. In other words, the attorney should ask him or herself: "Am I joining this organization simply because I enjoy it?" The answer must be a resounding "yes" or else the marketing value of the activity is wasted.

SEIZING THE OPPORTUNITIES

There is a great degree of camaraderie and fellowship to be enjoyed in groups ranging from Rotary Clubs to alumni associations, from golf clubs to Masonic Lodges. But without a plan to incorporate this activity into an overall business-development program, their value is often overrated by marketers and by the attorneys themselves.

If clients are members of the same organizations to which an attorney belongs, those joint memberships improve the personal relationships of all concerned. The attorney receives a bonus in improved working relationships and no doubt stronger client loyalty.

The joining of groups and social activities is not a mandatory part of marketing. But since they are so commonplace, it is clear that opportunities present themselves through social activities and that some sort of plan to follow up on these situations is appropriate. Involvement should be voluntary. The value lies in the building of relationships, a lengthy process that will not occur if the attorney is participating out of a sense of obligation.

Other considerations for attorneys is that community-sponsored social activities can be very time consuming. Further, the attorney may find it hard to "stand out" among several competitors who are also involved in the same activity. Because of the large number of other activities that are probably just as enjoyable and potentially beneficial for the attorney, a reevaluation of these activities is in order.

See the membership grid in Figure 71-1 for recommendations on effective use of attorney time in professional and social activities.

APPENDIX 1
When Practice Development Doesn't Work

Practice development programs for attorneys are comprised of many things. Their success or failure is never the result of one isolated activity.

But when the program does not seem to be working, attorneys search for clues. Here is a checklist to isolate what is going wrong.

- The potential client is not purchasing your legal services for personal reasons that are beyond your control.
- The potential client is not purchasing your legal services for political, moral, social, or traditional reasons that are beyond your control.
- You're selling the wrong type of legal services.
- You're selling to the wrong person.
- You're selling to the wrong company.
- You're selling to the wrong industry.
- Your services are priced incorrectly.
- Your service quality is poor.
- Your delivery systems are poor (late, sloppy, etc.).
- Your location is poor.
- Your service is not available when the client wants it.
- Your service is not known by the potential client.
- Your service is not understood by the potential client.
- You or your firm is not known by the potential client.
- You or your firm is not understood by the potential client.
- Your profession has a bad reputation.
- You or your firm have a bad reputation.
- You or your firm lack experience.
- Your company lacks good referrals.
- Your promotional materials and techniques are unconvincing.
- Your promotional materials and techniques are ill timed.
- Your promotional materials and techniques are unappealing to the audience for which they were intended, that is, form or language are wrong.
- The potential client has no interest in your services.
- The potential client has no time to invest in your services.
- The potential client has no need for your services.
- The potential client has no *immediate* need for your services.
- The potential client has no money to purchase your services.
- The potential client is purchasing legal services from someone else and sees no advantage to purchasing your services.
- If none of the above is true, the potential client thinks they are.

APPENDIX 2
Introduction to Real-World Programs

This section contains business development programs and budgets for

1. a sole practitioner in a medium-sized city.
2. a 6-attorney firm in the suburbs of a large city.
3. a 15-attorney firm in a large city.
4. a 30-attorney firm in a secondary market.
5. a 150-attorney firm in a large metropolitan area.

Each plan is a result of analysis of the individual attorneys in each situation. The plans set forth here suggest specific marketing activities and respective costs. Review of them will ease consideration of some elements involved with business development for attorneys. Details on setting budgets and tracking costs for the business-development program are explained in Chapters 35, 36, and 37 of this book.

These plans were developed for attorneys and firms that had accomplished three prerequisites of good practice development: they understood the basic theory of business development, they assessed their situation, and they took care of internal consensus building before embarking on these programs.

The length of time and adequacy of investment will vary according to a variety of circumstances, which have been identified in Chapter 38.

TIME REQUIRED

In the five examples here, it is assumed that the attorneys budgeted themselves for a certain number of billable hours annually. The attorneys therefore planned for "lost revenue" as a cost of the marketing program, that is, that attorney time devoted to marketing would otherwise be billable. Because of the huge "cost" of marketing this represented, attorneys were encouraged to add the marketing hours onto their billable-hour requirements. For budget purposes, the hourly rates for timekeepers were shown at billable rates. Hourly rates for nontimekeepers were shown at cost.

APPENDIX 3
Marketing Budget for the Sole Practitioner

A sole practitioner, sharing an office with two other attorneys, practiced general retail law in a town of 20,000. The town's economy was based on heavy manufacturing and agriculture. The attorney was able to develop a comfortable life-style and working environment through work in family law and bankruptcy. Occasional work in tenant/landlord and labor also came his way. His average billable hours were 1,200, somewhat low compared to the big-city attorneys. But with administrative and other duties necessary to run the practice, the attorney seemed to have little other choice.

The population of the town was growing, but so was the number of attorneys moving in. The net result was a very stable market for each attorney. Everyone seemed to get their fair share. Few of the 25 attorneys in the community were starving, yet few were getting rich. The biggest local firm had 5 attorneys.

However, the amount of legal fees paid by local businesses was increasing steadily. As businesses became involved in more complicated issues ranging from environmental law to labor issues, the local businesses turned to the larger law firms in the metropolitan area, 150 miles away. In the eyes of the business owners, the local attorneys did not have the expertise to handle complex issues.

The amount of legal work in the community available to each attorney was not growing. The sole practitioner realized that growth in his practice could occur only through an aggressive and focused marketing program.

Once this decision was made, the attorney analyzed how the total dollars for legal work were spent in the community. He immediately recognized that the greatest opportunity for the larger fees and more professional challenge lay in capturing some business that was going out of town. This was the speciality work purchased by local businesses from the larger, out-of-town firms.

The sole practitioner realized that he must narrowly define an area of emphasis, then develop a plan to communicate his experience and skill in this area to local business. What would be the area that the attorney found desirable and at the same time lucrative? In analyzing his past work, the attorney acknowledged that he enjoyed the few labor law issues that he handled. He had studied independently in this area and had once written an article on the subject for a bar bulletin.

To raise awareness of his expertise in labor, the attorney selected an aggressive program. He conducted informal research to find which area might bear the most results. He contacted other attorneys in the area for their opinions. He also called law school classmates who worked for the larger firms.

At the same time, news media throughout the state had been reporting on several statewide labor issues. One problem was the exploding rates of worker's compensation insurance for employers, due to mismanagement by a state-controlled insurance organization. Another was widespread abuse of the program by individual employees.

Since the attorney had a background and some experience in worker's compensation, the attorney decided to make a marketing effort to increase his defendant work in this area. The attorney would continue his general practice, which was mostly the result of referrals, and continue work from existing clients.

Activities	Portion of Total Effort
Writing of specific marketing plan with clearly defined goals, to include budget and precise schedule of activities	5%
Development, writing, and printing of a fact sheet on worker's compensation experience and services	10
Development of a direct-mail program to draw attention to attorney's work, sent to past and potential clients	20
Personal relationship-building activities with CEOs and human resource managers	30
Personal selling activities to other attorneys for referrals	25
News releases and media relations with local editor on labor law and worker's compensation stories (who always wanted a "local angle" on the statewide events	10

Time Required	Lost Revenue or Cost
Attorney—120 hours @ $100	$12,000
Staff—220 hours @ $25	$5,500
	$17,500

Out-of-Pocket Costs	
Direct Mail	$3,500
Entertainment, travel	1,000
Fact sheet design and production	1,200
News releases and media relations	600
Personal selling activities	800
Expenses and supplies	2,000
	$9,100
Total:	$26,600

APPENDIX 4
Marketing Budget for a 6-Attorney Firm

Six attorneys pooled their libraries, office equipment, and talents to form a new firm. Their office was on the suburban fringe of a medium-sized town. The firm was named for three of the founding partners; all six were partners and very entrepreneurial. There were no associates. They had an excellent group of five paralegals and legal secretaries, plus a good support staff.

Each attorney had his or her general practice and was known individually as doing excellent work. If there was a uniting bond, it was real estate. Clients were mostly middle class, and there were many of them. The office of the attorneys was designed to encourage drop-ins. They advertised in the Yellow Pages ($400 a month) and on average took on about 15 new cases, each, a month.

When their landlord came around with a three-year renewal lease on the 2,500-square-foot space, the attorneys met to discuss their future together. With average fees at $100/hour and each attorney billing and collecting 1,400 hours annually, they agreed that their practices were successful and they made comfortable livings. But some of them were not fully satisfied professionally. Their work and the cases they brought to trial were beginning to seem all the same. The intellectual challenges were fewer and fewer.

Further discussion revealed diverging interests among the six. Individually, each attorney expressed personal and financial needs that were different from the others. There was no common goal in sight. Further, none of the attorneys had a plan of how to reach their individual goals. Each attorney agreed that they enjoyed the camaraderie of the group and liked the working conditions, office location, staff support, and so on. In other words, nothing was terribly wrong but changes were needed.

Collectively, there was no clear pathway for future direction. Without viable options, the attorneys reluctantly agreed to sign the lease and continue along as before.

Soon after the meeting, one partner sensed that if the firm took no action to meet the personal goals of the attorneys, the group would begin to deteriorate and the loss would be felt by all.

In further discussing this topic with the other attorneys, a modest program was undertaken to create internal consensus regarding their strategic plan and to begin a proactive marketing program to attract a more upscale client base.

The managing partner drafted a basic plan for business development. The attorneys met one Friday afternoon to agree that they would work to build a one-year plan and budget. Their first activity was an all-day Saturday meeting at a partner's home to consider future options. Here is their intitial plan.

First-Year Activities	Portion of Total Effort
To hire a management consultant to analyze individual attorney needs and goals, and to develop a business plan to unify and reach these goals	20%
With help of consultant, to write a marketing plan for the firm and for each individual	25
To write, produce, and distribute a folder containing descriptions of the firm's various services and biographies of each attorney	10
To develop news releases and media relations with the editor of the suburban newspaper to generate articles that mention the firm or any of the attorneys in it	10
To volunteer for more community activities aimed at business people and upper-middle-class groups; to take on a more active leadership role in the local chamber of commerce	15
To deliver speeches and seminars on real estate to establish firm's expertise and encourage referrals	15
To redirect advertising to reach more upscale clients	5

Time Required	Lost Revenue or Cost
Named partners A, B, and C—200 hours each @ $110	$66,000
Other partners D, E, and F—160 hours each @ $90	$43,200
Staff A—300 hours @ $20	$6,000
	$115,200

Out-of-Pocket Costs	
Consultant fees	$6,500
Business plan development, writing (consultant)	3,500
Folder design and production	4,500
News releases, media relations (partially handled by consultant)	2,000
Community involvement, membership dues	1,200
Speeches, seminars	5,500
Advertising	6,000
Entertainment, travel	3,500
Expenses and supplies	1,000
	33,700
Total:	148,900

APPENDIX 5
Marketing Budget for the 15-Attorney Firm

Almost invisible to all but a few clients was a 15-attorney firm in a large metropolitan area. The founding partner of the firm, on whose reputation more than half the firm's work rested, was still active. Through early retirement, three of the other senior partners had left the firm. The managing partner was 50 and other named partners were all in their forties.

A cautious and conservative group of younger associates was attracted to the firm by its reputation. They enjoyed the comfortable, steady working atmosphere and the grind-it-out orientation of the firm. Four of the attorneys were litigators. The firm required 1,600 billable hours from all timekeepers and got it.

The attorneys in the firm worked hard and the firm was profitable. The firm had built a regional reputation on the senior partner's work in municipal bonds. The other major areas of emphasis were transportation law (where the litigators were) and tax law.

The firm lacked orientation toward new business development. They had done excellent work for their existing clients and had fortunately continued to receive additional work from them. The managing partner and one of the associates continually brought up the subject of marketing to the partners but to little avail. There was no serious need to "get new business." Everyone realized that the departure within the next five years of the senior partner would have an impact on the firm. At the same time, the solid and deep relationships they felt existed between them and client organizations were sufficient to ensure a continual flow of work.

The partnership finally agreed to prepare a client retention plan, reflecting the conservative nature of the firm (never was the word "marketing" mentioned in the plan or in discussions among attorneys). The plan aimed entirely at retaining existing clients. One of its objectives was to ensure the smooth transition of work following the departure of the senior partner.

As the firm carried out its client retention plan, it began to attract the attention of other potential client companies who had similar legal needs. Through exclusive client-focused activity, the firm was able to establish a solid basis for growth.

While the firm acknowledged that attorney time would be required to carry out the plan, no formal budget developed until after the first year. At that time, the firm learned what it had spent on their program. Because of their success, they were able to schedule more activities in the second year and begin to take other steps to increase their visibility before potential clients.

Here is the firm's first-year plan.

Activities	Portion of Total Effort
Client survey to obtain direct feedback on the firm's performance	25%
More active role in client trade associations	30
Meetings with clients to ask for referrals within client's business area	15
Sponsorship of a half-day seminar on current legal issues for clients	25
Holiday luncheon buffets, served in the attorneys' offices, one for each of the three major client groups	5

Time Required	Lost Revenue or Cost
Partner A—60 hours @ $125	$ 7,500
Partners B and C—40 hours each @ $110	$ 8,800
Partner D—200 hrs @ $100	$20,000
All other partners (4)—75 hrs each @ $85 average	$25,500
Associate A—100 hrs @ $80	$ 8,000
All other associates (6)—50 hrs each @ $75 average	$22,500
Staff A—600 hours @ $25	$15,000
Staff B—180 hours @ $20	$ 3,600
Other staff (5)—100 hours each @ $20 average	$10,000
	$120,900

Out-of-Pocket Costs	
Seminars, including materials	6,000
Client survey	2,500
Trade association memberships	2,750
Upgrade of graphics, resumes, fact sheet	4,500
Tombstone and other selected advertising	9,000
Referral sources	1,500
Holiday buffets	3,100
Entertainment, travel	5,000
Expenses and supplies	3,000
	37,350
Total:	158,250

Appendix 6
Marketing Budget for a 30-Attorney Firm

A 30-attorney firm had established a previously solid but slowly eroding practice in a top ten market. The firm was a blend of about 10 aggressive and highly visible attorneys, with the remainder effectively practicing law in their specialty areas.

The firm had gained a reputation among its existing clients for superior work and was used for general services by several large corporate clients. The firm was counsel to several smaller corporations but attracted only specialty work from the larger companies. The key attorneys had developed long-term relationships with corporate counsel within the firm and consistently referred work to them. At an average of 1,800 hours annually billed by each attorney, the firm was profitable.

But the practice was eroding because of slowly changing market conditions and attrition among key clients who were retiring or transferred out of the area. Since the firm's strength built on personal relationships, it was vulnerable to situations out of its control.

The firm was conservative, did outstanding work, and received good referrals from time to time because of this. But there was no comprehensive marketing effort. The marketing budget consisted almost exclusively of entertainment items—tickets to sporting and cultural events (about half given to clients and the rest used by the attorneys themselves); annual fishing trips on a charter boat; and numerous meals, social receptions, and parties.

While the individual attorneys all had their own enjoyment from the practice of law, there was no common goal of the firm, either written or spoken. Each practice group had their clients and practice emphasis. One or two partners led each group, with two or three associates to help them. Associates rarely saw clients. In essence, the firm functioned as approximately ten individual practices within the larger organization.

Some attorneys were concerned about the eroding client base. They saw the situation because of social and political factors, which in essence it was. The attorneys' work was always superior and no client ever told them that it wasn't.

The managing partner, concerned as much for a secure retirement program as for anything else, decided to look at a business-development program. The partner realized the importance of building a "firm," rather than maintaining what essentially was a dozen or so individual practices. He also realized that a closer look at the future market in the firm's practice areas, perhaps by talking to clients, might be helpful.

But where to start? The managing partner asked a consultant to provide broad-based recommendations for future action. Based on an analysis of the firm's situation, the consultant recommended the following program:

Activities	Portion of Total Effort
Weekend retreat to build internal consensus about the firm's strategic plan, and also to impress upon all attorneys the importance of a unified effort to maintain firm integrity and longevity	10%
Market trend survey to gain insights into future changes in the attorneys' specialty areas	5
Client surveys to gain information on exactly the quality of work performed and client suggestions that may be helpful to increase the firm's work for them	25
Development of marketing plan	15
Writing, producing, and distributing a brochure	15
Announcements/tombstones	5
Sponsorship of two forums for clients to build relationships and increase visibility of associates: one forum to consist of a celebrity speaker, noted for strong views in an area of the attorney's work; the other to consist of a private debate between local politicians on solutions to a regional land use issue	20
"Image" advertising	5

Time Required	Lost Revenue or Cost
Partner A—300 hours @ $120	$36,000
Partners B and C—140 hours each @ $100	28,000
Partner D—400 hours @ $80	32,000
All other partners (6)—100 hours each @ $80 (average)	48,000
Associate A—500 hours @ $65	32,500
Associate B—300 hours @ $65	19,500
All other associates (18)—60 hours each @ $65 (average)	70,200
Staff A—900 hours @ $25	22,500
Staff B—400 hours @ $20	8,000
Other staff (5)—60 hours each @ $20 (average)	6,000
	$302,700

Out-of-Pocket Costs	
Retreat facilitator	2,000
Research consultation and survey instrument development	1,500
Entertainment, travel	4,500
Brochure design and production	13,500
VIP forums including materials	4,000
Client survey	3,500
Announcements	4,500
Advertising	6,500
Expenses and supplies	2,000
	42,000
	$344,700

APPENDIX 7
Marketing Budget for the 150-Attorney Firm

It was not hard for the attorneys in the 150-attorney firm to stay busy. Three of the five named partners were extraordinary rainmakers and all five were well known and active in the social and professional community. The firm held a reputation of excellence among clients.

Founded 25 years earlier, the firm celebrated its silver anniversary last year with a gala in a downtown hotel ballroom. As the fourth largest firm in a metropolitan area of three million, the firm commanded high visibility and name recognition among community leaders.

Its clients were loyal and continued to send work to the firm. The firm was general counsel to several well-known businesses in the community, both in high technology and apparel. The firm had built its initial reputation on insurance defense, but had since branched out to other areas and provided full legal services, even highly specialized areas such as entertainment law and patent law. While there may not have been much work, for instance, in these two areas, the firm's commitment to full service required that it have expertise in-house.

Consequently, the firm never hesitated to add laterals. It quickly built new departments or sections to meet emerging markets, such as environmental law and international trade. In addition, recruitment of the top one-third from the best law schools was not difficult for the firm. Often, the top 10 percent of students applied and were hired.

Several years ago, the firm asked an exceptionally bright paralegal if she could take on additional duties of business development. By last year, the position had evolved into a three quarters marketing and one quarter paralegal duties.

The coordinator had produced an eight-page brochure for the firm, describing the firm's various services. It cost $28,000 for photography, design, and printing. Although everyone agreed the brochure looked professional, it was not extensively used. Of the 1,000 copies printed, a little more than two-thirds remained in a storage closet a year later.

The work load on younger attorneys and associates approached 2,200 hours a year. The working stress level was high. Burnout was more common than most of the attorneys cared to admit. There was internal competition for additional staff and firmwide resources among the departments. Occasionally the conflicts reached a level where the managing partner needed to intervene to handle internal conflicts and smooth out areas of tension.

The firm was neither seeking a merger nor considering opening an office in another city, although it had acquired other small firms along the way to maintain its full-service status. It had seen several larger mergers occur among firms within its own city. Firms from other areas also opened local branches. A recent merger created a larger firm, moving the firm from the third-largest spot it had held for the last five years. All this activity drew media attention and was cause for many announcments, open houses, and general marketing efforts by the other firms.

Competition for the firm came not from other full-service firms but from the medium-sized firms that had developed a solid expertise in two or three areas of the law. Vigorous marketing by these smaller firms had brought their expertise to the attention of corporate counsel and the business community. Although direct solicitation of the firm's clients had not occurred (and was unlikely), the managing partners realized that any client dissatisfaction could result in a loss of business to the more aggressive specialty firms.

If the firm had an image in the community, it was "conservative and lacking innovation." While the firm brochure represented a forward step in business development, the firm conducted its marketing in much the same way it had for years. It relied heavily on the three rainmaking partners to bring in the business. The firm had a regular holiday party for clients and was generous in its pro bono work and charity to nonprofit groups. But there were no coordinated efforts in these contributions.

Overall, the firm sensed that it was threatened by changes in the legal market that were out of its control. It was no longer possible to conduct regular business.

Although the firm was growing steadily, the managing partner was not wholly satisfied with what the future held. He convinced the executive committee that some sort of action must be taken. After considering "marketing" as an agenda item (a first in the history of the firm) for several meetings, the partners agreed to the following approach to a budget for the next 12 months of business development.

Activities	Portion of Total Effort
Practice planning sessions for executive committee at a setting away from the firm: four a year, over two days (one business day and a weekend); retreats devoted to many topics, but at least one-third devoted exclusively to business development; include efforts to make existing activities more effective for marketing (holiday party, donations, etc.)	11%

Revision of graphic identity and application to letterhead, business cards, and all printed materials representing the firm	4
Sales training for junior rainmakers—hiring a sales trainer to instruct aggressive partners and selected associates on specific sales techniques for attorneys	3
Client surveys to gain information on work performed and suggestions to increase the firm's work for existing clients	6
Customer service training for staff members on office procedures, client response, and importance of first impressions.	5
Revisions to and improvement of the firm's job description for the marketing coordinator; development of a firm policy toward business development and preparation of a formalized and detailed marketing plan	4
Direct-mail programs to clients and friends around holiday themes, with goal of being memorable and dramatic, showing both creativity and contemporary thinking	10
Announcements/tombstones	5
Brochure distribution program, requiring selected attorneys (about 60%) to distribute materials to existing clients and referral sources	2
Sponsorship of four executive forums for the community, to draw attention to the firm's diverse talents and multinational interests	13
Active article-writing program (a "publish or perish policy") with goal of having 40% of attorneys published in legal or trade publications during the first year of the program	7
Aggressive media relations program to gain visibility among client groups; pursued by hiring of public relations firm to generate publicity opportunities	9
Initiation of a scholarship program for high school students interested in business	4
Affinity marketing program (joint sponsorship) of a community good health day with local bank (a client)	12
"Image" advertising	5

Time Required	Lost Revenue or Cost
Partners A, B, C, and D—300 hours each @ $120	$144,000
Partners E and F—100 hours each @ $100	20,000
Partner G—500 hours @ $90	45,000
All other partners (43)—60 hours each @ $90 (average)	232,200
Associates A, B, and C—200 hours @ $80 (average)	48,000
Other associates (10)—80 hours each @ $75 (average)	60,000
All other associates (87)—40 hours each @ $75 (average)	261,000
Staff A—1,600 hours @ $30	48,000
Staff B—400 hours @ $20	8,000
Other staff (10)—160 hours each @ $20 (average)	32,000
Other staff (15)—60 hours each @ $20 (average)	18,000
	$916,200

Out-of-Pocket Costs	
Revisions to graphics and applications	$2,200
Sales training consultant	1,500
Client survey	5,500
Customer Service training for staff	1,800
Direct-mail programs	11,500
Announcements, tombstones	4,500
Executive forums (4) including materials	18,000
Media relations (PR firm)	9,000
Student scholarship program	6,000
Affinity marketing program	6,000
Image advertising	7,000
Entertainment, travel	14,500
Expenses and supplies	6,000
	$93,500
	$1,009,700

APPENDIX 8
Introduction to Information Sources for the Client-Focused Attorney

Part of being client focused is understanding the economic activity of former, present, and potential clients. Most attorneys have access to a number of readily available sources of seldom-used information regarding economic patterns and trends. There is also a vast amount of information with regard to many organizations, businesses and nonprofits alike, which can provide clues for increased learning about client characteristics, needs, and financial positions. Reference sources provide descriptive pieces to the client puzzle.

Most of these sources are available at city libraries and public community college and university libraries. Contrary to common understanding, libraries at public educational institutions are usually open to nonstudents. Most libraries also have reference librarians willing to and capable of providing assistance.

Several commercial data base services provide much the same service through computer terminal modems. Computer research can be a considerable time-saver, whereas do-it-yourself library research is less expensive. Attorneys can determine which method best suits their needs by consulting their computer software provider or legal research source.

SOURCES OF INFORMATION

The following list of sources and information is available to any attorney (as well as the general public):

Specific Firms and Industry Listings. Both the *Reader's Guide to Periodical Literature* and the *Business Periodical Index* list by subject articles relevant to specific organizations, industries, and geographic location, as well as almost any other subject or interest. Some libraries also have "Findex" which has references by industries, products, and services usually in relation to predictions appearing in the press.

Directories. There are several directories which can be valuable in researching publicly owned firms including Standard & Poors, *Fortune* 500, and *Business Week* Global 1000 lists. All substantial companies, publicly owned or not, are likely to appear in *Thomas Register of American Manufacturers* and Dun & Bradstreet's *Million Dollar Directory* and *Contacts Influential.* Information provided in these sources is straight factual information, that is, officer names, principal business, size/locations, and so on.

Dun & Bradstreet Reports. This report also includes reported confidential information on closely held organizations (available to subscribers).

General Business and Economic Patterns. Many sources are available, but two of the most valuable for relative economic strength of a region have proven to be *County Business Patterns* (published by the U.S. Department of Commerce) and *Survey of Buying Power* (published by *Sales and Marketing Management* Magazine).

Legal References. Sources such as *The Legal Resource Index, Westlaw,* and *Lexis* can give court records for specific prospective clients and their principals which may indicate not only conflicts but litigious trends.

The process of researching existing and prospective clients is based on the premise that people prefer to do business with those who understand their situation, including background and peripheral information. Being well informed regarding client interests demonstrates to the client a genuine sense of caring.

There is one simple reason to learn as much as possible about existing ideal clients: so the attorney can understand them better and find more just like them.

General methods exist to help attorneys cross-reference larger groups of people. Two general methods are SIC (Standard Industrial Classification) codes and demographic analysis. These methods have been used by marketing and business professionals for years to increase market shares; they are also appropriate methods for lawyers.

APPENDIX 9
Standard Industrial Classification Codes

Standard Industrial Classification (SIC) codes are numerical classifications assigned to all businesses in the United States, originally developed by the U.S. Department of Commerce for census purposes. Their use has expanded to utilization in market and labor studies on both local and national scales. The simplicity of the system lends itself to a wide variety of uses in analytical studies of a given market or industry.

In the SIC code process, all business are assigned a four-digit number with each digit indicating a particular detail.

A sample of the general SIC codes assigned to various industries and specific list of SIC codes follows:

Contents

B. MINING

Code	*Short Title*
10	METAL MINING
101	**Iron Ores**
1011	Iron ores
102	**Copper Ores**
1021	Copper ores
103	**Lead and Zinc Ores**
1031	Lead and zinc ores
104	**Gold and Silver Ores**
1041	Gold ores
1044	Silver ores
106	**Ferroalloy Ores, Except Vanadium**
1061	Ferroalloy ores, except vanadium
108	**Metal Mining Services**
1081	Metal mining services
109	**Miscellaneous Metal Ores**
1094	Uranium-radium-vanadium ores
1099	Metal ores, nec
12	COAL MINING
122	**Bituminous Coal and Lignite Mining**
1221	Bituminous coal and lignite—surface
1222	Bituminous coal—underground
123	**Anthracite Mining**
1231	Anthracite mining
124	**Coal Mining Services**
1241	Coal mining services
13	OIL AND GAS EXTRACTION
131	**Crude Petroleum and Natural Gas**
1311	Crude petroleum and natural gas
132	**Natural Gas Liquids**
1321	Natural gas liquids
138	**Oil and Gas Field Services**
1381	Drilling oil and gas wells
1382	Oil and gas exploration services
1389	Oil and gas field services, nec
14	NONMETALLIC MINERALS, EXCEPT FUELS
141	**Dimension Stone**
1411	Dimension stone
142	**Crushed and Broken Stone**
1422	Crushed and broken limestone
1423	Crushed and broken granite
1429	Crushed and broken stone, nec
144	**Sand and Gravel**
1442	Construction sand and gravel
1446	Industrial sand
145	**Clay, Ceramic, & Refractory Minerals**
1455	Kaolin and ball clay
1459	Clay and related minerals, nec
147	**Chemical and Fertilizer Minerals**
1474	Potash, soda, and borate minerals
1475	Phosphate rock
1479	Chemical and fertilizer mining, nec
148	**Nonmetallic Minerals Services**
1481	Nonmetallic minerals services
149	**Miscellaneous Nonmetallic Minerals**
1499	Miscellaneous nonmetallic minerals

C. CONSTRUCTION

Code	*Short Title*
15	GENERAL BUILDING CONTRACTORS
152	**Residential Building Construction**
1521	Single-family housing construction
1522	Residential construction, nec
153	**Operative Builders**
1531	Operative builders
154	**Nonresidential Building Construction**
1541	Industrial buildings and warehouses
1542	Nonresidential construction, nec
16	HEAVY CONSTRUCTION, EX. BUILDING
161	**Highway and Street Construction**
1611	Highway and street construction
162	**Heavy Construction, Except Highway**
1622	Bridge, tunnel, & elevated highway
1623	Water, sewer, and utility lines
1629	Heavy construction, nec
17	SPECIAL TRADE CONTRACTORS
171	**Plumbing, Heating, Air-Conditioning**
1711	Plumbing, heating, air-conditioning
172	**Painting and Paper Hanging**
1721	Painting and paper hanging
173	**Electrical Work**
1731	Electrical work

NUMERICAL LIST OF SHORT TITLES

Code	Short Title
174	**Masonry, Stonework, and Plastering**
1741	Masonry and other stonework
1742	Plastering, drywall, and insulation
1743	Terrazzo, tile, marble, mosaic work
175	**Carpentry and Floor Work**
1751	Carpentry work
1752	Floor laying and floor work, nec
176	**Roofing, Siding, and Sheet Metal Work**
1761	Roofing, siding, and sheet metal work
177	**Concrete Work**
1771	Concrete work
178	**Water Well Drilling**
1781	Water well drilling
179	**Misc. Special Trade Contractors**
1791	Structural steel erection
1793	Glass and glazing work
1794	Excavation work
1795	Wrecking and demolition work
1796	Installing building equipment, nec
1799	Special trade contractors, nec

D. MANUFACTURING

Code	Short Title
20	FOOD AND KINDRED PRODUCTS
201	**Meat Products**
2011	Meat packing plants
2013	Sausages and other prepared meats
2015	Poultry slaughtering and processing
202	**Dairy Products**
2021	Creamery butter
2022	Cheese, natural and processed
2023	Dry, condensed, evaporated products
2024	Ice cream and frozen desserts
2026	Fluid milk
203	**Preserved Fruits and Vegetables**
2032	Canned specialties
2033	Canned fruits and vegetables
2034	Dehydrated fruits, vegetables, soups
2035	Pickles, sauces, and salad dressings
2037	Frozen fruits and vegetables
2038	Frozen specialties, nec
204	**Grain Mill Products**
2041	Flour and other grain mill products
2043	Cereal breakfast foods
2044	Rice milling
2045	Prepared flour mixes and doughs
2046	Wet corn milling
2047	Dog and cat food
2048	Prepared feeds, nec
205	**Bakery Products**
2051	Bread, cake, and related products
2052	Cookies and crackers
2053	Frozen bakery products, except bread
206	**Sugar and Confectionery Products**
2061	Raw cane sugar
2062	Cane sugar refining
2063	Beet sugar
2064	Candy & other confectionery products
2066	Chocolate and cocoa products
2067	Chewing gum
2068	Salted and roasted nuts and seeds
207	**Fats and Oils**
2074	Cottonseed oil mills
2075	Soybean oil mills
2076	Vegetable oil mills, nec
2077	Animal and marine fats and oils
2079	Edible fats and oils, nec
208	**Beverages**
2082	Malt beverages
2083	Malt
2084	Wines, brandy, and brandy spirits
2085	Distilled and blended liquors
2086	Bottled and canned soft drinks
2087	Flavoring extracts and syrups, nec
209	**Misc. Food and Kindred Products**
2091	Canned and cured fish and seafoods
2092	Fresh or frozen prepared fish
2095	Roasted coffee
2096	Potato chips and similar snacks
2097	Manufactured ice
2098	Macaroni and spaghetti
2099	Food preparations, nec
21	TOBACCO PRODUCTS
211	**Cigarettes**
2111	Cigarettes
212	**Cigars**
2121	Cigars
213	**Chewing and Smoking Tobacco**
2131	Chewing and smoking tobacco
214	**Tobacco Stemming and Redrying**
2141	Tobacco stemming and redrying
22	TEXTILE MILL PRODUCTS
221	**Broadwoven Fabric Mills, Cotton**

DIVISION C

Construction

The Division as a Whole

This division includes establishments primarily engaged in construction. The term construction includes new work, additions, alterations, reconstruction, installations, and repairs. Construction activities are generally administered or managed from a relatively fixed place of business, but the actual construction work is performed at one or more different sites. If a company has more than one relatively fixed place of business from which it undertakes or manages construction activities and for which separate data on the number of employees, payroll, receipts, and other establishment-type records are maintained, each such place of business is considered a separate construction establishment.

Three broad types of construction activity are covered: (1) building construction by general contractors or by operative builders; (2) heavy construction other than building by general contractors and special trade contractors; and (3) construction activity by other special trade contractors. Special trade contractors are primarily engaged in specialized construction activities, such as plumbing, painting, and electrical work, and work for general contractors under subcontract or directly for property owners. General contractors usually assume responsibility for an entire construction project, but may subcontract to others all of the actual construction work or those portions of the project that require special skills or equipment. General contractors thus may or may not have construction workers on their payroll.

Building construction general contractors are primarily engaged in the construction of dwellings, office buildings, stores, farm buildings, and other building construction projects. Operative builders who build on their own account for resale are also included in this division. However, investment builders who build structures on their own account for rental are classified in Real Estate, Major Group 65, but separate establishments primarily engaged in construction for the investment builder are classified in this division.

General contractors and special trade contractors for heavy construction other than building are primarily engaged in the construction of highways; pipelines, communications and power lines, and sewer and water mains; and other heavy construction projects. Special trade contractors are classified in heavy construction other than building if they are primarily engaged in activities such as grading for highway and airport runways; guardrail construction; installation of highway signs; asphalt and concrete construction of roads, highways, streets and public sidewalks; trenching; cable laying; conduit construction; underwater rock removal; pipeline wrapping; or land clearing and leveling.

Major Group 15.—BUILDING CONSTRUCTION—GENERAL CONTRACTORS AND OPERATIVE BUILDERS

The Major Group as a Whole

This major group includes general contractors and operative builders primarily engaged in the construction of residential, farm, industrial, commercial, or other buildings. General building contractors who combine a special trade with the contracting are included in this major group.

Industry Group No. | Industry No.

152 **GENERAL BUILDING CONTRACTORS—RESIDENTIAL BUILDINGS**

1521 **General Contractors—Single-Family Houses**

General contractors primarily engaged in construction (including new work, additions, alterations, remodeling, and repair) of single-family houses.

Building alterations, single-family—general contractors
Building construction, single-family—general contractors
Custom builders, single-family houses—general contractors
Designing and erecting combined: single-family houses—general contractors
Home improvements, single-family—general contractors
House construction, single-family—general contractors
House: shell erection, single-family—general contractors
Mobile home repair, on site—general contractors
Modular housing, single-family (assembled on site)—general contractors
One-family house construction—general contractors
Prefabricated single-family houses erection—general contractors
Premanufactured housing, single-family (assembled on site)—general contractors
Remodeling buildings, single-family—general contractors
Renovating buildings, single-family—general contractors
Repairing buildings, single-family—general contractors
Residential construction, single-family—general contractors
Rowhouse (single-family) construction—general contractors
Townhouse construction—general contractors

1522 **General Contractors—Residential Buildings, Other Than Single-Family**

General contractors primarily engaged in construction (including new work, additions, alterations, remodeling, and repair) of residential buildings other than single-family houses.

Apartment building construction—general contractors
Building alterations, residential: except single-family—general contractors
Building construction, residential: except single-family—general contractors
Custom builders, residential: except single-family—general contractors
Designing and erecting, combined: residential, except single-family—general contractors
Dormitory construction—general contractors
Home improvements, residential: except single-family—general contractors
Hotel construction—general contractors
Motel construction—general contractors
Prefabricated building erection, residential: except single-family—general contractors
Remodeling buildings, residential: except single-family—general contractors
Renovating buildings, residential: except single-family—general contractors
Repairing buildings, residential: except single-family—general contractors
Residential construction, except single-family—general contractors

Major Group 16.—HEAVY CONSTRUCTION OTHER THAN BUILDING CONSTRUCTION—CONTRACTORS

The Major Group as a Whole

This major group includes general contractors primarily engaged in heavy construction other than building, such as highways and streets, bridges, sewers, railroads, irrigation projects, flood control projects and marine construction, and special trade contractors primarily engaged in activities of a type that are clearly specialized to such heavy construction and are not normally performed on buildings or building-related projects. Specialized activities that are covered here include grading for highways and airport runways; guardrail construction; installation of highway signs; trenching; underwater rock removal; and asphalt and concrete construction of roads, highways, streets and public sidewalks. Establishments primarily engaged in specialized activities that may be performed on buildings or on other heavy construction projects are classified in Major Group 17. These include contractors primarily engaged in painting (including bridge painting and traffic lane painting), electrical work (including work on bridges, power lines, and power plants), and carpentry work.

Industry Group No. | Industry No.

161 HIGHWAY AND STREET CONSTRUCTION, EXCEPT ELEVATED HIGHWAYS

1611 Highway and Street Construction, Except Elevated Highways

General and special trade contractors primarily engaged in the construction of roads, streets, alleys, public sidewalks, guardrails, parkways, and airports. Special trade contractors primarily engaged in the construction of private driveways and sidewalks are classified in Industry 1771.

Airport runway construction—general contractors
Alley construction—general contractors
Asphalt paving: roads, public sidewalks, and streets—contractors
Concrete construction: roads, highways, public sidewalks, and streets—contractors
Grading for highways, streets, and airport runways—contractors
Guardrail construction on highways—contractors
Highway construction, except elevated—general contractors
Highway signs, installation of—contractors
Parkway construction—general contractors
Paving construction—contractors
Resurfacing streets and highways—contractors
Road construction, except elevated—general contractors
Sidewalk construction, public—contractors
Street maintenance or repair—contractors
Street paving—contractors

162 HEAVY CONSTRUCTION, EXCEPT HIGHWAY AND STREET CONSTRUCTION

1622 Bridge, Tunnel, and Elevated Highway Construction

General contractors primarily engaged in the construction of bridges; viaducts; elevated highways; and highway, pedestrian, and railway tunnels. General contractors engaged in subway construction are classified in Industry 1629. Special trade contractors primarily engaged in guardrail construction or installation of highway signs is classified in Industry 1611.

Abutment construction—general contractors
Bridge construction—general contractors
Causeway construction on structural supports—general contractors
Highway construction, elevated—general contractors

APPENDIX 10
Demographic Analyses Using U.S. Census Data

Demographics is the study and resultant grouping of the general public into catagories such as age, gender, education, occupation, income, marital status, and such. Demographic information is by its very nature quantifiable because it is a science of statistics and percentages.

The U.S. Census Bureau provides the most definitive demographic data available. The significance of demographic data is that it can be broken down into geographic segments. For an attorney exploring possible new practice areas, a demographic study showing increasing age in a particular area could very well indicate a potential for estate and probate work. A trend toward young families could impact several practice areas.

A number of reports regarding census data are available. Sample listings follow.

1980 Census of Population

General Social and Economic Characteristics

UNITED STATES SUMMARY

PC80-1-C1

Contents

(Page numbers listed here omit the report prefix number which appears as part of the page number for each page. The prefix for this report is 1)

MAPS AND CHARTS Page

Figure

MAPS AND CHARTS Page

Contents

Table 72. Summary of Social Characteristics: 1980

[Data are estimates based on a sample; see Introduction. For meaning of symbols, see Introduction. For definitions of terms, see appendixes A and B]

United States Urban and Rural and Size of Place Inside and Outside SMSA's	Total persons			Persons 5 years and over					Persons 25 years old and over					
	Number	Percent foreign born	Native persons—Percent born in State of residence	Percent living in different house in 1975	Percent who speak a language other than English at home	Persons 3 years old and over enrolled in kindergarten or elementary school—Percent in private school	Civilian persons 16 to 19 years old—Percent not enrolled in school, not high school graduates	Persons 18 to 24 years old—Percent enrolled in school	Percent high school graduates	Percent completed 4 or more years of college	Persons 60 years and over—Percent living alone	Families—Percent with own children under 6 years	Persons under 18—Percent living with two parents	Children ever born per 1,000 women 35 to 44 years
United States	**226 545 805**	**6.2**	**68.2**	**46.4**	**11.0**	**11.8**	**13.4**	**31.8**	**66.5**	**16.2**	**24.2**	**22.3**	**76.7**	**2 639**
URBAN AND RURAL AND SIZE OF PLACE														
Urban	**167 054 638**	**7.7**	**65.2**	**48.0**	**13.0**	**13.8**	**13.1**	**34.5**	**68.6**	**18.1**	**25.3**	**22.1**	**73.7**	**2 561**
Inside urbanized areas	139 182 696	8.6	64.0	47.7	13.9	15.1	12.9	34.1	69.7	18.8	24.8	21.9	73.2	2 522
Central cities	67 035 742	9.6	65.3	48.2	16.6	16.8	15.5	35.8	64.9	17.3	28.2	22.6	64.9	2 565
Urban fringe	72 146 954	7.8	62.9	47.2	11.3	13.5	10.5	32.2	74.1	20.2	21.2	21.2	80.4	2 488
Outside urbanized areas	27 871 942	3.2	70.6	49.6	8.4	7.9	13.6	36.7	63.0	14.1	27.4	23.3	76.2	2 780
Places of 10,000 or more	13 480 685	3.5	69.4	51.9	8.7	8.8	12.8	42.6	64.6	15.6	27.7	23.6	75.0	2 740
Places of 2,500 to 10,000	14 391 257	3.0	71.7	47.4	8.0	7.0	14.3	29.7	61.5	12.8	27.2	23.1	77.2	2 817
Rural	**59 491 167**	**2.0**	**76.1**	**41.9**	**5.3**	**6.8**	**14.2**	**22.0**	**60.4**	**11.0**	**20.8**	**22.8**	**84.0**	**2 849**
Places of 1,000 to 2,500	7 034 378	2.3	75.4	42.9	6.5	5.4	13.8	22.2	60.0	11.3	27.0	22.3	79.6	2 865
Other rural	52 456 789	1.9	76.2	41.8	5.2	6.9	14.3	22.0	60.5	11.0	19.7	22.9	84.6	2 847
Rural farm	5 617 903	1.3	84.4	23.0	5.6	10.5	8.2	26.0	62.0	9.6	12.8	16.7	92.8	3 021
INSIDE AND OUTSIDE SMSA's														
Inside SMSA's	**169 430 577**	**7.6**	**65.6**	**47.3**	**12.6**	**13.6**	**12.9**	**32.8**	**69.0**	**17.9**	**24.1**	**22.1**	**75.4**	**2 563**
Urban	145 451 315	8.5	64.2	47.9	13.7	14.7	13.0	34.0	69.5	18.6	24.9	22.0	73.5	2 531
Central cities	67 854 918	9.7	65.0	48.3	16.8	16.8	15.6	35.7	64.8	17.2	28.1	22.6	64.9	2 566
Not in central cities	77 596 397	7.3	63.6	47.5	11.0	13.0	10.7	32.2	73.6	19.8	21.7	21.5	80.5	2 505
Rural	23 979 262	2.6	73.6	44.1	5.7	8.3	12.5	24.1	65.7	13.4	18.9	22.8	85.8	2 732
Outside SMSA's	**57 115 228**	**2.0**	**75.3**	**43.7**	**6.2**	**6.5**	**14.7**	**28.5**	**59.0**	**11.2**	**24.3**	**22.9**	**80.1**	**2 887**
Urban	21 603 323	2.9	71.3	49.0	7.9	8.1	13.6	37.9	62.4	14.1	27.9	23.0	75.0	2 789
Rural	35 511 905	1.5	77.7	40.4	5.1	5.7	15.4	20.6	56.9	9.4	21.8	22.9	82.8	2 940

Table 73. Summary of Economic Characteristics: 1980

[Data are estimates based on a sample, see Introduction. For meaning of symbols, see Introduction. For definitions of terms, see appendixes A and B]

United States Urban and Rural and Size of Place Inside and Outside SMSA's	Percent in labor force						Workers 16 years and over				Median income in 1979 (dollars)			Income in 1979 below poverty level	
	Male, 16 years and over	Female, 16 years and over: Total	Female, 16 years and over: With own children under 6 years	Nonworkers per 100 workers	Civilian labor force—Percent unemployed	Employed persons 16 years and over—Percent in manufacturing industries	Percent worked outside area of residence	Percent in carpools	Percent using public transportation	Families—Percent with no workers in 1979	Households	Families	Per capita income in 1979 (dollars)	Percent of persons for whom poverty status is determined	Percent of families
United States	**75.1**	**49.9**	**45.7**	**114**	**6.5**	**22.4**	...	**19.7**	**6.4**	**12.8**	**16 841**	**19 917**	**7 298**	**12.4**	**9.6**
URBAN AND RURAL AND SIZE OF PLACE															
Urban	**75.7**	**51.4**	**46.5**	**108**	**6.4**	**21.5**	...	**18.7**	**8.2**	**12.8**	**17 159**	**20 653**	**7 645**	**12.1**	**9.2**
Inside urbanized areas	76.4	52.1	45.9	105	6.3	21.3	...	18.3	9.5	12.6	17 738	21 243	7 887	11.8	9.0
Central cities	73.2	51.2	47.4	111	7.3	19.7	...	17.7	14.5	15.1	14 914	18 379	7 166	16.5	12.9
Urban fringe	79.2	53.0	44.6	101	5.4	22.7	...	18.8	5.2	10.5	20 790	23 639	8 557	7.4	5.7
Outside urbanized areas	72.1	47.6	49.1	123	6.9	22.5	...	21.2	1.1	13.9	14 501	17 791	6 439	14.0	10.2
Places of 10,000 or more	72.4	49.0	50.1	118	6.8	21.7	...	20.2	1.3	13.1	14 608	18 118	6 527	14.3	10.2
Places of 2,500 to 10,000	71.9	46.3	48.1	128	7.0	23.2	...	22.2	0.9	14.6	14 402	17 501	6 356	13.6	10.2
Rural	**73.7**	**45.4**	**43.6**	**130**	**7.0**	**25.4**	...	**22.8**	**0.8**	**12.6**	**15 954**	**17 995**	**6 322**	**13.2**	**10.6**
Places of 1,000 to 2,500	71.3	44.9	46.5	133	7.0	24.5	...	23.3	0.8	15.1	14 220	17 205	6 227	13.2	10.0
Other rural	74.0	45.5	43.3	130	7.0	25.5	...	22.8	0.8	12.2	16 202	18 110	6 335	13.2	10.6
Rural farm	78.1	40.3	37.9	119	3.6	13.4	...	13.3	0.4	8.1	16 498	17 730	6 851	14.7	12.5
INSIDE AND OUTSIDE SMSA's															
Inside SMSA's	**76.4**	**51.5**	**45.5**	**108**	**6.3**	**22.1**	...	**19.0**	**8.1**	**12.3**	**17 880**	**21 128**	**7 743**	**11.4**	**8.7**
Urban	76.3	52.0	46.0	106	6.3	21.5	...	18.5	9.2	12.6	17 683	21 165	7 838	11.7	9.0
Central cities	73.3	51.2	47.3	111	7.3	20.0	...	17.7	14.3	15.1	14 955	18 398	7 158	16.5	12.9
Not in central cities	78.9	52.6	44.8	102	5.5	22.7	...	19.1	4.9	10.6	20 488	23 303	8 433	7.6	5.8
Rural	77.0	48.2	42.8	119	6.3	26.2	...	22.0	1.0	10.3	19 088	20 940	7 165	9.3	7.4
Outside SMSA's	**71.3**	**45.1**	**46.2**	**132**	**7.2**	**23.5**	...	**22.3**	**0.8**	**14.1**	**14 040**	**16 592**	**5 977**	**15.4**	**12.0**
Urban	71.2	47.4	49.8	124	6.9	21.6	...	20.5	1.1	14.2	13 937	17 302	6 346	14.8	10.8
Rural	71.4	43.6	44.2	138	7.5	24.8	...	23.4	0.6	14.1	14 104	16 204	5 753	15.8	12.7

Table 95. **Income in 1979, 1969, and 1959 of Persons by Sex and Race: 1960 to 1980**

[In 1979 dollars. Data are estimates based on a sample; see Introduction. For meaning of symbols, see Introduction. For definitions of terms, see appendixes A and B]

United States Regions	Number: United States	Number: Northeast	Number: North Central	Number: South	Number: West	Percent distribution: United States	Percent distribution: Northeast	Percent distribution: North Central	Percent distribution: South	Percent distribution: West
TOTAL										
1980										
Persons 15 years and over	**175 307 629**	**38 765 075**	**45 260 854**	**57 933 216**	**33 348 484**	**100.0**	**100.0**	**100.0**	**100.0**	**100.0**
Without income	28 120 985	6 352 922	6 901 509	9 735 790	5 130 764	16.0	16.4	15.2	16.8	15.4
With income	147 186 644	32 412 153	38 359 345	48 197 426	28 217 720	84.0	83.6	84.8	83.2	84.6
$1 to $999 or loss	10 271 583	2 146 080	2 808 853	3 404 809	1 911 841	5.9	5.5	6.2	5.9	5.7
$1,000 to $1,999	10 468 598	2 135 775	2 710 376	3 843 334	1 779 113	6.0	5.5	6.0	6.6	5.3
$2,000 to $2,999	11 138 093	2 313 782	2 839 564	4 211 335	1 773 412	6.4	6.0	6.3	7.3	5.3
$3,000 to $3,999	10 428 856	2 480 139	2 666 715	3 399 722	1 882 280	5.9	6.4	5.9	5.9	5.6
$4,000 to $4,999	8 582 855	1 959 792	2 148 373	2 706 435	1 768 255	4.9	5.1	4.7	4.7	5.3
$5,000 to $5,999	7 763 691	1 713 483	1 926 424	2 657 275	1 466 509	4.4	4.4	4.3	4.6	4.4
$6,000 to $6,999	7 522 474	1 584 501	1 813 445	2 709 483	1 415 045	4.3	4.1	4.0	4.7	4.2
$7,000 to $9,999	19 247 318	4 196 644	4 703 905	6 774 733	3 572 036	11.0	10.8	10.4	11.7	10.7
$7,000 to $7,999	6 825 168	1 483 344	1 657 789	2 437 348	1 246 687	3.9	3.8	3.7	4.2	3.7
$8,000 to $8,999	6 641 418	1 442 331	1 620 967	2 340 132	1 237 988	3.8	3.7	3.6	4.0	3.7
$9,000 to $9,999	5 780 732	1 270 969	1 425 149	1 997 253	1 087 361	3.3	3.3	3.1	3.4	3.3
$10,000 to $24,999	~~61 763 176~~	~~13 881 957~~	~~16 741 690~~	~~18 490 300~~	~~12 649 229~~	~~35.2~~	~~35.8~~	~~37.0~~	~~31.9~~	~~37.9~~
$10,000 to $14,999	23 508 570	5 327 284	6 043 694	7 673 881	4 463 711	13.4	13.7	13.4	13.2	13.4
$15,000 to $24,999	25 296 783	5 728 897	7 216 305	7 159 342	5 192 239	14.4	14.8	15.9	12.4	15.6
$25,000 or more	12 957 823	2 825 776	3 481 691	3 657 077	2 993 279	7.4	7.3	7.7	6.3	9.0
$25,000 to $34,999	7 888 927	1 708 292	2 238 148	2 144 309	1 798 178	4.5	4.4	4.9	3.7	5.4
$35,000 to $49,999	2 923 246	636 827	738 373	855 720	692 326	1.7	1.6	1.6	1.5	2.1
$50,000 to $74,999	1 328 592	299 393	313 219	404 054	311 926	0.8	0.8	0.7	0.7	0.9
$75,000 or more	817 058	181 264	191 951	252 994	190 849	0.5	0.5	0.4	0.4	0.6
Median	$8 089	$8 270	$8 375	$7 479	$8 699	...	...	...	...	...
Mean	$11 232	$11 332	$11 389	$10 518	$12 126	...	...	...	...	...
Males 15 years and over	**83 824 951**	**18 170 740**	**21 647 802**	**27 664 163**	**16 342 246**	**100.0**	**100.0**	**100.0**	**100.0**	**100.0**
Without income	6 527 504	1 550 434	1 464 653	2 334 502	1 177 915	7.8	8.5	6.8	8.4	7.2
With income	77 297 447	16 620 306	20 183 149	25 329 661	15 164 331	92.2	91.5	93.2	91.6	92.8
$1 to $999 or loss	3 538 456	746 522	954 485	1 167 375	670 074	4.2	4.1	4.4	4.2	4.1
$1,000 to $1,999	3 249 306	668 045	812 195	1 197 722	571 344	3.9	3.7	3.8	4.3	3.5
$2,000 to $2,999	3 482 081	671 816	851 558	1 384 848	573 859	4.2	3.7	3.9	5.0	3.5
$3,000 to $3,999	3 588 160	756 267	874 569	1 292 215	665 109	4.3	4.2	4.0	4.7	4.1
$4,000 to $4,999	3 291 975	692 236	786 893	1 127 900	684 946	3.9	3.8	3.6	4.1	4.2
$5,000 to $5,999	3 184 756	656 737	747 559	1 141 850	638 610	3.8	3.6	3.5	4.1	3.9
$6,000 to $6,999	3 188 005	637 200	721 234	1 184 961	644 610	3.8	3.5	3.3	4.3	3.9
$7,000 to $9,999	8 804 123	1 847 483	2 030 233	3 249 848	1 676 559	10.5	10.2	9.4	11.7	10.3
$7,000 to $7,999	2 995 631	626 872	688 234	1 105 703	574 822	3.6	3.4	3.2	4.0	3.5
$8,000 to $8,999	3 027 691	629 291	696 476	1 121 869	580 055	3.6	3.5	3.2	4.1	3.5
$9,000 to $9,999	2 780 801	591 320	645 523	1 022 276	521 682	3.3	3.3	3.0	3.7	3.2
$10,000 to $24,999	~~44 970 585~~	~~9 944 000~~	~~12 404 423~~	~~13 582 942~~	~~9 039 220~~	~~53.6~~	~~54.7~~	~~57.3~~	~~49.1~~	~~55.3~~
$10,000 to $14,999	13 411 030	2 983 910	3 408 424	4 583 322	2 435 374	16.0	16.4	15.7	16.6	14.9
$15,000 to $24,999	19 797 764	4 418 788	5 773 292	5 694 601	3 911 083	23.6	24.3	26.7	20.6	23.9
$25,000 or more	11 761 791	2 541 302	3 222 707	3 305 019	2 692 763	14.0	14.0	14.9	11.9	16.5
$25,000 to $34,999	7 117 717	1 518 116	2 064 885	1 933 029	1 601 687	8.5	8.4	9.5	7.0	9.8
$35,000 to $49,999	2 680 524	579 737	688 508	780 285	631 994	3.2	3.2	3.2	2.8	3.9
$50,000 to $74,999	1 214 381	275 206	290 747	364 327	284 101	1.4	1.5	1.3	1.3	1.7
$75,000 or more	749 169	168 243	178 567	227 378	174 981	0.9	0.9	0.8	0.8	1.1
Median	$12 192	$12 532	$13 217	$10 909	$12 774	...	...	...	...	...
Mean	$15 124	$15 372	$15 535	$14 063	$16 079	...	...	...	...	...
Females 15 years and over	**91 482 678**	**20 594 335**	**23 613 052**	**30 269 053**	**17 006 238**	**100.0**	**100.0**	**100.0**	**100.0**	**100.0**
Without income	21 593 481	4 802 488	5 436 856	7 401 288	3 952 849	23.6	23.3	23.0	24.5	23.2
With income	69 889 197	15 791 847	18 176 196	22 867 765	13 053 389	76.4	76.7	77.0	75.5	76.8
$1 to $999 or loss	6 733 127	1 399 558	1 854 368	2 237 434	1 241 767	7.4	6.8	7.9	7.4	7.3
$1,000 to $1,999	7 219 292	1 467 730	1 898 181	2 645 612	1 207 769	7.9	7.1	8.0	8.7	7.1
$2,000 to $2,999	7 656 012	1 641 966	1 988 006	2 826 487	1 199 553	8.4	8.0	8.4	9.3	7.1
$3,000 to $3,999	6 840 696	1 723 872	1 792 146	2 107 507	1 217 171	7.5	8.4	7.6	7.0	7.2
$4,000 to $4,999	5 290 880	1 267 556	1 361 480	1 578 535	1 083 309	5.8	6.2	5.8	5.2	6.4
$5,000 to $5,999	4 578 935	1 056 746	1 178 865	1 515 425	827 899	5.0	5.1	5.0	5.0	4.9
$6,000 to $6,999	4 334 469	947 301	1 092 211	1 524 522	770 435	4.7	4.6	4.6	5.0	4.5
$7,000 to $9,999	10 443 195	2 349 161	2 673 672	3 524 885	1 895 477	11.4	11.4	11.3	11.6	11.1
$7,000 to $7,999	3 829 537	856 472	969 555	1 331 645	671 865	4.2	4.2	4.1	4.4	4.0
$8,000 to $8,999	3 613 727	813 040	924 491	1 218 263	657 933	4.0	3.9	3.9	4.0	3.9
$9,000 to $9,999	2 999 931	679 649	779 626	974 977	565 679	3.3	3.3	3.3	3.2	3.3
$10,000 to $24,999	~~16 792 591~~	~~3 937 957~~	~~4 337 267~~	~~4 907 358~~	~~3 610 009~~	~~18.4~~	~~19.1~~	~~18.4~~	~~16.2~~	~~21.2~~
$10,000 to $14,999	10 097 540	2 343 374	2 635 270	3 090 559	2 028 337	11.0	11.4	11.2	10.2	11.9
$15,000 to $24,999	5 499 019	1 310 109	1 443 013	1 464 741	1 281 156	6.0	6.4	6.1	4.8	7.5
$25,000 or more	1 196 032	284 474	258 984	352 058	300 516	1.3	1.4	1.1	1.2	1.8
$25,000 to $34,999	771 210	190 176	173 263	211 280	196 491	0.8	0.9	0.7	0.7	1.2
$35,000 to $49,999	242 722	57 090	49 865	75 435	60 332	0.3	0.3	0.2	0.2	0.4
$50,000 to $74,999	114 211	24 187	22 472	39 727	27 825	0.1	0.1	0.1	0.1	0.2
$75,000 or more	67 889	13 021	13 384	25 616	15 868	0.1	0.1	0.1	0.1	0.1
Median	$5 263	$5 374	$5 164	$5 025	$5 697	...	...	...	...	...
Mean	$6 928	$7 080	$6 786	$6 590	$7 533	...	...	...	...	...
1970										
Persons 14 years and over	**149 398 189**	**36 622 743**	**41 236 848**	**45 959 312**	**25 579 286**	**100.0**	**100.0**	**100.0**	**100.0**	**100.0**
Without income	35 292 578	8 453 271	9 569 906	11 514 088	5 755 313	23.6	23.1	23.2	25.1	22.5
With income	114 105 611	28 169 472	31 666 942	34 445 224	19 823 973	76.4	76.9	76.8	74.9	77.5
$1 to $999 or loss	10 144 708	2 215 281	2 821 229	3 445 387	1 662 811	6.8	6.0	6.8	7.5	6.5
$1,000 to $1,999	10 107 003	2 209 504	2 810 124	3 430 085	1 657 290	6.8	6.0	6.8	7.5	6.5
$2,000 to $2,999	7 877 541	1 837 105	2 161 236	2 556 630	1 322 569	5.3	5.0	5.2	5.6	5.2
$3,000 to $3,999	7 775 594	1 812 871	2 131 543	2 523 363	1 307 817	5.2	5.0	5.2	5.5	5.1
$4,000 to $4,999	5 394 258	1 246 806	1 437 960	1 746 275	963 216	3.6	3.4	3.5	3.8	3.8
$5,000 to $5,999	5 366 630	1 241 031	1 427 432	1 745 910	952 256	3.6	3.4	3.5	3.8	3.7
$6,000 to $6,999	4 941 999	1 152 271	1 265 623	1 740 285	783 820	3.3	3.1	3.1	3.8	3.1
$7,000 to $9,999	13 352 964	3 254 784	3 430 216	4 563 430	2 104 533	8.9	8.9	8.3	9.9	8.2
$7,000 to $7,999	4 885 423	1 144 324	1 251 527	1 715 290	774 281	3.3	3.1	3.0	3.7	3.0
$8,000 to $8,999	8 467 541	2 110 460	2 178 689	2 848 140	1 330 252	5.7	5.8	5.3	6.2	5.2
$9,000 to $9,999	(1)	(1)	(1)	(1)	(1)	(1)	(1)	(1)	(1)	(1)

(1) Included in preceding category.

Table 230. Summary of Social Characteristics for Regions, Divisions, and States: 1980

[Data are estimates based on a sample; see Introduction. For meaning of symbols, see Introduction. For definitions of terms, see appendixes A and B]

United States Regions and Divisions States	Total persons			Persons 5 years and over					Persons 25 years old and over					
	Number	Percent foreign born	Native persons—Percent born in State of residence	Percent living in different house in 1975	Percent who speak a language other than English at home	Persons 3 years old and over enrolled in kindergarten or elementary school—Percent in private school	Civilian persons 16 to 19 years old—Percent not enrolled in school, not high school graduates	Persons 18 to 24 years old—Percent enrolled in school	Percent high school graduates	Percent completed 4 or more years of college	Persons 60 years and over—Percent living alone	Families—Percent with own children under 6 years	Persons under 18—Percent living with two parents	Children ever born per 1,000 women 35 to 44 years
United States	**226 545 805**	**6.2**	**68.2**	**46.4**	**11.0**	**11.8**	**13.4**	**31.8**	**66.5**	**16.2**	**24.2**	**22.3**	**76.7**	**2 639**
REGIONS AND DIVISIONS														
Northeast Region	49 135 283	9.2	76.5	38.3	14.5	15.8	10.2	35.4	67.1	17.2	24.2	20.1	76.5	2 499
New England	12 348 493	7.8	71.4	40.9	13.0	10.9	10.0	37.3	70.5	19.2	24.1	20.1	79.1	2 555
Middle Atlantic	36 786 790	9.6	78.2	37.4	15.0	17.4	10.2	34.7	66.0	16.6	24.2	20.1	75.7	2 480
North Central Region	58 865 670	3.6	74.4	44.6	6.4	12.9	11.2	31.9	68.0	14.7	25.2	23.1	79.6	2 750
East North Central	41 682 217	4.2	75.0	44.0	7.2	13.6	11.7	31.6	67.3	14.5	24.7	22.9	78.2	2 736
West North Central	17 183 453	2.0	73.1	46.1	4.6	11.2	10.1	32.7	69.6	15.3	26.1	23.6	82.9	2 787
South Region	75 372 362	3.8	67.5	47.6	8.2	9.7	16.5	29.7	60.2	15.0	23.4	22.2	74.5	2 675
South Atlantic	36 959 123	4.7	60.2	47.3	6.2	10.2	15.5	30.2	61.3	15.7	22.6	20.4	73.0	2 565
East South Central	14 666 423	1.0	77.6	44.0	1.9	10.5	17.9	29.1	55.3	12.1	24.1	22.8	74.4	2 740
West South Central	23 746 816	4.3	72.3	50.4	15.5	8.4	17.1	29.2	61.5	15.5	24.5	24.8	76.6	2 813
West Region	43 172 490	10.6	50.7	56.2	17.9	9.6	14.5	31.4	74.5	19.3	24.0	24.0	76.7	2 596
Mountain	11 372 785	4.3	46.0	57.3	14.6	5.6	15.2	30.0	75.2	18.8	23.2	26.2	80.5	2 845
Pacific	31 799 705	12.8	52.5	55.8	19.1	11.1	14.3	31.9	74.3	19.4	24.3	23.2	75.2	2 510
STATES														
New England Division														
Maine	1 124 660	3.9	75.7	43.1	10.8	5.4	10.6	30.0	68.7	14.4	24.2	22.0	80.6	2 813
New Hampshire	920 610	4.4	51.6	48.4	10.4	11.0	11.6	33.9	72.3	18.2	23.4	22.3	82.7	2 632
Vermont	511 456	4.1	64.2	45.6	6.6	6.2	9.0	36.8	71.0	19.0	24.5	23.3	81.2	2 730
Massachusetts	5 737 037	8.7	78.6	39.0	13.0	10.9	8.8	40.4	72.2	20.0	24.9	19.7	78.4	2 531
Rhode Island	947 154	8.9	74.0	39.5	16.5	16.3	13.9	38.2	61.1	15.4	24.8	19.5	78.4	2 585
Connecticut	3 107 576	8.6	63.2	41.0	14.3	12.2	10.4	34.5	70.3	20.7	22.3	19.1	78.6	2 458
Middle Atlantic Division														
New York	17 558 072	13.6	80.2	38.5	20.1	17.4	10.7	38.1	66.3	17.9	25.6	20.9	73.1	2 436
New Jersey	7 364 823	10.3	62.9	38.5	15.9	15.8	10.2	33.4	67.4	18.3	21.8	19.7	76.2	2 452
Pennsylvania	11 863 895	3.4	84.4	35.0	6.9	18.4	9.6	30.7	64.7	13.6	23.7	19.3	79.2	2 573
East North Central Division														
Ohio	10 797 630	2.8	74.6	43.3	5.2	13.2	10.4	30.9	67.0	13.7	25.0	22.3	79.4	2 691
Indiana	5 490 224	1.9	72.3	45.2	4.1	10.0	13.7	30.4	66.4	12.5	25.4	23.3	79.8	2 764
Illinois	11 426 518	7.2	74.3	44.5	11.5	15.7	12.9	31.3	66.5	16.2	25.1	22.9	75.8	2 660
Michigan	9 262 078	4.5	75.6	43.6	6.5	11.1	11.5	33.0	68.0	14.3	23.8	23.0	76.4	2 797
Wisconsin	4 705 767	2.7	79.5	43.8	5.8	18.8	9.5	32.4	69.6	14.8	24.3	23.6	83.1	2 877
West North Central Division														
Minnesota	4 075 970	2.6	76.9	44.4	5.6	11.9	7.3	35.4	73.1	17.4	25.5	24.2	85.4	2 804
Iowa	2 913 808	1.6	78.9	44.4	3.4	10.0	8.4	33.4	71.5	13.9	26.1	23.6	85.2	2 859
Missouri	4 916 686	1.7	71.4	46.0	3.1	13.7	13.9	30.5	63.5	13.9	26.6	22.0	78.3	2 676
North Dakota	652 717	2.3	74.6	48.3	11.3	8.6	8.0	32.6	66.4	14.8	25.0	26.9	87.7	3 039
South Dakota	690 768	1.4	71.7	47.1	7.8	6.8	11.1	31.4	67.9	14.0	25.8	26.4	83.5	3 109
Nebraska	1 569 825	2.0	71.6	46.9	4.8	11.3	7.8	34.0	73.4	15.5	26.5	24.8	84.2	2 846
Kansas	2 363 679	2.0	64.3	49.8	4.7	8.0	11.6	31.5	73.3	17.0	26.0	23.2	82.5	2 723
South Atlantic Division														
Delaware	594 338	3.2	53.3	43.0	5.5	19.8	11.5	34.5	68.6	17.5	22.8	21.1	75.0	2 601
Maryland	4 216 975	4.6	56.3	44.5	6.2	13.6	12.1	32.5	67.4	20.4	22.1	20.2	73.0	2 475
District of Columbia	638 333	6.4	41.1	41.8	7.9	15.7	12.7	45.5	67.1	27.5	30.0	18.0	41.6	2 161
Virginia	5 346 818	3.3	62.0	49.0	4.4	8.0	13.9	31.5	62.4	19.1	21.6	21.4	75.9	2 480
West Virginia	1 949 644	1.1	80.1	39.1	2.1	4.0	17.4	27.5	56.0	10.4	25.2	22.8	82.2	2 730
North Carolina	5 881 766	1.3	77.1	43.1	2.4	6.2	16.3	30.4	54.8	13.2	22.9	20.9	74.0	2 558
South Carolina	3 121 820	1.5	73.7	42.5	2.5	10.7	14.4	30.5	53.7	13.4	23.3	23.0	71.7	2 769
Georgia	5 463 105	1.7	72.2	47.5	2.6	9.7	17.8	26.6	56.4	14.6	24.0	23.2	71.5	2 651
Florida	9 746 324	10.9	35.0	53.8	13.2	13.5	16.8	29.1	66.7	14.9	21.6	16.9	71.5	2 541
East South Central Division														
Kentucky	3 660 777	0.9	80.0	45.6	1.8	10.1	21.5	24.5	53.1	11.1	24.4	24.0	79.2	2 739
Tennessee	4 591 120	1.1	72.7	45.8	1.9	8.3	16.7	29.9	56.2	12.6	23.2	21.3	74.8	2 555
Alabama	3 893 888	1.0	79.8	42.4	1.9	11.6	16.3	31.6	56.5	12.2	24.2	22.2	73.0	2 755
Mississippi	2 520 638	0.9	79.4	41.0	1.9	12.8	17.5	30.4	54.8	12.3	24.9	24.5	69.1	3 089
West South Central Division														
Arkansas	2 286 435	1.0	69.9	46.9	1.8	5.8	16.7	28.2	55.5	10.8	24.3	22.2	75.6	2 845
Louisiana	4 205 900	2.0	79.7	43.0	10.0	17.6	17.3	27.3	57.7	13.9	24.9	26.0	71.4	3 014
Oklahoma	3 025 290	1.9	64.2	52.4	4.0	4.2	14.3	30.3	66.0	15.1	27.0	23.1	79.1	2 646
Texas	14 229 191	6.0	72.2	52.7	21.8	6.8	17.6	29.7	62.6	16.9	23.8	25.2	77.9	2 785
Mountain Division														
Montana	786 690	2.3	58.3	52.7	5.2	4.5	10.8	31.4	74.4	17.5	26.0	25.3	83.0	2 909
Idaho	943 935	2.5	50.3	55.6	5.6	4.0	14.8	28.4	73.7	15.8	23.4	28.4	84.0	3 074
Wyoming	469 557	2.0	39.5	61.6	6.3	3.2	15.2	22.2	77.9	17.2	26.4	29.2	84.4	2 876
Colorado	2 889 964	3.9	43.5	60.2	10.6	6.9	13.1	30.7	78.6	23.0	24.8	24.3	79.8	2 550
New Mexico	1 302 894	4.0	54.0	49.7	37.8	6.9	16.5	26.3	68.9	17.6	23.4	27.2	77.0	2 998
Arizona	2 718 215	6.0	35.1	58.1	20.1	7.2	18.2	31.8	72.4	17.4	20.7	22.9	77.6	2 807
Utah	1 461 037	3.5	68.6	54.2	7.4	2.1	13.7	36.0	80.0	19.9	22.6	37.0	86.7	3 515
Nevada	800 493	6.7	23.0	65.2	9.7	4.7	18.6	20.2	75.5	14.4	23.3	21.3	74.0	2 502
Pacific Division														
Washington	4 132 156	5.8	50.9	56.3	6.9	7.6	12.9	30.8	77.6	19.0	25.3	23.3	79.3	2 598
Oregon	2 633 105	4.1	46.2	58.6	5.4	8.9	15.4	30.5	75.6	17.9	24.5	22.9	78.4	2 607
California	23 667 902	15.1	53.4	55.4	22.6	11.9	14.7	32.7	73.5	19.6	24.4	22.9	73.9	2 483
Alaska	401 851	4.0	33.3	67.8	12.5	3.3	12.9	17.4	82.5	21.1	22.4	32.7	79.9	2 683
Hawaii	964 691	14.2	67.4	50.7	25.8	16.9	7.1	27.4	73.8	20.3	14.3	25.8	78.1	2 479

Table 231. **Summary of Economic Characteristics for Regions, Divisions, and States: 1980**

[Data are estimates based on a sample; see Introduction. For meaning of symbols, see Introduction. For definitions of terms, see appendixes A and B]

United States Regions and Divisions States	Percent in labor force						Workers 16 years and over				Median income in 1979 (dollars)			Income in 1979 below poverty level	
		Female, 16 years and over													
	Male, 16 years and over	Total	With own children under 6 years	Nonworkers per 100 workers	Civilian labor force—Percent unemployed	Employed persons 16 years and over—Percent in manufacturing industries	Percent worked outside area of residence	Percent in carpools	Percent using public transportation	Families—Percent with no workers in 1979	Households	Families	Per capita income in 1979 (dollars)	Percent of persons for whom poverty status is determined	Percent of families
United States	**75.1**	**49.9**	**45.7**	**114**	**6.5**	**22.4**	**...**	**19.7**	**6.4**	**12.8**	**16 841**	**19 917**	**7 298**	**12.4**	**9.6**
REGIONS AND DIVISIONS															
Northeast Region	74.2	49.1	39.1	113	6.7	25.3	...	18.5	14.2	13.8	17 310	20 651	7 475	11.2	8.7
New England	76.3	52.7	43.1	103	5.3	28.2	...	20.4	6.3	12.0	17 435	20 724	7 436	9.6	7.4
Middle Atlantic	73.5	47.9	37.8	117	7.1	24.2	...	17.8	17.1	14.4	17 267	20 626	7 488	11.7	9.2
North Central Region	76.3	50.3	45.5	112	7.4	25.9	...	18.5	4.9	11.6	17 753	20 988	7 422	10.5	8.0
East North Central	76.4	50.0	43.8	113	8.2	28.8	...	18.2	5.7	11.9	18 437	21 569	7 565	10.3	7.9
West North Central	76.2	50.9	49.7	110	5.4	19.0	...	19.3	3.1	11.0	16 310	19 589	7 074	11.0	8.2
South Region	73.9	49.1	49.8	119	5.7	20.6	...	22.5	3.3	13.3	15 318	17 857	6 725	15.4	11.9
South Atlantic	73.3	50.4	52.1	114	5.6	20.7	...	22.9	4.3	14.2	15 700	18 219	6 963	13.9	10.7
East South Central	71.8	46.2	48.7	131	7.7	25.2	...	23.5	2.0	13.7	13 623	16 155	5 893	18.7	14.8
West South Central	76.1	48.7	47.5	120	4.6	17.8	...	21.1	2.3	11.6	15 718	18 501	6 870	15.6	12.1
West Region	76.7	52.0	45.2	106	6.6	17.7	...	18.1	5.0	12.2	17 831	20 974	7 925	11.3	8.5
Mountain	77.2	51.0	43.9	114	6.0	12.2	...	20.1	2.7	11.2	16 868	19 656	7 123	11.9	8.9
Pacific	76.6	52.3	45.8	104	6.8	19.6	...	17.5	5.7	12.6	18 230	21 491	8 212	11.1	8.4
STATES															
New England Division															
Maine	73.1	47.9	45.3	122	7.6	27.3	3.1	24.6	1.5	12.8	13 816	16 167	5 768	13.0	9.8
New Hampshire	78.2	54.5	49.7	101	4.8	31.9	13.1	23.7	1.3	10.3	17 013	19 723	6 966	8.5	6.1
Vermont	75.2	51.8	48.1	111	6.3	23.9	5.0	24.9	1.4	11.2	14 790	17 205	6 178	12.1	8.9
Massachusetts	75.7	52.9	41.8	103	5.0	26.0	2.6	19.1	9.3	12.4	17 575	21 166	7 458	9.6	7.6
Rhode Island	75.3	52.4	45.0	104	7.0	32.5	8.4	21.4	4.3	13.4	16 097	19 448	6 897	10.3	7.7
Connecticut	78.3	53.6	40.8	98	4.7	31.0	4.2	19.6	5.1	11.2	20 077	23 149	8 511	8.0	6.2
Middle Atlantic Division															
New York	72.5	48.2	37.5	118	7.1	20.9	2.0	15.9	26.5	15.2	16 647	20 180	7 498	13.4	10.8
New Jersey	76.6	50.6	39.1	107	6.7	24.9	10.9	18.3	9.2	12.5	19 800	22 906	8 127	9.5	7.6
Pennsylvania	73.2	45.7	37.4	121	7.4	28.6	2.8	20.2	8.2	14.3	16 880	19 995	7 077	10.5	7.8
East North Central Division															
Ohio	76.0	48.0	42.2	117	8.0	30.1	2.0	17.3	4.0	12.1	17 754	20 909	7 285	10.3	8.0
Indiana	77.1	50.4	47.1	113	7.8	30.9	3.8	20.0	1.7	10.3	17 582	20 535	7 142	9.7	7.3
Illinois	77.3	51.6	43.3	108	7.2	25.8	2.4	17.9	12.0	11.5	19 321	22 746	8 066	11.0	8.4
Michigan	75.3	48.8	41.6	119	11.0	30.3	1.2	17.8	2.5	13.3	19 223	22 107	7 688	10.4	8.2
Wisconsin	76.4	52.7	48.6	108	6.6	28.5	2.3	19.2	3.9	11.5	17 680	20 915	7 243	8.7	6.3
West North Central Division															
Minnesota	77.1	54.0	50.4	104	5.4	20.2	1.6	19.0	5.5	10.4	17 761	21 185	7 451	9.5	7.0
Iowa	76.3	50.1	49.1	112	5.0	20.2	3.4	18.4	1.9	10.8	16 799	20 052	7 136	10.1	7.5
Missouri	74.2	49.3	50.5	115	6.9	21.9	3.9	21.8	3.8	12.8	15 581	18 784	6 917	12.2	9.1
North Dakota	75.6	47.3	47.2	119	5.3	5.8	2.6	16.4	0.7	8.8	15 293	18 023	6 417	12.6	9.8
South Dakota	75.4	49.3	50.9	117	4.9	9.6	2.0	14.3	0.4	9.9	13 156	15 993	5 697	16.9	13.1
Nebraska	78.0	51.3	49.4	107	3.7	13.8	1.8	17.8	2.5	9.8	15 925	19 122	6 936	10.7	8.0
Kansas	77.5	51.0	48.3	106	4.0	19.2	6.9	19.2	1.0	10.3	16 362	19 707	7 350	10.1	7.4
South Atlantic Division															
Delaware	76.6	51.6	48.8	108	6.3	23.6	8.8	21.3	4.1	10.7	17 846	20 817	7 449	11.9	8.9
Maryland	77.7	54.6	50.9	100	5.8	14.4	16.7	23.1	8.8	10.2	20 281	23 112	8 293	9.8	7.5
District of Columbia	69.0	58.2	62.1	96	6.8	4.5	19.1	15.7	38.0	15.5	16 211	19 099	8 960	18.6	15.1
Virginia	76.7	52.4	49.8	105	5.0	19.0	11.0	25.2	5.1	10.5	17 475	20 018	7 478	11.8	9.2
West Virginia	68.4	36.5	31.6	158	8.4	18.4	6.5	24.7	1.9	17.3	14 564	17 308	6 141	15.0	11.7
North Carolina	75.8	53.9	58.3	106	5.5	32.8	1.6	24.7	1.5	10.5	14 481	16 792	6 133	14.8	11.6
South Carolina	75.5	52.9	58.1	113	6.1	32.6	3.5	25.6	1.3	11.0	14 711	16 978	5 886	16.6	13.1
Georgia	75.8	52.3	53.9	114	5.9	24.1	2.4	22.1	3.9	11.5	15 033	17 414	6 402	16.6	13.2
Florida	67.0	45.8	50.7	126	5.1	12.6	1.2	20.3	2.7	21.8	14 675	17 280	7 270	13.5	9.9
East South Central Division															
Kentucky	71.8	43.8	41.9	135	8.5	22.5	5.9	22.8	2.5	14.5	13 965	16 444	5 978	17.6	14.6
Tennessee	73.3	48.9	51.0	119	7.4	26.7	3.2	23.2	2.5	12.7	14 142	16 564	6 213	16.5	13.1
Alabama	71.8	45.4	49.0	134	7.5	26.1	3.4	23.4	1.4	14.0	13 669	16 347	5 894	18.9	14.8
Mississippi	69.3	46.2	54.4	144	7.1	24.6	4.8	25.3	1.2	14.1	12 096	14 591	5 183	23.9	18.7
West South Central Division															
Arkansas	68.3	44.6	51.0	140	6.9	25.1	2.7	22.6	0.8	16.5	12 214	14 641	5 614	19.0	14.9
Louisiana	73.6	44.2	44.0	137	6.0	14.4	1.8	21.4	4.3	13.4	15 227	18 088	6 430	18.6	15.1
Oklahoma	74.2	47.3	47.2	120	4.1	16.7	2.1	20.3	1.0	12.9	14 750	17 668	6 858	13.4	10.3
Texas	78.4	51.0	48.1	112	4.0	17.9	0.8	21.1	2.3	10.0	16 708	19 618	7 205	14.7	11.1
Mountain Division															
Montana	75.2	49.0	44.6	117	8.3	7.4	1.0	17.3	1.1	10.3	15 420	18 413	6 589	12.3	9.2
Idaho	77.2	49.0	43.5	123	8.0	13.9	3.2	17.4	2.5	10.5	15 285	17 492	6 248	12.6	9.6
Wyoming	83.0	51.6	41.5	104	4.1	5.4	1.5	22.8	1.9	6.6	19 994	22 430	7 927	7.9	5.8
Colorado	80.0	55.2	46.4	96	5.0	14.1	1.0	20.2	4.2	9.2	18 056	21 279	7 998	10.1	7.4
New Mexico	74.3	46.5	42.5	131	7.1	7.4	1.8	20.2	1.8	12.8	14 654	16 928	6 119	17.6	14.0
Arizona	72.6	47.8	44.5	124	6.2	14.5	1.0	19.8	2.0	15.9	16 448	19 017	7 041	13.2	9.5
Utah	79.8	49.5	37.4	133	5.5	15.8	1.0	22.8	3.5	8.7	17 671	20 024	6 305	10.3	7.7
Nevada	81.1	60.1	54.1	85	5.9	5.9	1.3	19.5	1.9	8.8	18 211	21 311	8 453	8.7	6.3
Pacific Division															
Washington	76.6	50.6	42.7	108	7.4	19.5	2.6	18.9	5.3	12.1	18 367	21 696	8 073	9.8	7.2
Oregon	74.9	50.2	43.1	112	8.3	19.5	1.3	17.6	5.0	13.1	16 780	20 027	7 557	10.7	7.7
California	76.6	52.6	46.3	103	6.5	20.3	0.7	16.9	5.8	12.9	18 243	21 537	8 295	11.4	8.7
Alaska	81.7	59.7	47.4	96	9.7	6.3	0.7	21.5	3.2	4.3	25 414	28 395	10 193	10.7	8.6
Hawaii	78.3	57.8	51.5	95	4.7	7.9	2.2	23.2	8.3	9.3	20 473	22 750	7 740	9.9	7.8

APPENDIX 11
Acknowledgment Letter

(date)

Name
Title
Company
Address
City, State

RE: ____

Dear Name:

On behalf of the firm, I want to thank you for giving us the opportunity to serve you.

Our preliminary cost estimate of $ __________ for the project is based upon our current understanding of the relative complexity of the matter, that complete relevant information will be readily available, and that we encounter no other unforeseen circumstances. Should we encounter any unusual difficulties, we will contact you to discuss a revised estimate. To confirm our understanding, the enclosed fee agreement has been prepared, which I request you sign and return in the enclosed envelope.

____________________(if other than the signatory) will be the lawyer primarily responsible for your legal work, although other firm personnel may assist. It is our objective to provide the best value and highest-quality work. As a result, some tasks may be delegated to other lawyers and legal assistants in order to control the total cost of the job without affecting the quality.

We will send you monthly statements. Payment is due upon receipt. Bills will include a description of services and the date they were provided. Each bill will be reviewed before it is sent to ensure that you have been fairly charged.

In order to develop and maintain a good relationship, we believe that open communication between our firm and you is essential, and I encourage you to call me should any questions arise about either our billing or service.

We look forward to serving you.

Very Truly Yours,

____

cc: ____________________

APPENDIX 12
Contingent Fee Retainer Agreement

DATE: ____________________

CLIENT: ______________________________

ATTORNEYS: ____

RESPONSIBLE ATTORNEY: ________________________________

RETAINER: ____________ DATE RETAINER DUE: ____________

AGREEMENT:

Client hereby retains Attorneys and authorizes them to act on Client's behalf in all matters relating to ____

____

1. Legal representation

Attorneys agree to represent Client concerning personal injuries and loss of services arising from ____

____

with ________________________ on ________________________.

Client authorizes Attorneys to take all actions appropriate to assert Client's interests in this matter. Client specifically authorizes Attorneys to commence and litigate such civil actions as may be necessary, to associate other qualified persons as necessary to further Client's cause, and to choose which attorneys shall represent Client on any specific task. Client also specifically authorizes Attorneys to negotiate and settle Client's claim, but no settlement or compromise shall be made unless Client approves.

2. Legal fees

The parties agree that Attorneys will be entitled to a fee for services performed only if a recovery is obtained for Client. To the extent that Client does receive a recovery, Client agrees to pay Attorneys a percentage of any recovery obtained as Attorney's fee. Attorney's fee shall be a percentage of the actual recovery, including attorney's fees and all other sums awarded by the court, except as provided in paragraph 3 below. The percentage will vary according to the stage of the proceedings at which recovery is obtained, as follows:

(a) Before filing a complaint ________________

(b) After filing a complaint and prior to trial ________________

(c) Settlement during trial, or after verdict or judgment ________________

(d) If an appeal is filed ________________

Client agrees to pay when billed all costs and expenses incurred in preparation for or during litigation of this matter, including expert witness fees, transportation, lodging, and incidental expenses, regardless of the success or failure of Client's claim.

3. Reservation of rights

Client reserves the right to discharge Attorneys from representing him/her/them/it on this matter at any time before recovery, upon payment of a fee for all work that has been performed, and payment of all costs advanced and out-of-pocket expenses incurred by Attorneys on the case. In the event Attorneys are discharged, their fee will be calculated at the standard hourly rate for services when they were performed.

Attorneys reserve the right to cease representation of client at any time that Client has failed to pay in full within 30 days the amounts billed as costs and expenses incurred, and will assert an Attorney's lien on all material in the file until the same is paid. Attorneys reserve the right to cease representation of Client if Client refuses a settlement offer which in the opinion of Attorneys is both reasonable and in Client's best interests to accept, or if in the opinion of Attorneys, continued work on this matter would be detrimental to Client's or Attorneys' best interests, or is not justified. If Client does refuse a settlement offer which has been recommended by the attorneys and the case goes to trial and there is a judgment for less than the settlement offer, then the legal fees determined by paragraph 2 above shall be based on the amount of the refused offer rather than the judgment.

4. Assignment of rights

Client assigns to Attorneys any recovery by way of settlement, judgment or otherwise, to the extent of legal fees, costs and expenses owed to Attorneys by Client. Client agrees that when Attorneys receive any recovery on behalf of client, any amounts due Attorneys for legal fees, costs, and expenses, including but not limited to costs of investigation; court costs; and costs of securing evidence, expert testimony, any and all medical and hospital bills, and charges which are unpaid or unreimbursed shall be deducted before the balance of the recovery is paid to Client.

Client authorizes Attorneys to be his/hers/their/its attorney in fact to receive in Client's name any recovery due by way of judgment or settlement; to issue satisfaction of judgment, releases, and dismissals; and to exercise other rights of client as may be required by the court or the other party.

5. Disclaimer

The parties agree that neither Attorneys nor any of their employees have made any guarantee regarding the success or failure of any litigation involved in this matter. All discussions regarding the anticipated outcome of the case are merely an opinion of the attorneys working on the matter and are not a guarantee of any specific result.

6. Attorney fees

If any suit, action, or other proceeding shall be instituted relating to any term or condition of this Agreement or relating to any of the rights, duties, or obligations arising under it, the prevailing party or parties shall be entitled to recover from the other party, and the other party or parties agree to pay to the prevailing party, whether or not the matter proceeds to final judgment or decree, in addition to costs and disbursements allowed by law, such sum as the trial and each appellate court may adjudge reasonable as an attorney's fee in such suit, action, or other proceeding, and in any appeal thereof. Such sum shall include an amount estimated by the court as the reasonable costs and fees to be incurred by the prevailing party in collecting any monetary judgment or award or otherwise enforcing each order, judgment, or decree entered in such suit, action, or other proceeding.

SIGNATURES:

The parties have demonstrated their assent to all the terms of this agreement by affixing their signatures to it.

____

Client

______________________________ By ______________________________

Client Partner

____

Client

APPENDIX 13
Attorney Employment and Fee Agreement (general)

DATE: ______________________

CLIENT: ______________________________

ATTORNEYS: ____

RETAINER: ____________ DATE RETAINER DUE: ____________

AGREEMENT:

Client hereby retains Attorneys and authorizes them to act on Client's behalf in all matters relating to ____

____

1. Basis of fees

For legal services rendered in the above entitled matter, Client promises to pay fees of \$30.00 an hour for paralegal and law clerk services and fees between \$65.00 and \$125.00 per hour for services provided by attorneys. Client understands that attorney fees charged may be higher than the normal hourly rate and will take into consideration the uniqueness of the matter, the responsibility undertaken by the attorney, the expertise required, the result obtained, and whether urgent action is required on the matter.

2. Client's payment of costs

In addition to payment of attorney's fees, Client shall be responsible for and shall promptly pay upon request any costs and disbursements advanced by Attorneys on Client's behalf. These items include such things as filing fees, long-distance telephone charges, computer legal research, necessary travel expenses, copying costs, deposition charges, and any other out-of-pocket expenses related to the matter. Client will be responsible for paying all such costs before or at the time they are incurred.

3. Retainer fee deposits

Client agrees to make an initial retainer fee deposit of $ __________ and such additional retainer fee deposits as are requested by Attorneys. CLIENT UNDERSTANDS AND AGREES THAT ATTORNEYS WILL PERFORM NO SERVICES FOR CLIENT ON THIS MATTER UNTIL ANY INITIAL RETAINER FEE REQUESTED BY ATTORNEYS HAS BEEN DEPOSITED BY CLIENT. The retainer fee shall be deposited to Client's account and will first be applied to costs advanced; any balance may be applied to fees due.

4. Termination of attorney-client relationship

Client shall retain the right at any time to terminate Attorneys' services on Client's behalf by delivery of a signed letter notifying Attorneys of the termination of the Attorney-Client relationship. Client shall remain liable for and shall promptly pay all fees incurred and costs advanced through the time and date of Attorneys' receipt of such notice of termination. Similarly, Attorneys shall retain the right to withdraw as Attorneys for Client at any time, for any reason, including (but not limited to) nonpayment of Attorneys' fees and costs advanced when due. CLIENT SPECIFICALLY UNDERSTANDS AND AGREES THAT ATTORNEYS ARE WILLING AND ABLE TO UNDERTAKE REPRESENTATION OF CLIENT ON THIS MATTER ONLY ON THE BASIS THAT ALL OF ATTORNEYS' BILL (INCLUDING REQUESTS FOR FURTHER RETAINER FEES OR ADVANCE DEPOSITS) SHALL BE PAID IN FULL WHEN DESIGNATED; IF NOT SO PAID, ATTORNEYS MAY IN THEIR SOLE AND COMPLETE DISCRETION WITHHOLD PERFORMANCE OF FURTHER SERVICES AND BE FREE TO TERMINATE THE ATTORNEY-CLIENT RELATIONSHIP AND WITHDRAW AS ATTORNEYS OF RECORD. In order to afford Client an opportunity to obtain other representation, Attorneys will make reasonable effort not to withdraw during or immediately prior to a trial or a hearing without written notice to Client and approval by the Court.

5. Miscellaneous provisions

(a) The primary Attorney will have initial responsibility for the matter. However, Client agrees that any attorney that is a member of or employed by Attorneys may take responsibility for any part of the case and that the decision to involve another attorney or attorneys shall be within the discretion and professional judgment of Attorneys.

(b) If there is more than one individual or organization in the position of Client under and pursuant to this Agreement, all individuals and/or organizations being represented as Client will be jointly and severally bound by this Agreement.

(c) If any suit, action, or other proceeding shall be instituted relating to any term or condition of this Agreement or relating to any of the rights, duties, or obligations arising under it, the prevailing party or parties shall be entitled to recover from the other party and the other party or parties agree to pay to the prevailing judgment or decree, in addition to costs and disbursements allowed by law, such sum as the trial and each appellate court may adjudge reasonable as an attorney's fee in such suit, action, or other proceeding, and in any appeal thereof. Such sum shall include an amount estimated by the court as the reasonable costs and fees to be incurred by the prevailing party in collecting any monetary judgment or award or otherwise enforcing each order, judgment, or decree entered in such suit, action, or other proceeding.

(d) BILLINGS FROM ATTORNEYS ARE DUE AND PAYABLE UPON RECEIPT. ANY BALANCE NOT PAID WITHIN 30 DAYS WILL BE SUBJECT TO A LATE PAYMENT CHARGE OF 1.5% PER MONTH (18% ANNUALLY).

By: ______________________________ ______________________________

Partner Client

____

Client

____

Client

Appendix 14
Limited Attorney Employment and Fee Agreement

DATE: ______________________

CLIENT: ______________________________

ATTORNEYS: ____

RETAINER: ______________ DATE RETAINER DUE: ______________

AGREEMENT:

Client hereby retains Attorneys and authorizes them to act on Client's behalf in all matters relating to ____

____

1. Limitation

Attorney will only represent Client in matters relating to worker's compensation.

2. Basis of fees

For legal services rendered in the above entitled matter, Client promises to pay fees of $30.00 an hour for paralegal and law clerk services and fees between $65.00 and $125.00 per hour for services provided by attorneys. Client understands that attorney fees charged may be higher than the normal hourly rate and will take into consideration the uniqueness of the matter, the responsibility undertaken by the attorney, the expertise required, the result obtained, and whether urgent action is required on the matter.

3. Client's payment of costs

In addition to payment of attorneys' fees, Client shall be responsible for and shall promptly pay upon request any costs and disbursements advanced by Attorneys on Client's behalf. These items include such things as filing fees, long-distance telephone charges, computer legal research, necessary travel expenses, copying costs, deposition charges, and any other out-of-pocket expenses related to the matter. Client will be responsible for paying all such costs before or at the time they are incurred.

4. Retainer fee deposits

Client agrees to make an initial retainer fee deposit of $ __________ and such additional retainer fee deposits as are requested by Attorneys. CLIENT UNDERSTANDS AND AGREES THAT ATTORNEYS WILL PERFORM NO SERVICES FOR CLIENT ON THIS MATTER UNTIL ANY INITIAL RETAINER FEE REQUESTED BY ATTORNEYS HAS BEEN DEPOSITED BY CLIENT. The retainer fee shall be deposited to Client's account and will first be applied to costs advanced; any balance may be applied to fees due.

5. Termination of attorney-client relationship

Client shall retain the right at any time to terminate Attorneys' services on Client's behalf by delivery of a signed letter notifying Attorneys of the termination of the Attorney-Client relationship. Client shall remain liable for and shall promptly pay all fees incurred and costs advanced through the time and date of Attorneys' receipt of such notice of termination. Similarly, Attorneys shall retain the right to withdraw as Attorneys for Client at any time, for any reason, including (but not limited to) nonpayment of Attorneys' fees and costs advanced when due. CLIENT SPECIFICALLY UNDERSTANDS AND AGREES THAT ATTORNEYS ARE WILLING AND ABLE TO UNDERTAKE REPRESENTATION OF CLIENT ON THIS MATTER ONLY ON THE BASIS THAT ALL OF ATTORNEYS' BILL (INCLUDING REQUESTS FOR FURTHER RETAINER FEES OR ADVANCE DEPOSITS) SHALL BE PAID IN FULL WHEN DESIGNATED; IF NOT SO PAID, ATTORNEYS MAY IN THEIR SOLE AND COMPLETE DISCRETION WITHHOLD PERFORMANCE OF FURTHER SERVICES AND BE FREE TO TERMINATE THE ATTORNEY-CLIENT RELATIONSHIP AND WITHDRAW AS ATTORNEYS OF RECORD. In order to afford Client an opportunity to obtain other representation, Attorneys will make reasonable effort not to withdraw during or immediately prior to a trial or a hearing without written notice to Client and approval by the Court.

6. Miscellaneous provisions

(a) The primary Attorney will have initial responsibility for the matter. However, Client agrees that any attorney that is a member of or employed by Attorneys may take responsibility for any part of the case and that the decision to involve another attorney or attorneys shall be within the discretion and professional judgment of Attorneys.

(b) If there is more than one individual or organization in the position of Client under and pursuant to this Agreement, all individuals and/or organizations being represented as Client will be jointly and severally bound by this Agreement.

(c) If any suit, action, or other proceeding shall be instituted relating to any term or condition of this Agreement or relating to any of the rights, duties, or obligations arising under it, the prevailing party or parties shall be entitled to recover from the other party and the other party or parties agree to pay to the prevailing judgment or decree, in addition to costs and disbursements allowed by law, such sum as the trial and each appellate court may adjudge reasonable as an attorney's fee in such suit, action, or other proceeding, and in any appeal thereof. Such sum shall include an amount estimated by the court as the reasonable costs and fees to be incurred by the prevailing party in collecting any monetary judgment or award or otherwise enforcing each order, judgment, or decree entered in such suit, action, or other proceeding.

(d) BILLINGS FROM ATTORNEYS ARE DUE AND PAYABLE UPON RECEIPT. ANY BALANCE NOT PAID WITHIN 30 DAYS WILL BE SUBJECT TO A LATE PAYMENT CHARGE OF 1.5% PER MONTH (18% ANNUALLY).

By: ______________________________ ______________________________

Partner Client

____

Client

____

Client

Appendix 15
Glossary of Terms for Advertising and Printing

Accordion Fold. In binding, a term used for two or more parallel folds which open like an accordion.

Art or Artwork. Refers to illustrations, photographs, tables, charts, graphs, or other similar nontextual materials.

Basis Weight. The weight in pounds of a ream (500 sheets) of paper cut to a given standard size for that grade: 25 inches by 38 inches for book papers, 20 inches by 26 inches for cover papers, $22\frac{1}{2}$ inches by $28\frac{1}{2}$ inches or $22\frac{1}{2}$ inches by 35 inches for bristols, $25\frac{1}{2}$ inches by $30\frac{1}{2}$ inches for index. For example, 500 sheets, 25 inches by 38 inches of 80-pound coated will weight 80 pounds.

Black and White. Originals or reproductions in single color, as distinguished from multicolor.

Bleed. If the printed image extends to the trim edge of the sheet or page, it is called a bleed.

Blind Embossing. A design which is stamped without metallic leaf or ink, giving a bas-relief effect.

Bindery. Facility where books, brochures, and other printed materials are collated, folded, and bound as required. Usually located separate from the printing operation.

Classified Advertising. Separate section of small advertisements arranged by category in printing media; the "want ads" (as opposed to display advertising).

Coated Paper. Paper having a surface coating which produces a smooth finish. Surfaces vary from eggshell to glossy (see also Uncoated Paper).

Column Inch. Print media measurement of advertising or newsprint, 1 inch by 1 column wide.

Commercial Printer. A printing operation capable of producing high-quality, printed materials. Usually capable of printing in full color, using dies, embossing, and so on (see also Quick Printer).

Copy. Any typewritten manuscript to be used in the production of printed materials.

Cost per Thousand. Standard measurement of cost of media to reach 1,000 viewers, readers, or listeners.

Debossing. The process of depressing an image into paper to achieve a depressed surface (see Embossing).

Die-Cutting. The use of sharp steel rules to cut special shapes like labels, boxes, and containers from printed sheets.

Display Advertising. Advertising used in the editorial content sections of printed media, usually containing art or graphic designs. Also called point of sale, the advertisement in conjunction with product displays (as opposed to classified advertising).

Embossing. Impressing an image in relief to achieve a raised surface, either over printing or on blank paper (which is called blind embossing) (see Debossing).

Focus Group. A technique using a small group of people representative of the target audience, with homogeneous interests, who are interviewed in-depth as a group to test measure suppositions, for marketing planning.

Galley Proof. A proof taken of type standing in a galley, before being made up into pages.

Halftone. The reproduction of continuous-tone artwork, such as a photograph, through a cross-line or contact screen, which converts the image into dots of various sizes.

Insert. A printed piece prepared for insertion into a publication or another printed piece.

Institutional Advertising. Designed to improve or change firm or company image but not sell directly.

Layout. The drawing or sketch of a proposed printed piece.

Logotype (or Logo). The name of a company or product in a special design used as a trademark in advertising.

Mechanical. A term for a camera-ready pasteup of artwork. It includes type, photos, line art, and so on, all on one piece of artboard.

Process Colors. In printing, the subtractive primaries: yellow, magenta, and cyan, plus black in four-color process printing.

Proof. An impression of the material prepared for print, to be approved as a last check for arrangement, accuracy of information, and so on, before printing.

QUICK PRINTER. A small printing operation, specializing in high-speed photocopying and limited printing capabilities. Can usually handle printing up to two colors (see also COMMERCIAL PRINTER).

REVERSE. In visual media, when the normal background and letter colors are reversed.

SADDLE STITCH. In binding, to fasten a booklet by wiring it through the middle fold of the sheets. Commonly called "stapling."

SERIF AND SANS SERIF. A serif is the short cross-lines at the ends of the main strokes of many letters in some type faces. All letters are with serif or sans ("without" in French) serif.

UNCOATED PAPER. Paper having no surface coating and generally having some sort of rough or textured feel (see also COATED PAPER).

WHITE SPACE. The space without printing in an advertisement or brochure to focus attention on the information presented. A very important element in good design.

APPENDIX 16
P.I.C.'S National Law List

SPECIAL PRACTICE INDEX TOPICS

Administrative Law; Utilities; Municipal; Governmental; Legislative; Advocacy
Admiralty; Maritime
Aerospace
Agricultural and Cooperative
Alternate Dispute Resolution
Antitrust; Class Actions; Securities Litigation; Trade Regulation; Trade Name Protection
Appeals; Appellate Practice
Architectural Law (See Construction)
Asbestos Litigation
Association Law
Aviation; Marine
Banking; Commercial Finance; Leasing (See also Savings and Loan)
Bankruptcy; Creditors' Rights; Commercial Insolvency; Reorganization
Bond and Financing
Business Torts; Unfair Competition; Bad Faith
Business; Mergers; Acquisitions; Tax; Corporate; Planning; Technology
Casualty Defense (See Litigation)
Civil Trial Law (See Litigation)
Commercial Law (See Banking)
Commodities (See Securities)
Communications (FCC); Cable Television

Computer Industry
Construction; Architectural Law
Corporate Law; Banking; Business; Securities; Syndications; Tax; Finance
Criminal Defense
Debt Financing
Defamation Defense
Domestic Relations (See Family Law)
Education
Election Law
Employment; Civil Rights; Discrimination
Energy and Minerals; Wind and Geo-Thermal Energy (See Oil-Gas and Real Estate and Environmental)
Entertainment (See Sports; Entertainment)
Environmental Law; Natural Resources (See also Oil-Gas and Real Estate)
Estate Planning; Administration; Probate; Trusts; Taxation; Farm; Ranch
Family Law; Matrimonial Law; Domestic Relations (See also Estate Planning)
Federal Contracting
Fidelity and Surety Law
Finance; Commercial (See Banking)
First Amendment
Food and Drug
Franchising
General Practice
Governmental Relations; Contracts
Health Care; Hospital
Housing; Cooperatives; Condominiums
Immigration
Insolvency and Reorganization; Commercial Insolvency (See Bankruptcy)
Institutional Lending
Insurance; Contract Interpretation; Defense; Reinsurance Litigation; Self-Insurance; Trusts; Off Shore Captives; Regulation; Fraud
Intellectual Property
International Transactions
Investment Funds; Foreign
Labor Law; Employee Benefit Plans; Employment Practices; Executive Compensation; Wrongful Termination; EEO; Pensions; ERISA; ESOPs
Landlord/Tenant
Leasing; Equipment
Legislative and Administrative (See Administrative)
Liability; Professional (See Malpractice)
Libel Litigation
Literary Property
Litigation; Civil; Commercial; Business; Corporate; Energy; Labor; Casualty Defense; Multi-District; Complex; General; Disaster
Malpractice; Professional; Legal; Medical; Architect; Engineer
Management (See Labor)
Maritime and Casualty (See Admiralty)
Matrimonial (See Family Law)
Media
Mergers and Acquisitions (See Business)
Motor Carrier
Municipal Finance; Bonds
Municipal; Administrative Law (See Administrative)
Negligence; Professional
Non Profit Organizations
Oil and Gas; Energy; Minerals (See also Real Estate and Environmental)
Patent (See Trademark)
Personal Injury; Property Litigation; Subrogation; Insurance Fraud
Probate and Estate Planning (See Estate Planning)
Product Safety
Products Liability
Public Finance (See Securities)
Public Law and Government Agencies
Railroad Defense
Real Estate Development; Litigation; Commercial; Residential; Natural Resources; Zoning; Planning; Finance; Leasing; Land Use
Real Estate Tax Assessment and Condemnations
Real Estate; Foreclosure
Savings and Loan; Regulation
Secured Transactions
Securities; Commodities; SEC; Finance; Bonds (See also Antitrust and Corporate)
Sports; Entertainment
Subrogation (See Personal Injury)
Tax Exempt Organizations
Tax; Federal; State; Local; Corporate Planning; Estate; Tax Exempt Financing (See also Business, Corporate and Estate Planning)
Telecommunications
Torts; Toxio
Trade Association
Trade Regulation (See Antitrust)
Trademark; Patent; Copyright
Transportation
Trusts and Estates (See Estate Planning)
Utility Regulation
Venture Capital and Securities (See also Securities)
White Collar Criminal Defense
Workers' Compensation

BIBLIOGRAPHY

ALBRECHT, KARL, AND RON ZEMKE. *Service America! Doing Business in the New Economy.* Homewood, IL: Dow Jones-Irwin, 1985.

ALESSANDRA, TONY, PHIL WEXLER, AND RICK BARRERA. *Non-Manipulative Selling,* 2nd ed. Englewood Cliffs, NJ: Prentice Hall, 1987.

BLANCHARD, KENNETH, AND SPENCER JOHNSON. *The One-Minute Manager.* Berkeley, CA: Berkeley Books, 1981.

BOLLES, RICHARD. *Where Do I Go from Here with My Life?* Berkeley, CA: 10 Speed Press, 1974.

BOLLES, RICHARD N. *What Color Is Your Parachute?* Berkeley, CA: 10 Speed Press, 1989.

BREEN, GEORGE EDWARD, AND A. B. BLANKENSHIP. *Do-It-Yourself Marketing Research,* 2nd ed. New York: McGraw-Hill, 1982.

COHEN, HERB. *You Can Negotiate Anything.* New York: Bantam Books, 1980.

CONNER, RICHARD A., JR. *Marketing Your Consulting and Professional Services.* New York: John Wiley,

COXE, WELD. *Marketing Architectural and Engineering Services,* 2nd ed. New York, NY: Van Nostrand Reinhold Co., 1983.

DESATNICK, ROBERT L. *Managing to Keep the Customer: How to Achieve and Maintain Superior Customer Service Throughout the Organization.* San Francisco: Jossey-Bass, 1987.

DOOHER, JOSEPH M., AND MARQUIS VIVIENNE. *Effective Communication on the Job.* American Management Association, 1956.

DRUCKER, PETER F. *The Effective Executive.* New York: Harper & Row, 1966.

DUNN, S. W., AND A. M. BARBAN. *Advertising: Its Role in Modern Marketing,* 4th ed. The Dryden Press, 1978.

GRONROOS, CHRISTIAN. *Internal Marketing—Theory and Practice,* Swedish School of Economics. Research report presented at the American Marketing Association's Third Conference/Services Marketing, Helsinki, Finland.

GRONROOS, CHRISTIAN. A Service Quality Model and Its Marketing Implications," *European Journal of Marketing,* Vol. 18, No. 4, 1984.

GRONROOS, CHRISTIAN. *A Relationship Approach to Marketing: The Need for a New Paradigm,* Swedish School of Economics, Helsinki, Finland February 1989.

GRONROOS, CHRISTIAN. *Service Management and Marketing: Managing the Moments of Truth in Service Competition* D.C. Heath/Lexington Books, Lexington, Mass. 1990.

HAYNSWORTH, HARRY J. *Expanding Your Law Practice: The Ethical Risks* American Bar Association, Chicago IL 1990

KOTLER, PHILIP. "Mega-Marketing," *Harvard Business Review,* May/April 1986.

KOTLER, PHILIP, AND BLOOM, PAUL, *Marketing Professional Services.* Englewood Cliffs, NJ: Prentice Hall, 1984.

LAKEIN, ALAN. *How to Get Control of Your Time and Your Life.* P. H. Wyden, 1973.

LEBOEUF, MICHAEL. *How to Win Customers and Keep Them for Life.* G. P. Putnam's Sons, New York, NY; 1987.

MCCARTHY, E. JEROME. *Basic Marketing.* Richard D. Irwin, Inc. Homewood IL. 1971.

PETERSON, ROBIN. *Marketing: A Contemporary Introduction.* New York: John Wiley, 1977.

REED, RICHARD C. EDITOR. *Beyond the Billable Hour.* American Bar Association, Chicago IL 1990.

REIS, AL, AND TROUT, JACK. *Positioning: The Battle for Your Mind.* New York: McGraw-Hill, 1981.

REIS, AL, AND TROUT, JACK. *Marketing Warfare.* New York: McGraw-Hill, 1986.

SIMMONS, S. H. *How to Be the Life of the Podium.* Amacom, 1982.

SMITH, HOMER. *A Salesman's Guide to More Effective Selling.* S&MM, 1977.

SMITH, ROGER F. *Entrepreneur's Marketing Guide. Bigger Sales Power for Smaller Firms.* Reston, VA: Reston, 1984.

SMITH, ROGER F. *Sales Management, A Practitioner's Guide.* Englewood Cliffs, NJ: Prentice Hall, 1987.

STEVENS, ART. *The Persuasion Explosion. Your Guide to the Power & Influence of Contemporary Public Relations.* Acropolis Books Ltd., Washington, D.C.; 1985.

TAYLOR, ROBERT F. *Back to Basic Selling. Unique Sales Tips for Sure-fire Success.* Englewood Cliffs, NJ: Prentice Hall, 1985.

The Preventative Lawyer, available from the University of Denver College of Law, 7039 E. 18th Street, Denver, CO 80220.

VON OECH, ROGER. *A Whack on the Side of the Head. How to Unlock Your Mind for Innovation.* New York: Warner Books, 1983.

Index

Y